Criminal Law

Criminal Law

by Joshua Dressler
Frank R. Strong Chair in Law
Michael E. Moritz College of Law
The Ohio State University

FIRST EDITION

THOMSON

WEST

Mat #40234999

© 2005 Thomson/West
　　610 Opperman Drive
　　P.O. Box 64526
　　St. Paul, MN 55164–0526
　　800–328–9352

ISBN 0–314–15233–4

 PRINTED ON 10% POST CONSUMER RECYCLED PAPER

Dedication

To Lucy Belle

*

Preface

This "Black Letter" is designed to help a law student recognize and understand the basic principles and issues of law covered in a law school course. It can be used both as a study aid when preparing for classes and as a review of the subject matter when studying for an examination.

Each "Black Letter" is written by experienced law school teachers who are recognized national authorities on the subject covered.

The law is succinctly stated by the authors of this "Black Letter." In addition, the exceptions to the rules are stated in the text. The rules and exceptions have purposely been condensed to facilitate quick and easy recollection. For an in-depth study of a point of law, citations to major student texts are given.

If the subject covered by this text is a code or code-related course, the code section or rule is set forth and discussed wherever applicable.

FORMAT

The format of this "Black Letter" is specially designed for review. (1) **Text.** First, it is recommended that the entire text be studied and, if deemed necessary, supplemented by the student texts cited. (2) **Capsule Summary.** The Capsule Summary is an abbreviated review of the subject matter which can be used both before and after studying the main body of the text. The headings in the Capsule Summary follow the main text of the "Black Letter." (3) **Table of Contents.** The Table of Contents is in outline form to help you organize the details of the subject and the Summary of Contents gives you a final overview of the materials. (4)

Sample Examination. The Sample Examinations in Appendix A give you the opportunity to test yourself with the type of questions asked on an exam and compare your answer with a model answer.

In addition, a number of other features are included to help you understand the subject matter and prepare for examinations:

Perspective: In this feature, the authors discuss their approach to the topic, the approach used in preparing the materials, and any tips on studying for and writing examinations.

Analysis: This feature, at the beginning of each section, is designed to give a quick summary of a particular section to help you recall the subject matter and to help you determine which areas need the most extensive review.

Examples: This feature is designed to illustrate, through fact situations, the law just stated. This, we believe, should help you analytically approach a question on the examination.

Glossary: This feature is designed to refamiliarize you with the meaning of a particular legal term. We believe that the recognition of words of art used in an examination helps you to better analyze the question. In addition, when writing an examination you should know the precise definition of a word of art you intend to use.

We believe that the materials in this "Black Letter" will facilitate your study of a law school course and assure success in writing examinations not only for the course but for the bar examination. We wish you success.

THE PUBLISHER

Summary of Contents

■ PART ONE: INTRODUCTORY PRINCIPLES

■ PART TWO: *ACTUS REUS*

■ PART THREE: *MENS REA*

■ PART FOUR: *MENS REA* AND MISTAKES OF FACT OR LAW

■ PART SEVEN: DEFENSES TO CRIME: EXCUSES

■ PART EIGHT: INCHOATE CONDUCT

■ PART NINE: COMPLICITY

■ PART TEN: CRIMINAL HOMICIDE

■ PART ELEVEN: RAPE

■ PART TWELVE: THEFT

APPENDICES

App.

*

Table of Contents

■ PART ONE: INTRODUCTORY PRINCIPLES

■ PART TWO: *ACTUS REUS*

■ PART THREE: *MENS REA*

■ PART FOUR: *MENS REA* AND MISTAKES OF FACT OR LAW

■ PART FIVE: CAUSATION

■ PART SIX: DEFENSES TO CRIME: JUSTIFICATIONS

■ PART SEVEN: DEFENSES TO CRIME: EXCUSES

■ PART EIGHT: INCHOATE CONDUCT

PART NINE: COMPLICITY

■ PART TEN: CRIMINAL HOMICIDE

■ PART ELEVEN: RAPE

■ PART TWELVE: THEFT

Capsule Summary of Criminal Law

■ PART ONE: INTRODUCTORY PRINCIPLES

I. CRIMINAL LAW OVERVIEW

A. "Criminal" versus "Civil"

    1. The Essence of the Criminal Law

What distinguishes a criminal from a civil sanction and all that distinguishes it, is the judgment of community condemnation that accompanies and justifies its imposition. A "crime" is (or, at least should be) limited to conduct that, if duly shown to have taken place, will incur a formal and solemn pronouncement of the moral condemnation of the community.

B. Sources of the Criminal Law

1. Common Law

"Common law" is judge-made law. For the most part, British common law became American common law.

2. Statutes

Today, all criminal lawyers in this country turn first to a book—often characterized as a "penal code"—that contains legislatively-drafted definitions of crimes, defenses to crimes, and other relevant doctrines of criminal law, which apply in that lawyer's jurisdiction.

3. Model Penal Code

The Model Penal Code (typically abbreviated as "MPC") is a code created in the 1950s and adopted in 1962 by the American Law Institute, a prestigious organization composed of top judges, scholars, and lawyers.

C. Limits on the Criminal Law

State and federal legislation is subject to the strictures of the United States Constitution (and, with state laws, the constitution of the relevant state). Some of these strictures are discussed throughout this Outline.

D. Burden of Proof: Basics

A basic American principle of criminal law is that a defendant is presumed innocent. The Due Process Clauses of the Fifth and Fourteenth Amendments of the Constitution require that, to convict a defendant, the government must persuade the factfinder beyond a reasonable doubt of every fact necessary to constitute the crime charged.

E. Judge versus Jury

1. Constitutional Law

The Sixth Amendment to the United States Constitution provides that "in all criminal prosecutions, the accused shall enjoy the right to a speedy and public trial, by an impartial jury." Despite the phrase "in *all* criminal prosecutions," the Supreme Court has generally limited the right to a jury trial to prosecutions for crimes for which the maximum potential punishment exceeds incarceration of six months.

2. Jury Nullification

Jury nullification occurs when the jury decides that the prosecution has proven its case beyond a reasonable doubt, but for reasons of conscience it disregards the facts and/or the law and acquits the defendant.

II. "TOOLS" OF THE CRIMINAL LAW

A. Theories of Punishment

1. Different Theories

Two broad theories of punishment exist: *utilitarianism* and *retribution*.

2. Principles of Utilitarianism

a. Augmenting Happiness

Utilitarianism holds that the general object of all laws is to augment the total happiness of the community by excluding, as much as possible, everything that subtracts from that happiness, *i.e.*, everything that causes "mischief" (pain).

b. Role of Punishment

Both crime and punishment are evils, because they both result in pain to individuals and to society as a whole. Therefore, the pain of punishment is undesirable unless its infliction is likely to prevent a greater amount of pain in the form of future crime.

c. Forms of Utilitarianism

i. General Deterrence

A person is punished in order to send a message to others (the general society or, at least, persons who might be contemplating criminal conduct) that crime does not pay.

ii. Specific Deterrence

D is punished in order to deter *D* from future criminal activity. This is done in either of two ways: by *incapacitation* (incarceration of *D* prevents her from committing additional crimes in the general community for the duration of her sentence); and/or by *intimidation* (*D*'s punishment serves as a painful reminder, so that upon release *D* will be deterred from future criminal conduct).

iii. Rehabilitation

Advocates of this form of utilitarianism believe that the criminal law can prevent future crime by reforming an individual, by providing her with employment skills, psychological aid, etc., so that she will not want or need to commit offenses in the future.

3. Principles of Retribution

a. Just Deserts

Punishment of a wrongdoer is justified as a deserved response to wrongdoing. Retributivists punish *because* of the wrongdoing—the criminal gets his just deserts—regardless of whether such punishment will deter future crime.

b. Rationale

Wrongdoing creates a moral disequilibrium in society. The wrongdoer obtains the benefits of the law (namely, that other people have respected *his* rights), but he does not accept the law's burdens (respecting others' rights). Proportional punishment of the wrongdoer—"paying his debt"—brings him back into moral equilibrium. Another justification is that both crime and punishment are forms of communication: one who commits a crime sends an implicit message to the victim that the wrongdoer's rights are more important than others' rights; punishment is a symbolic way of showing the criminal—and reaffirming for victims—that this message was wrong. Punishment proportional to the offense defeats the offender: it brings him down to his proper place in relation to others.

B. Proportionality of Punishment

1. General Principle

A general principle of criminal law is that punishment should be proportional to the offense committed.

2. Utilitarian Meaning

Punishment is proportional if it involves the infliction of no more pain than necessary to fulfill the law's deterrent goal of reducing a greater amount of crime.

3. Retributive Meaning

Punishment should be proportional to the harm caused on the present occasion, taking into consideration the actor's degree of culpability for causing the harm.

4. Constitutional Law

The Eighth Amendment Cruel and Unusual Punishment Clause prohibits grossly disproportional punishment.

a. Death Penalty Cases

The Supreme Court has held that death is grossly disproportional punishment for the crime of rape of an adult woman, because the latter offense does not involve the taking of human life.

b. Imprisonment Cases

According to the Supreme Court's most recent pronouncement, there is only a very "narrow proportionality principle" outside the context of the death penalty. The legislature (not the judiciary) has primary authority in setting punishments. No non-capital incarcerative punishment will be declared unconstitutional unless there are objective grounds—not simply a judge's own subjective views of the propriety of the punishment—for determining that the punishment is grossly disproportionate to the crime.

C. Legality

1. Requirement of Previously Defined Conduct

a. General Principle

The so-called "principle of legality" is that there can be no crime without (pre-existent) law, no punishment without (pre-existent) law.

b. Constitutional Law

The principle of legality not only is a common law doctrine, but has deep constitutional roots. Legislatures are prohibited by the Ex Post Facto Clause of the United States Constitution from enacting laws that would punish conduct that was lawful at the time of its commission, or that increases the punishment for an act committed before the law took effect. In turn, courts are prohibited from enlarging the scope of criminal statutes by the Due Process Clause.

2. Fair Notice

A corollary of the legality principle is that a person may not be punished for an offense unless the statute is sufficiently clear that a person of ordinary intelligence can understand its meaning. This is a fundamental common law concept, with constitutional roots as well in the Due Process Clause.

3. Nondiscriminatory Enforcement

Another corollary of the legality principle is that a criminal statute should not be so broadly worded that it is susceptible to discriminatory enforcement by law enforcement officers.

D. Burden of Proof

1. Burden of Production

This burden relates to the question of which party—the defendant or the government—has the obligation to first introduce evidence on a given issue. The party with this obligation, who fails to satisfy this burden, loses on the issue.

2. Burden of Persuasion

Once the burden of production has been satisfied, the next question becomes: who has the burden of persuading the factfinder on the particular issue? The party with the burden of *production* need not have the burden of *persuasion*.

a. Degree of Burden

i. Elements of a Crime

The Due Process Clause of the Constitution requires that the government carry the burden of persuasion, beyond a reasonable doubt, as to "every *fact* necessary to constitute the crime charged." The Court has limited the word "fact"—and, thus, the prosecutor's constitutional obligation to carry the burden of production beyond a reasonable doubt—to elements of an offense, and not to defenses and mitigating factors.

ii. Defenses to Crimes

A legislature is free to place the burden of persuasion regarding a criminal law defense on either party—the defendant or government—and to set the burden very high (proof beyond a reasonable doubt), somewhat high (clear and convincing evidence) or low (proof by preponderance of the evidence).

■ PART TWO: *ACTUS REUS*

I. *ACTUS REUS*: OVERVIEW

A. Definition

The *"actus reus"* of an offense is the physical, or external, component of a crime—what society does not want to occur.

B. Two Elements

The *actus reus* of a crime consists of two components, both of which must be proved by the prosecutor.

1. Voluntary Act or Legal Omission

Generally speaking, there can be no crime in the absence of conduct. But, only a certain type of conduct qualifies, namely, conduct that includes a voluntary act. In rare circumstances, a person may be prosecuted because of what he or she did *not* do—an absence of conduct. An "omission" substitutes for a voluntary act when the defendant has a legal duty to act.

2. Social Harm

People are not punished for conduct (or omissions), but rather for conduct (or omissions) that result in "social harm."

II. VOLUNTARY ACT

A. General Rule

A person is not ordinarily guilty of a criminal offense unless his conduct includes a voluntary act.

1. Common Law Definition of Voluntary Act

A "voluntary act" is a willed muscular contraction or bodily movement by the actor. An act is "willed" if the bodily movement was controlled by the mind of the actor.

2. Model Penal Code

The MPC does not define "voluntary act." It provides examples of involuntary actions: a reflex or convulsion; bodily movement while unconscious or asleep; conduct during hypnosis or as a result of hypnotic suggestion; and/or "a bodily movement that otherwise is not a product of the effort or determination of the actor, either conscious or habitual."

3. **Constitutional Law**

The Supreme Court has never expressly held that punishment of an involuntary actor is unconstitutional. However, it has invalidated statutes that criminalize a "status" or "condition" (such as being a drug addict), rather than conduct.

4. **Important Study Point**

To be guilty of an offense, it is sufficient that the person's conduct *included* a voluntary act. *It is not necessary that all aspects of his conduct be voluntary.*

B. **Rationale of Voluntary Act Requirement**

1. **Utilitarian**

A person who acts involuntarily cannot be deterred. Therefore, it is useless to punish the involuntary actor. It results in pain without the benefit of crime reduction.

2. **Retribution**

A more persuasive justification for the voluntary act requirement is that blame and punishment presuppose free will: a person does not deserve to be punished unless she *chooses* to put her bad thoughts into action.

III. OMISSIONS

A. **General Rule**

Ordinarily, a person is not guilty of a crime for failing to act, even if such failure permits harm to occur to another, and even if the person could act at no risk to personal safety.

B. **Rationale for the General Rule**

1. **Proving the Omitter's State of Mind**

Criminal conduct requires a guilty state of mind (*mens rea*). It is unusually difficult to determine the state of mind of one who fails to act.

2. Line-drawing problems

Difficult line-drawing problems—which omitters should be prosecuted?—arise in omission cases.

3. Promoting individual liberty

In a society such as ours, premised on individual liberties and limited government, the criminal law should be used to prevent persons from causing positive harm to others, but it should not be used to coerce people to act to benefit others.

C. Exceptions to the General Rule

Notwithstanding the general rule, a person has a legal duty to act in limited circumstances, if he is physically capable of doing so.

1. Crimes of Omission: Statutory Duty

Some statutes expressly require a person to perform specified acts. Failure to perform those acts constitutes an offense. Such an offense may be characterized as a "crime of omission."

2. Crimes of Commission

The criminal law sometimes permits prosecution for a crime of commission (an offense that, by definition, appears to require proof of conduct, rather than an omission), although the basis of the prosecution is an omission. Thus, we have a case of what might be characterized as commission-by-omission.

a. Duty by Status

A person has a common law duty to protect another with whom he has a special status relationship, typically, one based on dependency or interdependency, such as parent-to-child, spouse-to-spouse, and master-to-servant.

b. Duty by Contract

A person may have an express contract to come to the aid of another, or such a contract may be implied-in-law.

c. Duty by Voluntary Assumption

One who voluntarily assumes the care of another must continue to assist if a subsequent omission would place the victim in a worse position than if the good samaritan had not assumed care at all.

d. Duty by Risk Creation

One who creates a risk of harm to another must thereafter act to prevent ensuing harm.

IV. SOCIAL HARM

A. Definition

"Social harm" may be defined as the destruction of, injury to, or endangerment of, some socially valuable interest.

B. Identifying the Social Harm

You can determine the "social harm" of an offense by looking at the definition of the crime and identifying the elements of it that describe the external conduct that constitutes the crime.

C. Breaking Down the Social Harm Into Categories

It is sometimes essential for a lawyer (especially in jurisdictions that follow the Model Penal Code) to be able to look at the definition of a crime, more specifically the *actus reus* portion, and divide up the "social harm" elements into one or more of the following three categories.

1. "Result" Elements (or Crimes)

Some crimes prohibit a specific result, such as the death of another person.

2. "Conduct" Elements (or Crimes)

Some crimes prohibit specific conduct, whether or not tangible harm results thereby, such as offenses that prohibit drunk driving.

3. "Attendant Circumstance" Elements

A "result" or "conduct" is not an offense unless certain "attendant circumstances" exist. An "attendant circumstance" is a fact that exists at the time of the actor's conduct, or at the time of a particular result, and which is required to be proven in the definition of the offense.

■ PART THREE: *MENS REA*

I. *MENS REA*: GENERAL PRINCIPLES

A. Meaning of *"Mens Rea"*

1. Broad ("Culpability") Meaning

A person has acted with *"mens rea"* in the broad sense of the term if she committed the *actus reus* of an offense with a "vicious will," "evil mind," or "morally blameworthy" or "culpable" state of mind.

2. Narrow ("Elemental") Meaning

"Mens rea" exists in the narrow sense of the term if, but only if, a person commits the *actus reus* of an offense with the particular mental state set out expressly in the definition of that offense. This may be called the "elemental" definition of *mens rea*.

B. Rationale of the *Mens Rea* Requirement

1. Utilitarian Argument

It is frequently asserted that a person who commits the *actus reus* of an offense without a *mens rea* is not dangerous, could not have been deterred, and is not in need of reform. Therefore, her punishment would be counter-utilitarian.

2. Retributive Argument

The *mens rea* requirement is solidly supported by the retributive principle of just deserts. A person who commits the *actus reus* of an offense in a morally innocent manner, *i.e.*, accidentally, does not deserve to be punished, as she did not choose to act unlawfully.

II. COMMON LAW

A. "Intentionally"

1. Definition

A person commits the social harm of an offense "intentionally" if: (1) it was her conscious object to cause the result; or (2) if she knew that the result was virtually certain to occur because of her conduct.

2. Transferred Intent Doctrine

Courts frequently speaks of a "transferred intent" doctrine: A person acts "intentionally" as the term is defined above, if the result of her conduct differs from that which she desired only in respect to the identity of the victim.

B. "Knowledge" or "Knowingly"

1. Definition

Some offenses require proof that the actor had knowledge of an attendant circumstance. At common law, a person acts "knowingly" regarding an existing fact (an "attendant circumstance") if she either: (1) is aware of the fact; (2) correctly believes that the fact exists; or (3) suspects that the fact exists and purposely avoids learning if her suspicion is correct. The latter form of "knowledge" is sometimes called "wilful blindness."

C. Risk-Taking: "Recklessness" and "Criminal Negligence"

1. Overview

Risk-taking is properly divisible into various types: justifiable risk-taking; unjustifiable risk-taking that may properly result in tort damages; and unjustifiable risk-taking that may also result in criminal punishment. The latter forms of risk-taking are frequently described as "negligent" risk-taking and "reckless" risk-taking.

2. Unjustified Risk–Taking

In order to determine whether risk-taking is justifiable or not, one must look at three factors: the *gravity of harm* that a reasonable person would foresee might occur as the result of the risk-taking conduct; the *probability* that this harm will occur; and the *reason* for the proposed conduct, *i.e.*, the benefit to the individual or society of taking the risk. A risk is unjustifiable if the gravity of the foreseeable harm, multiplied by the probability of its occurrence, outweighs the foreseeable benefit from the conduct.

3. "Criminal Negligence"

A person acts in a "criminally negligent" manner if she should be aware that her conduct creates a substantial and unjustifiable risk of social harm. Synonyms for "criminal negligence," include "gross negligence" and "culpable negligence."

4. "Recklessness"

a. Holmes's View

Oliver Wendell Holmes, Jr., believed that a person acts "recklessly" if she should be aware that she is taking a *very* substantial and unjustifiable risk. This is simply a heightened version of "criminal negligence." Notice: "civil negligence" involves unjustifiable risk-taking; "criminal negligence" is *substantial* and unjustifiable risk-taking; and "recklessness" (as defined here) is *very* substantial and unjustifiable risk-taking.

b. Modern Definition

Although Holmes's definition is still followed by some courts, most courts now provide that a person acts "recklessly" if she *consciously* disregards a substantial and unjustifiable risk that her conduct will cause the social harm of the offense. Under this definition, "recklessness" differs from "criminal negligence" in that it requires that the actor subjectively be aware of the substantial and unjustifiable risk.

D. "Malice"

A person acts with "malice" if she intentionally or recklessly causes the social harm of an offense, as the latter *mens rea* terms are defined above.

E. "Specific Intent" and "General Intent"

The common law distinguishes between "general intent" and "specific intent" crimes. The distinction is critical, because some defenses apply only, or more broadly, in the case of so-called "specific intent" offenses.

1. "Specific Intent" Offenses

In most cases, a "specific intent" offense is one that *explicitly* contains one of the following *mens rea* elements in its definition: (1) the intent to commit some act over and beyond the *actus reus* of the offense; (2) a special motive for committing the *actus reus* of the offense; or (3) awareness of a particular attendant circumstance.

2. "General Intent" Offenses

Any offense that requires proof of a culpable mental state, but which does not contain a specific intent, is a "general intent" offense. Sometimes, such an offense will have no explicit *mens rea* term in the definition of the offense; it is enough that the defendant committed the *actus reus* with *any* culpable state of mind.

F. Statutory Construction

A common issue in criminal law litigation is whether a *mens rea* term in the definition of an offense applies to all or only some of the *actus reus* elements in the definition of the crime. In the absence of explicit rules, common law courts have struggled to interpret modern statutes.

1. Common Law Interpretive Rules Of Thumb

a. Legislative intent

The ultimate issue for any court today—*always*—is to determine what the legislature intended. A court will try to resolve interpretive problems by ascertaining the intention of the drafters of the law, sometimes by looking through legislative history. Often, however, evidence regarding legislative intent is non-existent or ambiguous, so courts must look elsewhere.

b. Position of the *Mens Rea* term in Definition of Offense

Courts often look at the placement of the *mens rea* term in the definition of the offense, in order to ascertain legislative intent. See the Main Outline for a useful example.

c. Punctuation

Sometimes punctuation is relied upon to determine that a phrase set off by commas is independent of the language that precedes or follows it.

d. Attendant Circumstances

Frequently, courts assume that, absent evidence to the contrary, *mens rea* terms in the definitions of offenses do *not* apply to "attendant circumstance" elements of the crime.

III. MODEL PENAL CODE

A. Section 2.02, Subsection 1

1. Language

In general, "a person is not guilty of an offense unless he acted purposely, knowingly, recklessly, or negligently, as the law may require, with respect to each material element of the offense."

2. Significance of Subsection

a. Role of *Mens Rea*

In general, the MPC requires proof of *mens rea*. More significantly, it requires proof of some particular *mens rea*—purpose, knowledge, recklessness, or negligence—as to *each* material element of the offense. This contrasts with the common law, where there might be a *mens rea* requirement as to one element but no *mens rea* required as to other elements. In other words, with the MPC, *each actus reus* element should be "covered" by some *mens rea* requirement.

B. Culpability Terms Defined

1. Purposely

The common law term "intentionally" is not used in the Model Penal Code. Instead, the MPC subdivides "intent" into its two alternative components, and calls them "purposely" and "knowingly." A person causes a result "purposely" if it is her conscious object to cause the result.

2. Knowingly

a. Results

A person "knowingly" causes a result if she is aware that the result is "practically certain" to occur from her conduct.

b. Attendant Circumstances

A person acts "knowingly" as to an attendant circumstance if he is aware that the circumstance exists, or if he is aware "of a high probability of its existence, unless he actually believes that it does not exist." The latter provision is the Code version of the "wilful blindness" doctrine discussed earlier.

3. Recklessly

a. Basic Definition

A person is said to have acted recklessly if "he consciously disregards a substantial and unjustifiable risk that the material element exists or will result from his conduct."

b. Standard for Evaluating Conduct

The Code provides, basically, that the standard discussed earlier—measuring the gravity of foreseeable harm, the probability of its occurrence, and the reasons for taking the risk—should be applied. One is reckless when the risk-taking "involves a gross deviation from the standard of care that a reasonable person would observe in the actor's situation."

4. Negligently

A person acts negligently when he *should be aware* of a "substantial and unjustifiable risk." This is a risk that constitutes "a gross deviation from the standard of care that a reasonable person would observe in the actor's situation." The critical difference between recklessness and negligence under the Code is that in the former case, the actor is consciously aware of the substantial and unjustifiable risk, but proceeds anyway; in the case of negligence, the actor is *not* aware of the risk, but *should* be.

C. Interpretative Rules

1. Default Position

The MPC requires some *mens rea* term for each element of an offense (§ 2.05 aside). If the statute defining an offense is silent regarding the issue of *mens rea* as to one or more of the *actus reus* elements, the Code provides that "such element is established if a person acts purposely, knowingly, or recklessly with respect thereto." In essence, you fill in the blank with "purposely, knowingly, or recklessly."

2. When Just One *Mens Rea* Term is Mentioned

If the definition of a MPC statute only sets out a single *mens rea* element in the definition of the offense, that *mens rea* term applies to *every* material element of the offense, *unless* a contrary legislative intent "plainly appears."

IV. STRICT LIABILITY

A. Nature of a Strict Liability Offense

An offense is "strict liability" in nature if commission of the *actus reus* of the offense, without proof of a *mens rea*, is sufficient to convict the actor.

B. Public Welfare Offenses

Strict liability most often applies in relation to "public welfare" offenses.

1. Characteristics of Most Public Welfare Offenses

a. Nature of the Conduct

Such offenses typically involve *malum prohibitum* conduct, *i.e.*, conduct that is wrongful only because it is prohibited (*e.g.*, motor vehicle laws), as distinguished from *malum in se* conduct, *i.e.*, inherently wrongful conduct (*e.g.*, murder).

b. Punishment

The penalty for violation of a public welfare offense is usually minor, such as a monetary fine or a very short jail sentence.

c. Degree of Social Danger

A single violation of a public welfare offense often threatens the safety of many persons, *e.g.*, transportation of explosives on a highway not designated for such use.

C. Non–Public Welfare Offenses

On rare occasion, *non*-public welfare offenses are considered strict liability in nature. Statutory rape is the most common example of such an offense.

D. Constitutionality of Strict Liability Offenses

Strict-liability offenses are not *per se* unconstitutional. Nonetheless, there is a strong presumption against strict liability as to offenses that have their roots in the common law (*i.e.*, *non*-public-welfare offenses). In such circumstances, a court will not assume (absent evidence to the contrary) that the legislature intended to abandon the common law *mens rea* requirement, even if the statute is silent regarding this element.

■ PART FOUR: *MENS REA* AND MISTAKES OF FACT OR LAW

I. MISTAKE OF FACT

A. Common Law

1. Specific–Intent Offenses

A defendant is not guilty of a specific-intent crime if her mistake of fact negates the specific-intent element of the offense. Even an unreasonable mistake of fact—a mistake that a reasonable person would *not* make— may exculpate the actor, assuming the mistake negatives the *mens rea* required for the offense.

2. General–Intent Offenses

a. Ordinary Rule

A defendant is not guilty of a general-intent offense if her mistake of fact was reasonable. An *unreasonable* mistake of fact does *not* exculpate.

b. Exception: "Moral Wrong" Doctrine

Although the principle stated above is the general rule, on occasion a court will convict a defendant of an offense, although her mistake of fact was reasonable, if her conduct violates the "moral wrong" doctrine. This doctrine provides that there should be no exculpation for a mistake where, if the facts had been as the actor believed them to be, her conduct would be immoral, albeit legal. By knowingly committing a morally wrong act, an actor assumes the risk that the facts are not as she believed them to be, *i.e.*, that her actions are not just morally wrong, but also legally wrong.

c. Alternative Exception: "Legal Wrong" Doctrine

Occasionally, a court will convict a defendant of an offense, al-though her mistake of fact was reasonable, if her conduct violates the "legal wrong" doctrine. This rule substitutes the word "illegal" for "immoral" in the description of the moral-wrong doctrine, but is otherwise applied in the same manner. Thus, a person is guilty of criminal offense X, despite a reasonable mistake of fact, if she would be guilty of a different, *albeit lesser*, crime Y, if the factual situation were as she supposed.

3. Strict-Liability Offenses

A mistake of fact, whether reasonable or unreasonable, is never a defense to a strict-liability offense. This rule is logical: a strict-liability offense is one that requires no proof of *mens rea*. Therefore, there is no *mens rea* to negate. A defendant's mistake of fact is legally irrelevant.

B. Model Penal Code

1. General Rule

Subject to the exception noted below, a mistake of fact is a defense to a crime if the mistake negates a mental state element required in the definition of the offense. The Code dispenses with the common law distinction between "general intent" and "specific intent" offenses: the mistake-of-fact rule applies to all offenses in the same manner.

2. Exception to the General Rule

In a variation on the common law legal-wrong doctrine, the defense of mistake-of-fact is inapplicable if the defendant would be guilty of a lesser offense had the facts been as she believed them to be. Under such circumstances—unlike the common law—the defendant will be punished at the level of the lesser, rather than the greater, offense.

II. MISTAKE OF LAW

A. General Principles

1. General Rule

In general, knowledge of the law is not an element of an offense. Moreover, a mistake of law—even a reasonable one!—does not ordinarily relieve an actor of liability for the commission of a criminal offense.

2. Purported Justifications for the Rule

a. Certainty of the Law

The law is definite. Therefore, any mistake of law is inherently unreasonable. See the Main Outline for rebuttal arguments.

b. Concern about Fraud

If a mistake-of-law defense were recognized, it would invite fraud. Every defendant would assert ignorance or mistake, and it would be nearly impossible to disprove the claim. See the Main Outline for rebuttal arguments.

c. Promoting Knowledge of the Law

We want people to learn the law. To promote education—to deter ignorance—the law must apply strict liability principles. See the Main Outline for rebuttal arguments.

B. Exceptions to the General Rule

1. Mistakes That Negate the *Mens Rea*

A defendant is not guilty of an offense if his mistake of law, whether reasonable or unreasonable, negates an element of the crime charged.

2. Authorized–Reliance Doctrine

A person is not guilty of a criminal offense if, at the time of the offense, he reasonably relied on an official statement of the law, later determined to be erroneous, obtained from a person or public body with responsibility for the interpretation, administration, or enforcement of the law defining the offense.

a. On Whom or What Body is Reliance Reasonable

Although the common law is less clear than the Model Penal Code in this regard, apparently a defendant may reasonably rely on an official statement of the law found in a statute, judicial opinion, administrative ruling, or an official interpretation of the law given by one who is responsible for the law's enforcement or interpretation, such as the United States or State Attorney General.

3. Due Process Clause

In very rare circumstances, it offends due process to punish a person for a crime of which she was unaware at the time of her conduct. The Due Process Clause apparently is violated if three factors exist: (1) the "unknown" offense criminalizes an omission; (2) the duty to act is based on a status condition rather than conduct; and (3) the offense is *malum prohibitum* in nature.

■ PART FIVE: CAUSATION

I. ACTUAL CAUSE (CAUSE–IN–FACT)

A. General Principles

1. Rule

A person is not guilty of an offense unless she is an actual cause of the ensuing harm. Both the common law and the Model Penal Code provide that conduct is the "actual cause" of the prohibited result if the result would *not* have occurred but for the actor's conduct.

B. Steps for Determining the "Actual Cause"

1. Identifying the Relevant Conduct

Determine what is (are) the relevant voluntary act(s) committed by *D*. If the case is based on an omission, determine what the omission is, and substitute that for the "voluntary act" in the following discussion.

2. Frame the Question Properly

Ask the question: "But for *D*'s voluntary act(s) would the social harm have occurred when it did?" If the social harm would have occurred when it did even if *D* had not acted, *D* is *not* the actual cause of the harm and, therefore, is not guilty of the offense. In a sense, "yes" means "no" (no criminal liability). If the social harm would *not* have occurred when it did but for *D*'s voluntary act(s), *D* *is* an actual cause of the social harm, in which case you move on to the remaining causation issue (proximate cause).

C. Multiple Actual Causes

There usually are multiple actual causes of a result. A person who dies of lung cancer, for example, might not have died *when she did* but for her smoking habit *and* living in a smog-polluted city. It can also be the case that two persons—two potential defendants—are the actual cause of a result. See the Main Outline for useful examples.

D. Concurrent Sufficient Causes

In rare circumstances, the "but for" test may fail to reach the morally sensible result. The problem arises when two acts, either one of which is sufficient to cause the resulting harm when it did, occur concurrently. See the Main Outline for useful examples.

1. Substantial Factor Test

In such cases, many courts resort to the "substantial factor" test, a standard that is often used in tort cases. The question to be asked is: "Was *D*'s conduct a substantial factor in the resulting harm?"

2. Model Penal Code

The MPC does not apply the substantial factor test—it uses the "but for" test in all cases. However, the Commentary to the Code explains that, in deciding whether a defendant was a "but for" cause of a "result," one would state the "result" with specificity. See the Main Outline for details.

II. PROXIMATE CAUSE (LEGAL CAUSE)

A. General Principles

1. Role of "Proximate Cause" In Legal Analysis

A person who is an actual cause of resulting harm is not responsible for it unless she is also the proximate (or "legal") cause of the harm. When the law states that a defendant was the proximate cause of a result, this is a shorthand way of saying that it is morally just to hold this person responsible for the harm.

2. Common Law, Model Penal Code, and Study Point

As with any "what is just" analysis, there is no single or straightforward answer. The common law provides various potential factors to consider. The drafters of the Code have another way of handling the issue: they treat "proximate causation" as a culpability, rather than causal, issue. The MPC issue is whether the defendant can be said to have purposely, knowingly, recklessly, or negligently (whichever is relevant in a particular case) caused "a particular result" if the "result" occurs in an odd or unexpected manner. The Code takes all of the common law factors discussed below and basically roles them into one, explicit, policy question for the jury: Was "the actual result . . . too remote or accidental in its occurrence to have a [just] bearing on the actor's liability or on the gravity of the offense."

B. Direct Cause

A direct cause is a but-for cause, in which no other cause intervenes between it and the resulting social harm. A voluntary act that is a direct cause of the social harm is also a proximate cause of it. This is because there is no other candidate for causal responsibility.

C. Intervening Cause

1. Definition

An "intervening cause" is an actual cause (a "but for" cause) of social harm that arises *after D's* causal contribution to the result.

2. General Role of Intervening Causes

An intervening cause does not necessarily relieve a defendant of causal responsibility for the resulting harm. At common law, various factors come into play in proximate causation analysis.

3. Nature of Intervening Cause

It is useful, *although not always dispositive*, to determine whether the intervening cause was "dependent" or "independent" of the defendant's act.

a. "Dependent" and "Independent" Distinguished

An intervening cause is *dependent* if it occurs in response to the defendant's earlier conduct. An intervening cause is *independent* if the factor would have come into play even in the absence of the defendant's conduct.

b. Legal Significance of Terminology

Generally speaking, a defendant is responsible for a *dependent* intervening cause, *unless* the dependent intervening act was not only unforeseeable but freakish. In contrast, a defendant is *not* ordinarily responsible for an *independent* intervening cause, *unless* its occurrence was foreseeable to a reasonable person in the defendant's situation.

4. Other Important Factors

a. Intended Consequences Doctrine

In general, a defendant is the proximate cause of a result, even if there is an intervening cause, if the defendant intended the result that occurred. But, one should be very precise in stating what result the defendant intended: a person may want someone dead in a particular manner, in which case this doctrine only applies if the result occurs in the desired manner.

b. Free, Deliberate, Informed Human Intervention

In general, a defendant is *not* the proximate cause of a result if a free, deliberate, and informed act of another human being intervenes.

■ PART SIX: DEFENSES TO CRIME: JUSTIFICATIONS

I. JUSTIFICATION DEFENSES: GENERALLY

A. Definition

A justification defense is one that indicates society's belief that the defendant's conduct was morally good, socially desirable, or (at least) not wrongful.

B. Basic Structure of Justification Defenses

In general, a justification defense contains three components.

1. Necessity

Ordinarily, use of force against another is not justifiable unless it is necessary.

2. Proportionality

Ordinarily, a person may not use force that is disproportional to the threat that motivates the use of force. For example, deadly force should not be used to repel a non-deadly threat.

3. Reasonable Belief

Ordinarily, a defendant must possess a reasonable (even if incorrect) belief that the use of force is necessary and proportional to the supposed threat.

II. SELF–DEFENSE

A. Common Law

1. General Rule

Subject to clarification below, a person is justified in using *deadly force* against another if: (a) he is not the *aggressor*; and (b) he *reasonably believes* that such force is *necessary* to repel the *imminent* use of *unlawful deadly force* by the other person.

2. Definition of "Deadly Force"

The term "deadly force"—whether applied to the actions of the aggressor or the person resisting aggression—is typically defined as "force likely to cause, or intended to cause, death or serious bodily harm."

3. "Aggressor"

An aggressor may not use deadly force in self-defense. It is possible, however, for an aggressor to purge himself of his status as an aggressor and regain the right of self-defense.

a. Definition

An "aggressor" may be defined as one who commits an "unlawful act reasonably calculated to produce an affray foreboding injurious or fatal consequences."

b. Losing the "Aggressor" Status

i. Nondeadly Aggressors

A, a nondeadly aggressor, may regain her right of self-defense against *B*, if *B* responds to *A*'s nondeadly aggression by threatening to use excessive—deadly—force in response. Courts differ, however, regarding how *A* regains the right to use deadly force.

(1) Majority Rule

A immediately regains her right of self-defense, as soon as *B* threatens excessive force.

(2) Minority Rule

If *B* responds to *A*'s nondeadly aggression by threatening to use deadly force against *A*, *A* may not use deadly force in self-defense unless *A* first retreats, and *B* continues to threaten *A* with deadly force. If no safe retreat is possible, however, *A* may immediately use deadly force.

ii. Deadly Aggressor

A, a deadly aggressor, loses the right of self-defense in a conflict unless she abandons her deadly design and communicates this fact to *B*.

4. Proportionality of Force: Deadly Against Deadly

Deadly force may never be used in response to a nondeadly threat, even if this is the only way to repel the nondeadly threat.

5. "Unlawful Force"/"Unlawful Threat"

A person has no right to defend herself against lawful—justified—force. She may only respond to unlawful threats of force.

6. "Imminency"

Although modern courts are somewhat less strict than their predecessors, generally speaking a person may not use deadly force in self-defense unless the aggressor's threatened force will occur immediately, almost at that instant.

7. Necessity to Use Deadly Force

A person may not use deadly force unless it is necessary.

a. Use of Less Force

A person may not use deadly force to repel an unlawful deadly attack if more moderate (nondeadly) force will do the job.

b. Retreat?

Must non-aggressors retreat—flee to a safe place—rather than stand their ground and use deadly force? Today, there is a conflict on this subject in non-Model Penal Code jurisdictions. A majority of non-MPC jurisdictions do *not* have a retreat requirement. A minority of jurisdictions provide that, with one key exception, a non-aggressor may *not* use deadly force to repel an attack if she knows of a completely safe place to which she can retreat. The exception is that a non-aggressor is never required to retreat from her own home.

8. "Reasonable Belief"

a. General Rule

The self-defense rules discussed above are modified by the "reasonable belief" principle, which provides that a person may use deadly force in self-defense is she has reasonable grounds to believe, and actually believes, that she is in imminent danger of death or serious bodily harm, and that use of deadly force is necessary to protect herself, *even if her reasonable beliefs in these regards are incorrect.*

b. What Is a "Reasonable Belief"?

A reasonable belief is a belief that a reasonable person would hold in the actor's situation. But, that only shifts the question to the issue:

who is a "reasonable person"? Ordinarily, the defendant's physical characteristics may be incorporated into the "reasonable person." Many courts today also subscribe to the view that prior experiences of the defendant that help the defendant evaluate the present situation are relevant.

c. Battered Women and Self–Defense

How should the law deal with the situation of a woman, physically abused for years by her husband or live-in partner, who kills her abuser at a moment when she is not, in fact, under imminent attack, for example, when the batterer is sleeping? Can we say that the battered woman *reasonably* believed that the batterer represented an imminent threat in such nonconfrontational circumstances?

i. Legal Trends

Most courts prohibit an instruction on self-defense if the homicide occurred in nonconfrontational circumstances, on the ground that no reasonable juror could believe that the defendant, *as a reasonable person*, would believe that a sleeping man represents an *imminent* threat. But, some courts now do permit such cases to go to the jury, if Battered Woman Syndrome evidence is introduced to show that the defendant, as a battered woman, suffered from this condition. See the Main Outline for discussion of this syndrome evidence.

B. Model Penal Code

1. General Rule

Subject to the limitations discussed below, a person is not justified in using deadly force against another unless she believe that such force is immediately necessary to protect herself against the exercise of unlawful deadly force, force likely to cause serious bodily harm, a kidnapping, or sexual intercourse compelled by force or threat, by the other person on the present occasion. See the Main Outline for a comparison of this rule to the common law.

2. Limitations on General Rule

Even if deadly force is otherwise permitted, it is impermissible in two key circumstances.

a. Defendant as Aggressor

As with the common law, the defense is not permitted if the actor is the aggressor, which the Code defines as one who "provokes" the use of force against herself "in the same encounter" for the "purpose of causing death or serious bodily injury."

b. Retreat

The Code follows the minority common law position that a non-aggressor must retreat if she knows that she can thereby avoid the need to use deadly force with complete safety to herself. This retreat requirement, however, is itself subject to various exceptions, most notably that a person need not retreat from her own dwelling.

c. Other "Non–Necessity" Circumstances

The Code explicitly provides that deadly force may not be used if, subject to various exceptions, the defendant can avoid doing so "by surrendering possession of a thing to a person asserting a claim of right thereto or by complying with a demand that he abstain from any action that he has no duty to take."

III. DEFENSE–OF–THIRD–PARTIES

A. Common Law

1. General Rule

A person is justified is using deadly force to protect a third party from unlawful use of force by an aggressor. The intervenor's right to use force parallels the third party's *apparent* right of *self*-defense. That is, the third party may use force when, and to the extent that, she reasonably believes that the third party would be justified in using force to protect herself.

2. Minority Rule

Some jurisdictions provide that a person may only use force to defend a third party if the person being defended would *in fact* have been justified in using the same degree of force in self-defense. That is, the intervenor is placed in the shoes of the party whom she is seeking to defend. If the other person has no right of self-defense, *even though the intervenor reasonably believes that she does*, the intervenor loses her claim.

B. Model Penal Code

A person is justified in using deadly force to protect another if: (1) the intervenor would be justified in using such force to protect herself, if the facts were as she believed them to be; (2) according to the facts as the intervenor believes them to be, the third person would be justified in using such force to protect herself; (3) the intervenor believes force is necessary for the third party's protection; and (4) if the third party would be required to retreat under the Code self-protection rules, the intervenor must attempt to cause the third party to retreat before using deadly force.

IV. DEFENSES OF PROPERTY AND HABITATION

A. Defense of Property

1. Common Law

A person is never justified in using deadly force to defend her real or personal property. A person *is* justified in using *non*deadly force if she reasonably believes that such force is necessary to prevent the imminent, unlawful dispossession of the property. Some jurisdictions also provide that, prior to using force, the property defender must ask the dispossessor to desist from his conduct, unless such a request would be futile or dangerous.

a. Important Clarification

With one exception, the defender must be in lawful possession of the property at the time force is used. If she has already been dispossessed of the property, force may *not* be used to *recapture* the property. Instead, the victim of dispossession must seek judicial redress. The exception is that nondeadly force *is* permitted in fresh pursuit of a dispossessor of property. In such circumstances, the use of force to recapture the property is treated as an extension of the original effort to prevent dispossession.

b. Another Important Clarification

The defender's right to use force is based on her rightful *possession* of the property; she does not need to have title to it.

2. Model Penal Code

The MPC differs from the common law in various key respects.

a. Belief Requirement

As with other justifications defenses, the right to use force to protect property is based on the actor's subjective belief, subject to the provisions of § 3.09, previously discussed in the Main Outline.

b. Recapture of Property

With one exception, the MPC goes further than the common law in that it generally authorizes use of nondeadly force to retake possession of land or recapture personal property, *even after fresh pursuit has ended*, if the actor believes that the dispossessor has no claim of right to the property. The exception is that in the case of land, a recapturer may *not* use force unless she believes that it would constitute an "exceptional hardship" to delay re-entry until she can obtain a court order.

c. Deadly Force

The Code authorizes the use of deadly force if *D* believes that *V*: (1) intends to dispossess *D* of his dwelling other than under a claim-of-right to possession; or (2) intends to commit arson, burglary, robbery or felonious theft inside the dwelling and (2a) *V* "has employed or threatened deadly force against or in the presence" of *D* or (2b) the use of *non*deadly force to prevent commission of the crime would expose *D* or another to substantial risk of serious bodily harm.

B. Defense of Habitation

1. Common Law

a. Older, Broader Rule

D is justified in using deadly force against *V* if the actor reasonably believes that: (1) *V* intends unlawfully and imminently to enter *D*'s dwelling; (2) *V* intends to commit a felony inside, or to cause bodily injury, no matter how slight, to any occupant; and (3) deadly force is necessary to prevent the entry.

b. Narrower Rule

Many jurisdictions no longer apply the broad rule set out above and instead hold that deadly force is limited to circumstances in which *D* believes that *V* will commit an atrocious (violent) felony inside the dwelling if *V* enters.

2. Model Penal Code

The Code does not recognize a separate interest in habitation, as distinguished from defense of property. See the comments above in regard to the MPC defense-of-property claim.

C. Special Issue: Spring Guns

1. Common Law

A person may use a spring gun to inflict deadly force on another "where an intrusion is, *in fact*, such that a person, were he present, would be justified in taking the life or inflicting the bodily harm with his own hands." As the italicized words suggest, the user of the spring gun acts at her peril: the deadly force must be necessary. Reasonable appearances will not suffice.

2. Model Penal Code

The justifiable use of force does not extend to any mechanical device that is intended to use, or is known to create, a significant risk of causing death or serious bodily injury.

V. LAW ENFORCEMENT DEFENSES

A. Crime Prevention

1. Common Law

a. Original (Now Minority) Approach

The original common law rule, followed today in a few jurisdictions, is that a police officer or private citizen is justified in using deadly force upon another if she reasonably believes that: (1) the other person is committing *any* felony; and (2) deadly force is necessary to prevent commission of the crime. This version of the defense is controversial because it can authorize use of force grossly disproportional to the threat caused by the felon.

b. Modern (Majority) Approach

The majority rule differs from the original rule in one critical way: deadly force is only permitted if the actor reasonably believes that the other person is about to commit an "atrocious" felony, *i.e.,* a felony that involves a significant risk of serious bodily harm to an innocent person. Among the felonies that are considered atrocious are: murder, manslaughter, robbery, arson, rape, and burglary.

2. Model Penal Code

A police officer or private party may not use deadly force to prevent a felony unless she believes that: (1) there is a substantial risk that the suspect will cause death or serious bodily harm to another unless commission or consummation of the offense is prevented; (2) the force is immediately necessary to prevent commission of the offense; and (3) use of deadly force presents no substantial risk of injury to bystanders. As with other Code justification defenses, the defense is based on the actor's subjective belief, subject always to Code provisions that permit prosecution for reckless or negligent homicide if the actor's beliefs were reckless or negligent, as the case may be.

B. Arrest

1. Common Law

a. Majority Rule

A police officer is justified in using deadly force against another if she reasonably believes that: (1) the suspect committed any felony; and (2) such force is necessary to immediately effectuate the arrest. As discussed below, this rule is now unconstitutional as it relates to the actions of police officers.

b. Special Problem of "Citizen Arrests"

Common law jurists were hesitant to permit private citizens to use deadly force in "citizen arrests." Therefore, although the rules vary considerably by jurisdiction, limitations on the use of deadly force by private parties are common. These may include: (i) limitation of the use of deadly force to atrocious felonies; (ii) a requirement that the private person give notice of her intention to make the arrest; and (iii) denial of the defense if the suspect *in fact* did not commit the felony, even if the private party reasonably believed that she did.

2. Model Penal Code

Deadly force may *never* be used by private citizens acting on their own to make an arrest or to prevent a suspect's escape. However, a police officer (or private citizen assisting the officer) may use deadly force to effectuate an arrest if she believes that: (1) the force can be applied at no risk to innocent bystanders; (2) such force is immediately necessary to make the arrest; and either (3a) the felony for which the person is being arrested included the use or threatened use of deadly force; or (3b) a substantial risk exists that the suspect will cause serious bodily harm to another if she is not apprehended immediately.

C. *Tennessee v. Garner*

1. Constitutional Rule

The Supreme Court ruled in *Tennessee v. Garner* that it is unconstitutional for a police officer to use deadly force to prevent the escape of a fleeing felony suspect unless: (1) the force is necessary to prevent the suspect's successful flight; (2) if it is practical to do so, the officer warns the suspect of her intention to use deadly force; and (3), the officer has probable cause to believe that the suspect, if not immediately apprehended, poses a significant threat of death or serious injury to the officer or others. The term "probable cause" is a constitutional term of art: it is enough for current purposes to state that it involves less than a fifty percent degree of likelihood.

2. Court Examples of Permissible Deadly Force

The constitutional rule is set out above, but the Court provided two examples of circumstances in which deadly force, if otherwise necessary (and assuming a prior warning is given, if possible), would be reasonable: (1) if the suspect threatens the officer with a weapon; or (2) the officer has probable cause to believe that the suspect has committed a crime involving the actual or threatened infliction of serious physical harm to another.

VI. NECESSITY

A. Common Law

1. Elements of the Defense

a. Lesser–Evils Analysis

The actor must be faced with a choice of evils or harms, and he must choose to commit the lesser of the evils. Put differently, the harm that *D* seeks to *prevent* by his conduct must be greater than the harm he reasonably expects to *cause* by his conduct. The balancing of the harms is conducted by the judge or jury; the defendant's belief that he is acting properly is not in itself sufficient.

b. Imminency of Harm

The actor must be seeking to avoid imminent harm. This rule is strictly enforced: if there is sufficient time to seek a lawful avenue, the actor *must* take that route.

c. Causal Element

The actor must reasonably believe that his actions will abate the threatened harm.

d. Blamelessness of the Actor

Many courts and/or statutes provide that the actor must not be at fault in creating the necessity.

2. Homicide Prosecutions

It is unclear whether the defense of necessity applies to the crime of murder. Fortunately, the issue has only rarely arisen. The leading case—and the one most likely to be in your casebook—is *Regina v. Dudley and Stephens*. Read the Main Outline for discussion of this case.

B. Model Penal Code

1. Elements

A person is justified in committing an act that otherwise would constitute an offense if: (a) the actor believes that the conduct is necessary to avoid harm to himself or another; (b) the harm that the actor seeks to avoid is greater than that sought to be avoided by the law prohibiting his conduct; and (c) there does not plainly exist any legislative intent to exclude the justification claimed by the actor. If the actor was reckless or negligent in bringing about the emergency, the defense is unavailable in a prosecution for any offense for which recklessness or negligence, as the may be, is sufficient to prove guilt.

2. Comparison to Common Law

Under the Code, the threatened harm need not be imminent. Moreover, the Commentary to the Code expressly states that this defense *is* available in homicide prosecutions.

■ PART SEVEN: DEFENSES TO CRIME: EXCUSES

I. EXCUSE DEFENSES: GENERALLY

A. Excuse: Defined

An excuse defense is one that indicates that, although the actor committed the elements of the offense, and although his actions were unjustified—wrongful—the law does not blame him for his wrongful conduct.

B. Justification versus Excuse

A justification defense tends to focus on the wrongfulness of an *act* or a result; an excuse defense focuses on the *actor*. The distinction between the two categories of defenses—justifications and excuses—is an important one.

II. DURESS

A. Rationale of the Defense: Justification or Excuse?

1. Duress as a Justification Defense

A few courts and treatises treat duress as if it were sub-species of the necessity defense and, thus, as a justification defense. According to this view, the only meaningful difference between necessity and duress is that the former defense involves natural, *i.e.*, non-human, pressures, whereas duress involves human-based threats (*e.g.*, a terrorist demanding an innocent person to commit a crime against other innocent persons; a criminal forcing an innocent person to rob a bank).

2. Duress as an Excuse Defense

Most courts and treatises treat duress as an excuse defense, and not as a justification defense. Intuitively, most people believe that a coerced person (based on the definition of duress discussed below) is morally blameless, but not that she has done nothing wrong. The essence of the duress defense is that a person is not to blame for her conduct if, because of an unlawful threat, she lacks a fair opportunity to conform her conduct to the law.

B. Common Law

1. Elements of Defense

Generally speaking, a defendant will be acquitted of an offense *other than murder* on the basis of duress if she proves that she committed the offense because: (a) another person unlawfully threatened imminently to kill or grievously injure her or another person unless she committed the crime; and (b) she is not at fault in exposing herself to the threat. See the Main Outline for more details.

2. Coerced Homicides

The common law duress defense does not apply to the offense of murder. The no-defense rule is sometimes defended on the utilitarian ground that the drive for self-preservation, although strong, is not irresistible; therefore, people should be persuaded (by the threat of punishment) to resist such coercion. The rule is also defended on the moral ground that it is better to die than to kill an innocent person. However, this latter argument only serves to show that a person is not *justified* in killing an innocent person. It does not explain why a coerced actor should not be *excused* on the ground that virtually anyone, short of a saintly hero, would succumb to the coercion.

3. Intolerable Prison Conditions

a. The Issue

Suppose a prisoner is threatened by another inmate with sexual or physical assault, is denied critical medical care by prison officials, or is placed in some other intolerable condition. Therefore, the inmate escapes confinement, but is caught and returned to prison. She is now prosecuted for the offense of prison escape. The inmate wishes to avoid conviction by arguing that she fled as a result of the intolerable prison condition. The frequently litigated issue is whether the inmate may make such a claim in court; and, if she may, is her claim one of necessity (justification) or excuse (duress)?

b. The Law

Originally, courts did not permit inmates to raise prison conditions as a defense to their escape. Today most courts recognize a limited defense. Some courts, however, require the escapee to turn herself in after the escape, once the prison condition "has lost its coercive force," or else the defense is lost. Other courts are more lenient and treat's an escapee's failure to turn herself in as one factor to be considered by the jury in determining whether the escapee should be acquitted. Some states will not recognize the defense if the prisoner uses any violence against other persons during the escape.

c. Nature of the Defense

Courts are fairly evenly divided on the question of whether the defense claim is basically one of duress or necessity. See the Main

Outline for the conceptual problems and practical significance relating to framing the defense as a justification or, alternatively, as an excuse.

C. Model Penal Code

1. Defense

The Model Penal Code unambiguously treats duress as an excuse, and not a justification, defense. Thus, the defense may be raised although the defendant did not commit the lesser of two evils. Instead, the defendant must show that: (a) he committed an offense because he was coerced to do so by another person's use, or threat to use, unlawful force against him or a third party; and (b) a person of reasonable firmness would have committed the offense. The Code further provides that the defense is lost if the coerced actor put himself in a situation "in which it was probable that he would be subjected to duress." Furthermore, if he was negligent in placing himself in the situation, the defense is unavailable if he is prosecuted for an offense for which negligence is sufficient to prove guilt. See the Main Outline for further details.

2. Coerced Homicides

Unlike the common law, there is no bar to use of the duress defense in murder prosecutions.

III. INTOXICATION

A. Common Law: Voluntary Intoxication

1. Definition of "Intoxication"

Intoxication may be defined as a disturbance of an actor's mental or physical capacities resulting from the ingestion of *any* foreign substance, most notably alcohol or drugs, including lawfully prescribed medication.

2. Not an Excuse Defense

A person is never *excused* for his criminal conduct on the ground that he became voluntarily intoxicated. Indeed, the act of getting intoxicated enhances, rather than mitigates, culpability.

3. *Mens Rea* Defense

Although voluntary intoxication is *not* an excuse for criminal conduct, most jurisdictions following the common law provide that a person is not guilty of a *specific-intent* offense if, as the result of voluntary intoxication, he lacked the capacity or otherwise did not form the specific intent required for the crime. However, voluntary intoxication does *not* exculpate for general-intent offenses.

a. Exceptions to Rule

A minority of states today have statutes that bar a defendant from introducing evidence of voluntary intoxication to avoid conviction for a specific-intent offense.

4. "Temporary" Insanity

A defendant is *not* entitled to argue that, due to voluntary intoxication, he did not know right from wrong, or did not know what he was doing, at the time of the offense, even though such a mental state *would* result in acquittal on *insanity* grounds if he suffered from a mental illness.

5. "Fixed" Insanity

Long-term use of alcohol or drugs can cause brain damage or cause the individual to suffer from chronic mental illness. In such circumstances, the defendant who seeks acquittal is not claiming he should be exculpated because he was voluntarily intoxicated at the time of the crime, but rather that, because of long-term use of intoxicants, he is insane (whether he is currently sober or intoxicated). Such a claim *is* recognized by the common law, but the applicable defense is insanity, and not intoxication.

B. Model Penal Code: "Self–Induced" (Voluntary) Intoxication

Subject to one exception, voluntary intoxication is a defense to any crime if it negates an element of the offense.

1. Exception to General Rule

If the defendant is charged with an offense for which recklessness suffices to convict, she cannot avoid conviction by proving that, because of intoxication, she was unaware of the riskiness of her conduct. That is, even if the defendant's actual culpability is that of negligence—she *should have been aware* that her conduct created a substantial and unjustifiable risk of harm—she may be convicted of an offense requiring recklessness (which ordinarily requires *actual awareness* of the risk), if the reason for her failure to perceive the risk is her self-induced intoxication.

C. Involuntary Intoxication

1. What Makes Intoxication Involuntary?

Intoxication is involuntary if: (a) *coercion*: the actor is forced to ingest the intoxicant; (b) *mistake*: the actor innocently ingests an intoxicant; (c) *prescribed medication*: the actor becomes unexpectedly intoxicated from ingestion of a medically prescribed drug, perhaps due to an allergic reaction; or (d) *pathological intoxication*: the actor's intoxication is "grossly excessive in degree, given the amount of intoxicant, to which the actor does not know he is susceptible."

2. When Does Involuntary Intoxication Exculpate?

a. Lack of *Mens Rea*

The defendant will be acquitted if, as a result of involuntary intoxication, the actor lacks the requisite mental state of the offense for which she was charged, whether the offense could be denominated as specific-intent or general-intent. This is the common law and MPC rule.

b. "Temporary Insanity"

Unlike the rule with voluntary intoxication, a defendant *will* be exculpated on the ground of "temporary insanity" if, due to involuntary intoxication rather than mental illness, she otherwise satisfies the jurisdiction's insanity test (*e.g.*, she did not know right from wrong, or did not understand what she was doing, because of involuntary intoxication). This is the common law and Model Penal Code rule.

IV. INSANITY

A. Rationale of Defense

1. Utilitarian Argument

A person who suffers from a severe cognitive or volitional disorder, *i.e.*, a disorder that undermines the actor's ability to perceive reality (cognition) or to control her conduct (volition), is undeterrable by the threat of punishment. Therefore, punishment is inefficacious. See the Main Outline for counter-arguments.

2. Retributive Argument

The insanity defense distinguishes the mad from the bad; it separates those whom we consider evil from those whom we consider sick. A person is not a moral agent, and thus is not fairly subject to moral condemnation, if she lacked the capacity to make a rational choice to violate the law or if she lacks the capacity to control her conduct.

B. The *M'Naghten* Test of Insanity

1. Rule

A person is legally insane if, at the time of the act, he was laboring under such a defect of reason, from disease of the mind, as: (1) not to know the nature and quality of the act he was doing; or, (2), if he did know it, that he did not know what he was doing was wrong. See the Main Outline for criticisms of the *M'Naghten* test.

2. Clarification of the Rule

a. "Know" versus "Appreciate"

Although the *M'Naghten* test originally was phrased in terms of whether the defendant "knew" the nature and quality of his action or "knew" right from wrong, many jurisdictions now use the word "appreciate." "Appreciate" is a word intended to convey a deeper, or broader, sense of understanding than simple "knowledge." See the Main Outline for clarification.

B. "Right/Wrong" Prong

Courts have split fairly evenly on whether this prong refers to legal or moral wrongfulness. In jurisdictions that use the "moral wrong" test, the relevant issue is *not* whether the defendant believed that his act was morally right, but rather when he knew (or appreciated) that *society* considered his actions morally wrong.

C. The "Irresistible Impulse" ("Control") Test of Insanity

1. Rule

In general, this supplement to *M'Naghten* provides that a person is insane if, as the result of mental illness or defect, she "acted with an irresistible and uncontrollable impulse," or if she "lost the power to choose between . . . right and wrong, and to avoid doing the act in question, as that [her] free agency was at the time destroyed." See the Main Outline for criticisms of the test.

D. The "Product" (*Durham*) Test of Insanity

1. Rule

A person is excused if his unlawful act was the product of a mental disease or defect. As subsequently defined, "mental disease or defect" is "any abnormal condition of the mind which substantially affects mental or emotional processes and substantially impairs behavior controls." Thus, to be acquitted according to this rule, two matters must be proved: the defendant suffered from a mental disease or defect at the time of the crime; and, but for the mental disease or defect, he would not have committed the crime. See the Main Outline for criticisms of the test.

E. Model Penal Code Test of Insanity

1. Rule

The MPC test represents a broadened version of the *M'Naghten* and irresistible impulse tests. With modifications, it retains the second prong of *M'Naghten* and adds to it a volitional prong. The Code provides that is person is not responsible for her conduct if, at the time of the criminal act, as the result of a mental disease or defect (a term left undefined), she lacked the substantial capacity either: (1) to appreciate the criminality (or, in the alternative, wrongfulness) of her actions; or (2) to conform her conduct to the dictates of the law.

2. Closer Analysis

a. Avoiding All-or-Nothing Judgments

Both MPC prongs are modified by the phrase "lacks *substantial* capacity." Total cognitive or volitional incapacity is not required.

b. Cognitive Prong

First, the Code uses the word "appreciate" rather than *M'Naghten*'s "know," to permit a deeper, fuller analysis of the individual's cognitive capacity. Second, the drafters chose not to decide between "legal wrong" and "moral wrong": they invited legislators, in adopting the Code provision, to choose between the words "criminality" (legal wrong) and "wrongfulness" (moral wrong).

c. Volitional Prong

This prong is phrased to avoid the undesirable or potentially misleading words "irresistible" and "impulse." A person who has a very strong, but not irresistible, desire to commit a crime, including one who acts non-impulsively after considerable thought, can fall within the language of the MPC.

V. DIMINISHED CAPACITY

A. Putting "Diminished Capacity" in Context

1. *Mens Rea* Version

A defendant may raise a claim of "diminished capacity" in order to show that he lacked the requisite *mens rea* for an offense. In that manner, "diminished capacity" works like mistake-of-fact or voluntary intoxication—it does not excuse the wrongdoer, but serves to show that the prosecutor has failed to prove an essential element of an offense.

2. Partial Responsibility Version

"Diminished capacity" may also serve as a highly controversial excuse defense, used exclusively in criminal homicide prosecutions, as a basis for reducing the severity of the offense.

B. Diminished Capacity and *Mens Rea*

A sane person may suffer from a mental disability (*e.g.*, mental illness, mental retardation, Alzheimer's) that arguably prevents him from forming the mental state required for the commission of an offense.

1. Model Penal Code Approach

As a matter of logic, a defendant should be acquitted of any offense for which he lacked the requisite *mens rea*, including those cases in which he lacked the mental state because of a mental disability, whether that disability is permanent or temporary. This is the position taken by the Model Penal Code.

2. Common Law

Logic notwithstanding, most states permit evidence of an abnormal mental condition, *if at all*, in order to negate the *specific* intent in a specific-intent offense. Psychiatric evidence is inadmissible in the prosecution of general-intent offenses. A minority of jurisdictions do not permit diminished capacity to be claimed in *any* case. See the Main Outline for the reasons for judicial hostility to the doctrine of diminished capacity.

C. Partial Responsibility

1. Common Law

In this country, the partial defense was originated in California and adopted by a small number of other courts. This rule, no longer followed in California, provides that a person who commits a criminal homicide and suffers from some mental illness or abnormality short of insanity may have her offense reduced because of her diminished mental capacity. States that recognize the partial-responsibility claim usually permit reduction of the offense from first-degree to second-degree murder, or from murder to manslaughter. The underlying rationale of the partial responsibility doctrine is that a person who does not meet a jurisdiction's definition of insanity, but who suffers from a mental abnormality, is less deserving of punishment than a killer who acts with a normal state of mind. Therefore, she should be convicted of a lesser offense.

2. Model Penal Code

The Code provides that a homicide that would otherwise be murder is reduced to manslaughter if the homicide was the result of "extreme mental or emotional disturbance for which there is a reasonable explanation or excuse." This language is intended to permit courts to recognize a partial responsibility defense.

VI. ENTRAPMENT

A. Overview

Entrapment issues arise when law enforcement agencies use undercover police officers to investigate crimes. The issue is how far may the police go in such undercover activity. Over time, two different approaches have developed, one called the "subjective" approach, which is followed in federal courts and many state courts; the other is the "objective" approach followed by some states.

B. Subjective Test

1. Test

Entrapment is proved if the government agent implants in the mind of an innocent person the disposition to commit the alleged offense and induces its commission in order that the government may prosecute. According to the Supreme Court, the police may employ "artifice and stratagem" to trap an unwary criminal, but it is improper when a criminal design, originating with the government, is used to induce an innocent person.

a. Predisposition of the Defendant

Applying the subjective test, entrapment does not occur if the government agent induces a "predisposed" person to commit the offense. A person is criminally "predisposed," if, when he is first approached by the government, he is ready and willing to commit the type of crime charged, should a favorable opportunity to do so present itself.

2. Rationale of the Subjective Test

The Supreme Court justifies the subjective version of entrapment on the ground that Congress did not intend its criminal sanctions to be applied to innocent persons induced by government officials to commit criminal offenses. See the Main Outline for the criticisms of the subjective test.

C. "Objective" Test

1. Test

In states that apply this standard, the test generally seeks to determine whether "the police conduct falls below standards, to which common feelings respond for the proper use of government power." Some states provide that entrapment only exists if the police conduct is sufficiently egregious that it would induce an ordinary law-abiding individual to commit the offense.

2. Rationale of the Objective Test

Two arguments are raised. First, the defense should be used to deter police overreaching. Second, some argue that a court should protect "the purity of its own temple" by making sure that guilt is not proved by ignoble means. See the Main Outline for the criticisms of the objective test.

D. Procedural Aspects of "Entrapment"

Although entrapment is a criminal law defense, some jurisdictions (primarily those that apply the objective test) permit the defendant to raise the defense in a pre-trial hearing before a judge. If the judge determines that the defendant was entrapped, the prosecution is barred. No trial is held. In most jurisdictions, entrapment is treated like all other defenses: the defendant has the burden to raise the entrapment defense and present evidence in support of the claim at trial. If the factfinder determines that the defendant was entrapped, it brings back a not-guilty verdict.

E. Entrapment and the Due Process Clause

Although entrapment is not a constitutional doctrine, the Supreme Court has stated in dictum that police conduct could become so outrageous as to violate the Due Process Clause of the United States Constitution. More than once, however, the Court has refused to find a due process violation in entrapment-like circumstances.

■ PART EIGHT: INCHOATE CONDUCT

I. ATTEMPT

A. Common Law

1. General Principles

a. Basic Definition

In general, an attempt occurs when a person, with the intent to commit a criminal offense, engages in conduct that constitutes the beginning of the perpetration of, rather than mere preparation for, the target (*i.e.*, intended) offense.

b. Grading of Offense

A criminal attempt was a common law misdemeanor in England, regardless of the seriousness of the target offense. Today, modern statutes provide that an attempt to commit a felony is a felony, but it is considered a lesser felony that the target offense.

c. Merger Doctrine

A criminal attempt merges into the target offense, if it is successfully completed.

2. *Actus Reus*

There is no single common law test of when an attempt occurs. Most, but not all, of the common law tests focus on how close the actor is to completing the target offense.

a. Last Act Test

The rule used to be that a criminal attempt only occurred when a person performed all of the acts that she believed were necessary to commit the target offense. Today, there is general agreement that an attempt occurs *at least* by the time of the last act, but no jurisdiction requires that it reach this stage on all occasions.

b. Dangerous Proximity Test

Oliver Wendell Holmes announced the "dangerous proximity to success" test. This standard is not satisfied unless the conduct "is so near to the result that the danger of success is very great." In this regard, courts consider three factors: the nearness of the danger; the substantiality of the harm; and the degree of apprehension felt. The more serious the offense, the less close the actor must come to completing the offense to be convicted of attempt.

c. Physical Proximity Test

To be guilty of attempt under this test, an act "must go so far that it would result, or apparently result in the actual commission of the crime it was designed to effect, if not extrinsically hindered or frustrated by extraneous circumstances." Or, stated differently, the actor's conduct must approach sufficiently near to the completed offense "to stand either as the first or some subsequent step in a *direct movement* toward the commission of the offense after the preparations are made."

d. "Unequivocality"/"Res Ipsa Loquitur" Test

This test provides that a person is not guilty of a criminal attempt until her conduct ceases to be equivocal, *i.e.*, her conduct, standing alone, demonstrates her criminal intent.

e. Probable Desistance Test

A person is guilty of attempt if she has proceeded past "the point of no return," *i.e.*, the point past which an ordinary person is likely to abandon her criminal endeavor.

3. *Mens Rea*

a. Dual Intent

A criminal attempt involves two "intents." First, the actor must intentionally commit the acts that constitute the *actus reus* of an attempt, as discussed above. Second, the actor must commit the *actus reus* of an attempt with the specific intent to commit the target offense.

b. Comparing *Mens Rea* of Attempt to Target Offense

An attempt sometimes requires a *higher* level of *mens rea* than is necessary to commit the target offense. Second, "attempt" is a specific-intent offense, even if the target crime is general-intent.

c. Special Problem: Attendant Circumstances

At common law, it is unclear what *mens rea*, if any, an actor must possess regarding an attendant circumstance to be guilty of attempt. Some courts hold that a person may be convicted of a criminal attempt if he is reckless with regard to an attendant circumstance. Other courts believe that it is sufficient that the actor is as culpable regarding an attendant circumstance as is required for that element of the target crime. See the Main Outline for clarification.

4. Special Defense: Impossibility

a. General Rule

The common law distinguished between "factual" and "legal" impossibility. The latter was a defense to an attempt; the former was not.

b. Factual Impossibility

Factual impossibility, which is not a defense, may be defined as occurring when an actor's intended end constitutes a crime, but he fails to complete the offense because of a factual circumstance unknown to him or beyond his control. One way to phrase this is:

if the facts had been as the defendant believed them to be, would his conduct have constituted a crime? If yes, then this is a case of factual impossibility.

c. Legal Impossibility

There are two varieties of "legal impossibility."

i. Pure Legal Impossibility

This form of impossibility applies when an actor engages in lawful conduct that she incorrectly believes constitutes a crime.

ii. Hybrid Legal Impossibility

The more typical case of legal impossibility occurs when an actor's goal *is* illegal (this distinguishes it from pure legal impossibility), but commission of the offense is impossible due to a mistake by the actor regarding the *legal* status of some *factual* circumstance relevant to her conduct. See the Main Outline for examples.

B. Model Penal Code

1. General Principles

a. Grading of Offense

Unlike the common law and non-MPC statutes, the MPC generally treats inchoate offenses as offenses of the same degree, and thus subject to the same punishment, as the target offense. The one exception is that, for a felony characterized as a "felony of the first degree" under the Code—basically, an offense that carries a maximum punishment of life imprisonment—an attempt to commit such an offense is a felony of the *second* degree, *i.e.,* a lesser offense.

b. Merger

The common law merger doctrine applies as well under the Code.

2. *Actus Reus*

The Code abandons all of the common law tests described above and replaces them with a *substantial step* standard. Specifically, one has gone far enough to constitute an attempt if the act or omission constitutes a substantial step in the course of conduct planned to culminate in the commission of the crime. One significant difference between the substantial step test and the various common law standards is that, in general, the common law looked to see how close the defendant was to completing the crime, whereas the MPC looks to see how far the defendant has gone from the point of initiation of the target offense.

3. *Mens Rea*

Please see the Main Outline for clarification of certain inartfully drafted, but critically important, aspects of the MPC criminal attempt statute.

a. Rule

The Code uses slightly different language than the common law, but the analysis is essentially the same. A person is not guilty of attempt unless he: "*purposely* engages in conduct that would constitute the crime"; acts "with the *purpose* of causing" or "with the *belief* that it will cause" the criminal result; or "*purposely* does . . . an act . . . constituting a substantial step" in furtherance of the offense.

b. Special Problem: Attendant Circumstances

The "purpose" requirement for an attempt does *not* apply to attendant circumstances. As to attendant circumstances, a person is guilty of an attempt if she "act[s] with the kind of culpability otherwise required for commission of the [target] crime." In short, the actor need only be as culpable regarding an attendant circumstance as is required for the target offense.

4. Special Defense: Impossibility

The MPC has abandoned the hybrid legal impossibility defense. *Pure* legal impossibility remains a defense.

5. Special Defense: Renunciation of Criminal Purpose

The Code (but not the common law) recognizes a defense of "renunciation of criminal purpose." A person is not guilty of a criminal attempt, even if her actions constitute a substantial step in the commission of an offense, if: (1) she abandons her effort to commit the crime or prevents it from being committed; and (2) her conduct manifests a complete and voluntary renunciation of her criminal purpose. This defense is sometimes described as the "abandonment" defense.

II. CONSPIRACY

A. Common Law

1. General Principles

a. Definition

A common law conspiracy is an agreement between two or more persons to commit an unlawful act or series of unlawful acts.

b. Grading

At original common law, conspiracy was a misdemeanor. Today, conspiracy to commit a felony is usually a felony, but typically is a lesser offense than the target crime.

c. Rationale of the Offense

i. Preventive Law Enforcement

Like other inchoate offenses, recognition of the offense of conspiracy provides a basis for the police to arrest people before they commit another offense.

ii. Special Dangerousness

Group criminality is considered more dangerous than individual wrongdoing. The thesis is that when people combine to commit an offense, they are more dangerous than an individual criminal, because of their combined resources, strength, and expertise. They are also thought to be less likely to abandon their criminal purpose if they know that other persons are involved.

d. Merger

A common law conspiracy does *not* merge into the attempted or completed offense that is the object of the agreement.

2. *Actus Reus:* Basics

The gist of a conspiracy is the agreement by the parties to commit an unlawful act or series of unlawful acts together.

a. Overt Act

A common law conspiracy is committed as soon as the agreement is made. No act in furtherance of it is required. Today, many statutes provide that a conspiracy does not occur unless at least one party to the agreement commits an overt act in furtherance of it.

b. Method of Forming the Agreement

The conspiratorial agreement need not be in writing, nor even be verbally expressed. It may be implied from the actions of the parties.

c. Nature of Agreement

The object of the agreement must be unlawful. For purposes of conspiracy, an "unlawful" act is a morally wrongful act; *it need not be a criminal act*.

3. *Mens Rea*: The Basics

a. General Rule

Conspiracy is a dual-intent offense. First, the parties must intend to form an agreement (the *actus reus* of the conspiracy). Second, they must intend that the object(s) of their agreement be achieved. This second intent makes conspiracy a specific-intent offense.

b. Purpose versus Knowledge

i. The Issue

An issue that arises in some conspiracy prosecutions is whether a person may be convicted of conspiracy if, with *knowledge* that another person intends to commit an unlawful act, *but with indifference as to whether the crime is committed*, he furnishes an instrumentality for that offense or provides a service to the other person that aids in its commission.

ii. Case Law

The law is split on this issue. Most courts will not convict a person unless he acts with the *purpose* of promoting or facilitating the offense. Knowledge, coupled with indifference as to whether the offense is committed, is insufficient. But, sometimes one can infer purpose from knowledge. See the Main Outline.

4. Plurality Requirement

No person is guilty of conspiracy unless *two or more persons* possess the requisite *mens rea*. However, the plurality doctrine does not require that two persons be prosecuted and convicted of conspiracy. It is satisfactory that the prosecutor proves beyond a reasonable doubt that there were two or more persons who formed the agreement with the requisite *mens rea*.

5. Parties to an Agreement

Even if it is clear that a conspiracy exists, it is sometimes difficult to determine *who* is a party to the conspiracy. The Main Outline, through examples, discusses so-called "wheel," "chain," and "chain-wheel" conspiracies.

6. Objectives of a Conspiracy

Since the gist of a conspiracy is an agreement, what if the parties to the agreement intend to commit more than one offense. Is this one conspiracy or more? In general, there are as many (or as few) conspiracies as there are agreements made.

7. Special Defense: Wharton's Rule

a. Rule

If a crime *by definition* requires two or more persons as willing participants, there can be no conspiracy to commit that offense if the only parties to the agreement are those who are necessary to the commission of the underlying offense. This is Wharton's Rule, a common law defense to conspiracy.

b. Wharton's Rule Exceptions

There are two major exceptions: (1) Wharton's Rule does not apply if the two conspirators are not the parties necessary to commission of the offense; and (2) Wharton's Rule does not apply if more persons than are necessary to commit the crime are involved in the agreement to commit the crime.

c. Breakdown of the Rule

Wharton's Rule is increasingly disliked by courts. The Supreme Court has stated that in federal courts the doctrine is no more than a judicially-created rebuttable presumption. If there is evidence that the legislature intended to reject Wharton's Rule, then the doctrine will not be enforced.

8. Special Defense: Legislative–Exemption Rule

A person may not be prosecuted for conspiracy to commit a crime that is intended to protect that person.

9. Special Defense?: Impossibility

Case law here is particularly thin, but it has been stated that neither factual impossibility nor legal impossibility is a defense to a criminal conspiracy.

10. Special Defense?: Abandonment

a. No Defense to Crime of Conspiracy

At common law, the crime of conspiracy is complete as soon as the agreement is formed by two or more culpable persons. There is no turning back from that. Once the offense of conspiracy is complete, abandonment of the criminal plan by one of the parties is not a defense to the crime of conspiracy.

b. Relevance of Abandonment

Although abandonment, or withdrawal, from a conspiracy is not a defense to prosecution of the *crime* of conspiracy, a person who withdraws from a conspiracy may avoid conviction for subsequent offenses committed in furtherance of the conspiracy by other members of the conspiracy, if the abandoning party communicates his withdrawal to every other member of the conspiracy (a near impossibility in many-member conspiracies).

B. Model Penal Code

1. General Principles

a. Definition

The MPC provides that "a person is guilty of conspiracy with another person or persons to commit a crime" if that person, "with the purpose of promoting or facilitating" commission of the crime, "agrees with such other person or persons that they or one or more of them will engage in conduct that constitutes such crime or an attempt or solicitation to commit such crime," or if that person agrees to aid the other person or persons in commission of the offense or of an attempt or solicitation to commit such crime.

b. Grading

A conspiracy to commit any offense other than a felony of the first degree is graded the same as the crime that is the object of the conspiracy.

c. Merger

Unlike the common law, a conspirator may *not* be convicted of both conspiracy and the target offense(s), unless the conspiracy involves a continuing course of conduct.

2. *Actus Reus*: How It Differs from Common Law

a. Overt Act

In contrast to the common law, an overt act is required except for felonies of the first and second degree.

b. Nature of Agreement

In contrast to the common law, the object of the agreement must be a crime, and not merely an "unlawful" act.

3. *Mens Rea*

A person is not guilty of conspiracy unless she acts with the *purpose* of promoting or facilitating the commission of the conduct that constitutes a crime. One who furnishes a service or instrumentality with mere *knowledge* of another's criminal activities is not guilty of conspiracy.

4. Plurality Rule

The most influential feature of the MPC is its rejection of the common law plurality requirement. The Code defines the offense in unilateral terms: "*A person* is guilty of conspiracy with another person . . . [if he] agrees with such other person . . . ." It takes two people to agree, but it takes only one person to be *guilty* of conspiracy.

5. Parties to Agreement

Two aspects of the Code need to be kept in mind in determining the parties to a conspiracy. First, conspiracy is a unilateral offense, as discussed above. Second, the MPC provides that if a person guilty of conspiracy knows that the person with whom he has conspired has, in turn, conspired with another person or persons to commit the *same* crime, the first person is also guilty of conspiring with the other persons or person, whether or not he knows their identity. See the Main Outline for a discussion of how these provisions work to determine whether a person is party of an existing conspiracy.

6. Objectives of a Conspiracy

The Code provides that there is only one conspiracy between parties, even if they have multiple criminal objectives, as long as the multiple objectives are part of the same agreement or of a "continuous conspiratorial relationship."

7. Special Defenses

The MPC does not recognize Wharton's Rule, nor any impossibility defense.

a. Legislative–Exemption Rule

The Code provides that it is a defense to a charge of conspiracy "that if the criminal object were achieved, the actor would not be guilty of a crime under the law defining the offense or as an accomplice." The effect of this language is to permit a defense if enforcement of the conspiracy law would frustrate a legislative intention to exempt that party from prosecution.

b. Renunciation of Criminal Purpose

A person is not guilty of conspiracy under the Code if he renounces his criminal purpose, and then thwarts the success of the conspiracy "under circumstances manifesting a complete and voluntary renunciation of his criminal purpose."

III. SOLICITATION

A. General Principles

1. Definition

At common law, a person is guilty of solicitation if he intentionally invites, requests, commands, or encourages another person to engage in conduct constituting a felony or a misdemeanor involving a breach of the peace or obstruction of justice.

a. Model Penal Code

The Code definition of "solicitation" is broader than the common law in that it applies to solicitation to commit *any* misdemeanor (as well as all felonies).

2. Grading

At common law, a criminal solicitation was a misdemeanor, even when the offense solicited was a felony. Today, a solicitation to commit a felony is often treated as a felony, but of a lesser degree than the felony solicited.

a. Model Penal Code

As with other inchoate offenses, the MPC treats a solicitation to commit any offense other than a felony of the first degree as an offense of equal grade as the target offense.

3. Merger

The concept of merger applies to the crime of solicitation, just as it does to the offense of attempt.

B. *Actus Reus*

1. General Rule

The *actus reus* of a solicitation is consummated when the actor communicates the words or performs the physical act that constitutes the invitation, request, command, or encouragement of the other person to commit an offense.

2. Unsuccessful Communications

At common law, a solicitation does not occur unless the words or conduct of the solicitor are successfully communicated to the solicited party. In contrast, the Code provides that one who unsuccessfully attempts to communicate a solicitation is guilty of solicitation.

3. Relationship of Solicitor to Solicited Party

At common law, a person is not guilty of solicitation if she merely asks another person to *assist* in the crime, that is, to be an accomplice in the crime. To be guilty, a solicitor must ask the other person to actually perpetrate the offense herself. In contrast, the MPC provides that a person *is* guilty of solicitation if she requests the other person to do some act that would establish the latter person's complicity as an accomplice in the offense.

C. *Mens Rea*

1. Common Law

Solicitation is a specific-intent offense at common law. The solicitor must intentionally commit the *actus reus* (request, encourage, etc., another to commit the crime), with the specific intent that the person solicited commit the target offense.

2. Model Penal Code

The Model Penal Code does not deal in concepts of "specific intent" and "general intent." However, the analysis is the same: a person is not guilty of solicitation unless she acts with the purpose of promoting or facilitating the commission of the solicited offense.

D. Defense: Renunciation

The Model Penal Code—but not the common law—provides a defense to the crime of solicitation if the soliciting party: (1) completely and voluntarily renounces her criminal intent; and (2) persuades the solicited party not to commit the offense or otherwise prevents her from committing the crime.

IV. OTHER INCHOATE OFFENSES

A. Assault

1. Common Law Definition

A common law assault is an attempted battery. (A battery is unlawful application of force to the person of another.) However, the common law recognized "assault" as an offense before criminal attempt law developed, so attempt doctrines do not apply to it. To be guilty of assault, a person must engage in conduct that is in closer proximity to completion than is generally required for other attempt offenses.

2. Modern Statutes

Nearly all states have broadened the definition of assault to include the tort definition of assault: intentionally placing another person in reasonable apprehension of an imminent battery.

B. Inchoate Offenses in Disguise

1. Burglary

Common law burglary involves "breaking and entering the dwelling house of another at night with the intent to commit a felony therein." Thus, burglary only occurs if a person not only breaks into another person's dwelling at night, but has the further specific intention to commit a serious crime inside the dwelling. *The latter felony is inchoate* at the time that the *actus reus* of burglary (breaking and entering) occurs.

2. Larceny

Common law larceny is the trespassory taking and carrying away of the personal property of another with the intent to steal the property, *i.e.* permanently deprive the other of the property. The ultimate harm of theft comes when the wrongdoer *permanently* deprives the person of the property. *That* harm has not occurred at the moment when the thief nonconsensually "takes and carries away" the personal property.

■ PART NINE: COMPLICITY

I. ACCOMPLICE LIABILITY: COMMON LAW

A. General Principles

1. General Rule

Subject to clarification below, a person is an accomplice in the commission of an offense if she intentionally assists another person to engage in the conduct that constitutes the offense.

2. Accomplice Liability as Derivative Liability

Accomplice liability is derivative in nature. That is, an accomplice's liability derives from the primary party to whom she provided assistance. The accomplice is ordinarily convicted of the offense committed by the primary party.

3. Justification for Derivative Liability

Accomplice liability is loosely based on the civil concept of agency. That is, when a person intentionally assists another person in the commission of an offense, she manifests thereby her willingness to be held accountable for the conduct of the other person, *i.e.*, she allows the perpetrator of the crime to serve as her agent.

4. Common Law Terminology

There are four common law categories of parties to criminal offenses.

a. Principal in the First Degree

He is the person who, with the requisite *mens rea*, personally commits the offense, or who uses an innocent human instrumentality to commit it. The "innocent instrumentality doctrine" provides that a person is a principal in the first degree if she dupes or coerces an innocent human being to perform the acts that constitute an offense.

b. Principal in the Second Degree

She is the person who intentionally assists the principal in the first degree to commit the offense, and who is actually or constructively present during its commission. A person is "constructively" present if she is close enough to assist the principal in the first degree during the crime.

c. Accessory Before the Fact

She is one who intentionally assists in the commission of the offense, but who is not actually or constructively present during its commission.

d. Accessory After the Fact

She is one who knowingly assists a felon to avoid arrest, trial, or conviction.

B. What Makes a Person an Accomplice: Assistance

A person "assists" in an offense, and thus may be an accomplice in its commission, if she solicits or encourages another person to commit the crime, or if she aids in its commission.

1. If No Assistance

A person is not an accomplice unless her conduct *in fact* assists in commission of the crime.

2. Trivial Assistance

If a person intentionally aids in the commission of an offense, she is liable as an accomplice, although her assistance was trivial. *Indeed, an accomplice is liable even if the crime would have occurred without her assistance, i.e., she is guilty although her assistance did not cause the commission of the offense.* Because any actual assistance, no matter how trivial, qualifies, a person may be an accomplice merely by providing psychological encouragement to the perpetrator.

3. Presence at the Scene

A person who is present at the scene of a crime, *even if she is present in order to aid in commission of the offense,* is not an accomplice unless she *in fact* assists in the crime. Although "mere presence" does not constitute assistance, it does not take much to convert presence into trivial assistance. In some circumstances, a person's presence could provide psychological encouragement to the principal, which is enough to trigger accomplice liability.

4. Omissions

Although a person is not generally an accomplice if she simply permits a crime to occur, one may be an accomplice by failing to act to prevent a crime when she has a duty to so act.

C. What Makes a Person an Accomplice: *Mens Rea*

1. Rule

A person is an accomplice in the commission of an offense if she possesses two mental states. She must: (1) intentionally engage in the acts of assistance; and (2) act with the level of culpability required in the definition of the offense in which she assisted.

2. Crimes of Recklessness or Negligence

The prosecutor does not have to prove that the accomplice *intended* a crime of recklessness to occur: it is enough that she was reckless in regard to the ensuing harm; as for a crime of negligence, it is enough to show that the would-be accomplice was negligent in regard to the ensuring harm.

3. Natural–And–Probable–Consequences Doctrine

An accomplice is guilty not only of the offense she intended to facilitate or encourage, but also of any reasonably foreseeable offense committed by the person she aided. That is, once the prosecutor proves that *A* was an accomplice of *P* in the commission of Crime 1 (using the analysis discussed so far), *A* is also responsible for any other offense committed by *P* that was a natural and probable consequence of Crime 1.

D. Accomplice Liability: If the Perpetrator Is Acquitted

1. If No Crime Occurred

If a jury finds that the alleged crime never occurred and, therefore, acquits the principal in the first degree, it logically follows that any accomplice must be acquitted as well, as there is no guilt to derive—one cannot be an accomplice to a nonexistent crime.

2. If Perpetrator Is Acquitted on Grounds of a Defense

If a jury acquits the alleged perpetrator of a crime on the ground that he was justified in his actions, then the accomplice should also be acquitted, as this means she aided in a justified (proper) act. But, if the jury acquits the perpetrator on the ground of an excuse, the jury has determined that a crime *has* occurred. The perpetrator's excuse claim is personal to him, and should not protect the accomplice.

E. Perpetrator and Accomplice: Degrees of Guilt

The common law rule used to be that an accessory before the fact could not be convicted of a more serious offense, or a higher degree of an offense, than that for which the principal was convicted. (It has nearly always been the case that an accomplice may be convicted of a *lesser* degree of crime than the principal in the first degree.) This rule is breaking down. Even in an earlier era, however, most courts treated criminal homicides differently: on the proper facts, courts were and are prepared to convict an accomplice of a higher degree of criminal homicide than the perpetrator.

F. Special Defense: Legislative–Exemption Rule

A person may not be convicted as an accomplice in her own victimization.

II. CONSPIRACY LIABILITY

A. The *Pinkerton* Doctrine

At common law, a person may be held accountable for the actions of others either as an accomplice, discussed above, or as a conspirator. A controversial feature of conspiracy law in many jurisdictions is the *Pinkerton* doctrine, named after the Supreme Court ruling in *Pinkerton v. United States*. This doctrine provides that a conspirator is responsible for any crime committed by any other member of the conspiracy, whether or not he assisted, if the offense was an object of the conspiracy or a reasonably foreseeable consequence thereof.

III. MODEL PENAL CODE

A. Forms of Complicity Liability

1. Innocent–Instrumentality Doctrine

A person is guilty of an offense that she did not personally commit if, acting with the requisite *mens rea*, she "causes an innocent or irresponsible person" to commit the crime. This is equivalent to the common law innocent-instrumentality rule discussed earlier.

2. Accomplice Liability

A person is guilty of an offense that she did not personally commit if she is an accomplice of another person in the commission of the offense.

3. *Pinkerton* Rule

The *Pinkerton* conspiracy doctrine discussed above is not recognized in the Code.

B. What Makes a Person an Accomplice: Assistance

1. Rule

To be an accomplice in the commission of an offense, the person must: (a) solicit the offense; (b) aid, agree to aid, or attempt to aid in its commission; or (c) fail to make a proper effort to prevent commission of the offense (assuming that she has a legal duty to act). See the Main Outline for a comparison of the MPC to the common law.

C. What Makes a Person an Accomplice: *Mens Rea*

1. Rule

To be an accomplice, the person must act "with the purpose of promoting or facilitating the commission of the offense."

2. Exception to the Requirement of Purpose

The MPC handles the issue of accomplice liability for a crime of recklessness or negligence with the following provision: A person who is an accomplice in the commission of *conduct* that causes a criminal *result*, is also an accomplice in the *result* thereof, if she has the level of culpability regarding the *result* required in the definition of the offense. See the Main Outline for an example of how this provision works.

D. Accomplice Liability: If the Perpetrator Is Acquitted

The Code provides that an accomplice in the commission of an offense may be convicted of that offense, even if the alleged perpetrator "has been convicted of a different offense or degree of offense or . . . or has been acquitted." One must be very careful in reading this provision: *if there has been no offense*, then one is not an accomplice "in the commission of *the offense*."

E. Special Defenses

1. Legislative–Exemption Rule

Like the common law, the MPC applies the legislative-exemption rule.

2. Inevitable Incidence

An accomplice is not guilty of an offense if her conduct is an inevitable incident to the commission of the offense, such as a customer in the act of prostitution.

3. Abandonment

A person is not an accomplice in the commission of a crime if she terminates her participation before the crime is committed, and if she either neutralizes her assistance, gives timely warning to the police of the impending offense, or in some other manner prevents commission of the crime.

F. Special Provision to Consider: Relationship of Accomplice Liability to Criminal Attempts

The Code goes well beyond the common law by permitting an accomplice to be convicted of a criminal attempt, if she attempts to aid in commission of an offense, *although the other person does not commit or even attempt the offense.*

■ PART TEN: CRIMINAL HOMICIDE

I. CRIMINAL HOMICIDE: OVERVIEW

A. "Homicide"

1. Definition

The English common law defined "homicide" as "the killing of a human being by a human being." In American common law, it is "the killing of a human being by *another* human being."

2. "Criminal Homicide"

A criminal homicide is a homicide committed without justification (*e.g.,* in self-defense) or excuse (*e.g.,* as the result of insanity).

B. "Human Being"

1. At the Start of Life

The common law provides that a fetus is not a human being until it is born alive.

2. At the End of Life

At common law, a person is legally dead (and, therefore, ceases to be a "human being") when there is a total stoppage of the circulation of the blood and a permanent cessation of the functions of respiration and heart pulsation. Today, virtually every state provides that a person may be deemed legally dead if he experiences an irreversible cessation of breathing and heartbeat (the common law definition), *or* suffers from "brain death syndrome," which occurs when the whole brain (not just one portion of it) permanently loses the capacity to function.

C. Year–and–A–Day Rule

At common law, a homicide prosecution may only be brought if the victim dies within one year and a day of the injury inflicted by the accused. Today, in light of medical advances and life-support machinery, many states have abolished or modified the rule.

II. COMMON LAW: MURDER

A. Definition of "Murder"

Common law murder is a killing of a human being by another human being *with malice aforethought*.

1. "Malice"

A person acts with "malice" if she unjustifiably, inexcusably, and in the absence of any mitigating circumstance, kills a person with any one of four mental states: (a) the intention to kill a human being; (b) the intention to inflict grievous bodily injury on another; (c) an extremely reckless disregard for the value of human life (often called "depraved heart" at common law); or (d) the intention to commit a felony during the commission or attempted commission of which a death accidentally occurs (the "felony-murder rule"). These four categories of malice are considered below.

2. "Aforethought"

Originally, the term "aforethought" meant that the actor thought about the killing beforehand, *i.e.,* that he premeditated the killing. Over time, the term lost significance.

B. Murder: Intent to Kill

1. General Rule

In view of the definition of "malice aforethought" set out above, an intentional killing that is unjustifiable (*e.g.,* not committed in self-defense), inexcusable (*e.g.,* not committed by an insane person), and unmitigated (*e.g.,* not the result of sudden heat of passion) constitutes common law murder.

2. Proving Intent

The prosecutor must prove beyond a reasonable doubt that the killer *purposely* or *knowingly* took another's life. Until 1979, juries were often instructed in murder prosecutions that "the law presumes that a person *intends* the natural and probable consequences of his voluntary acts." However, this instruction violates the Due Process Clause of the United States Constitution, because it improperly shifts the burden of proof regarding an element of the offense (malice aforethought, via a finding of intent-to-kill) from the prosecutor to the defendant. Nonetheless, the jury instruction simply points out the obvious. Therefore, even without an instruction, a jury may infer (*but not presume*) intent in such circumstances.

3. Statutory Reform: "Wilful, Deliberate, Premeditated" Formula

In many states that by statute divide murder into degrees, a "wilful, deliberate, premeditated" killing is first-degree murder.

a. Wilful

In the context of murder statutes, this term means, simply, "intentional."

b. Premeditated

To "premeditate" is "to think about beforehand." Some courts state that "no time is too short" for a person to premeditate; "an intent to kill need exist only for an instant." In contrast, others courts more properly require proof that the actor thought about the killing "some appreciable time."

c. Deliberate

Unfortunately, courts rarely distinguish "premeditation" from "deliberation"—they treat it as a single entity. When courts do draw a distinction, as they should, the latter term means "to measure and evaluate the major facets of a choice or problem." Notice: to satisfy this standard of deliberation, a person would have to premeditate longer than an instant.

d. What If . . .

If a jury concludes that the defendant acted wilfully—intended to kill—but did *not* premeditate and/or deliberate, the defendant is guilty of *second*-degree murder in states with murder statutes of the sort being considered here. It is murder because the killing was intentional (remember: intent-to-kill is one form of malice aforethought); since the killing was not premeditated and/or deliberate, it is not first-degree murder. So, by matter of elimination, it drops to second-degree.

C. Murder: Intent to Inflict Grievous Bodily Injury

A person acts with malice aforethought if she intends to inflict grievous bodily injury on another human being. Therefore, if a death results from her conduct, she is guilty of murder.

1. "Grievous bodily injury"

This term has been defined as injury "that imperils life," "is likely to be attended with dangerous or fatal consequences," or is an injury that "gives rise to the apprehension of danger to life, health, or limb."

2. Statutory Approach

In states that distinguish between degrees of murder, one who kills another person with this state of mind is usually guilty of second-degree murder.

D. Murder: "Depraved Heart" (Extreme Recklessness)

1. General Rule

A person who acts with what the common law colorfully described as a "depraved heart" or an "abandoned and malignant" heart is one who acts with malice aforethought. If a person dies as a result of such conduct, the actor is guilty of murder, although the death was unintended.

2. What is "Depraved Heart"/"Extreme Recklessness"?

Common law judges did not provide a clear definition of "depraved heart" or "abandoned and malignant heart" behavior. In general terms, it is conduct that manifests an extreme indifference to the value of human life. Although no single definition of such extreme indifference can explain all of the common law decisions, today most courts would probably agree that an actor manifests an extreme indifference to the value of human life if he *consciously* takes a *substantial and unjustifiable foreseeable risk* of causing human death.

3. Statutory Approach

In states that divide murder into degrees pursuant to the traditional model, a depraved-heart homicide ordinarily is second-degree murder.

E. Felony–Murder Rule

1. General Rule

At common law, a person is guilty of murder if she kills another person, even accidentally, during the commission or attempted commission of any felony.

a. Statutory Approach

Many states that divide murder into degrees have a dual approach to felony-murder. The murder statute will often provide that a killing that occurs during the commission of certain specifically listed felonies (most commonly: arson, robbery, rape, and burglary) is first-degree murder; a death during the commission of any non-enumerated felony constitutes murder of the second-degree.

2. Rationale of the Rule

The most plausible deterrence argument—the one that is used most often to defend felony-murder—is that the harshness of the rule will cause felons to commit their crimes in a less dangerous manner, thereby decreasing the risk that deaths will ensue.

3. Limitations On Felony–Murder Rule

Because the felony-murder rule is unpopular, many courts have limited its scope.

a. Inherently-Dangerous-Felony Limitation

Many states limit the felony-murder rule to killings that arise during the commission of "inherently dangerous" felonies. Courts disagree, however, on how to determine whether a felony is inherently dangerous. Some courts consider the felony in the abstract: they look at the definition of the crime and ask whether the offense *could* be committed without creating "a high probability" of loss of life, or *could* be committed without creating a "substantial risk" that someone will die. Other courts consider a felony inherently dangerous if it is dangerous in the abstract *or* in light of the circumstances surrounding the particular case.

b. Independent-Felony Limitation

Some courts require that the felony that serves as the predicate for the felony-murder rule be "independent" of the homicide. A felony that is *not* independent "merges" with the homicide. The most obvious and least controversial example of a felony that merges is assault with a deadly weapon.

i. The Difficult Cases

Many violent offenses include assaultive conduct. For example, armed robbery basically consists of the offense of larceny + assault with a deadly weapon; rape involves assaultive conduct. In order that the "independent felony/merger" limitation does not eat up the felony-murder rule, courts have followed either of two approaches: some limit the merger principle to crimes of assault; some courts define a felony as independent— thus, a felony that will support the felony-murder rule, even if it is assaultive—if it involves an "independent felonious purpose."

c. *Res Gestae* Limitation

Many courts provide that the mere fact that a death occurs, in a temporal sense, "during" the commission of a felony, is insufficient to trigger the felony-murder rule. There must also be a causal connection between the felony and the death.

d. Killing by a Non–Felon

Some jurisdictions provide that the felony-murder rule does not apply if the person who commits the homicide is a non-felon resisting the felony.

i. Judicial Approach to Issue

Many courts apply the "agency" theory of felony-murder. That is, a felon is only responsible for homicides committed *in furtherance* of the felony, by a person acting as the felon's "agent." Therefore, a homicide committed by a police officer, felony victim, or bystander falls outside the felony-murder rule: they are antagonists, not agents of the felon. In contrast, some court apply a "proximate causation" rule, which holds that a felon may be held responsible for a homicide perpetrated by a non-felon if the felon proximately caused the shooting.

III. COMMON LAW: MANSLAUGHTER

A. Manslaughter: General Principles

1. Definition of "Manslaughter"

Common law manslaughter is an unlawful killing of a human being by another human being *without* malice aforethought.

2. Categories of manslaughter

The common law recognized two type of manslaughter, "voluntary" and "involuntary." Once punished alike, today voluntary manslaughter is the more serious offense.

B. Voluntary Manslaughter: Provocation ("Heat–of–Passion")

1. General Rule

An intentional, unjustified, inexcusable killing, which ordinarily is murder, constitutes manslaughter (or "voluntary manslaughter") if it is committed in sudden heat of passion, as the result of adequate provocation. Thus, the provocation doctrine functions as a full defense to murder, and as a partial defense overall (as the defendant is guilty of manslaughter).

2. Rationale of the Provocation Doctrine

Courts and commentators disagree regarding why an intentional killing in heat of passion is reduced to manslaughter.

a. Partial Justification

Currently the minority view, some courts in the past seemed to believe—and some scholars have expressly argued—that the provocation doctrine functions as a partial justification for a killing, *i.e.*, that the death of the provoker-victim constitutes less of a social harm than the killing of an entirely "innocent" person.

b. Partial excuse

Most commentators today now characterize the defense as a partial excuse, as a concession to normal human frailty: the social harm is unmitigated, but the culpability of the actor is reduced because of the provocation. Why is this so? If the provocation is serious enough (what the common law calls "adequate provocation"), "we are prepared to say that an ordinary person in the actor's circumstances, even an ordinarily law-abiding person . . . , might become sufficiently upset by the provocation to experience substantial impairment of his capacity for self-control and, as a consequence, to act violently." See the Main Outline for discussion of criticisms of the provocation defense.

3. Elements of the Defense

a. Adequate Provocation

A person may not claim the defense simply because he was provoked. The provocation must be such that it might "inflame the passion of a reasonable man and tend to cause him to act for the moment from passion rather than reason." Or, the provocation must be such that it "might render ordinary men, of fair average disposition, liable to act rashly or without due deliberation or reflection, and from passion, rather than judgment."

i. Fixed Categories

At original common law, the judge, rather than the jury, determined the adequacy of the provocation. Only a few types of provocation were considered adequate. The most common were: a serious battery; mutual combat; and observation by the husband of his wife in an act of adultery. "Adequate provocation" was *not* proved if the husband was informed of the adultery but did not see it. And, a rigid rule existed: words alone, no matter how insulting, were insufficient grounds for reducing a homicide to manslaughter.

ii. Modern Trend

Today, most jurisdictions go beyond the limited categories of "adequate provocation" of the original common law. The issue is now typically left to juries to decide whether the alleged provocation would render an ordinary or reasonable person liable to act rashly. (However, most jurisdictions continue to hold that words alone are never adequate provocation for a homicide.) An increasingly critical legal issue in this context is the nature of the "reasonable person" or "ordinary person" mentioned in judicial instructions to juries. See the Main Outline for discussion.

b. State of Passion

For the provocation doctrine to apply, the defendant must kill the victim while in a state of passion. Although the typical "passion" is anger, any over-wrought emotional state, including fear, jealousy, or even deep depression, may qualify.

c. Suddenness

The killing must occur in *sudden* heat of passion. That is, the defendant must not have had reasonable time to cool off.

d. Causal Connection

A causal link between the provocation, the passion, and the fatal act must be proved.

C. Involuntary Manslaughter: Criminal Negligence

1. General Rule

A person who kills another person in a criminally negligent manner is guilty of involuntary manslaughter. This offense often blurs into the depraved-heart version of reckless murder.

D. Involuntary Manslaughter: Unlawful–Act Doctrine

1. General Rule

In an analogue to the felony-murder rule, a person is guilty of involuntary manslaughter if she kills another person during the commission or attempted commission of an unlawful act that does not otherwise trigger the felony-murder rule.

2. Scope of the Rule

a. Broad Version

Some states apply the doctrine to all misdemeanors, as well as to any felony that is excluded from the felony-murder rule due to a limitation on the felony-murder rule. A few jurisdictions go so far as to apply the doctrine if the conduct that causes the death is wrongful (immoral), albeit not illegal.

b. Limitations

Some jurisdictions limit the rule to *mala in se* misdemeanors, such as petty theft, or to "dangerous" misdemeanors, *i.e.*, offenses entailing "a reasonably foreseeable risk of appreciable physical injury."

IV. MODEL PENAL CODE

A. Criminal Homicide: Overview

The MPC provides that a person is guilty of criminal homicide if she takes the life of another human being purposely, knowingly, recklessly, or negligently.

Unlike the common law, the Code divides criminal homicide into *three*, rather than two, offenses: murder, manslaughter, and negligent homicide.

B. Murder

1. Rule

In general, a homicide constitutes murder if the killing is committed: (a) purposely; (b) knowingly; or (c) "recklessly under circumstances manifesting an extreme indifference to the value of human life." Unlike many modern statutes, the MPC does *not* divide murder into degrees.

2. Common Law versus MPC

a. Types of murder

The common law term "malice aforethought" is abandoned. What about the underlying concept of malice aforethought? Consider the four common law forms:

i. Intent to Kill

This form *is* recognized under the MPC: as noted above, a criminal homicide is murder under the Code if the killing is committed purposely or knowingly. In essence, this is equivalent to the common law "intent to kill" form of *mens rea*.

ii. Intent to Commit Grievous Bodily Injury

Virtually any case that would qualify as common law murder according to this form of malice, will fit under the MPC "extreme recklessness" umbrella.

iii. Depraved Heart

The MPC extreme recklessness provision is similar to the depraved heart form of common law murder, except that it is explicit in requiring proof of advertent risk-taking, and that the risk-taking be "substantial and unjustifiable."

iv. Felony–Murder

The Code abandons the felony-murder rule. As a compromise, the Code provides that reckless indifference to human life may be presumed if the person causes the death during commission of one of the felonies enumerated in the Code (robbery, arson, burglary, kidnapping, felonious escape, or rape or deviate sexual intercourse by force or threat of force). This presumption is rebuttable.

C. Manslaughter

Criminal homicide constitutes manslaughter in two circumstances.

1. Recklessness

A homicide committed recklessly constitutes manslaughter. The difference between reckless manslaughter and reckless murder is that here the conduct, although reckless, does *not* manifest an extreme indifference to human life.

2. Extreme Mental or Emotional Disturbance

The Code recognizes a much broader version of the common law provocation doctrine, and also allows states to recognize a "partial responsibility" diminished capacity defense, if they wish to do so. The Code provides that a murder constitutes manslaughter if the actor kills under the influence of an "extreme mental or emotional disturbance" (EMED), for which there is a "reasonable explanation or excuse."

a. Comparison to Common Law

i. Common Law Rigidity/Narrowness Rejected

The EMED provision is wide open: The MPC permits a jury, if it chooses to do so, to reduce the offense to manslaughter without considering the rigid common law categories of adequate provocation; also, "words alone" can qualify. Indeed, the defense applies *even if there is no provocation at all*, as long as the jury concludes that there is a reasonable explanation or excuse for the actor's EMED. There is also no "reasonable cooling off" requirement.

ii. Mixed Subjectivity and Objectivity

The Code provides that the reasonableness of the defendant's explanation or excuse for the EMED should be determined from the perspective of a person "in the actor's situation under the circumstances as he believes them to be." This allows for considerable subjectivization of the objective standard, although the Commentary to the Code concedes that the words "in the actor's situation" are "designedly ambiguous," so as to permit common law development of the subjective/objective issue.

3. What is "Missing"

There is no "unlawful-act" manslaughter provision under the MPC. As for criminally negligent homicides, they represent a reduced offense, discussed immediately below.

D. Negligent Homicide

A criminally negligent killing—involuntary manslaughter at common law—is the lesser offense of "negligent homicide" under the Code.

■ PART ELEVEN: RAPE

I. COMMON LAW: FORCIBLE RAPE

A. In General

Blackstone defined rape as "carnal knowledge of a woman forcibly and against her will." Today, it is more accurate to characterize this as *forcible* rape. Rape is a general-intent offense.

1. Statutory Law

The traditional rape statute is apt to provide that forcible rape is sexual intercourse by a male, with a female not his wife, by means of force or threat of force, against her will, and without her consent.

B. *Actus Reus* in Detail

1. Sexual Intercourse By Male With Female

The common law offense was not complete in the absence of penetration by a male of the female's vagina. Nonconsensual oral and anal sexual penetration constituted the separate offense of sodomy.

a. Modern Reform Statutes

Many states that have reformed their law have re-named the offense "sexual assault" or "sexual battery." These offenses typically prohibit *all* forms of forcible sexual penetration, and not simply vaginal intercourse. They also tend to be gender-neutral: male-on-male and female-on-female sexual penetration is included, as is nonconsensual female-on-male sexual penetration. Also, some states prohibit "sexual contact"—undesired contact that does not result in penetration—as a lesser degree of the offense.

2. Marital Immunity

At original common law, a husband was immune from prosecution for rape of his wife. He could be convicted as an *accomplice* in the rape of his wife, but could not convicted for personally committing the crime. See the Main Outline for the rationale, and rebuttal arguments, for this rule.

3. Nonconsent

The essence of rape is the nonconsensual nature of the sexual intercourse. "Nonconsent" is an element of the crime, rather than consent being a defense. This means that the prosecutor must prove nonconsent beyond a reasonable doubt.

4. Force

a. General Rule

The crime of forcible rape is not complete simply upon proof that the intercourse was nonconsensual. It must also be shown that the male acted forcibly or by threat of physical force. *Nonconsent and force are separate elements.*

b. How Much Force

Originally, the prosecutor had to prove that the male used or threatened substantial force upon the female in order for a forcible rape prosecution to succeed. In this regard, the common law developed a resistance requirement. Essentially, the rule was: if the male uses or threatens to use force likely to cause death or serious bodily injury to the female, she is not required to resist. If the male uses lesser force, the female *is* required to resist the rapist "to the utmost," or "until exhausted or overpowered."

c. Moving Away From Force

i. Requiring Less Force

Some states have begun to reshape forcible rape law by requiring far less proof of force, at least in cases involving unusual facts.

ii. Changing the Resistance Requirement

A few states have abolished the resistance requirement. Most states still retain the requirement, but only require "reasonable resistance," which leaves it to the jury to determine the sufficiency of the female's resistance.

iii. Abandoning the Force Requirement Altogether

One state has gone so far as to hold that the force inherently involved in the sexual act itself is sufficient proof of "force" to permit a forcible rape conviction. The effect of this decision is to make *all* cases of sexual intercourse "forcible." The only remaining issue is whether the intercourse was nonconsensual. Furthermore, this court has held that forcible rape is proved upon evidence of sexual intercourse, unless the female, by words or conduct, reasonably appears to give permission for the intercourse.

C. *Mens Rea*

1. General Rule

Rape is a general-intent offense. Therefore, most jurisdictions provide that a person is not guilty of rape if, at the time of intercourse, he entertained a genuine and *reasonable* belief that the female voluntarily consented.

2. Minority Rules

a. No Mistake-of-Fact "Defense"

A few states provide that even a defendant's *reasonable* mistake of fact is not a defense.

b. Unreasonable Mistake-of-Fact as a "Defense"

At the other end of the spectrum, the English House of Lords ruled that even an *unreasonable* mistake of fact is a defense to rape. No American state has adopted this reasoning. Moreover, in light of public upset, the Parliament redrafted its rape statute to permit conviction for rape if the male was at least reckless in regard to the female's lack of consent.

II. COMMON LAW: RAPE BY NONFORCIBLE MEANS

A. Statutory Rape

1. Statutory Background

All states provide that intercourse by a male with an underage female to whom he is not married constitutes rape. Neither force nor the underage female's lack of consent is an element of the offense. The definition of "underage" varies by jurisdiction. Today, many states divide statutory rape into degrees of offense, based on the age of the female and, often, on the basis of the difference of age between the female and the male. The most severe penalties are imposed when the male is an adult and the female is pre-pubescent.

2. Rationale

An early rationale of statutory rape laws, especially in the Victorian era, was that such laws were needed to protect "chaste maidens" from becoming "fallen women." In recent years, statutory rape laws have been defended on a different ground: recent studies reveal that there is a high pregnancy rate among underage females as a result of sexual relations with adult males. At least in these cases, prosecution of statutory rape laws arguably might serve as a deterrent against adult exploitation and resulting pregnancies of young females.

3. Mistake of Fact Regarding Age

Nearly all jurisdictions treat statutory rape as a strict-liability offense. Therefore, the defendant is guilty of the offense, even if he reasonably believed that the victim was old enough to consent.

B. Rape by Fraud

1. Fraud-in-the-Inducement

At common law, a seducer is not a rapist. More specifically, a male is not guilty of rape even if he fraudulent induces the female to consent to intercourse with him.

2. Fraud-in-the-Factum

In contrast to fraud-in-the-inducement, consent to engage in sexual intercourse is invalid if, as the result of fraud, the victim is unaware that she has consented to an act of sexual intercourse. Therefore, in these so-called fraud-in-the-factum cases, consent is vitiated and a rape prosecution will lie.

III. MODEL PENAL CODE

A. Forcible Rape

1. Definition

"A male who has sexual intercourse with a female not his wife is guilty if . . . he compels her to submit by force or by threat of imminent death, serious bodily injury, extreme pain or kidnapping, to be inflicted on anyone." As this definition shows, the Code is gender-specific and recognizes the marital immunity rule. The term "sexual intercourse," however, is defined elsewhere to include oral and anal sexual relations, which is broader than the common law.

2. Looking a Little Deeper

Notice that the Code does not use the term "nonconsent." Instead, it uses the word "compels." Although, of course, compulsion by the male implies nonconsent by the female, the drafters believed that, as with other violent crimes, attention should be focused on the alleged perpetrator's actions—his acts of compulsion—and not on how the alleged victim responded. Thus, the MPC does *not* include a resistance requirement.

3. Grading Rape

The Code grades rape as a felony of the second degree except in two circumstances, in which it is aggravated to a felony of the first degree. It is first degree if: (1) the male actually inflicts serious bodily injury upon anyone during the course of the rape; or, very controversially today, (2) the female was *not* a "voluntary social companion of the actor upon the occasion of the crime and had not previously permitted him sexual liberties."

B. Other Forms of Rape

The Code also prohibits nonforcible sexual intercourse by a male with a female not his wife in other circumstances: (1) if he "substantially impaired her power to appraise or control her conduct by administering or employing without her knowledge drugs, intoxicants, or other means for the purpose of preventing resistance"; (2) if she was unconscious at the time of the intercourse; or (3) if she is under ten years of age. In the latter case, it is no defense that the male reasonably believed "the child to be older than 10."

C. Gross Sexual Imposition

The MPC drafters defined a new sexual offense, less serious than rape, to deal with three circumstances in which a male secures sexual intercourse with a female not his wife: (1) if "he compels her to submit by any threat that would prevent resistance by a woman of ordinary resolution"; (2) if he knows that she suffers from mental disease "which renders her incapable of appraising the nature of her conduct"; or (3) if "he knows that she is unaware that a sexual act is being committed upon her or that she submits because she mistakenly supposed that he is her husband."

1. Clarification

The first version of gross sexual imposition set out above is intended to criminalize less serious *bodily* threats than are encompassed under the rape statute as well as non-bodily threats—economic, reputational, and the like. The limitation—that the threat would prevent resistance by a "woman of ordinary resolution"—is intended to reduce the risk that criminal prosecutions will be brought in cases of relatively trivial threats.

The third form above covers cases of fraud-in-the-factum and one specific issue that bedeviled common law courts: cases in which a female has intercourse with a man whom she incorrectly believes is her husband.

■ PART TWELVE: THEFT

I. LARCENY

A. General Principles

1. Common Law Definition

Larceny is the trespassory taking and carrying away of the personal property of another with the intent to permanently deprive the other person of the property (for shorthand, with the "intent to steal" the property).

a. Possession

Larceny is a crime of possession not of title. If a wrongdoer wrongfully obtains title to another person's property, the offense of false pretenses, discussed later, may be implicated.

b. *Mens Rea*

Larceny is a specific-intent offense. The defendant is not guilty of the crime unless he commits the *actus reus* with the specific intent to steal the property.

2. Grade of the Offense

Common law larceny was a felony. However, the crime was divided up between "grand" and "petty" larceny. The death penalty applied to grand larceny. In modern statutes, petty larceny is a misdemeanor; grand theft is a felony.

B. *Actus Reus* in Detail

1. Trespass

The taking of another person's personal property is not larceny unless the taking is trespassory in nature. A trespass occurs if the defendant takes possession of the personal property of another, *i.e.*, she dispossesses another person, without the latter's consent or in the absence of a justification for the nonconsensual taking.

a. Taking Possession by Fraud

A person who secures property deceitfully acts trespassorily, *i.e.*, the fraud vitiates the consent of the original possessor of the property. Larceny by fraud is sometimes called *larceny by trick*.

2. Taking Possession ("Caption")

Larceny implicates the trespassory taking of personal property. More specifically, a "taking" involves the wrongful taking of *possession*, rather than mere *custody*, of property. This distinction—possession versus custody—is critical to understanding larceny law.

a. Possession versus Custody: Drawing the Distinction

i. Possession

A person is in "possession" of property if she has sufficient control over it to use it in a generally unrestricted manner. Possession may be actual or constructive. It is "actual" if a person has physical control over the property. It is "constructive" if she does not have physical control over it, but nobody else is in actual possession of it.

ii. Custody

A person is in "custody" of property if she has physical control of the property, but her right to use it is substantially restricted. In the ordinary situation, a person has custody rather than possession of property if she has temporary and limited right to use the property in the possessor's presence.

b. Special Possession/Custody Rules In Employment Relationship

i. Employer to employee

When an employer (the "master") furnishes his personal property to his employee (the "servant") for use in the employment relationship, the common law ruled that the employer retains constructive possession of the property. The employee has mere custody.

ii. Third Person to Employee for Employer

When a person furnishes personal property to *another* person's employee, in order that it will be delivered to the employer, he transfers *possession* of the property to the *employee*.

c. Bailments: The Breaking Bulk Doctrine

When a bailee is entrusted by the bailor with a container for delivery to another person, the bailee receives possession of the container, but mere custody of its contents. Therefore, if the bailee wrongfully opens the container and removes its contents, *i.e.*, breaks bulk, he takes possession of the contents at that moment. As with other areas of theft law, the precise facts of the case can turn a larceny into a non-larceny, or vice-versa. See the Main Outline for examples.

3. Carrying Away ("Asportation")

A person is not guilty of larceny unless he carries away the property. Virtually any movement of property away from the place where possession was taken constitutes asportation. However, the asportation must consist of "carrying away" movement.

4. Personal Property of Another

a. "Personal Property"

i. Personal versus Real Property

Larceny is not committed if a person takes property attached to the land, such as trees and crops, because such property is *real* rather than *personal* in nature. When real property is severed from the land, however, it becomes personal property, and the first person to take possession of it in that form is in lawful possession of it.

ii. Animals

At common law, domestic animals were protected by larceny law; animals in the state of nature (*ferae naturae*), such as wild deer and birds, were not considered to be personal property belonging to another.

iii. Intangible property

Intangible personal property—property that, by definition, cannot be taken and carried away—is not protected by the common law of larceny, but is covered in most modern statutes.

b. "Of Another"

Larceny involves the taking of another person's personal property. For purposes of larceny law, the "another" is the person who has lawful possession of the property. Ownership is not the key.

C. *Mens Rea*: "Intent to Steal"

1. General Rule

A person is not guilty of larceny when he wrongfully takes and carries away another person's personal property, unless he possesses the specific intent to permanently deprive the other person of the property.

a. Recklessness

Often, a court will find that the requisite intent is proven if the actor takes property, and then abandons it under circumstances in which he knows that the property will probably not be returned to its owner. In such circumstances, it is more accurate to describe the actor's *mens rea* as "reckless deprivation of another person's property."

2. Concurrence Requirement

In general, the intent to steal must *concur* with the taking of the property.

a. "Continuing Trespass" Doctrine

The concurrence requirement is subject to the "continuing trespass" doctrine. This legal fiction provides that when a person trespassorily takes possession of property, she commits a new trespass every moment that she retains wrongful possession of it. Therefore, even if the wrongdoer does not have the intent to steal the property when she originally takes it, the concurrence requirement is met if she later decides to steal the property.

D. Special Problem: Lost or Mislaid Property

1. Lost Property

The rights of a finder of lost property depend on two factors: the possessory interest of the person who lost the property at the time the property is discovered by the finder; and the finder's state of mind when he retrieves the lost property.

a. Possessory Interest of the Owner

A person retains constructive possession of his lost property if there is a reasonable clue to ownership of it when it is discovered. A reasonable clue to ownership exists if the finder: (1) knows to whom the lost property belongs; or (2) has reasonable ground to believe, from the nature of the property or the circumstances under which it is found, that the party to whom it belongs can reasonably be ascertained.

b. State of Mind of the Finder

As with other larceny cases, it is important to determine the finder's state of mind when he takes possession of the lost property. See the Example in the Main Outline for clarification.

2. Mislaid Property

An object is "mislaid" if it is intentionally put in a certain place for a temporary purpose, and then accidentally left there when the owner leaves. The two factors just discussed regarding lost property also apply to mislaid property. However, in regard to the "reasonable clue to ownership" factor, the common law is more protective of the owner of mislaid property than of lost property: The common law provides that there is *always* a clue to ownership of mislaid property.

II. EMBEZZLEMENT

A. Elements of the Offense

Today, embezzlement is a felony or a misdemeanor, depending on the value of the property embezzled. Because the offense is statutory in nature, and differs from jurisdiction to jurisdiction, the precise contours of the offense cannot be stated. However, in general the offense requires proof of two or three elements:

1. Manner of Obtaining Possession

Embezzlement occurs when the actor takes possession of the personal property of another in a lawful—nontrespassory—manner.

2. Conversion

After securing lawful possession of the property, the actor converts the property to his own use, *i.e.*, he uses the property in a manner that manifests his intention to deprive another person of the property permanently.

3. Entrustment

Many embezzlement statutes provide that the actor must have obtained possession as a result of entrustment by another person.

B. Larceny Versus Embezzlement

The line between these two offenses is very thin, and depends in large part on the state of mind of the actor at the time he takes possession of property. See the Examples in the Main Outline for clarification.

III. FALSE PRETENSES

A. Elements of the Offense

The crime of "obtaining property by false pretense" is a felony or misdemeanor, depending on the value of the property taken. As with embezzlement, the statutory nature of the crime allows for only general description of the offense.

1. Title

With false pretenses, the victim transfers title, rather than mere possession, to the wrongdoer. This is the key difference between false pretenses, on the one hand, and larceny and embezzlement, on the other.

2. Nature of Fraud

False pretenses involves a false representation of an existing fact.

a. How the Misrepresentation Occurs

The misrepresentation may be in written or oral form, or can be the result of misleading conduct. Silence—nondisclosure of a fact—does not usually constitute false pretenses, even if D knowingly takes advantage of V's false impressions.

b. Fact versus Opinion

The misrepresentation must be of a fact and not of opinion.

c. Existing Fact versus a Promise of Future Conduct

The majority rule is that, to constitute false pretenses, a factual misrepresentation must pertain to an existing fact, and not involve a promise of future conduct. The minority rule, led by the Model Penal Code, is that a prosecution is permitted, even if the misrepresentation is in the form of a promise of future conduct. However, the intention to deceive cannot be proved solely on the basis of the promisor's failure to live up to his promise.

3. *Mens Rea*

The deceiver must make the false representation "knowingly" and with "the intent to defraud." That is, the actor must know that the representation is false; and he must make the false statement with the specific intent of defrauding the other person. This approximates the "intent to steal" concept in larceny.

*

Perspective

CONVERSATION WITH THE READER

When I was in law school (it seems ages ago, but really I remember it well), I liked it when a professor would start class with some introductory comments, perhaps giving us some idea of where we were planning to go in class that day or that week. It helped me to put the materials in context, and reduced my first-year angst just a bit.

Sometimes a professor would also tell us in that introduction that a particular topic we were about to consider was especially hard (because . . .), or especially interesting (because . . .), or especially controversial (because . . .), and so on. I liked having the professor talk to me (or us, really) that way. So, I plan to do the same here, by having these brief introductory "conversations" with you at the beginning of each Part of the Black Letter and, if the spirit moves me, more often. (Of course, it is generally a one-sided conversation—me to you—but you get the idea.) You can view these conversations as "off the record" comments.

To get us in the mood, I am going to carry on a "conversation" between us right now. But, to avoid it being entirely one-sided, I will ask "your" questions and then answer them.

BUYING THIS BLACK LETTER OUTLINE

FIRST THINGS FIRST. SHOULD I BUY AN OUTLINE?

That all depends. An outline is a helpful learning tool, but only if it is accurate, covers what is needed for your class, and is clear, and only if you will not misuse it. If these requirements are not met, you definitely should *not* buy an outline. If these requirements *are* met, then it may be suitable for purchase.

WAIT, AREN'T ALL OUTLINES ACCURATE?

When I went to law school (more years ago than I would like to remember, in the early 1970s), some of the outlines on the market were anonymously written. I later learned that there was good reason for this: the authors were third-year law students and recent law graduates whose knowledge of the subject was—to put it kindly—sparse.

When I became a teacher, I saw from the other side how a bad outline can hurt students. I began to find certain common mis-statements of law in some of my students' answers to my examination questions. At first, I worried that I had mis-spoken in class. Later, I discovered that the students were parroting back statements from a particular outline. Parroting is always bad. Parroting incorrect statements is worse than bad.

Since then, the "study aid market" has improved dramatically. Now, outlines published by the major law publishers are written by experts in the field. This does not mean that the outlines are error-free, any more than any other source of information—and, beyond the minor error here or there, legal experts in any subject will differ at times on matters of law—but today I really believe that students can use outlines, such as those in the Black Letter Series, with confidence. But, that moves us to the more important point: you must not misuse study aids, such as outlines.

WHAT DO YOU MEAN ABOUT MISUSING THE OUTLINES?

Let's start with a hackneyed example: a hammer is a good tool to use if you want to put a nail in a piece of wood, but it is an awful tool to use if you want to place a screw in a wall. And, it certainly is not sufficient to build an entire house.

My point simply is: An accurate, coherent, fairly complete law outline is a useful tool in learning a subject, but it is just one tool in the process. If you use the outline properly, it can help you. But, if you use it to do things for which it was not intended, you will hurt yourself. Therefore, before you buy an outline, and certainly before you use it, make sure that you are prepared to use it properly.

Perhaps the single most critical part of the law school process—certainly this is so in the first year of your legal education—is learning legal-reasoning skills ("learning to think like a lawyer"). This may seem hard for some of you to believe when you start your legal education, but law schools are more interested in honing your legal thinking skills than in teaching you the law itself. After all, there is too much law to learn in law school anyway, and the law is always changing, so what you need are the skills to be able to function as a lawyer.

That critical learning process comes through the daily reading of cases and class participation. An outline is *never* a substitute for the casebooks and any other books your teachers assign. It is *never* a substitute for classroom discussion as a learning tool. If you use the outline to avoid coming to class or as a substitute for reading and thinking deeply (I stress, *deeply*) about the assigned materials, you will hurt yourself in the class and on the examination.

Also, virtually no rule is as smooth as an outline may make it seem. Rules have a wonderful, at times mysterious, texture to them—rationales, complexities, exceptions, permutations—to which outlines should make you sensitive, so that you can read your casebook with special care, but they cannot provide that nuanced aspect of the law.

WOW, FROM WHAT YOU ARE SAYING IT SOUNDS TO ME LIKE YOU DON'T THINK I SHOULD BUY AN OUTLINE. CORRECT?

No, not at all. For most students, used properly, an outline is worth the cost. If your experience in law school is anything like my own, no matter how hard I worked to understand what was going on in class, I needed help. I needed help articulating the rules of law and, maybe more importantly, I needed help seeing how the rules fit together in a coherent manner.

That is where a good outline will serve you well. It can give you a good boost to understanding the law you are studying in class. By its nature, what an outline does best is to explain legal rules in a brief, clear, organized fashion. And, just as importantly, by seeing how the outline is organized, section by section, you can see how the pieces of the jigsaw fit together.

You may not need an outline for all of your classes (I suspect the publisher is not thrilled that I am saying this, but truth is truth)—I didn't—but inevitably there will be courses in which outlines will provide you that extra boost you need: to improve your understanding of the law, to enhance your confidence as you prepare for class or an examination.

OKAY, WHY SHOULD I BUY THIS OUTLINE?

I am not here to bury other outlines, only to praise my own.

It is accurate. (I have taught criminal law for more than a quarter of a century. I have written a great deal in the field. This does not mean that I do not make mistakes. It does mean that you can use this outline with a high degree of confidence.)

It is clear. Look at it and see.

It covers the subjects that you will be studying in your class.

And, it will make you sensitive to the special problems in the law, which will require your special care.

STUDYING CRIMINAL LAW

OKAY, ENOUGH OF ALL THAT. WHAT IS "CRIMINAL LAW"? IS THIS THE COURSE WHERE I LEARN ABOUT MIRANDA, CAR SEARCHES, AND WHETHER THOSE COPS I SEE IN ALL THOSE GREAT TV SHOWS ARE DOING THE RIGHT THING?

No. Most students are a little disappointed by that answer, but they shouldn't be, because this is a class in which you are asked to think about some of the most profound moral questions that arise in the law.

I tell my students on the first say of class that this is the course with the Big Questions: Why is it justifiable to punish people for their wrongdoing? When is it appropriate for the Government to take a person's life or liberty? When is it justifiable for an individual to take another person's life? Is it every proper to kill an innocent person? When should we excuse people for their wrongdoing? When is it fair to hold a person accountable for the actions of another? Do people possess free will? And so on. These are the sorts of questions with which lawyers have wrestled for centuries. More importantly perhaps, these are the sorts of questions that philosophers and theologians and scientists and poets and *just plain people* have wrestled with for centuries.

In terms of essentials, in this class you will likely learn about the basic components of any crime, the defenses to criminal conduct, the circumstances under which a person may be punished for conduct that falls short of attainment, and the concept of complicity (legal accountability of one person for the actions of another). You will also study various crimes in your class.

AH, A CRIME. WHAT IS A "CRIME"? IS THIS JUST ANOTHER "TORTS" CLASS?

Well, now you are moving into the Outline. I will cover that in Part I. I will say this much now: criminal law is (or, at least, should be) very different from tort law. Basically, a crime is a wrong, usually a moral wrong, committed against the society as a whole. Notice how criminal cases are titled in your casebook: *The People of the United States v. Jones* or *The People of the State of [x] v. Smith*. This distinguishes it from a tort action, which is a suit between private parties. Criminal prosecutions are brought in *our* name because *we* are the victims of crimes, both as individuals and as a community. And, it is *we* who punish the person convicted of the crime.

Tort actions are intended to compensate victims for their injuries. Criminal prosecutions are brought in order to punish wrongdoers. That difference is important to your appreciation of Criminal Law.

WHAT LAW WILL I HAVE TO LEARN IN MY CLASS? WILL I LEARN THE LAW OF MY OWN STATE?

Probably not. Basically, you will study the *common law* and perhaps the *Model Penal Code*. You will also learn some constitutional law principles that affect the criminal law. More on that in Part One.

(AS THE SEMESTER IS PROCEEDING:) I NEED HELP ORGANIZING MY THOUGHTS ABOUT CRIMINAL LAW. CAN YOU HELP?

Yes. First and foremost, use any technique that your teacher recommends. Here, however, is my own way of thinking about the subject.

First, learn the definitions of the crimes that are emphasized by your teacher or in your casebook as the semester proceeds. This job is easy: it is just a case of memorization. You will find most of the important crimes defined in this Outline.

Second, there are certain broad principles or concepts of criminal law that you are apt to need all semester. Become familiar with them, so that you can use them when you need them. In this Outline, I call them the "tools" of the Criminal Law, and they covered in Part One. They include: (1) theories of punishment; (2) the principle of legality; (3) the concept of proportionality; and (4) burdens of proof.

Third, you need to be able to analyze the relevant facts in relation to the basic "elements" of any crime. That is, in order to determine whether the defendant is guilty of a crime, you need to break up the crime you are considering into its constituent parts. As you will learn, there are five basic elements to most crimes. Unless your professor provides a different approach, which he or she may do, I recommend that you organize your analysis of the elements of a crime in the following order (as discussed in the outline):

1. Voluntary act (or omission) (Part Two)

2. Social harm (Part Two)

3. *Mens rea* (Parts Three and Four)

4. Actual causation (Part Five)

5. Proximate causation (Part Five)

Fourth, even if the elements of the crime are proved, the defendant may have a defense to his or her conduct. You should consider the defenses *after* you resolve the "elements." Organize your thoughts about the defenses in the following way:

1. Ask: Was the defendant *justified* in doing what (s)he did? The so-called justification defenses are considered in Part Six.

2. Ask: Should the defendant be *excused* for what (s)he did? The excuse defenses are covered in Part Seven.

Fifth, if the defendant did not successfully complete the offense, consider whether (s)he proceeded far enough along to be guilty of a so-called "inchoate" (or, incomplete or unsuccessful) offense. Generally speaking, there are three crimes to consider: (1) attempt; (2) conspiracy; and (3) solicitation. Part Eight covers this area. You should analyze these crimes like you would a completed crime: that is, by considering the elements of the crimes and defenses to them.

Sixth, if more than one person participated in the criminal enterprise, consider (Part Nine) whether the persons who did not personally commit the offense are accountable for the actions of the perpetrator. This requires you to determine whether the non-perpetrators are accomplices and/or co-conspirators in the crime.

I GUESS I AM READY TO START. BUT BEFORE I GET TOO DEEP INTO THE MATERIALS, ARE THERE OTHER SOURCES I CAN TURN TO BEYOND THE OUTLINE FOR HELP?

Of course. First, ask your professor for advice. *Your teacher is the best source for advice.* There is a lot out there: some of the materials are very good. Your professor can help you pick out the best materials to meet your needs.

One of the best sources of help are "hornbooks" or legal texts in the field. Some are directed at lawyers, others are aimed at students. Like an outline, they explain the general principles of law, but they do so in greater depth than is possible in an outline. The major hornbooks are usually on reserve in a law library, so you do not need to buy them. Sometimes, however, it will be worth the cost to purchase. Ask students who have already taken Criminal Law for advice. I would suggest two major texts:

1. Joshua Dressler, UNDERSTANDING CRIMINAL LAW (Lexis Nexis, 3rd Ed. 2001). (For some reason, I am partial to this one.)

2. Wayne LaFave, CRIMINAL LAW (Thomson West, 4th ed. 2003) (For some reason, my Black Letter publisher is partial to this one.)

If you want to look deeply into a very narrow subject, you will want to look at a book or law review article on the subject. Ask your professor for suggestions. Also, use the bibliography in your casebook, if there is one, to see what sources the author thinks are worth your time. Also, the Dressler Hornbook offers many source suggestions.

OKAY, ANY MORE ADVICE?

Yes, two things. First, in studying the criminal law, do not focus on the trees so much that you ignore the forest. The fun part of the study of the law ought to be when you ask yourself the Big Questions. A lawyer is not worth a damn in the larger picture unless (s)he cares about whether the laws that govern us are morally just and coherent.

Second, have fun. If this outline makes it possible for you to enjoy law school a little more, I will be pleased.

EXAMINATION PRACTICE–POINTERS

Examination-taking is an art. A very bright student—and a future fine lawyer—can do very poorly on a test because (s)he has not studied adequately or has not learned the art of examination-taking. The hard reality is that although a student who does not have a good grasp of the law cannot do too well on an examination, a student who understands the law in its full complexity will do less well than (s)he should if (s)he has not yet learned how to take law school examinations.

Another hard reality is that there is *no* single, foolproof way to take an essay examination. Talk to experienced law students and you are apt to find almost as many recipes for success as the number of cooks to whom you speak. Examination-taking, like studying for an examination, is very personal: what will work for you may not work for someone else; and, just as importantly, there are differences in expectations among professors.

Nonetheless, there are certain suggestions that probably have merit in most cases. What follows, therefore, is a summary of what I advise *my* students. I would look over these comments just before you take an essay examination.

Do's and Don't's In Essay Examination–Taking

1. **DO** read the facts in the essay question carefully.

Read over the essay facts twice. The first time, read the essay fairly quickly. The purpose of the first reading should be to get an overview of the facts and to see what the teacher wants you to do with the facts. The second reading is the key one: now you are poring over the facts in order to answer the question the professor has asked you.

2. **DO** read the "call" of the question carefully.

The "call" is the portion of the question, usually at the end, where your teacher tells you exactly what you are to do with the facts. It might say something very general: "Discuss the criminal liability of the parties." Or, it might be more specific, such as: "Jones is prosecuted for murder. Discuss her criminal liability for this crime." Or, it may be even more specific: "Jones is prosecuted for murder. What defenses might she raise at trial, and will they succeed?"

One of the great tragedies in examination-taking occurs when a student answers a question that was not asked (or, worse still does <u>not</u> answer the question that <u>was</u> asked). For example, a fact pattern may suggest a number of crimes committed by various parties. Students who do not read the call of the question carefully are apt to assume that the professor wants them to discuss every crime committed by every person discussed in the essay. Sometimes this assumption is correct. Often, however, the teacher has a narrower focus: (s)he may want more in-depth discussion of fewer crimes. Therefore, (s)he may ask you to discuss only certain specified aspects of the case. If a student discusses issues not asked, (s)he may not receive any credit for this; meanwhile, (s)he is not answering the question that was asked.

3. **DO NOT** rush to start answering the question.

Novice students often become fearful when they see someone nearby answering an essay question while they are still thinking about what to write. Of course, a student *can* spend too much time thinking and too little time writing an answer, but more often than not an inexperienced law student's "sin" is to think and organize too little, and write too much.

Organize your thoughts before you begin to write. To do so, you may want to prepare a brief outline before you write your "real" answer—just something that will help you remember what you plan to write about and in what order. Just write down a few words on each issue to remind you.

How much time should you spend in this organizational process? There is no sure answer. It depends on many factors, not the least of which is how fast a writer (or computer typist) you are. However, I would expect that you may want to spend about one-quarter of your time on this stage of your answer.

4. **DO** budget your time carefully.

Here is a common scenario: a student has three essay questions of equal value to write in three hours. Rather than spend one hour on each question as (s)he should, the student spends 70 minutes on each of the first two questions. Obviously, (s)he has little time—only 40 minutes—to read, think about, and answer the third question. *Almost without fail, the few extra points (s)he might earn on the first two questions because (s)he spent a little extra time on them are lost in spades in the third question!*

Remember this, if you remember nothing else from my comments: **Nobody can say everything that there is to say on any single essay question during an in-class examination.** (Or, perhaps, I should say: if you *do* have time to say everything you know, then maybe you know too little!) Therefore, be a tough taskmaster on yourself: if you should spend one hour on a question (for example, if the professor recommends an hour, or tells you that this question will count one-third of your grade on a three-hour exam), spend only one hour on it, *no matter what*. Strictly apportion your time during that hour. By looking at the outline you prepared (see above), you should be able to see in advance what needs to be said. By checking the time regularly to see where you are in the hour *and where you are in your answer*, you can decide when you will need to stop discussing an issue and move on. That is a far better situation than to write at the end of your last bluebook (as so many of my students have done over the years): "Sorry, Professor, I ran out of time."

5. If you are permitted to do so, **DO** skip pages in your blue book, *i.e.*, leave every other page blank.

The reason is simple: no matter how well you organize your answer in advance, you will forget to say something or a great idea will dart into your mind after you have moved on to another issue. Rather than stick those afterthoughts in at the end of the examination, go back to the spot where it belongs, draw an arrow to the blank page, and stick in the new thought. It may not be neat, but it is easier to follow than if you put it in at the end of your answer, where it definitely does *not* belong.

6. In answering a question, **DO NOT** add facts that are not there, and **DO NOT** create issues that are not reasonably apparent from the facts.

Let me start with an extreme—and downright silly—example, but one that actually happened. I gave an essay question that involved a fairly simple set of facts, in which John shot and instantly killed Jane, his wife. My student, perhaps assuming that I was planning to raise some weighty moral issues that I discussed in class wrote in her bluebook, "If Jane had been a fetus, then. . . . " The student then proceeded to discuss the definition of "human being" and the common law rule that a fetus not born alive is not a "human being" within the meaning of the common law. (We learned that in class.) Wonderfully interesting—and even true—but hardly relevant to the facts. As I have said, there is rarely enough time on an exam to say everything you could in a perfect world; you certainly *don't* have time to discuss non-issues. Use your time to discuss the issues that a lawyer would worry about in the real world.

Nostalgia Department: I remember the one and only practice examination I took as a first year student at UCLA. It was in Civil Procedure. I prepared feverishly for the examination, and I wrote an erudite answer, in which I provided my professor virtually everything there was to know about Civil Procedure (or, at least, that we had learned in class at that stage of the semester). I left the examination very proud of myself. Later, he returned our examinations. I received a "D." In red, at the end of my answer, was the following comment from my acerbic instructor: "If I had wanted *Corpus Juris Secundum* I would have asked for it." I had no idea what he meant, so I went sheepishly and asked. His answer: I had written an encyclopedic statement about Civil Procedure that had little to do with the facts in the essay question. I could have telephoned in my answer without even reading the facts. As I mentioned above, law professors want you to learn how to think like a lawyer, and not simply or primarily memorize rules and spit them back. That means you need to use the law you learn to analyze the facts given to you on the examination.

How do you know whether the facts call for discussion of a particular subject? It is not always easy to tell. For example, suppose the facts tell you that *D* left work, went to a bar, drove home, and there killed her husband. Assume that you are asked to discuss *D*'s possible criminal liability for the homicide. Is intoxication an issue? It is hard to say. If the facts had not mentioned that she went to a bar, the answer would clearly be that intoxication is not a viable issue. Perhaps you should ask yourself, "If I were a defense lawyer, and my client described these facts to me, what additional information would I need in order to properly defend her?" Almost certainly you would ask her questions, such as "What did you drink?" and "How many drinks did you have?" On an examination, therefore, it would be appropriate to write (in the appropriate place in the discussion): "The facts are unclear as to *D*'s possible state of intoxication. We know that she went to a bar, so it is reasonable to assume that she drank intoxicants. However, we do not know how much she drank or the quality of her mental processes thereafter. If the facts were to be found that. . . . " Then, you can discuss the hypothetical possibilities.

7.   **DO NOT** write conclusory answers.

You have probably already heard it more often than you want: Professors are more interested in how you get to your answer than what your answer is. Within limits, this is true. It is wholly unsatisfactory to say that Donald is guilty of murder unless you tell me why. It is wholly unsatisfactory to say that Donald is guilty of murder because he intentionally killed Victor, unless you tell me how you came to the conclusion that Donald intentionally killer Victor. In short, always listen to a little voice in the back of your mind that is asking you "Why?" whenever you make an assertion.

8.   **DO** define legal terms.

Remember what it is you are doing: you are trying to show your professor what you know. Therefore, it is important to show that you know what legal terms mean. Ideally, you should define terms in your discussion of them. For example, if you are attempting to show that the defendant acted recklessly, define "recklessness." If you do not expressly define legal terminology, then make sure that your factual discussion is sufficiently thorough that the professor can tell from it that you know what the term means.

9.   **DO NOT** write introductions and conclusions to your answers, unless your teacher tells you to do so.

You are not writing a brief for a court or a memorandum to an associate in a law firm: you are writing an answer to an examination under severe time pressures. Therefore, my advice (although there are teachers who feel differently) is: get directly into your answer. Skip introductions in which you say, "I am going to discuss. . . . I will show that. . . . " Skip conclusions, too.

10. **DO NOT** panic.

You will survive. Life goes on. No examination is worth the stress.

Writing a Criminal Law Examination

Here are a few pointers. (This advice will be of most use if you read it *after* you have studied the subject, not at the start.) Again, however, ignore my advice if your professor provides his or her own practice-pointers.

1. Separate out your thoughts (and ultimately your answer) by defendants and crimes.

That is, if the facts involve Ann and Bob, who arguably rob and kill Charles, you need to look at the problems in terms of Ann-Robbery, Ann-Murder, Bob-Robbery, and Bob-Murder. Talk about each defendant separately. And, with one exception noted at point 6 below, talk about each crime separately.

2. Be explicit about the crime and defendant under discussion.

For example, if you are discussing Ann's liability for the robbery, say so. The easiest way to do this is to write and underline in your blue book something like:

State v. Ann (robbery)

Then discuss Ann's liability for the robbery, element by element. By doing it this way, you tell the teacher (and remind yourself) what defendant and crime is under discussion. Then, when you are through with your discussion, you turn to the next problem, for example,

State v. Ann (murder)

and so on.

3. Discuss a crime in a logical order.

A. *Completed crimes.* Barring contrary advice from your professor, I recommend that you discuss any crime in the order listed earlier in this Perspective: (1) voluntary act (or omission); (2) social harm (that is, discuss the specific *actus reus* elements of the crime)[1]; (3) *mens rea* of the particular crime; (4) actual cause; and

---

1. For example, if you are discussing the common law crime of burglary, discuss separately each element of the *actus reus*: (1) breaking; (2) entering; (3) dwelling house; (4) of another; and (5) at night.

(5) proximate cause. Then discuss defenses, starting with any relevant justification defenses, and then moving to excuse defenses.

B. *Inchoate offenses.* If you are discussing an inchoate offense, such as attempt, your discussion can be more limited. Basically, you will need to discuss: (1) the *actus reus* (did the actor go far enough to constitute an attempt?); and (2) *mens rea* of attempt. Then discuss any possible defenses. Although the justification and excuse defenses might apply, be especially careful to look for the crime-specific defenses, e.g., legal impossibility and abandonment.

C. *Complicity.* If you are discussing a defendant's potential accomplice's liability, you will discuss the "elements" of accomplice liability: Did the defendant assist (the *actus reus* of complicity liability)?; and did the defendant act with the requisite *mens rea.* Defenses, where relevant, can then be discussed.

4. Discuss multiple defendants in a logical order.

If the facts involve multiple potential defendants, there is usually a logical order to discuss the defendants. As you learn(ed), an accomplice's liability is derived from the principal's liability. That is simply a matter of logic. If Ann actually robbed a bank, it would be illogical to discuss Bob's liability first, as his liability as a potential accomplice depends on finding that a robbery occurred. Therefore, always discuss the alleged perpetrator's liability first. Then, discuss the liability of the secondary party(ies).

5. If the question involves multiple crimes, discuss them in a logical order, if there is one.

Sometimes it does not matter in what order you discuss crimes. If Donald is charged with robbery and rape, you might discuss either one first. You may as well do them in chronological order.

But, sometimes you can see (especially if you have done your necessary pre-answer organization) that there is a logical order to the discussion. For example, if you have a potential robbery and murder charge against Defendant Linda, you may see that the prosecutor's murder charge could be based on felony-murder principles. If so, you would do well to discuss the felony first. Then, when you get to your murder discussion and, more particularly, to the felony-murder issue, you can simply say, "As discussed earlier, the defendant is (not) guilty of the felony of robbery. Therefore . . ."

6.   Special Problem: Criminal Homicide.

Unless your professor (or the "call" of the question) tells you otherwise, any time you discuss a defendant's possible guilt for the crime of murder, you will also want to discuss manslaughter and/or negligent homicide, lesser included offenses. As you learn(ed), an intentional killing can be murder or manslaughter. And, the line between a reckless murder and negligent manslaughter is thin.

There are two ways to handle your homicide discussion. First, you can discuss the defendant's liability for murder, element by element. Then, start all over again, this time discussing the defendant's liability for manslaughter, incorporating by reference all of your earlier discussion of "voluntary act," "social harm," "actual cause," "proximate cause," and the defenses. Simply discuss fully the issue of *mens rea*, as this is the only real difference between murder and manslaughter.

Alternatively—I personally prefer this—discuss the defendant's liability in terms of "criminal homicide": Discuss the elements of both crimes together, *since there is no difference between them*, except when you reach *mens rea*. At that point, you would "start at the top" by discussing the *mens rea* of murder, and then (assuming there is a plausible case for it) discussing the possibility that the defendant has the *mens rea* of manslaughter or negligent homicide. This is the one situation where it is acceptable to discuss two crimes together.

PART ONE

Introductory Principles

■ *ANALYSIS*

CONVERSATION WITH STUDENTS

There is a lot of important material in Part One. I will start by giving you an overview of the criminal law—a brief sketch of what matters in the study of the criminal law. I will then turn in Section II to the "tools" of the criminal law, by which I mean the overarching doctrines or concepts that you are apt to need all semester long to help understand and evaluate the criminal law. If one thinks of the criminal law as if it were a house, these are the tools one needs to construct that house and evaluate its worth. (By the way, if you have not already done so, it will be worth your time to read my Perspectives, which immediately precedes this.)

I. Criminal Law Overview

A. "Criminal" versus "Civil"

1. The Problem

What distinguishes a "crime" from, for example, a "tort" or "breach of contract"? In other words, what distinguishes the "criminal law" from "civil" areas of the law, such as Torts and Contracts?

2. Definition of "Crime"

According to two criminal law scholars, a "crime" is "any social harm defined and made punishable by law." Rollin M. Perkins & Ronald N. Boyce, Criminal Law 12 (3rd ed. 1982). But this is a nearly useless definition because it means that anything that is called a crime by lawmakers is a crime. What if lawmakers say sneezing is a crime? And, what distinguishes the "crime" of (for example) battery from the "tort" of battery, other than the label?

3. The Essence of the Criminal Law: A Preliminary Start

It is commonly pointed out that what distinguishes the criminal law from civil law is that *punishment* flows from violation of a crime, whereas those who commit torts or breach a contract pay *money damages*. This is an imperfect way of distinguishing the criminal from the civil law, since one form of "punishment" for violation of a "crime" is payment of a fine; and in limited circumstances, a person who violates a civil obligation may be temporarily jailed, and yet this is not called "punishment." So, we must look further.

4. The Essence of the Criminal Law: A Better Answer

"What distinguishes a criminal from a civil sanction and all that distinguishes it, it is ventured, is the judgment of community condemnation which accompanies and justifies its imposition." Henry M. Hart, *The Aims of the Criminal Law*, 23 Law & Contemp. Probs. 401 (1958). A "crime," therefore, is (or, at least should be) limited to conduct that "if duly shown to have taken place, will incur a formal and solemn pronouncement of the moral condemnation of the community." *Id.*

B. Sources of the Criminal Law

1. Common Law

American criminal law is British in its origins, and "common law" in nature. In this context, "common law" means, simply, judge-made law. Contrary to lawmaking today, judges—not legislators—in England defined the crimes, formulated the defenses to crimes, and developed all of the relevant doctrines relating to the field.

Actually, the judges of the time did not claim they were *defining* and *formulating* the criminal law. They said they were *discovering* the law, which implied that there was pre-existent criminal law. The criminal law was understood to derive from basic, moral principles that existed independent of the judges, perhaps from God. For our purposes, however, we can say that the roots of American law are found in the judge-made law of English soil. For the most part, British common law became American common law.

2. Statutes

a. A New Source

Judicial lawmaking (or law-discovering, if you wish) has given way to legislative lawmaking, both in England (where the Parliament enacts criminal laws) and in the United States (in which Congress at the federal level, and legislatures at the state level, enact criminal legislation). This process culminated at different times in different jurisdictions in the United States, but mostly in the late nineteenth and early twentieth century. Today, all criminal lawyers in this country turn first to a book—often characterized as a "penal code"—that contains the legislatively drafted definitions of crimes, defenses to crimes, and other relevant doctrines of criminal law, which apply in that lawyer's jurisdiction. *Therefore, when you read cases in your class, pay careful attention to any statute set out in the judicial opinion.*

b. **Common Law: Continuing Relevance**

Although criminal codes, enacted by legislators, are the primary source of law today, there are two reasons why modern lawyers (and, therefore, law students) still need to understand the common law.

i. **Gaps**

Unfortunately, some legislatures have enacted penal codes containing significant gaps. For example, a particular penal code may define the relevant crimes and defenses, but fail to deal with other critical doctrines, such as accomplice liability. Where gaps exist, courts often turn to the common law to fill the holes.

ii. **Statutory Interpretation**

When a statute needs clarification in some manner, one source of guidance is the common law, particularly if the statute is itself a codification of the common law.

Example: The California legislature defined "murder" in much the same way that the crime was defined at common law, as the killing of a "human being" by another human being with malice aforethought. The term "human being" was not defined in the California murder statute. In *Keeler v. Superior Court*, 2 Cal.3d 619, 87 Cal.Rptr. 481, 470 P.2d 617 (1970), *K* purposely kicked his estranged and pregnant wife in the abdomen, causing the immediate death of the fetus. The state supreme court had to determine whether *K* could be prosecuted for murder for the death of the fetus. In turn, the issue was whether a fetus is a "human being." The court held that, in the absence of a statutory definition, the term should be defined as it was at common law; at common law, only a viable fetus born alive constituted a "human being." Therefore, *K* could not be prosecuted for murder.

3. **Model Penal Code**

a. **What Is It?**

The Model Penal Code (typically abbreviated as "MPC") is a code created in the 1950s and adopted in 1962 by the American Law Institute (ALI), a prestigious organization composed of top judges, scholars, and lawyers.

b. **Why Does It Exist?**

Many state legislatures had enacted imperfect penal codes: leaving gaps in the law; sometimes adopting conflicting or overlapping statutes; providing ambiguous or no definitions to critical terms; and/or enacting laws without serious consideration of the underlying purposes of the criminal law. The hope of the ALI was that the MPC would serve as a model for better penal code legislation.

c. **Why Learn It?**

Most criminal law casebooks and many professors emphasize the Model Penal Code, even as you also learn the common law and perhaps become familiar with one or another state penal code. You are likely to find major portions of the MPC in the appendix of your casebook or interspersed throughout the book. The MPC, therefore, is likely to be a *very* important part of your course in Criminal Law. There are two major reasons for this: many states have adopted significant portions of the MPC (some state codes are almost entirely MPC-based); and the MPC serves as a useful device for thinking about and critiquing common law and existing non-MPC statutory law. Unless your professor indicates otherwise, be attentive to the MPC.

C. Limits on the Criminal Law

Legislatures have broad discretion in defining crimes, identifying and defining defenses to crimes (or, for that matter, deciding *not* to recognize defenses), enacting general criminal law doctrine, and setting punishment for violations of criminal laws. This discretion is not unlimited, however. State and federal legislation is subject to the strictures of the United States Constitution (and, with state laws, the constitution of the relevant state).

Examples: The federal Constitution prohibits *ex post facto* legislation. The First Amendment to the Constitution, which guarantees freedom of speech, assembly and religion, bars a state from making it a crime for a person to deface an American flag knowing that it "will seriously offend" others. *Texas v. Johnson*, 491 U.S. 397, 109 S.Ct. 2533, 105 L.Ed.2d 342 (1989). The Due Process Clause prohibits a state from criminalizing private adult consensual homosexual conduct. *Lawrence v. Texas*, 539 U.S. 558, 123 S.Ct. 2472, 156 L.Ed.2d 508 (2003). A state is not permitted to make the status of "being addicted" to a drug a criminal offense. *Robinson v. California*, 370 U.S. 660, 82 S.Ct. 1417, 8 L.Ed.2d 758 (1962) (applying the Eighth Amendment bar on cruel and unusual punishment).

D. Burden of Proof: Basics

Much more will be said on this subject (see II.E. below), but it is a basic American principle of criminal law that a defendant is presumed innocent. The Due Process Clauses of the Fifth and Fourteenth Amendments have been interpreted to require that, to convict a defendant, the government must persuade the factfinder "beyond a reasonable doubt of every fact necessary to constitute the crime charged." *In re Winship*, 397 U.S. 358, 90 S.Ct. 1068, 25 L.Ed.2d 368 (1970). This "bedrock 'axiomatic and elementary' principle" is "indispensable to commanding the respect and confidence of the community" in the criminal justice system; as Justice Harlan stated in *Winship*, "we do not view the social disutility of convicting an innocent man as equivalent to the disutility of acquitting someone who is guilty."

E. Judge Versus Jury

1. Constitutional Law

a. Rule

The Sixth Amendment to the United States Constitution provides that "in all criminal prosecutions, the accused shall enjoy the right to a speedy and public trial, by an impartial jury." Despite the phrase "in *all* criminal prosecutions," the Supreme Court has generally limited the right to a jury trial to prosecutions for crimes for which the maximum potential punishment exceeds incarceration of six months. *Sullivan v. Louisiana*, 508 U.S. 275, 113 S.Ct. 2078, 124 L.Ed.2d 182 (1993). A defendant may waive his right to trial by jury and have his case decided by a judge (a "bench trial").

b. Rationale for Jury Trial Right

Conviction of a crime involves the moral condemnation of the community (see I.A.4. above). It is proper, therefore, that the determination of innocence or guilt be determined by jurors, rather than a judge, since jurors serve as representatives of the community—the defendant's peers. The Supreme Court has also explained the jury-trial right in historical and political terms: "A right to jury trial is granted to criminal defendants in order to prevent oppression by the Government. Those who wrote our constitutions knew from history and experience that it was necessary to protect against unfounded criminal charges brought to eliminate enemies and against judges too unresponsive to the voice of higher authority." Further, "[i]f the defendant preferred the common-sense judgment of a jury to the more tutored but perhaps less sympathetic reaction of the single judge, he was to have it." *Duncan v. Louisiana*, 391 U.S. 145, 88 S.Ct. 1444, 20 L.Ed.2d 491 (1968).

2. Jury Nullification

a. What Is It?

Although a defendant is entitled to trial by jury, the judge remains the authority on the law. Before jury deliberation, the judge instructs the jury on the relevant law. Jury nullification occurs when the jury decides that the prosecution has proven its case beyond a reasonable doubt, but for reasons of conscience it disregards the facts and/or the law, and acquits the defendant. Typically, nullification occurs when the jury feels particularly sympathetic to the defendant, believes that the victim was significantly at fault for the events, or disagrees with the wisdom of the law that they are expected to apply.

b. The Law

The Fifth Amendment Double Jeopardy Clause provides that a defendant may not be reprosecuted after an acquittal. This rule applies even if the acquittal was the result of jury nullification. Thus, it is said that a jury has the *power* to nullify, but not the *right* to do so. That is, jurors take an oath to obey the judge's instructions on the law; jury nullification, therefore, constitutes a violation of the juror's oath. Because jurors do not have the *right* to nullify—only the naked power to do so—a defendant is not entitled to have the jury instructed that it may nullify the law if it chooses to do so.

II. "Tools" of the Criminal Law

A. Overview

As noted in my "conversation" above, there are various important overarching doctrines that you may need in your class to better understand and evaluate the law you are learning. These are, if you will, the "tools" for building the "criminal law house."

B. Theories of Punishment

1. Different Theories

Two broad theories of punishment exist: *utilitarianism* and *retribution*. Each theory has its adherents and critics. These theories help to determine why a society creates a criminal justice system; and, at least as importantly, these theories should guide lawmakers in developing general principles of criminal responsibility—the rules you will be learning in class—and in setting the penalties for violations of the criminal laws.

2. Principles of Utilitarianism

a. Augmenting Happiness

Utilitarianism holds that the general object of all laws is to augment the total happiness of the community by excluding, as much as possible, everything that subtracts from that happiness, *i.e.*, everything that causes "mischief" (pain).

b. Role of Punishment

Critical to appreciating utilitarianism is the point that both crime and punishment are evils, because they both result in pain to individuals and to society as a whole. Therefore, the pain of punishment is undesirable unless its infliction is likely to prevent a greater amount of pain in the form of future crime. *Notice that utilitarianism looks to the future: punishment is not inflicted as punishment for the prior wrongdoing, but in order to prevent future crime (pain).* If punishment of the criminal is unnecessary to prevent future crime, a utilitarian will let the wrongdoer go unpunished!

c. Forms of Utilitarianism

i. General Deterrence

Here, a person (call her *D*) is punished in order to send a message to others (the general society or, at least, persons who might be contemplating criminal conduct) that crime does not pay.

ii. Specific Deterrence

In contrast to general deterrence, *D* is punished in order to deter *D* from future criminal activity. This is done in either of two ways: by *incapacitation* (incarceration of *D* prevents her from committing additional crimes in the general community for the duration of her sentence); and/or by *intimidation* (*D*'s punishment serves as a painful reminder, so that upon release *D* will be deterred from future criminal conduct).

iii. Rehabilitation

Advocates of this form of utilitarianism believe that the criminal law can prevent future crime by reforming an individual, by providing her with employment skills, psychological aid, etc., so that she will not want or need to commit offenses in the future.

d. Underlying Premises

Utilitarianism—at least the deterrence versions—is founded on the belief that humans are hedonistic, in the sense that people ordinarily seek to augment their personal pleasure and avoid pain. Another critical premise is that human beings, as a species, generally are capable of rational calculation. Therefore, a potential wrongdoer will weigh the benefits (pleasure) she expects to receive from committing a crime against its "down-side" in the form of punishment. If the rational calculator believes that the risks of arrest, conviction and punishment outweigh the likely benefits of the proposed action, she will not commit the crime.

3. Principles of Retribution

a. Just Deserts

Retributivism is sometimes called the "just deserts" theory. Punishment of a wrongdoer is justified as a deserved response to wrongdoing. That is, unlike utilitarianism, which does not punish because of prior wrongdoing, but punishes in order to prevent *future* wrongdoing (the pain of crime), retributivists punish *because* of the wrongdoing—the criminal gets his just deserts—regardless of whether such punishment will deter future crime.

b. Rationale

One justification for retribution is that wrongdoing creates a moral disequilibrium in society. This is because the wrongdoer obtains the benefits of the law (namely, that other people have respected *his* rights), but he does not accept the law's burdens (respecting others' rights). Proportional punishment of the wrongdoer—"paying his debt"—brings him back into moral equilibrium. Another justification is based on the idea that both crime and punishment are forms of communication: one who commits a crime sends an implicit message to the victim that the wrongdoer's rights are more important than others' rights; punishment is a symbolic way of showing the criminal—and reaffirming for victims—that this message was wrong. Punishment proportional to the offense defeats the offender: it brings him down to his proper place in relation to others.

c. Underlying Premise

Critical to retributive theory is the belief that humans possess free will. As long as a person has freely chosen to commit an offense, punishment is justified. To the extent that a person lacks free choice, punishment is morally wrong.

4. Mixing the Theories: Hybrid Approach

a. Overview

Retributive and utilitarian theory frequently will result in the same outcome, albeit for different reasons. Frequently, however, these theories will lead lawmakers or judges in different, even opposite, directions. Some people advocate one theory at the exclusion of the other, but many people have sought to find a coherent way to combine the theories.

b. One Hybrid Approach

Some people distinguish between the *general justifying aim* of the criminal law (why we have a criminal justice system) and *distributive justice* (determining who should be punished, and how much punishment is proper). These hybrid advocates argue that one can be a utilitarian as to one issue, and a retributivist as to the other. For example, one might be a utilitarian as to the general justifying aim—we created a justice system to try to deter crime—and retributivist in determining who should be punished in the justice system, and in calculating the proper punishment to impose.

c. "Limiting Retributivism"

Another hybrid approach, although one limited to sentencing matters, starts from a retributivist perspective: lawmakers should make a rough determination of the proper retributive punishment for an offense by coming up with a sentencing range (identifying a certain level of punishment that is disproportionately high, and another level that is deemed disproportionately low), and then setting the *actual* punishment *within* the proportional range based on utilitarian considerations.

C. Proportionality of Punishment

1. General Principle

A general principle of criminal law is that punishment should be proportional to the offense committed. MPC § 1.02(2)(c). The difficulty lies in determining the meaning of the term "proportional."

2. Utilitarian Meaning

In a utilitarian system of criminal justice, punishment is proportional if it involves the infliction of no more pain than necessary to fulfill the law's deterrent goal of reducing a greater amount of crime.

Example: Assume that based on a utilitarian calculus it is determined that 10 units of crime can be prevented by the imposition, or threatened imposition, of 6 units of punishment. Six units of punishment constitutes proportional punishment (assuming that fewer units of punishment would not do the job as well); 7 or more units of punishment would be excessive (assuming it would not deter more units of crime).

3. Retributive Meaning

Proportionality of punishment is an especially critical concept in retributive theory. To retributivists, punishment should be proportional to the harm caused on the present occasion, taking into consideration the actor's degree of culpability for causing the harm.

Example: A murderer should be punished more than a robber, because murder causes more harm than robbery. But, as well, a person who kills another person negligently should be punished less severely than one who takes a life intentionally, because a negligent wrongdoer is less morally culpable in causing the harm than an intentional wrongdoer.

4. Difference In Outcome: An Example

Utilitarians and retributivists may reach different results in determining how much punishment is proportional to an offense. For example, in most states, a repeat offender ("recidivist") is punished more severely for an offense than a first-time violator. Thus, a third-time thief might be sentenced to 25–years-to-life imprisonment, although a first-time offender would receive a much more lenient sentence.

a. Utilitarian Analysis

The preceding example of a recidivist law might be valid: the *threat* of very long imprisonment may be necessary to deter a recidivist, who has been undeterred by lesser punishment in the past; in addition, a third-time felon—a person who has proven that he is likely to continue to transgress if allowed to do so—may need to be incapacitated for a longer period of time. However, it should be kept in mind that a utilitarian will only inflict this heightened pain if there is a reliable reason to believe that it is necessary for general or specific deterrent purposes.

b. Retributive Analysis

A wrongdoer should receive punishment proportional to the crime just committed, taking into consideration both the harm caused and the actor's culpability. The criminal paid his debt to society for his earlier offenses, so these crimes are irrelevant to the present punishment; and a retributivist would not punish a person for predicted future crimes. Therefore, it is unlikely that one can justify a sentence of 25–years-to-life for theft, even for a recidivist.

5. **Constitutional Law**

The Eighth Amendment Cruel and Unusual Punishment Clause prohibits grossly disproportional punishment.

a. Death Penalty Cases

The Supreme Court has held that death is grossly disproportional punishment for the crime of rape of an adult woman, because the latter offense does not involve the taking of human life. *Coker v. Georgia*, 433 U.S. 584, 97 S.Ct. 2861, 53 L.Ed.2d 982 (1977). Notice that this result is consistent with retributive theory: since the offender took no life, *his* life should not be taken. However, the rapist in *Coker* had previously killed one, and raped two, young women. Therefore, based on concepts of specific deterrence, the death penalty might have been justified on the basis of the defendant's personal dangerousness.

b. Imprisonment Cases

According to the Supreme Court's most recent pronouncement, there is only a very "narrow proportionality principle" outside the context of the death penalty. As explained by Justice Kennedy in *Harmelin v. Michigan*, 501 U.S. 957, 111 S.Ct. 2680, 115 L.Ed.2d 836 (1991) (concurring opinion), and later reaffirmed as guiding principles in *Ewing v. California*, 538 U.S. 11, 123 S.Ct. 1179, 155 L.Ed.2d 108 2003), the legislature (not the judiciary) has primary authority in setting punishments, particularly because it is the role of the legislature to determine whether to apply utilitarian, retributive, or hybrid penological goals. No non-capital incarcerative punishment will be declared unconstitutional, therefore, unless there are objective grounds—not simply a judge's own subjective views of the propriety of the punishment—for determining that the punishment is grossly disproportionate to the crime.

Example: In *Ewing, supra*, the Supreme Court had to determine whether California's "three strikes" recidivist law was unconstitutional because it resulted in *E*'s sentence of 25–years-to-life after he was convicted of shoplifting three golf clubs. *E* had previously been convicted and punished for various offenses, including theft, burglary, and unlawful possession of a firearm. By a vote of 5–4, the Court held that in light of *E*'s prior criminal conduct, and the legislature's primacy in setting penalties, and in further view of the right of California to apply utilitarian, specific deterrence principles in recidivist cases, *E*'s sentence was not grossly disproportionate.

D. Legality

1. Requirement of Previously Defined Conduct

a. General Principle

The so-called "principle of legality" is *nullem sine lege; nulla poena sine lege* or "no crime without (pre-existent) law, no punishment without (pre-existent) law. This principle has been characterized as *"the* first principle"—the most basic principle—of American law. Herbert L. Packer, The Limits of the Criminal Sanction 79–80 (1968). In current Anglo–American modern law, the principle has also come to mean that *judicial* crime-creation is no longer permitted.

b. Rationale

It is morally unjust to punish a person whose conduct was lawful when she acted, because she did not choose to violate the law. Furthermore, a law cannot have its desired deterrent effect unless people are put on notice of the illegality of their contemplated conduct. Also, from a political theory perspective, retroactive prosecution, conviction, and punishment of a person permits a government to punish its enemies, and is antithetical to a system of limited government.

c. Constitutional Law

The principle of legality not only is a common law doctrine, but has deep constitutional roots.

i. Ex Post Facto

Legislatures are prohibited by the Ex Post Facto Clause of the United States Constitution from enacting laws that punish conduct that was lawful at the time of its commission, or that increases the punishment for an act committed before the law took effect. (U.S. Constitution, Article I §§ 9, 10.)

Examples: *D* does legal act X on January 1. On January 2, the legislature prohibits X. It would violate the Ex Post Facto Clause to prosecute *D* for her January 1 conduct.

D commits murder, an offense punishable by life imprisonment, on January 1. On January 2, the legislature enacts a death penalty for the offense of murder. It would violate the Ex Post Facto Clause to sentence *D* to death for her offense.

ii. Due Process

Courts are prohibited from enlarging the scope of a criminal statute. To do so violates two aspects of the principle of legality: it results in retroactive criminalization and punishment; and, because it is the modern role of *legislatures* to enact criminal laws, the enlargement exceeds the modern authority of the judiciary.

Example: *D* struck *V*, a pregnant woman, in the abdomen with his knee in order to kill the viable fetus. The fetus was delivered stillborn. *D* was prosecuted for murder, statutorily defined as the "killing of a human being by another human being." The statutory term "human being" was interpreted to apply only to fetuses born alive. (See I.B.2.b.ii., *supra*.) The state supreme court refused to expand the definition of "human being" to include viable fetuses born dead: to do so would result in retroactive criminalization, a violation of the Due Process Clause; furthermore, the court stated it lacked jurisdiction to change the law, a matter for the legislature. *Keeler v. Superior Court*, 2 Cal.3d 619, 87 Cal.Rptr. 481, 470 P.2d 617 (1970).

2. Fair Notice

A corollary of the legality principle is that a person may not be punished for an offense unless the statute is sufficiently clear that a person of ordinary intelligence can understand its meaning. See MPC § 1.02 (1)(d). This is a fundamental common law concept, *In re Banks*, 295 N.C. 236, 244 S.E.2d 386 (1978), with constitutional roots as well.

a. Constitutional Law

An unduly vague statute violates the Due Process Clause. *Warning:* The void-for-vagueness doctrine ordinarily is not applied strictly. There is no way to capture through words precisely what a lawmaking body intends to prohibit; uncertainties lurk among all words and phrases. Furthermore, lawmakers need flexibility to draft laws to deal with novel forms of criminal activity. Therefore, courts hesitate to declare statutes unconstitutionally vague. However, if the law impinges on an especially valued right, such as freedom of speech, a court will typically demand greater-than-ordinary legislative clarity.

i. General Rule

A person has sufficient notice as to the meaning of a statute if its wording would put an ordinary law-abiding person on notice that her conduct comes near the proscribed area. If the statute meets this test, the law-abiding person is responsible to seek out further information to determine the meaning of the statute, including whether the statute has been previously clarified by a court.

Example: S was prosecuted under a Florida statute that prohibited, without defining, "the abominable and detestable crime against nature, either with mankind or beast." The Supreme Court held that the statute was not unconstitutionally vague, in part because Florida courts had previously held that the sexual act that S had committed fell within the meaning of the term "crime against nature." *Wainwright v. Stone*, 414 U.S. 21, 94 S.Ct. 190, 38 L.Ed.2d 179 (1973).

3. Nondiscriminatory Enforcement

Another corollary of the legality principle is that a criminal statute should not be so broadly worded that it is susceptible to discriminatory enforcement by law enforcement officers.

Example: The City of Chicago enacted an ordinance prohibiting "criminal street gang members" from "loitering" with one another or other persons in any public place. In turn, "loitering" was defined as "remaining in one place with no apparent purpose." The law required loiterers to disperse "from the area" upon police order. The Supreme Court in *City of Chicago v. Morales*, 527 U.S. 41, 119 S.Ct. 1849, 144 L.Ed.2d 67 (1999), ruled that the ordinance violated the Due Process Clause. It determined that the ordinance was "vague and standardless" and, as a result, "affords too much discretion to the police and too little notice to citizens who wish to use the public streets." Among other problems: the language "no apparent purpose" was too subjective and, thus, left too much to the discretion of individual police officers; the ordinance was too broad (it seemingly would apply to innocent behavior, such as a gang member and his father "loiter[ing] . . . just to get a glimpse of Sammy Sosa leaving the ballpark"); and the dispersal requirement was vague (what constitutes leaving "the area," and how long before dispersed parties may return?).

E. Burden of Proof

CONVERSATION WITH STUDENTS

Many (perhaps most) professors either will not cover this topic or cover it only sparingly (perhaps by lecture). It *is* a difficult topic anytime, but one that is especially hard to grasp if you are a first-year student (and even more so if you are a first *semester* student). A few professors (perhaps yours?) will cover this topic in considerable detail, but even if this occurs, you may find that the topic is broken up into parts, perhaps partially covered early in the semester, and more so when you reach discussion of criminal homicide and/or some of the criminal law defenses. There is no perfect place to cover the subject. (Notice that I have already divided up the discussion myself—look back to Section I.D., earlier in this Part of the Outline.) I urge you to return to these materials later in the semester. It will probably make more sense then. But, give it a try now.

1. Burden of Production

"Burden of proof" involves two different burdens, the first of which is "burden of production" (or "burden of producing evidence"). This speaks to the question of which party—the defendant or the government—has the obligation to first introduce evidence on a given issue. The party with this obligation who fails to satisfy this burden loses on the issue. Usually, the party with the burden of production on an issue is only required to introduce "some evidence" on the issue to meet the burden. In general, the government has the burden of producing evidence regarding the *elements* of a crime, and the defendant has the burden of producing evidence regarding *affirmative defenses*, as these italicized terms are explained later in this Outline.

Examples: *D* is prosecuted for Crime X, defined as "intentionally doing X." "Intent" is an element of this offense. Therefore, the prosecutor has the burden of introducing evidence on the issue of intent. If the prosecutor fails to introduce "some evidence" that *D* did kill X "intentionally," then the government has not satisfied its obligation in regard to this issue and, therefore, loses on the issue. Since the prosecutor must prove (beyond a reasonable doubt) *every* element of a crime, and the prosecutor has lost on one element of Crime X, the defendant must be acquitted.

On the other hand, assume that the government *does* satisfy its burden of production above. Now assume *D* wants to show that he was insane—a legal defense—when he intentionally did X. As insanity is an affirmative defense, the burden is on *D* to introduce some evidence of his legal insanity. If he fails to satisfy his burden of production on this issue, the insanity claim drops out of the case.

2. Burden of Persuasion

Once the burden of production has been satisfied—and, thus, an issue has been properly raised—the next question becomes: who has the burden of persuading the factfinder regarding the particular issue? The party with the burden of *production* may not necessarily have the burden of *persuasion*.

Example: In the example above, although *D* had the burden of production on the issue of insanity, the legislature, if it chooses to do so, might place the burden of *persuasion* on the issue of sanity on the *government*.

a.   Degree of Burden

i.   Elements of a Crime

As noted earlier in this Outline, the Due Process Clause of the Constitution requires that the government carry the burden of persuasion, beyond a reasonable doubt, as to "every *fact* necessary to constitute the crime charged." The Supreme Court has struggled to determine what "fact" means in this context. At one time it defined the term broadly, apparently to include at least some criminal law defenses and factors that have a substantial mitigating effect on a defendant's punishment. *Mullaney v. Wilbur*, 421 U.S. 684, 95 S.Ct. 1881, 44 L.Ed.2d 508 (1975). More recently, the Court has limited the word "fact"—and, thus, the prosecutor's constitutional obligation to carry the burden of production beyond a reasonable doubt—to expressed or implicit elements of an offense (as "elements" are discussed in this Outline), and not to defenses and mitigating factors. *Patterson v. New York*, 432 U.S. 197, 97 S.Ct. 2319, 53 L.Ed.2d 281 (1977). Therefore, the government must prove *every element* of the crime beyond a reasonable doubt. If it fails to satisfy that burden as to each element of the crime charged, the government loses: the defendant must be acquitted.

ii. **Defenses to Crimes**

Because defenses to crimes fall outside the *Patterson* principle stated above, a legislature is free to place the burden of persuasion regarding a criminal law defense on either party—the defendant or government—and to set the burden very high (proof beyond a reasonable doubt), somewhat high (clear and convincing evidence) or low (proof by preponderance of the evidence)

Example: The government may place the burden of persuasion of the issue of sanity/insanity on the defendant or the prosecutor, and then require the party to whom the burden has been allocated to prove its side of the case by any one of the three burden levels noted above.

iii. **Sentencing Facts**

The Supreme Court recently decided a complicated line of cases relating to the sentencing phase of a trial, *i.e.*, after the defendant has already been convicted of a crime. The Court held that the government is constitutionally required at the sentencing stage to prove beyond a reasonable doubt any fact (with one exception) that increases the penalty for a crime beyond the prescribed statutory maximum. (The one exception to this rule is that the burden of persuasion can be lower if the fact to be proven is that the defendant was previously convicted of an offense, that is, that the defendant is subject to a recidivist law.)

Example: *D* is convicted of Crime X, which carries a maximum sentence of five years' imprisonment. At sentencing, *D* is shown to have possessed a weapon during the commission of Crime X. State law provides that any person convicted of Crime X who is also found to have been in possession of a weapon during the offense, must receive a *10*-year prison sentence. Since the fact at issue here—was *D* in possession of a weapon—will increase the defendant's penalty for the crime beyond the prescribed statutory maximum (instead of 5 years, *D* will get 10 years), this fact must be proven by the government beyond a reasonable doubt. *Apprendi v. New Jersey*, 530 U.S. 466, 120 S.Ct. 2348, 147 L.Ed.2d 435 (2000).

III. Review Questions

[Answers Provided in Appendix A, page 357]

1. What is the definition of a "crime"?

2. T or F.   Jurors have the legal right to ignore a judge's legal instructions if they morally disagree with the law.

3. "We should punish Albert for raping Betty in order to send a message to other would-be rapists of what will happen to them if they get caught." This is a statement that would mostly like be made by an adherent of:

   a.   Retribution;

   b.   General deterrence;

   c.   Specific deterrence; or

   d.   Rehabilitation.

4. T or F.   Recidivist laws are more easily defended in a jurisdiction that applies retributivist principles than one that applies utilitarianism.

5. What is the principle of legality?

6. Which of the following statements, if any, is (or are) inaccurate?

a.   The prosecutor has the burden of producing evidence regarding the elements of a crime;

b.   The prosecutor is constitutionally required to carry the burden of persuasion, beyond a reasonable doubt, of every element of a crime charged;

c.   The defendant is constitutionally required to carry the burden of persuasion regarding affirmative defenses; and/or

d.   At sentencing, the prosecutor has the constitutional burden of persuasion, by clear and convincing evidence, to prove any fact that will increase the defendant's punishment beyond the statutory maximum.

PART TWO

Actus Reus

■ *ANALYSIS*

CONVERSATION WITH STUDENTS

We begin now to build the "criminal law" house. In this and the next three Parts of this outline, we will talk about the "elements"—or, ingredients—of a crime. In other words, subject to a few exceptions that will be noted, there are certain basic elements of *all* crimes, and this is what we will focus on now.

To begin with, all crimes contain an *"actus reus."* Unfortunately, lawyers (and, therefore, law professors) use this Latin term in various ways. Don't be worried, but be conscious of the definitional problem.

I. *Actus Reus*: Overview

A. Definition

The *"actus reus"* of an offense is the physical, or external, component of a crime—what society does not want to occur. It must be distinguished from the mental, or internal, component of the crime—the state of mind of the actor—which is called the *"mens rea,"* and which is the subject of Part Three of this outline.

Examples: The *actus reus* of the crime of murder is the taking of another person's life. The *actus reus* of the crime of larceny is the trespassory (non-consensual) taking and carrying away of the personal property of another. The *actus reus* of a criminal battery is harmful or offensive contact upon another person.

B. Two Elements

As defined here, the *actus reus* of a crime consists of two components, both of which must be proved by the prosecutor. Thus, we can say these are the first two elements of an offense.

1. Voluntary Act or Legal Omission

Generally speaking, there can be no crime in the absence of conduct. But, only a certain type of conduct qualifies, namely, conduct that includes a voluntary act. In rare circumstances, a person may be prosecuted because of what he or she did *not* do—an absence of conduct. An "omission" substitutes for a voluntary act when the defendant has a legal duty to act.

2. Social Harm

People are not punished for conduct (or omissions), but rather for conduct (or omissions) that result in "social harm." This term has a specialized meaning, as discussed below.

II. Voluntary Act

A. General Rule

A person is not ordinarily guilty of a criminal offense unless his conduct includes a voluntary act. This is a common law principle, and it is also the position of the Model Penal Code. MPC § 2.01(1).

1. Conduct

The preceding rule starts from the proposition that there ordinarily must be conduct. A person is never prosecuted solely for his thoughts, no matter now evil his ideas or dangerous his plans. There must be some externality of those thoughts.

2. Common Law Definition of Voluntary Act

A "voluntary act" is a willed muscular contraction or bodily movement by the actor.

a. Degree of movement required

The slightest muscular contraction or bodily movement constitutes an act.

Examples: A slight movement of a finger (as in pulling the trigger of a gun in a homicide prosecution) is sufficient. Even the movement of a person's tongue (the uttering of words in a prosecution, for example, of making a terrorist threat) is enough.

b. Meaning of "willed"

An act is "willed" if the bodily movement was controlled by the mind of the actor.

i. Unwilled acts

Some bodily movements are the result of impulses from the brain that direct the person's bodily movements. But, the brain may send out "unwilled" impulses, as when a person suffers from an epileptic seizure. Such acts are controlled by the *brain*, but not by the *mind*, and thus are "involuntary."

ii. Drawing the line

The difference between a willed/voluntary act and an unwilled/involuntary act may be sensed if you consider the difference between the statements: "I raised my hand" and "My hand came up." In the first case, the speaker is suggesting that she chose to raise her hand; it was a decision *she* made. In the second case, the speaker implies that the hand rose without her volition, perhaps unconsciously or as the result of a seizure.

3. Model Penal Code

The MPC does not provide a definition of "voluntary act." It defines an "act" ("a bodily movement whether voluntary or involuntary"). MPC § 1.13(2). The Code provides that " 'voluntary' has the meaning specified in Section 2.01." MPC § 1.13(3). But, Section 2.01 never defines "voluntary," except by providing examples of involuntary actions: a reflex or convulsion; bodily movement while unconscious or asleep; conduct during hypnosis or as a result of hypnotic suggestion; and/or "a bodily movement that otherwise is not a product of the effort or determination of the actor, either conscious or habitual." MPC § 2.01(2).

4. Constitutional Law

The Supreme Court has never expressly held that punishment of an involuntary actor is unconstitutional. However, it has invalidated statutes that criminalize a "status" or "condition," rather than conduct.

a. Punishment of drug addiction

It is unconstitutional cruel and unusual punishment for a state to make it a crime to be addicted to the use of narcotics. Robinson v. California, 370 U.S. 660, 82 S.Ct. 1417, 8 L.Ed.2d 758 (1962). According to the Supreme Court, a state lacks constitutional authority to punish a person for the illness of narcotics addiction, just as "even one day in prison would be cruel and unusual punishment for the 'crime' of having a common cold."

b. Punishment for public drunkenness

In contrast, in Powell v. Texas, 392 U.S. 514, 88 S.Ct. 2145, 20 L.Ed.2d 1254 (1968), the Supreme Court upheld the conviction of a person charged with the crime of being found in a state of intoxication in a public place. Although *P* asserted that he was an alcoholic and, therefore, should not be punished under the principles of *Robinson*, the Court distinguished *Robinson* on the ground that *P* was not prosecuted for his alcoholism, but rather for the *act* of getting intoxicated and going into a public place. Furthermore, the evidence in the case indicated that *P*'s first drink of the day was voluntary.

5. Avoiding Confusion

a. Coerced acts

An act is not involuntary, as discussed here, merely because the individual is compelled to perform the act.

Example: C points a loaded gun at D and orders her to steal V's watch. D does as she is ordered. Despite the deadly threat, the law treats the theft as a result of a voluntary act by D. Although D acted under extreme pressure, the muscular contractions that went in to stealing the watch were willed, in the sense that her mind told her that it was preferable to steal the watch than to die. D will be acquitted of the theft on the ground of duress, a criminal law defense, but the "voluntary act" requirement (an element of an offense) is satisfied.

b. Crimes of possession

Every penal code prohibits possession of certain articles, such as illegal drugs, obscene materials for dissemination, or burglar's tools. On its face, these statutes do not require proof of any act by the defendant.

Example: X plants an illegal drug on D's person. D is in possession of the illegal drug. Where is the voluntary act by D?

i. Solution

Penal codes define "possession" for current purposes as occurring if the possessor knowingly *procures* the article in question or *fails* to dispossess himself of it after he is made aware of its presence. MPC § 2.01(4). Thus, "possession" only arises if the person voluntarily takes control of the object (a voluntary act); or, alternatively, "possession" can be explained in terms of an omission, in which the person omits his duty to dispossess himself of the article. "Omissions" are discussed *infra*.

6. Important Study Point

Keep in mind that to be guilty of an offense, it is sufficient that the person's conduct *included* a voluntary act. *It is not necessary that all aspects of his conduct be voluntary.*

Example: D knew that he was an epileptic subject to sudden uncontrollable seizures. Nonetheless, he drove his automobile and killed pedestrians while suffering from a seizure. *D* was charged with the offense of "negligently driving a vehicle, so as to cause the death of a human being." (Assume for current purposes that *D*'s conduct was negligent, the "*mens rea*" of the crime.) Although the deaths occurred as the result of an involuntary act (the seizure), he may be convicted of the offense. The *actus reus* of the crime for which he was charged (remember, the "*actus reus*" is the external aspect of the crime—what society does not want to occur) was "driving a vehicle so as to cause the death of a human being." Therefore, *D*'s relevant conduct *included* the voluntary act of entering the car, turning on the ignition, and driving. *People v. Decina*, 2 N.Y.2d 133, 157 N.Y.S.2d 558, 138 N.E.2d 799 (1956).

B. Rationale of Voluntary Act Requirement

1. Utilitarian

A person who acts involuntarily cannot be deterred. Therefore, it is useless to punish the involuntary actor. It results in pain without the benefit of crime reduction.

a. Competing argument

It is true that persons cannot be deterred during their involuntary conduct, but the threat of punishment might deter persons from placing themselves in situations in which their involuntary conduct can cause harm to others, such as in *Decina, supra*.

2. Retribution

A more persuasive justification for the voluntary act requirement is that blame and punishment presuppose free will: a person does not deserve to be punished unless she *chooses* to put her bad thoughts into action.

III. Omissions

A. General Rule

Ordinarily, a person is not guilty of a crime for failing to act, even if such failure permits harm to occur to another, and even if the person could act at no risk to personal safety. This is also the Model Penal Code position. MPC § 2.01(3).

Example: D, an Olympic swimmer, stands by and watches V, a small child he does not know, drown in a wading pool. D's criminal responsibility, if any, for V's death would have to be grounded on the theory that he did not come to

V's aid, an omission. Although *D* almost certainly had a *moral* duty to act, he is not guilty of any crime because he lacked a *legal* duty to act.

B. Rationale for the General Rule

1. Proving the Omitter's State of Mind

Criminal conduct requires a guilty state of mind (*mens rea*). It is too difficult to determine the state of mind of one who fails to act.

Example: We can reasonably infer an intention to kill when *D* puts a loaded gun to the head of another person and voluntarily pulls the trigger. However, if *D* fails to come to another's aid, it is difficult to know why he stood by.

2. Line-drawing problems

Difficult line-drawing problems arise in omission cases.

Examples: Fifty strangers stand by silently while *X* attacks *V*. Difficult questions would arise if omitters could be held responsible: Should all 50 persons be held responsible? If not, how do we sensibly draw the line: only those who had the physical capacity to stop the assault; only those who fully understood the seriousness of the situation?

A homeless person dies of starvation on the street. Is everyone who walked by responsible? Only those who walked by on the day he actually died, or also those who observed his plight on earlier days?

3. Promoting individual liberty

In a society such as ours, premised on individual liberties and limited government, the criminal law should be used to prevent persons from causing positive harm to others, but it should not be used to coerce people to act to benefit others. Put another way, the criminal law—as distinguished from our religious and moral teachings—should be limited only to punishing the most serious moral wrong*doings*, and not *non*-doings.

C. Exceptions to the General Rule

Notwithstanding the general rule, a person has a legal duty to act in limited circumstances, if he is physically capable of doing so. MPC § 2.01(1).

1. Crimes of Omission: Statutory Duty

Some statutes expressly require a person to perform specified acts. Failure to perform those acts constitutes an offense. Such an offense may be characterized as a "crime of omission."

Example: States commonly require parents to provide food and shelter for their minor children. Failure to do so is a crime. MPC § 230.4.

2. Crimes of Commission

As distinguished from crimes of omission (statutes that by definition prohibit certain failures to act), the criminal law sometimes permits prosecution for a crime of commission (an offense that, by definition, appears to require proof of conduct, rather than an omission), although the basis of the prosecution is an omission. Thus, we have a case of what might be characterized as commission-by-omission.

Example: The *actus reus* of criminal homicide involves the *"killing* of a human being by another human being." The word "killing" would seem to require conduct on the part of the person charged with such an offense. However, in limited cases, discussed below, a person might be prosecuted for a crime-of-commission by way of omission.

a. Duty by Status

A person has a common law duty to protect another with whom he has a special status relationship, typically, one based on dependency or interdependency, such as parent-to-child, spouse-to-spouse, and master-to-servant.

Example: Parent fails to obtain needed medical attention for Sick Child. Sick Child dies. Parent may be prosecuted for some form of criminal homicide as a result of this omission. *State v. Williams*, 4 Wash.App. 908, 484 P.2d 1167 (1971).

b. Duty by Contract

A person may have an express contract to come to the aid of another, or such a contract may be implied-in-law (*e.g.*, a baby sitter has an implied contract to protect his ward).

b. Duty by Voluntary Assumption

One who voluntarily assumes the care of another must continue to assist if a subsequent omission would place the victim in a worse position than if the good samaritan had not assumed care at all.

Example: D takes V, a stranger, into her home to provide care. V becomes critically ill. D does not aid V, who dies. By assuming care and secluding V in her home so that V could not get other help, D had a duty to assist. See *Cornell v. State*, 159 Fla. 687, 32 So.2d 610 (1947).

d. Duty by Risk Creation

One who creates a risk of harm to another must thereafter act to prevent ensuing harm.

Example: Driver *D* strikes *V*, a pedestrian, causing minor injury. *D* now has a duty to come to *V*'s aid. If he does not, and *V*'s injuries are aggravated (or if *V* dies) as the result of the delay in obtaining medical care, *D* may be held criminally responsible for the ensuing harm, even if he was not criminally responsible for the original injury.

IV. Social Harm

CONVERSATION WITH STUDENTS

The criminal law does not punish people for conduct or omissions. It punishes people for conduct or omissions *that result in social harm.* After all, it is the harm to society that the criminal law seeks to deter and/or deserves retributive redress by way of punishment.

Notice, we call this *social* harm, because this is the *criminal* law: although an individual may be the direct victim of the harm, it is society that brings the prosecution because it is the community as a whole that is considered harmed as well; and thus it is the society as a whole that condemns the wrongdoer for the social arm. But, as we will see below, the term "social harm" has an unusual and broad meaning.

A. Definition

"Social harm" may be defined as the destruction of, injury to, or endangerment of, some socially valuable interest.

1. Breadth of Definition

Notice that under this definition there is social harm simply from endangerment to a socially valuable interest.

Example: If Alice tries to shoot Bob while he is asleep, but the pistol fails to discharge, Bob may suffer no physical or mental injury, but a socially valuable interest—human life—*was* endangered, so there is social harm.

B. Identifying the Social Harm

You can determine the "social harm" of an offense by looking at the definition of the crime and identifying the elements of it that describe the external conduct that constitutes the crime.

Examples: Common law burglary is defined as the "breaking and entering of the dwelling house of another at night, with the intent to commit a felony therein." The social harm of burglary occurs when a person "breaks and enters the dwelling house of another at night." If he does so as the result of conduct that includes a voluntary act, the *actus reus* of burglary is proved. (As is discussed in the next Part, "intent to commit a felony therein" is the culpable state of mind (the *mens rea*) that must be proven.)

Assume that a rape statute provides that a person is guilty of a felony if "he intentionally has sexual intercourse with a female, not his wife, without her consent." Here, the prohibited social harm occurs when a male has nonconsensual sexual intercourse with a female who is not his wife. Again, the *actus reus* is proven if this social harm occurs as the result of conduct that includes a voluntary act.

C. Breaking Down the Social Harm Into Categories

It is sometimes essential for a lawyer (especially in jurisdictions that follow the Model Penal Code) to be able to look at the definition of a crime, more specifically the *actus reus* portion, and divide up the "social harm" elements into one or more of the following three categories.

1. "Result" Elements (or Crimes)

Some crimes prohibit a specific result.

Example: The social harm of murder is the "death of another human being," *i.e.*, a harmful *result*.

2. "Conduct" Elements (or Crimes)

Some crimes prohibit specific conduct, whether or not tangible harm results thereby.

Example: A statute prohibiting "driving under the influence of alcohol" fits this category, as it prohibits a certain type of *driving* (driving while intoxicated), and not a result of that driving (such as death of another person or injury to property).

3. "Attendant Circumstance" Elements

A "result" or "conduct" typically is not an offense unless certain "attendant circumstances" exist. An "attendant circumstance" is a fact that exists at the time of the actor's conduct, or at the time of a particular result, and which is required to be proven in the definition of the offense.

Examples: In the "murder" example above in subsection 1., there is an attendant circumstance: the result (death) must be of "another human being." Thus, it is not murder to kill a dog or a cat; it is murder to cause the death of "another human being." The fact that exists, and which must be proven, is that the victim is a "human being."

In subsection 2., above, the conduct that is prohibited is not driving, but driving *under the influence of alcohol.* The italicized language constitutes the "attendant circumstance" element of this offense.

Sexual intercourse by a man with a woman does not constitute common law rape unless certain attendant circumstances exist: (1) the victim is a woman; (2) the victim is not the defendant's wife; and (3) the victim did not consent.

V. Review Questions

[Answers Provided in Appendix A, page 358]

1. What are the two components of the *actus reus* of an offense?

2. What is the definition of a "voluntary act"?

3. Alex is employed as a lifeguard. Alex observes Bob in peril in the water, but Alex prefers to stay out of the water and chat with Carla. Bob drowns.

   T or F.   Alex may properly be prosecuted for Bob's death in a common law jurisdiction.

4. "Any person who intentionally kills another by means of poison is guilty of murder." Take the preceding hypothetical definition and: (a) identify the words in it that represent the *actus reus* of the offense; (b) identify the social harm of the offense; and (c) break down the social harm into its sub-categories (result; conduct; attendant circumstances).

*

PART THREE

Mens Rea

■ *ANALYSIS*

Conversation with Students
I. *Mens Rea*: **General Principles**
    A.   Meaning of *"Mens Rea"*
    B.   Rationale of the *Mens Rea* Requirement
II. **Common Law**
    A.   "Intentionally"
    B.   "Knowledge" or "Knowingly"
    C.   Risk–Taking: "Recklessness" and "Criminal Negligence"
    D.   "Malice"
    E.   "Specific Intent" and "General Intent"
    F.   Statutory Construction
III. **Model Penal Code**
    Conversation with Students
    A.   Section 2.02, Subsection 1
    B.   Culpability Terms Defined
    C.   Interpretative Rules
IV. **Strict Liability**
    A.   Nature of a Strict Liability Offense
    B.   Public Welfare Offenses

CONVERSATION WITH STUDENTS

You have now considered the first ingredient of a crime, the physical or external component: *actus reus*. (Actually, as you learned, this "first" component consists of *two* elements: (1) a voluntary act (or, rarely, an omission when there is a duty to act); and (2) the resulting social harm.) Now we turn to the mental component: *mens rea*. There is no topic that you will consider more often during the semester.

In studying *mens rea*, you should focus on the subject both from a distance and up close. There are certain questions you can answer only by looking at the concept from afar, so that you see its place in the larger picture. Specifically, try to understand why the Supreme Court has said that *mens rea* "is no provincial or transient notion." *Morissette v. United States*, 342 U.S. 246, 72 S.Ct. 240, 96 L.Ed. 288 (1952). What purpose does *mens rea* play in a just system of punishment? Are there any good reasons to dispense with the *mens rea* requirement?

You must also consider "*mens rea*" up close. There are a number of very important "*mens rea*" terms, the precise definitions of which you need to be familiar with. Here, it is critical to separate out the common law of *mens rea* from the Model Penal Code, which not only greatly diverges from the common law, but has also had considerable influence on statutory and judicial reform.

I. *Mens Rea*: General Principles

A. Meaning of "*Mens Rea*"

The term "*mens rea*" has a general and a specific meaning. Both usages of the term are important.

1. Broad ("Culpability") Meaning

A person has acted with "*mens rea*" in the broad sense of the term if she committed the *actus reus* of an offense with a "vicious will," "evil mind," or "morally blameworthy" or "culpable" state of mind.

Example: D has nonconsensual sexual intercourse with V, a woman not his wife (the *actus reus* of common law rape). He genuinely but negligently (*i.e.*, unreasonably) believed that she consented to the sexual act. On these facts, D committed the *actus reus* of rape with "*mens rea*" in the broad sense of the term: it does not manner that D did not intend to act without *V*'s consent; his belief regarding *V*'s consent was negligent, so he possessed a culpable or morally blameworthy state of mind.

2. Narrow ("Elemental") Meaning

"Mens rea" exists in the narrow sense of the term if, but only if, a person commits the *actus reus* of an offense with the particular mental state set out expressly in the definition of that offense. This may be called the "elemental" definition of *mens rea*.

Example: Assume that rape is defined in State X as "sexual intercourse by a male, with a female not his wife, with *knowledge* that she did not consent." Assume further the facts set out in the *Example* immediately above. Under the narrow meaning of *"mens rea,"* D lacks the requisite *mens rea* of rape: this statute requires proof that the actor had *knowledge* that the female did not consent. As he did not act with this particular state of mind, he lacks *mens rea* in this narrow, elemental, sense. Notice, however, that he committed the *actus reus* of rape in a morally culpable manner (he unreasonably—foolishly—believed she consented), so he possessed *mens rea* in the broader, culpability, meaning of the term.

3. Practice Point

As you will see as you proceed through the semester, courts use the term *"mens rea"* in both senses of the term, so be careful! Also, you should expect your professor to use the term both ways, unless told otherwise. To a slight degree, the narrow approach—or what I am calling "elemental" sense of the term—is gaining prominence, especially as the result of the influence of the Model Penal Code.

B. Rationale of the *Mens Rea* Requirement

1. Utilitarian Argument

It is frequently asserted that a person who commits the *actus reus* of an offense without a *mens rea* is not dangerous, could not have been deterred, and is not in need of reform. Therefore, her punishment would be counter-utilitarian.

a. Contrary Argument

Although the preceding argument is accurate in many circumstances, it overstates the case. Some persons may be accident prone; although they cannot help what they do, they represent a danger to the community that may merit the application of the criminal law.

Furthermore, there may be deterrence value in punishing a person who innocently commits the *actus reus* of an offense as an object lesson to others who might believe that they could otherwise avoid punishment by fraudulently claiming a lack of *mens rea*. Abandonment of the *mens rea* requirement would also create an incentive for people to act with the greatest possible care.

2. Retributive Argument

The *mens rea* requirement is solidly supported by the retributive principle of just deserts. A person who commits the *actus reus* of an offense in a morally innocent manner, *i.e.*, accidentally, does not deserve to be punished, as she did not choose to act unlawfully.

a. The Supreme Court Speaks

According to the Court, the requirement of *mens rea* "is as universal and persistent in mature systems of law as belief in freedom of the human will and a consequent ability and duty of the normal individual to choose between good and evil." *Morissette v. United States, supra.* Nonetheless, as discussed later in this Part, the United State Constitution does *not* generally require proof of a *mens rea*, if a legislature wishes to forgo this doctrine.

II. Common Law

A. "Intentionally"

A frequently used common law *mens rea* term is "intentionally" or some variation of it (*e.g.*, "intent" or "intentional"). Typically, this term is used to describe a defendant's state of mind in relation to a socially harmful result, such as the death of another person (criminal homicide) or the destruction of a dwelling house (arson).

1. Definition

A person commits the social harm of an offense "intentionally" if: (1) it was her conscious object to cause the result; or (2) if she knew that the harm was virtually certain to occur as the result of her conduct.

Example: D plants a bomb in a room in order to kill *V. D* realizes that the explosion will kill not only *V* but the five other persons in the room. *D* does not want to kill these bystanders. The bomb explodes, killing all six persons. On these facts, *D* has *intentionally* killed all six people: he killed *V* "intentionally" because *V*'s death was *D*'s conscious object; *D* killed the other five persons "intentionally" because he knew that this result—their death—was virtually certain to occur from his actions.

a. Study Point

Notice in the definition above that the "intent" pertains to the social harm—the unwanted result—and not to the *act* that causes the result. A person may "intend" an act, but for purposes of analyzing *mens rea*, the issue is whether the person intended *the result* of the act.

Example: *A* goes to a target range to practice firing a weapon. She aims at a target and intentionally pulls the trigger. To *A*'s surprise, *V* walks in front of the target and is killed by a bullet from *A*'s gun. Here, *A* has caused the social harm of homicide—the death of another human being. But, *A* did *not* cause this *result* intentionally. It was *not* her conscious object to kill *V*, nor did she know that firing the gun would almost certainly result in a death. We would characterize the pulling of the trigger as a *voluntary* act, a part of the *actus reus*, but for purposes of determining *A*'s *mens rea*, we focus on her state of mind in relation to the social harm (here, the death). *A* may have some *mens rea* as to this death, but on these facts, it is *not* an "intentional" killing.

2. **Subjective Fault**

This *mens rea* term describes what may be characterized as *subjective* fault: the fault is "subjective" in that it describes the actor's actual morally blameworthy state of mind—what the actor wants to happen (the actor's conscious object) or is consciously aware is practically certain to happen.

3. **Transferred Intent Doctrine**

Courts frequently speaks of a "transferred intent" doctrine: A person acts "intentionally" as the term is defined above, if the result of her conduct differs from that which she desired only in respect to the identity of the victim.

Example: *D*'s conscious object is to kill *V*. With that purpose in mind, *D* fires a gun at *V*, but the bullet strikes and kills *X* instead. The intent to kill *V* is transferred to the actual victim, *X*.

a. Criticism of Doctrine

The doctrine is unnecessary. The *actus reus* of murder, for example, is the killing of *a* human being by another human being. In the example above, *D* intended to cause the death of *a* human being (*V*), and he *did* cause the death of *a* human being (*X*). The identify of the victim is not part of the definition of the offense, so there is no need to "transfer" victims. If the law mindlessly accepts the transferred-intent doctrine, it can lead to improper results.

Example: A law makes it an offense to "intentionally kill the President of the United States." Assume *D*'s conscious object is to kill the President's wife, but she misfires and kills the President instead. She is not guilty of this offense. Here, the law specifies the victim—the President—and it was not her intention to kill him. Therefore, *D* lacks the specified *mens rea* in this offense (the intent to kill the President). You shouldn't "transfer" the intent.

B. "Knowledge" or "Knowingly"

1. Definition

Some offenses require proof that the actor had knowledge of an attendant circumstance. At common law, a person acts "knowingly" regarding an existing fact (an "attendant circumstance") if she either: (1) is aware of the fact; (2) correctly believes that it exists; or (3) suspects that it exists and purposely avoids learning if her suspicion is correct. The latter form of "knowledge" is sometimes called "wilful blindness."

Example: It is a crime to "receive property with knowledge that it was stolen." This offense requires proof that the actor has "knowledge" of an attendant circumstance, namely, that the property received was stolen. *D* would have the requisite "knowledge" if, for example,: (1) she was aware that the received property was stolen, because she saw it being stolen; or (2) she correctly believed that the property was stolen, because she paid an extremely low price for it; or (3) she accurately suspects (although her suspicion is not strong enough to constitute a "belief") that the property was stolen, because she bought it from a known purveyor of stolen goods, and she told the seller, "Don't tell me where you got the property." The third example constitutes "wilful blindness."

a. Criticism of "Wilful Blindness" Doctrine

Notice in the definition above, it is accurate to characterize the actor as having "knowledge" in the first two cases—*D* subjectively knew or correctly believed the property was stolen. In the third case, with "wilful blindness," *D* suspected it was stolen and *purposely avoided knowledge,* so how can it be said that she had such knowledge? She clearly has a culpable state of mind—some *mens rea* (perhaps recklessness, as that concept is defined below)—but critics say that it is stretching to characterize it as "knowledge."

C. Risk-Taking: "Recklessness" and "Criminal Negligence"

1. Overview

The criminal law punishes some forms of risk-taking. But, it is important to keep in mind that life is filled with risks, and we all must, and in some cases wisely, take risks in our lives: to drive on the freeway or fly in an airplane, to go to law school, to undergo surgery; and so on. Our risk-taking may also jeopardize others. Therefore, risk-taking is properly divisible into various types: justifiable risk-taking; unjustifiable risk-taking that may properly result in tort damages; and unjustifiable risk-taking that may also result in criminal punishment. The latter forms of risk-taking are frequently described as "negligent" risk-taking and "reckless" risk-taking.

2. Unjustified Risk–Taking

In order to determine whether risk-taking is justifiable or not, one must look at three factors: the *gravity of harm* that a reasonable person would foresee might occur as the result of the risk-taking conduct; the *probability* that this harm will occur; and the *reason* for the proposed conduct, *i.e.,* the benefit to the individual or society of taking the risk. A risk is unjustifiable if the gravity of the foreseeable harm, multiplied by the probability of its occurrence, outweighs the foreseeable benefit from the conduct. *United States v. Carroll Towing Co.,* 159 F.2d 169 (2d Cir.1947).

Examples: As a practical joke, *D* takes a pistol and places a single bullet in the six-chamber gun. He points the gun at *V*, a friend, spins the cylinder, and pulls the trigger once. To *D*'s horror, he kills *V*. *D* took an unjustifiable risk. The gravity of harm risked: death of one human being. The probability of the harm occurring: one chance in six. The reason for taking the risk—the social benefit—is virtually nil.

A surgeon (with consent) conducts experimental brain surgery on a 30–year-old patient who will die within six months without the surgery. The surgeon estimates that there is a 50% chance that the patient will die during surgery, but if successful, the patient will live a healthy life. This may be a justifiable risk: the gravity of harm is high: death of the patient (who would otherwise die in six months); the probability of the harm occurring: 50%; the benefit from the risky conduct is that a patient who would die in six months may live a long life. Notice: the risks here are greater than in the first example, but here the benefit of the risk-taking is much greater.

3. Drawing Lines

Once ones determines that the risk-taking is unjustified, a matter that in an actual trial will be determined by the jury as factfinder, the analytical issue that remains is whether the risk-taking constitutes civil-level negligence; criminal-level negligence; or criminal-level recklessness. Unfortunately, there are no bright lines to separate these three categories. Even worse, there is no single, accepted common law definition of criminal negligence and recklessness. Indeed, some courts use the latter two terms interchangeably.

4. "Criminal Negligence"

A person acts in a "criminally negligent" manner if she should be aware that her conduct creates a substantial and unjustifiable risk of social harm. Modern synonyms for "criminal negligence," include "gross negligence" and "culpable negligence."

a. Degree of Risk

Because a criminal conviction typically results in loss of liberty and stigmatization of the wrongdoer, a higher level of culpability is usually required to convict a person of a crime on the basis of negligence than is necessary to prove civil (tort) negligence. The added culpability exists if the risk taken is a *substantial* and unjustifiable risk.

b. Objective Fault

Negligence constitutes objective fault. That is, a negligent actor is not blamed because he possessed a wrongful state of mind, but because he failed to live up to the objective standard of conduct of a reasonable person. To say that a person was negligent is to say that, by taking a substantial and unjustifiable risk, the defendant has failed to act like a reasonable person.

i. Subjectivizing the "Reasonable Person"

Courts have been reluctant to infuse the defendant's personal characteristics into the hypothetical "reasonable person" (or, as the term originally was stated, "reasonable *man*") standard. In general, courts are willing to consider an actor's unusual physical characteristics, *e.g.*, her blindness (so that the issue would be whether a reasonable *blind* person would have acted as *D* did). However, other factors, such as the actor's lack of education, economic status, and mental disabilities, are often not considered.

c. Debate Regarding Punishment For Negligence

i. Critique

The criminal law should not punish people for negligence. One who acts negligently does not choose to cause harm, so she does not deserve punishment: sue her in torts, but do not stigmatize and condemn her as a criminal wrongdoer. And, if a person does not intend to cause harm, she probably cannot be deterred; she certainly cannot be deterred if, due to mental incapacity, she is incapable of living up to the objective standard.

ii. Rebuttal

Punishment for negligence makes people act more carefully, therefore reducing future harm. As for the undeterrable person, she may be dangerous, so use of the law to incapacitate her may be beneficial. As for retribution, people who act negligently demonstrate by their unjustifiably risky conduct an indifference to the rights of others that morally justifies punishment.

5. "Recklessness"

Common law jurists were not of one mind as to the definition of "recklessness."

a. Holmes's View

Oliver Wendell Holmes, Jr., believed that a person acts "recklessly" if she should be aware that she is taking a *very* substantial and unjustifiable risk. This is simply a heightened version of "criminal negligence." Notice: "civil negligence" involves unjustifiable risk-taking; "criminal negligence" is *substantial* and unjustifiable risk-taking; and "recklessness" (as defined here) is *very* substantial and unjustifiable risk-taking.

b. Modern Definition

Although Holmes's definition is still followed by some courts, most courts now provide that a person acts "recklessly" if she *consciously* disregards a substantial and unjustifiable risk that her conduct will cause the social harm of the offense. Under this definition, "recklessness" differs from "criminal negligence" in that it requires that the actor subjectively be aware of the substantial and unjustifiable risk.

D. "Malice"

A person acts with "malice" if she intentionally or recklessly causes the social harm of an offense, as the latter *mens rea* terms are defined above.

Example: P throws a stone at V. The stone misses V, but breaks a window behind V. P is charged with the offense of "malicious damage to property." *Regina v. Pembliton*, 12 Cox C.C. 607 (Eng. 1874). To prove P's guilt, the prosecutor must show that P either intended to damage the property (the *actus reus* of the offense charged) or that P recklessly damaged it.

1. Special Definition

"Malice" has a specialized definition in the context of common law murder, the *mens rea* of which is "malice aforethought." This special definition is considered elsewhere in this Outline.

E. "Specific Intent" and "General Intent"

The common law distinguishes between "general intent" and "specific intent" crimes. The distinction is critical, because some defenses apply only, or more broadly, in the case of so-called "specific intent" offenses.

1. Terminological Confusion

Unfortunately, courts and lawyers use the terms "general intent" and "specific intent" in many different ways. Obviously, use whatever definitions your professor prefers. What follows is probably the most common way to distinguish between "general intent" and "specific intent" offenses.

2. "Specific Intent" Offenses

In most cases, a "specific intent" offense is one that explicitly contains one of the following *mens rea* elements in its definition: (1) the intent to commit some act over and beyond the *actus reus* of the offense; (2) a special motive for committing the *actus reus* of the offense; or (3) awareness of a particular attendant circumstance.

Examples: "Burglary" is a specific-intent offense of the first type. The offense is defined at common law as "breaking and entering the dwelling house of another at night, with the intent to commit a felony therein." The *actus reus* is "breaking and entering the dwelling house of another at night." The *mens rea*—"intent to commit a felony therein"—is a mental state pertaining to an act (commission of a felony) that is *not* part of the *actus reus* of the offense. That is, the crime of burglary is complete whether or not *D* ever commits a felony inside the house; but it is incomplete unless *D* has this "specific intent" of further conduct upon entering.

Common law larceny is an example of the second type of specific-intent offense. Larceny is the "trespassory (nonconsensual) taking and carrying away of the personal property of another with the intent to permanently deprive the owner of the property." It is a "specific intent" offense because the *actus reus* (trespassorily taking and carrying away the personal property of another) must occur with a specific motive—not simply to temporarily dispossess the other person of the property, but to permanently deprive her of it.

An example of the third variety of specific intent would be the offense, "receiving stolen property with knowledge it is stolen." The specific intent of this offense is that the actor must be aware (have knowledge) of the attendant circumstance that the property was stolen.

3. "General Intent" Offenses

Any offense that requires proof of a culpable mental state, but which does not contain a specific intent, is a "general intent" offense. Sometimes, such an offense will have no explicit *mens rea* term in the definition of the crime; it is enough that the defendant committed the *actus reus* with any culpable state of mind.

Examples: Common law battery is an "unlawful application of force upon the person of another." In this context, "unlawful" means that the actor "wrongfully" committed the *actus reus* of the offense. This means that the *actus reus* (application of the force upon the person of another) must be committed in a morally blameworthy manner. This is the "general intent" of the offense.

Today, "battery" might be defined with a particular mental state in its definition: *e.g.*, "*intentional* application of force to the person of another." This definitional change should not affect its characterization as a general-intent offense, because this *mens rea* term does not fit any of the three types of "specific intent" noted above.

F. Statutory Construction

A common issue in criminal law litigation is whether a *mens rea* term in the definition of an offense applies to all or only some of the *actus reus* elements in the definition of the crime. In the absence of explicit rules, common law courts have struggled to interpret modern statutes.

Example: Assume that a state defines "rape" as "intentional sexual intercourse by a man with a woman not his wife, without her consent." In this definition, the *actus reus* may be divided up as follows: "sexual intercourse" (element A); "with a woman" (element B); "not one's wife" (element C); and "without her consent" (element D). The question is: Does the word "intent" in this definition modify *each* of these elements? In many rape cases, X will intentionally have sexual intercourse (element A). Suppose, however, that X intends to have sexual intercourse, but he believes that he has the woman's consent and, indeed, does not intend to do it without her consent. In this case X lacks "intent" regarding element D. But, is such an intent required? That depends on how the statute is interpreted.

1. Common Law Interpretive Rules of Thumb

a. Legislative intent

The ultimate issue for any court today—*always*—is to determine what the legislature intended. A court will try to resolve interpretive problems by ascertaining the intention of the drafters of the law, sometimes by looking through legislative history. Often, however, evidence regarding legislative intent is non-existent or ambiguous, so courts must look elsewhere.

b. Position of the *Mens Rea* term in Definition of Offense

Courts often look at the placement of the *mens rea* term in the definition of the offense, in order to ascertain legislative intent.

Example: A federal statute provides that "whoever, in any matter within the jurisdiction of a federal agency, knowingly makes any false statement is guilty of an offense." Y knowingly made a false statement, but he did not know that his statement related to "any matter within the jurisdiction of a federal agency." The issue was whether such knowledge was required under the statute. Notice that the word "knowingly" in the statute follows, rather than precedes, the critical phrase "in any matter within the jurisdiction of a federal agency." The implication is that "knowingly" does *not* modify the earlier phrase. *United States v. Yermian*, 468 U.S. 63, 104 S.Ct. 2936, 82 L.Ed.2d 53 (1984). The interpretation might have been different if the word "knowingly" had been placed at the beginning of the statute.

c. Punctuation

Sometimes punctuation is relied upon to determine that a phrase set off by commas is independent of the language that precedes or follows it.

Example: A statute provides that "any person who intentionally confines another, without authority of law, in a state prison is guilty of false imprisonment." A punctuation-based reading of this statute is that the term "intentionally" modifies the words "confines another . . . in a state prison"; according to this interpretation, "intent" does *not* modify the phrase "without authority of law" because the latter words are set off by commas—it is as if the word "intent" flies over that phrase, skipping it. Thus, according to this reading, *D* is guilty if she intentionally confines another in a state prison under circumstances in which such confinement, in fact, is without authority of law; it is *not* necessary to show that *D intended* to act without authority of law.

d. Attendant Circumstances

Frequently, courts assume that, absent evidence to the contrary, *mens rea* terms in the definitions of offenses do *not* apply to "attendant circumstance" elements of the crime.

Example: Reconsider the *Example* above (beginning of subsection F.) regarding the offense of rape. In the *Example*, elements B, C, and D, are "attendant circumstance" elements. Therefore, under the rule described here, the "intent" in the definition of the offense would *not* apply to those elements: *D could* be convicted of rape although, for example, he did *not* intend that *V* not consent.

III. Model Penal Code

CONVERSATION WITH STUDENTS

The most influential feature of the Model Penal Code is Section 2.02, "General Requirements of Culpability." If your professor has you study the MPC in your class, this will be *the most important* section you study. Learn it well, because you will need to use the concepts and provisions of § 2.02 throughout the semester, whenever you apply the Code to a particular crime.

A. Section 2.02, Subsection 1

1. Language

"Except as provided in Section 2.05, a person is not guilty of an offense unless he acted purposely, knowingly, recklessly, or negligently, as the law may require, with respect to each material element of the offense."

a. Study Point

Students often ignore language in the Code, such as you have here, where it says "[e]xcept as provided in Section . . . " Some students skip right by it. But, why? It is there for a reason! Essentially, the other section noted here is incorporated by reference into the present section. So, § 2.05 is a part of § 2.02(1) (representing an exception to it). Don't ignore it. (Section 2.05 is discussed in the Strict Liability section below.)

2. Significance of Subsection

a. Role of *Mens Rea*

Except when § 2.05 applies, the MPC requires proof of *mens rea*. More significantly, it requires proof of some particular *mens rea*—purpose, knowledge, recklessness, or negligence—as to *each* material element of the offense. This contrasts with the common law, where there might be a *mens rea* requirement as to one element but no *mens rea* required as to other elements. In other words, with the MPC, *each actus reus* element should be "covered" by some *mens rea* requirement.

Example: Consider a hypothetical statute in which there are four *actus reus* elements, call them A, B, C, and D. Under § 2.02(1), the statute will contain a *mens rea* requirement as to each of these elements. It might be, for example, that the prosecutor must prove that the defendant *purposely* did A, B, C and D; or maybe the statute will be defined with different *mens rea* requirements as to each element. The point is: there is *some* culpability requirement as to *each* element.

b. Elemental Approach

Look back at pp. 145–146 of this Outline, at the difference between the "culpability" and "elemental" approach to *mens rea*. Section

2.02(1) demonstrates that the MPC uses the elemental approach. A person is not convicted simply because he committed the *actus reus* in a morally culpable manner: the prosecutor must instead prove that the defendant committed the *actus reus* with the very specific state(s) of mind—purpose, knowledge, recklessness, and/or negligence—set out in the definition of the crime.

c.   Fewer *Mens Rea* Terms

The common law and non-MPC statutes are replete with *mens rea* terms. Under the MPC, there are only the four terms set out here. Not only does this mean that there are fewer terms to learn, but there are definitions set out for each.

B.   Culpability Terms Defined

Subsection 2 of Section 2.02 of the Code provides definitions of the four culpability terms. But, be aware that it provides different definitions depending on whether the *actus reus* element under consideration involves a result (*e.g.*, death of a person, or damage or destruction of property), conduct (*e.g.*, driving a vehicle), or an attendant circumstance. What follows are some of the definitions, but you should look at the Code language more fully in your casebook.

1.   Purposely

The common law term "intentionally" is not used in the Model Penal Code. Instead, the MPC subdivides common law "intent" into its two alternative components, and calls them "purposely" and "knowingly." A person causes a result "purposely" if it is her conscious object to cause the result. MPC § 2.02(2)(a)(1).

2.   Knowingly

a.   Results

A person "knowingly" causes a result if she is aware that the result is "practically certain" to result from her conduct. MPC § 2.02(2)(b)(ii).

Example: Reconsider the bomb *Example* on page 147. Whereas all six killings at common law were deemed "intentional," under the Code, *D purposely* killed *V*, and *knowingly* killed the others.

b.   Attendant Circumstances

A person acts "knowingly" as to an attendant circumstance if he is aware that the circumstance exists (MPC § 2.02(2)(b)(i)), or if he is aware "of a high probability of its existence, unless he actually believes that it does not exist." MPC § 2.02(7). The latter provision is the Code version of the common law "wilful blindness" doctrine discussed earlier.

3. Recklessly

a. Basic Definition

A person is said to have acted recklessly if "he consciously disregards a substantial and unjustifiable risk that the material element exists or will result from his conduct." Notice that this definition conforms with the modern common law definition of the term.

b. Standard for Evaluating Conduct

The Code provides, basically, that the standard discussed earlier—measuring the gravity of foreseeable harm, the probability of its occurrence, and the reasons for taking the risk—should be applied. One is reckless when the risk-taking "involves a gross deviation from the standard of care that a reasonable person would observe in the actor's situation."

i. "In the Actor's Situation"

This phrase is intended to permit courts to incorporate some subjectivity into the objective standard, more than is permitted at common law. However, the Commentary to the Code indicates that the phrase is intentionally ambiguous, so that courts may determine for themselves which characteristics of the defendant (or "the defendant's situation") should be incorporated into the reasonable person.

4. Negligently

The Model Code definition of "negligence" generally conforms with the common law definition (see II.C.4.): a person acts negligently when he *should be aware* of a "substantial and unjustifiable risk." This is a risk that constitutes "a gross deviation from the standard of care that a reasonable person would observe in the actor's situation." MPC § 2.02(2)(d). Notice that the critical difference between recklessness and negligence under the Code is that in the former case, the actor is consciously aware of the substantial and unjustifiable risk, but proceeds anyway; in the case of negligence, the actor is *not* aware of the risk, but *should* be.

C. Interpretative Rules

The Code avoids some of the interpretative problems confronting courts and lawyers (and students!) when dealing with common law and non-MPC statutes, which were discussed earlier.

1. Default Position

As discussed above, the MPC requires some *mens rea* term for each element of an offense (§ 2.05 aside). If the statute defining an offense is silent regarding the issue of *mens rea* as to one or more of the *actus reus* elements, the Code provides that "such element is established if a person acts purposely, knowingly, or recklessly with respect thereto." MPC § 2.02(3). In essence, you fill in the blank with "purposely, knowingly, or recklessly."

Examples: Hypothetical Statute 1: "A person is guilty of an offense if he purposely restrains another [call this *actus reus* element A], thereby knowingly exposing the other to the risk of bodily injury [*actus reus* element B], and causing mental distress to the victim [*actus reus* element C]." Notice that this statute is structured this way: purposely A, knowingly B, and C." In light of § 2.02(3), this statute *really* reads: "Purposely A, Knowingly B, and Purposely or Knowingly or Recklessly C." That is, the prosecutor must prove that the defendant purposely restrained the victim, knowingly put the victim at risk of bodily injury, and purposely, knowingly, or recklessly (but not negligently) caused mental distress to the victim.

Hypothetical Statute 2: "A person is guilty if he restrains another, thereby exposing the other to the risk of bodily injury, and causing mental distress." This is the same *actus reus* as in Statute 1, but *no mens rea* terms are set out at all. But, there *must* be some *mens rea* term as to *each* material element of this crime, so this statute would be read as requiring proof that each element occurred purposely, knowingly, or recklessly.

2. When Just One *Mens Rea* Term is Mentioned

If the definition of a MPC statute only sets out a single *mens rea* element in the definition of the offense, that *mens rea* term applies to *every* material element of the offense, *unless* a contrary legislative intent "plainly appears." MPC § 2.02(4).

Examples: MPC § 212.3 defines the crime of false imprisonment, basically as follows: "knowingly restraining another so as to interfere substantially with his liberty." Thus, the material elements here are: restraining another; and substantially interfering with the other's liberty. Because one *mens rea* term is set out ("knowingly"), but there is a requirement of proof of *mens rea* as to *each* material element of an offense, we know here that the Code requires the prosecutor to prove that the defendant knowingly restrained the victim, *and* knowingly interfered substantially with the victim's liberty.

Suppose a statute is structured this way: "Anyone who does A, B, and knowingly C is guilty of an offense." In this case, "knowingly" is not set out at the start of the statute but near the end. Therefore, this might be a case where a contrary legislative intent "plainly appears." That is, the legislature probably intends that the word "knowingly" modify C, but not A and B. (Otherwise, why didn't the drafters of the statute put "knowingly" at the start of the sentence?) If so, then what do we do about elements A and B? We return to the default position discussed in subsection 1.: as to elements A and B, the prosecutor would need to prove that these elements occurred purposely, knowingly, or recklessly!

IV. Strict Liability

A. Nature of a Strict Liability Offense

Notwithstanding the general rule that a person is not guilty of an offense in the absence of *mens rea*, some crimes are denominated as "strict liability." An offense is "strict liability" in nature if commission of the *actus reus* of the offense, without proof of a *mens rea*, is sufficient to convict the actor.

Example: It is an offense for a driver of a motor vehicle to exceed the speed limit on a highway. No *mens rea* is required. Assume that *D* exceeds the speed limit because her speedometer is slightly inaccurate. Even if *D* had no reason to know that the speedometer was inaccurate, she is guilty of this strict liability offense.

1. Clarification

An offense is sometimes characterized as strict liability in nature if a single, critical element of the offense does not require proof of any *mens rea*.

Example: So-called "statutory rape"—sexual intercourse with an under-age female (what constitutes being underage varies by statute)—is often denominated as "strict liability" in nature. This is a correct description in the sense that, in most jurisdictions, a person may be convicted of this offense even if he lacks a culpable state of mind regarding the female's age (he reasonably believed she was old enough to consent to intercourse). The fact that the male *intentionally* had sexual intercourse is not the key: what makes the conduct wrongful is the female's underage status and, as to *this* attendant circumstance, a person may be convicted even if he has no *mens rea*.

B. Public Welfare Offenses

Strict liability most often applies in relation to "public welfare" offenses.

1. Characteristics of Most Public Welfare Offenses

a. Nature of the Conduct

Such offenses typically involve *malum prohibitum* conduct, *i.e.,* conduct that is wrongful only because it is prohibited (*e.g.,* motor vehicle laws), as distinguished from *malum in se* conduct, *i.e.,* inherently wrongful conduct (*e.g.,* murder).

b. Punishment

The penalty for violation of a public welfare offense is usually minor, such as a monetary fine or a very short jail sentence.

c. Degree of Social Danger

A single violation of a public welfare offense often threatens the safety of many persons, *e.g.,* transportation of explosives on a highway not designated for such use.

C. Non–Public Welfare Offenses

On rare occasion, *non*-public welfare offenses are considered strict liability in nature. Statutory rape is the most common example of such an offense.

D. Constitutionality of Strict Liability Offenses

Strict liability offenses are not *per se* unconstitutional. According to the Supreme Court, "the state may in the maintenance of a public policy provide 'that he who shall do [acts] shall do them at his peril.' "*United States v. Balint,* 258 U.S. 250, 42 S.Ct. 301, 66 L.Ed. 604 (1922).

1. Presumption Against Strict Liability

Although strict liability statutes are not unconstitutional *per se*, there is a strong presumption against strict liability as to offenses that have their roots in the common law (*i.e. non*-public-welfare offenses). In such circumstances, a court will not assume (absent evidence to the contrary) that the legislature intended to abandon the *mens rea* requirement, even if the statute is silent regarding this element. *Morissette v. United States,* 342 U.S. 246, 72 S.Ct. 240, 96 L.Ed. 288 (1952).

Example: In *Morissette,* M converted government property to his own use. M believed that the property had been abandoned. Therefore, he had no intention to steal the property. On its face, the offense did not require such an intent. The Court held, however, that the statutory offense of conversion was a variation on the common law crime of larceny, which *does* require a specific intent to steal. Consequently, the Court held that a specific intent to steal was an element of the offense, although it was not expressed in the statute.

E. Model Penal Code
The MPC abolishes strict criminal liability except as to "violations." MPC § 2.05. A "violation" is an "offense" (not a "crime") the violation of which involves "no other sentence than a fine, or fine and forfeiture or other civil penalty." MPC § 1.04(5).

1. Statutes that are Silent Regarding *Mens Rea*
As discussed earlier (III.C.1.), a crime (as distinguished from a "violation") that does not expressly include a *mens rea* term in its definition still has a *mens rea* requirement: the prosecutor must prove that the defendant acted purposely, knowingly, or recklessly as to each material element of the offense.

V. Review Questions

[Answers Provided in Appendix A, page 359]

1. What is the "culpability" meaning of *mens rea*?

2. If Albert "intentionally" kills Bob, what does "intentionally" mean in this context?

3. T or F.   "Rape with intent to kill" is a specific-intent offense.

4. Which is a more culpable form of *mens rea*, negligence or recklessness?

5. Does the Model Penal Code recognize strict liability for any crimes?

6. "A person is guilty of an offense if she purposely does X, Y, and Z." In order to convict a defendant of this statute under the Model Penal Code, the prosecutor must prove:

a. The defendant purposely did X, purposely did Y, and purposely did Z;

b. The defendant purposely did X, and purposely, knowingly, or recklessly did Y and Z;

c. The defendant purposely did X, and did Y and Z with any culpable state of mind; or

d. The defendant purposely did X; as for Y and Z, there is no *mens rea* requirement.

7. T or F.   Strict liability offenses are presumptively unconstitutional.

PART FOUR

Mens Rea and Mistakes of Fact or Law

■ *ANALYSIS*

CONVERSATION WITH STUDENTS

In Part Two of this Outline we studied the external component of a crime, the *actus reus*. We saw that there are two components to the *actus reus*: (1) conduct that includes a voluntary act (although, on rare occasion, a failure to act may substitute for the voluntary act); and (2) the social harm that results from the conduct. (Actually, there is a *third* component of the *actus reus*, which is implicit in the last sentence—a causal connection between the voluntary act (or omission) and the social harm. We will turn to the causation issue in Part Five.) Then, in Part Three, we looked at the mental element of most offenses, the *mens rea*.

We are not done with *mens rea*. Frequently, defendants will claim that they should not be convicted of an offense because they made a mistake. They may have been mistaken about some fact (attendant circumstance) or about the law (either the criminal law for which they have been charged or some other law relevant to the prosecution).

Why would a mistake exculpate the actor? The answer is that a mistake of fact or law *sometimes* negatives the requisite *mens rea* for the crime. Put another way, one who acts on the basis of incorrect factual or legal information sometimes lacks the *mens rea* for the crime *because of* the mistake of fact or law. So understood, courts frequently characterize "mistake" as a potential "defense" to a crime. It is a defense in one sense—it is up to the defendant to raise the issue of mistake. But, the ultimate issue is: Did the defendant possess the *mens rea* of the crime? And, remember: "*mens rea*" is an element of an offense; and, the burden of persuasion is on the *prosecutor* to prove every element of a crime. **So, the burden is actually on the government to convince the factfinder beyond a reasonable doubt that, notwithstanding any mistake of fact or law, the defendant possessed the requisite** *mens rea.*

One final point: in order to understand common law "mistake" doctrine, you need to be able to distinguish between "specific intent" and "general intent" offenses. You should also review the distinction between the "culpability" and "elemental" meanings of the term "*mens rea*." So, you may want to review these concepts from Part Three before proceeding.

I. Mistake of Fact

A. Common Law

1. Overview and Study Point

A defendant is not guilty of a crime if her mistake of fact negates the *mens rea* of the offense charged. Although this rule is simple to state, application of the rule can prove difficult because it is necessary at common law to distinguish between "specific intent" and "general intent" offenses. Indeed, whenever a mistake-of-fact claim is raised in the common law context, the first question you should ask yourself is: "Is the offense for which the defendant is charged one of 'specific intent' or 'general intent'?" Once you answer *that* question, you will know which rules to apply.

2. Specific–Intent Offenses

a. Rule

A defendant is not guilty of a specific-intent crime if her mistake of fact negates the specific-intent element of the offense. Even an unreasonable mistake of fact—a mistake that a reasonable person would *not* make—may exculpate the actor, assuming the mistake negatives the *mens rea* required for the offense.

Examples: N picked up wooden beams from a construction site, incorrectly believing that they had been abandoned by the original owner. In short, N mistakenly believed that the beams no longer belonged to anyone. N was charged with larceny of V's property. *People v. Navarro*, 160 Cal.Rptr. 692, 99 Cal.App.3d Supp. 1 (1979). Larceny is the trespassory (nonconsensual) taking of the personal property of another with the intent to steal. On these facts, N is not guilty of larceny. His mistaken belief that the beams had been abandoned negates the specific intent of larceny, *i.e.*, the intent to steal. N is not guilty regardless of whether his mistake was reasonable or unreasonable; in either case, he did not *intend* to steal. At most, he acted *recklessly* or *negligently* in regard to V's property.

D obtains cocaine from V, mistakenly believing that she is receiving heroin. D is charged with the specific-intent offense of "receiving property, knowing that it is contraband." D is guilty of this offense, notwithstanding her mistake: she knew that she was receiving contraband, the specific intent of the offense. Her mistake related only to the nature of the contraband.

b. Study Point

With specific-intent offenses, the common law uses an "elemental" meaning of the term *"mens rea."* Either a defendant has, or doesn't have, the specific-intent required in the definition of the offense. Notice in the first *Example* above: N may have been negligent or reckless in his belief that the beams had been abandoned. If so, he had *"mens rea"* in the broader, "culpability," sense of the term. But, N is acquitted because he lacked the *mens rea* in the "elemental" sense. For specific-intent offenses, *that* is the key.

3. General–Intent Offenses

A defendant is not guilty of a general-intent offense if, as the result of her mistake of fact, she committed the *actus reus* of the offense with a morally blameless state of mind, *i.e.,* if she acted without a *"mens rea"* in the "culpability" sense of the latter term.

a. Ordinary Rule

A defendant is not guilty of a general-intent offense if her mistake of fact was reasonable. An *unreasonable* mistake of fact does *not* exculpate.

Example: D drives V's car, without V's consent. D is charged with "unauthorized use of a vehicle belonging to another." D claims that when she used the car she mistakenly believed that she had V's consent, *i.e.,* that her use of the car was authorized. Based on the rule under discussion, D should be acquitted if her mistake was reasonable, but not if her mistake was unreasonable. This follows from that fact that if her mistake was unreasonable (she was negligent or reckless in her belief), then she acted with a culpable state of mind (with *mens rea*). If her was mistake was reasonable, she acted without *mens rea*.

b. Exception: "Moral Wrong" Doctrine

Although the rule stated above is the general rule, on occasion a court will convict a defendant of an offense, although her mistake of fact was reasonable, if her conduct violates the "moral wrong" doctrine. This doctrine provides that there should be no exculpation for a mistake where, if the facts had been as the actor believed them to be, her conduct would be immoral, albeit legal. By knowingly committing a morally wrong act, an actor assumes the risk that the facts are not as she believed them to be, *i.e.*, that her actions are not just morally wrong, but are also legally wrong.

Example: D has intercourse with girl-friend V, reasonably but incorrectly believing that V consented to the intercourse. D is charged with rape ("sexual intercourse by a male, with a female not his wife, without her consent"), a general-intent offense. Because D's mistake-of-fact was reasonable, he is not guilty of rape under the general rule. However, under the moral-wrong doctrine, if a court chose to apply it, he might be convicted, as explained below.

i. How to Apply the Doctrine

The doctrine involves a two-step process. First, the facts: look at the facts from the mistaken actor's perspective. That is, we assume the facts were as the defendant reasonably believed them to be. Second, the moral judgment: Looking at the facts as the defendant understood them to be, was the defendant's conduct morally wrong? In this context, the issue is *not* whether the actor believes that his or her actions were morally wrong, but whether society so adjudges the conduct.

Example: In the present hypothetical, we would look at the situation through D's eyes: the court would assume that V *had* consented to intercourse, which is what D reasonably believed. Turning to the moral judgment: The issue is whether *consensual* sexual intercourse by a male with female not his wife is morally wrong. If society believes that it is, then D would be convicted of rape, assuming a court decided to apply the moral-wrong doctrine rather than the ordinary mistake-of-fact rule.

c. Alternative Exception: "Legal Wrong" Doctrine

Occasionally, a court will convict a defendant of an offense, although her mistake of fact was reasonable, if her conduct violates the "legal wrong" doctrine. This rule substitutes the word "illegal" for "immoral" in the description of the moral-wrong doctrine, but is otherwise applied in the same manner. Thus, a person is guilty of criminal offense X, despite a reasonable mistake of fact, if she would be guilty of a different, *albeit lesser*, crime Y, if the factual situation were as she supposed.

Example: In the rape hypothetical, suppose consensual intercourse with a female out of wedlock (the act *D* thought he was committing) constituted the misdemeanor offense of "fornication." Or, assume *D* was a married man, so his actions constituted misdemeanor adultery. Thus, even looking at the facts as *D* reasonably believed them to be, *D* committed a crime, albeit a misdemeanor. Under the legal-wrong doctrine, because *D* knowingly committed fornication (or adultery), he could be convicted of the more serious offense of rape. Essentially, the *actus reus* of rape *was* committed; *D*'s *mens rea* was that of being a fornicator or adulterer, a lesser offense. Under this doctrine, he will be convicted of the greater offense.

4. Strict-Liability Offenses

A mistake of fact, whether reasonable or unreasonable, is never a defense to a strict-liability offense. This rule is logical: a strict-liability offense is one that requires no proof of *mens rea*. Therefore, there is no *mens rea* to negate. A defendant's mistake of fact is legally irrelevant.

B. Model Penal Code

1. General Rule

Subject to the exception noted below, a mistake of fact is a defense to a crime if the mistake negates a mental state element required in the definition of the offense. MPC § 2.04(1)(a). The Code dispenses with the common law distinction between "general intent" and "specific intent" offenses: the mistake-of-fact rule applies to all offenses in the same manner.

Example: D has sexual intercourse with *V*, unreasonably believing that she consented. He is prosecuted under the following statute: "A man is guilty of rape if he recklessly compels a woman not his wife to have sexual intercourse with him." Based on this statute, *D* is guilty of rape if his mistake regarding her lack of consent constituted recklessness (in which case he "recklessly compelled" her to have intercourse with him); he would *not* be guilty of rape if his mistake was negligent (because, in these circumstances, he does not have the requisite *mens rea* of recklessness).

2. Exception to the General Rule

In a variation on the common law legal-wrong doctrine, the defense of mistake-of-fact is inapplicable if the defendant would be guilty of a lesser offense had the facts been as she believed them to be. Under such circumstances—unlike the common law—the defendant will be punished at the level of the lesser, rather than the greater, offense. MPC § 2.04(2).

Example: D has sexual intercourse with an 11–year-old girl, although he believed that the girl was 14. Assume that under state law, D is guilty of first-degree statutory rape if he purposely or knowingly has sexual intercourse with a girl under the age of 12; D is guilty of second-degree statutory rape if he purposely or knowingly has sexual intercourse with a girl between the ages of 12 and 16. Under MPC § 2.04, D will be punished as if he had committed *second*-degree statutory rape, the crime he believed that he was factually committing. In contrast, under the common law "legal wrong" doctrine, D would be convicted of *first*-degree statutory rape.

II. Mistake of Law

CONVERSATION WITH STUDENTS

Every schoolchild has heard the refrain, "Ignorance of the law is no excuse." For once, a shibboleth is correct or, at least, nearly so. As you will see, there are only two common law exceptions, and one constitutional limitation, to this rule. The Model Penal Code differs only marginally from the common law, so they are discussed together.

One other point before we proceed: the law treats ignorance of the law, and mistakes regarding the meaning of the law, interchangeably. Therefore, whenever the term "mistake" is used, the comments apply as well to claims of ignorance.

A. General Principles

1. General Rule

In general, knowledge of the law is not an element of an offense. MPC § 2.02(9). Moreover, a mistake of law—even a reasonable one!—does not ordinarily relieve an actor of liability for the commission of a criminal offense.

2. Purported Justifications for the Rule

a. Certainty of the Law

The law is definite. Therefore, any mistake of law is inherently unreasonable.

i. *Rebuttal*

Perhaps this rationale was accurate at original common law when there were few crimes and all of them involved *malum in se* conduct. Today, however, there are almost countless criminal statutes, many of which involve *malum prohibitum* conduct, and some of which are exceedingly complex. It is perfectly reasonable today to be unaware of some laws or to be confused as to their meaning.

b. Concern about Fraud

If a mistake-of-law defense were recognized, it would invite fraud. Every defendant would assert ignorance or mistake, and it would be nearly impossible to disprove the claim.

i. *Rebuttal*

The risk of fraud exists in many aspects of civil and criminal litigation. For example, the doctrines of *mens rea* and insanity are susceptible to fraudulent claims, but we trust juries to determine which claims are fraudulent.

c. Promoting Knowledge of the Law

We want people to learn the law. To promote education—to deter ignorance—the law must apply strict liability principles. As Holmes put it, "justice to the individual is rightly outweighed by the larger interests on the other side of the scales." O. Holmes, THE COMMON LAW 48 (1881).

i. *Rebuttal*

The strict liability rule may be counter-utilitarian. If citizens knew that they could avoid punishment if they made *reasonable* efforts to learn the law, but that they would be punished for *unreasonable* mistakes of law, they would have an incentive to learn the law. But, under current law, they are punished even for reasonable mistakes of law, so they may not make the initial effort to educate themselves. Beyond this, retributivists would argue that unless a person chooses to do wrong, he should not be punished; if a person does not knowingly commit a wrong (or, at least, act unreasonably in learning the law), society has no basis for exacting retribution.

B. Exceptions to the General Rule

1. Mistakes That Negate the *Mens Rea*

A defendant is not guilty of an offense if his mistake of law, whether reasonable or unreasonable, negates an element of the crime charged. See MPC § 2.04(1)(a).

Examples: D1, an airline pilot, was charged with multiple counts of "willfully" failing to file a federal income tax return. Under federal law, "willfulness" was defined as an "intentional violation of a known legal duty." Thus, to be convicted, the prosecutor had to prove that D1 intentionally violated a known legal duty to file a federal income tax return. D1 testified at trial that he believed that his wages were not "income" within the meaning of the Internal Revenue Code and, therefore, he did not realize that he had a duty to report his wages. *Cheek v. United States*, 498 U.S. 192, 111 S.Ct. 604, 122 L.Ed.2d 617 (1991). The Supreme Court held that D1 was entitled to have the jury instructed that, if D1 genuinely (albeit unreasonably) believed that wages were not income, D1 was not guilty of the offense charged. In such circumstances, D1's mistake regarding the legal meaning of the term "income" negates the element of "willfulness," in that he did not intentionally violate a *known* legal duty.

D2, an apartment tenant, installed floor boards in his home with the landlord's permission. When D2 moved out, he tore out the boards, believing that he had a legal right to do so. However, under his jurisdiction's landlord-tenant law, the floor boards, although constructed by D2, legally belonged to the landlord. D2 was prosecuted for "purposely, knowingly, or recklessly destroying the property of another." If D2's mistake regarding property law (*i.e.*, regarding who owned the floor boards) was a reasonable one or, at most, negligent, he should be acquitted. In such circumstances, his mistake of property law proves that D2 did not purposely, knowingly, or recklessly destroy the "property of another"—he innocently or negligently believed he was destroying his own property!

a. Rationale

Either a person has, or does not have, the requisite *mens rea* of an offense. It is rare that knowledge of some law is an element of an offense, but when it is, the prosecutor must prove such knowledge!

2. Authorized–Reliance Doctrine

A person is not guilty of a criminal offense if, at the time of the offense, he reasonably relied on an official statement of the law, later determined to be erroneous, obtained from a person or public body with responsibility for the interpretation, administration, or enforcement of the law defining the offense. MPC § 2.04(3)(b); *Commonwealth v. Twitchell*, 416 Mass. 114, 617 N.E.2d 609 (1993).

a. On Whom or What Body is Reliance Reasonable

Although the common law is less clear than the Model Penal Code in this regard, apparently a defendant may reasonably rely on an official statement of the law found in a statute, judicial opinion, administrative ruling, or an official interpretation of the law given by one who is responsible for the law's enforcement or interpretation, such as the United States or State Attorney General.

Examples: A state supreme court rules that a statute prohibiting conduct X is unconstitutional. In reliance on that opinion, *D1* performs X. Later, the court overrules itself and concludes that the statute is constitutional, *i.e.*, that conduct X is unlawful. *D1* is prosecuted under the now valid statute. *State v. O'Neil*, 147 Iowa 513, 126 N.W. 454 (1910). Because *D1* reasonably relied on the court's original interpretation of the law (that the statute was invalid), *D1* is entitled to acquittal.

D2 requests an official opinion of the State Attorney General regarding whether it is lawful to commit act X. The Attorney General furnishes *D2* with an official "opinion letter" stating that it is legal to do X. *D2* acts on the basis of this letter. Subsequently, a court rules that the Attorney General's legal interpretation was incorrect, *i.e.*, that conduct X is *unlawful*. If prosecuted for committing act X, *D2* should be acquitted: she acted on the basis of an official interpretation of the law issued by a person with authority to render such an opinion.

In *Hopkins v. State*, 193 Md. 489, 69 A.2d 456 (1949), a local prosecutor informed *D3* that it was lawful to erect a particular sign. In reliance, *D3* erected the sign. Thereafter, the prosecutor charged *D3* with violation of the law. The court held that *D3* was not entitled to a mistake-of-law defense. Unlike in *D2*'s case, there was no evidence here that the local prosecutor provided *D3* with a formal, or official, interpretation of the law. The prosecutor may have provided an off-the-cuff informal interpretation, which is insufficient.

3. Due Process Clause

In very rare circumstances, it offends due process to punish a person for a crime of which she was unaware at the time of her conduct. *Lambert v. California*, 355 U.S. 225, 78 S.Ct. 240, 2 L.Ed.2d 228 (1957).

a. Facts of *Lambert*

L, a Los Angeles resident, had previously been convicted of a felony while she lived in the city. She was unaware of an ordinance that required ex-felons residing in the city to register with the police. She failed to register and was prosecuted under the ordinance.

b. Holding

The Supreme Court agreed that the ordinary ignorance-of-the-law-is-no-excuse rule is "deep in our law," but it warned that the Due Process Clause occasionally limits its application. In this case, the Court concluded that it violated due process to convict *L* in the absence of "actual knowledge of the duty to register or proof of the probability of such knowledge."

c. Scope of the Holding

The scope of the *Lambert* principle is uncertain. However, due process probably is not violated unless three factors co-exist: (1) the "unknown" offense criminalizes an omission (here, the failure to register); (2) the duty to act is based on a status condition rather than conduct (here, mere presence in Los Angeles triggered the duty); and (3) the offense is *malum prohibitum* in nature.

III. Review Questions

[Answers Provided in Appendix A, page 360]

1. Dennis breaks and enters Barbara's home at night believing that it is his own home. ("Gee, I wonder why my key doesn't work. I will have to break in.") Dennis is charged with burglary ("breaking and entering a dwelling house of another with the purpose to commit a felony therein"). At common law, Dennis is:

   a. Not guilty, if his mistake is reasonable; guilty if his mistake is unreasonable;

   b. Not guilty, whether his mistake is reasonable or unreasonable; or

   c. Guilty, whether his mistake is reasonable or unreasonable.

2. Answer question 1 under the Model Penal Code.

3. T or F. At common law, a person may never be convicted of a general-intent offense if his mistake of fact is reasonable.

4. When will an *unreasonable* mistake of *law* exculpate an actor at common law or under the Model Penal Code?

PART FIVE

Causation

■ *ANALYSIS*

CONVERSATION WITH STUDENTS

Previously you learned that a crime is composed of an *"actus reus"* and, in most circumstances, a *"mens rea."* In turn, you learned that the *"actus reus"* of an offense includes two elements: a "voluntary act" (or, in limited circumstances, an "omission") and "social harm." But, these two elements— "voluntary act" and "social harm"—do not exist independently of each other: it is not enough for the prosecutor to prove that a defendant committed a voluntary act and that social harm occurred. For the defendant to be convicted, there must be a *link* between his voluntary act and the social harm. Put differently, the defendant's voluntary act must have *caused* the prohibited social harm. That link—causation—is the subject at hand. In turn, as discussed below, "causation" is divisible into two elements, "actual cause" and "proximate cause."

Once we have completed this Part, you will have all of the basic components— elements—of a crime: (1) voluntary act (or, rarely, omission); (2) social harm; (3) *mens rea*; (4) actual causation; and (5) proximate causation.

Although "causation" can be said to be an element of all offenses (since all offenses require some form of social harm, even if such social harm is merely the endangerment of some socially valuable interest), as a practical matter "causation" only proves to be a serious issue when a person is charged with a "result" crime, most especially criminal homicide (the "result" being the death of another human being).

I. Actual Cause (Cause–In–Fact)

A. General Principles

1. Rule

A person is not guilty of an offense unless she is an actual cause of the ensuing harm. Both the common law and the Model Penal Code provide that conduct is the "actual cause" of the prohibited result if the result would *not* have occurred but for the actor's conduct. MPC § 2.03(1)(a). This is the so-called "but for" or *"sine qua non"* test of causation.

2. Study Point

"Actual cause" (or "cause-in-fact"—perhaps a more useful but less often stated way of describing this element) is an empirical issue. That is, we are looking in the real world to identify which person (or persons) or natural forces were necessary for the result (for example, the death of a person) to occur. Frequently, the answer comes from experts—a medical examiner, for example, who can provide the "cause of death."

B. Steps for Determining the "Actual Cause"

1. Identifying the Relevant Conduct

Determine what is (are) the relevant voluntary act(s) committed by *D*. If the case is based on an omission, determine what the omission is, and substitute that for the "voluntary act" in the following discussion.

2. Frame the Question Properly

Ask the question: "But for *D*'s voluntary act(s) would the social harm have occurred when it did?"

a. Significance of "Yes"

If the social harm would have occurred when it did even if *D* had not acted, *D* is *not* the actual cause of the harm and, therefore, is not guilty of the offense. In a sense, "yes" means "no" (no criminal liability).

b. Significance of "No"

If the social harm would *not* have occurred when it did but for *D*'s voluntary act(s), *D* *is* an actual cause of the social harm, in which case you move on to the remaining causation issue (proximate cause), discussed in II.

Example: *D* fires a gun at *V*, intending to kill him. A split-second before the bullet reaches *V*, lightning strikes and instantly kills *V*. Ask: "But for *D*'s voluntary act of firing the gun in the direction of *V*, would *V* have died when he did?" The answer here is "Yes": even if *D* had not fired the gun, *V* would have died when he did as the result of lightning. Therefore, *D* is *not* an actual cause of *V*'s death. He is *not* guilty of murder. (*D* is guilty of *attempted* murder, however, a matter for discussion elsewhere—but he is not guilty of murder, because he did not cause *that* result, the death of *V*.)

C. Multiple Actual Causes

There usually are multiple actual causes of a result. A person who dies of lung cancer, for example, might not have died *when she did* but for her smoking habit *and* living in a smog-polluted city. It can also be the case that two persons—two potential defendants—are the actual cause of a result.

Example: Donald shoots *V* in the abdomen. Medical testimony will show that, based on this wound alone, *V* would have died from loss of blood in two hours. Simultaneously, Denise (who is not acting in concert with Donald—she has her own grudge against *V*) also shoots *V*. According to medical testimony, this wound alone would have killed *V* in five hours. *V* dies as the result of both wounds in one minute. Based on these facts, both *D1* and *D2* are actual causes of the death.

To see how this is the case, follow the procedure from above. Ask: "But for Donald's voluntary act [of shooting *V* in the abdomen] would *V* have died *when he did* [in one minute]? The answer: "No." If Donald had *not* shot *V*, *V* would have died in five hours from Denise's voluntary act. Thus, Donald accelerated *V*'s death. This is sufficient to prove "actual cause."

Now ask: "But for Denise's voluntary act [of shooting *V*], would *V* have died when he did [in one minute]? The answer, again, is "No." *V* would have died in two hours from Donald's voluntary act. Thus, Denise also accelerated *V*'s death. She, too, is an actual cause.

1. Study Point

In the real world, a hypothetical like the last one—two people, entirely independently of each other, shooting a victim simultaneously—is more a law-professor's dream than reality. (Indeed, one also wonders whether experts could provide the type of precise testimony hypothesized here.) In reality, if two people shoot the victim at the same time, they are likely working in concert—co-conspirators, according to concepts discussed elsewhere in this Outline. If they *were* working in concert, they would sink or swim together. That is, they would be treated as if they were just one person, so you would not have to go through this separate analysis. But, in the hypothetical, they were acting independently, so the analysis must be independent of each other.

D. Concurrent Sufficient Causes

In rare circumstances, the "but for" test may apparently fail to reach the morally sensible result. The problem arises when two acts, either one of which is sufficient to cause the resulting harm when it did, occur concurrently.

Example: *D1* and *D2*, not acting in concert, shoot *V* simultaneously. A bullet from *D1*'s gun strikes *V* in the head; *D2*'s bullet strikes *V* in the heart. *V* dies instantly. Medical testimony indicates that either wound would have killed *V* instantly. Application of the "but for" test will show that *neither D1 nor D2* "caused" *V*'s death, because *V* would have died *when he did*—instantly—as the result of either wound.

1. Substantial Factor Test

In such cases, many courts resort to the "substantial factor" test, a standard that is often used in tort cases. The question to be asked is: "Was *D*'s conduct a substantial factor in the resulting harm?" In the example above, *D1* and *D2* are each substantial factors in *V*'s death, because each inflicted a mortal wound.

2. Model Penal Code

The MPC does not apply the substantial factor test—it uses the "but for" test in all cases. However, the Commentary to the Code explains that, in deciding whether a defendant was a "but for" cause of a "result," one would state the "result" with specificity. In the current hypothetical, one would describe the result as "death by a bullet to the head and one to the heart." Explained *that* way, *D1* and *D2* *are* both actual causes of the result, because *V* would not have died from two bullet wounds but for each defendant's conduct!

II. Proximate Cause (Legal Cause)

A. General Principles

1. Role of "Proximate Cause" In Legal Analysis

A person who is an actual cause of resulting harm is not responsible for it unless she is also the proximate (or "legal") cause of the harm.

a. Relationship of "Proximate Cause" to "Actual Cause"

"Actual cause" analysis identifies the potential candidates for legal responsibility for a result. The purpose of "proximate causation" is to determine who among these candidates should be held accountable for the harm. Which "cause" will we pick out of the "lineup"?

b. Proximate Causation and Justice

As discussed above, "actual cause" is a matter hopefully susceptible to empirical verification. This is not the case with "proximate cause." Ultimately, when the law states that a defendant was the proximate cause of a result, this is a shorthand way of saying that the jury has determined it is morally just to hold this person responsible for the harm.

2. Common Law, Model Penal Code, and Study Point

The discussion that follows focuses on common law analysis of "proximate causation" doctrine. As you will see, as with any "what is just" analysis, there is no single or straightforward answer. The drafters of the Code have another way of handling the issue. They treat "proximate causation" as a culpability, rather than causal, issue. (Technically, the only "causal" issue under the Code is the but-for test discussed above.) The MPC issue is whether the defendant can be said to have purposely, knowingly, recklessly, or negligently (whichever is relevant in a particular case) caused "a particular result" if the "result" occurs in an odd or unexpected manner. This is essentially asking the same question as the common law does with "proximate causation" analysis (as you will see below). And, the Code takes all of the common law factors discussed below and basically roles them into one, explicit, policy question for the jury: Was "the actual result . . . too remote or accidental in its occurrence to have a [just] bearing on the actor's liability or on the gravity of the offense." MPC § 2.03 (2)(b) and (3)(b). The word "just" is in brackets—a legislature might include or exclude this word.

B. Direct Cause

1. Looking For a "Direct Cause"

In proximate causation analysis, look at the facts in the case and determine whether there was any actual (but-for) cause of the result that came into the picture *after* D's voluntary act. If there was none, D may be described as the "direct cause" of the social harm.

Example: D shoots V. D dies instantly. As no other but-for causal force occurred after D's relevant voluntary act, D is the direct cause of V's death.

2. Significance of Identifying a Direct Cause

A voluntary act that is a direct cause of the social harm is also a proximate cause of it. This is because there is no other candidate for causal responsibility. Thus, in the last hypothetical, D is the actual and proximate cause of V's death. If D possessed the requisite *mens rea*, he may be convicted of some form of criminal homicide (assuming no defense).

C. Intervening Cause

1. Definition

An "intervening cause" is an actual cause (a "but for" cause) of social harm that arises *after* D's causal contribution to the result.

Examples: D shoots V. D is taken to a hospital where X, a physician, attends to V's wound. Shortly thereafter, V dies. X might, or might not, be an "intervening cause." One possibility is that X had nothing to do with causing V's death. For example, X may have provided excellent medical care that extended (or, at least, did not shorten) V's life. If so, X is *not* an actual cause of V's death—she is not an "intervening cause." This leaves D as the direct cause of V's death (unless we can point to some other cause).

However, suppose that D did not mortally wound V, and V died due to negligent medical care by X. If so, D remains an actual cause of the death (but for D shooting V, V would not have been taken to the hospital, and thus would not have died at X's hands). But, X is *also* an actual cause of the death. Therefore, as X's actions occurred *after* D shot V, X's conduct constitutes an intervening cause. We now have a proximate causation issue—who should be help causally and legally responsible for the death?

2. General Role of Intervening Causes

An intervening cause does not necessarily relieve a defendant of causal responsibility for the resulting harm. At common law, various factors come into play in proximate causation analysis. Those factors are discussed below. The point to stress here is that these are factors—not rigid tests!

3. Nature of Intervening Cause

It is useful, *although not always dispositive*, to determine whether the intervening cause was "dependent" or "independent" of the defendant's act.

a. "Dependent" and "Independent" Distinguished

An intervening cause is *dependent* if it occurs in response to the defendant's earlier conduct. An intervening cause is *independent* if the factor would have come into play even in the absence of the defendant's conduct.

Examples: D1 shoots V1. V1 is taken to a hospital for medical care where X1, a surgeon, conducts negligent surgery on V1. V1 dies as the result of the surgery. X1's conduct is a *dependent* intervening cause, as his actions were a medical response to D1's act of shooting V1.

D2 shoots *V2*. *V2* is taken to a hospital for medical care, where *X2*, another patient, has an insane delusion and walks into patients' rooms and kills everyone in sight, including *V2*. *X2* is an *independent* intervening cause. *X2*'s actions were not in response to *D2*'s conduct: *X2* was going to kill everyone in sight regardless. He was even going to come into *V2*'s room regardless. *D2* simply put *V2* in the wrong place at the wrong time.

b. Legal Significance of Terminology

Generally speaking, a defendant is responsible for a *dependent* intervening cause, *unless* the dependent intervening act was not only unforeseeable but freakish in its occurrence. In contrast, a defendant is *not* ordinarily responsible for an *independent* intervening cause, *unless* its occurrence was foreseeable to a reasonable person in the defendant's situation.

Examples: In the surgery example above, *D1* is the proximate cause of *V1*'s death, although *X1* was negligent. *X1*'s conduct was dependent on *D1*; and negligence by a doctor, although actionable in tort law, cannot be described as so rare as to be freakish. In contrast, if *X1* conducted the surgery while under the influence of heroin, this could be considered so unusual or bizarre that *X1*, rather than *D1*, would be considered the proximate cause of the death.

In the insane delusion example above, *D2* is not the proximate cause of the death: *X2* was an independent intervening cause, and his intervention was unforeseeable to a reasonable person in *D2*'s situation.

4. **Other Important Factors**

Remember that there is no absolutely dispositive test for determining proximate causation, and that includes the dependent/independent analysis above. Here are some other factors to consider. (Your professor or casebook may discuss others, too.)

a. Intended-Consequences Doctrine

In general, a defendant is the proximate cause of a result, even if there is an intervening cause, if the defendant intended the result that occurred. But, one should be very precise in stating what "result" the defendant intended: a person may want someone dead in a particular manner, in which case the "intended consequences" doctrine only applies if the result occurs in the manner desired.

Example: *M* wants *V*, her nine-month-old child, dead by poisoning. She obtains poison, which she furnishes to *X*, *V*'s nurse, in the guise of medication. She instructs *X* to administer it to *V* later that day. *X* does not follow instructions, and instead places the "medication" on a table, where *Y*, a child too young to understand the consequences of his actions, picks it up and administers the poison to *V*. *V* dies. *Regina v. Michael*, 169 Eng. Rep. 48 (1840). Although there were two intervening causes in this case (*X*'s perhaps negligent act of placing the poison on a table in *Y*'s reach; and *Y*'s act of administering the poison to *V*), the court affirmed *M*'s conviction for the death of her child. This is consistent with the intended-consequence doctrine. The unstated premise is that *M* got what she wanted (the death of her child) in the very manner in which she wanted it (by poisoning). The fact that this result occurred in an unforeseeable manner (at the hands of *Y*, rather than *X*), did not relieve *M* of responsibility for the death. If *Y* had somehow obtained a gun and shot *V* to death, this might *not* qualify under the "intended consequences" rule.

b.   Free, Deliberate, Informed Human Intervention
     In general, a defendant is *not* the proximate cause of a result if a free, deliberate, and informed act of another human being intervenes. H. Hart & H. Honore, Causation in the Law 326 (2d ed. 1985). This doctrine is based on the retributive theory that free will is a critical factor in the determination of moral responsibility for social harm. When a person acts of her own free will, she should accept full responsibility for the results of her actions.

     Example: *D* strikes *V* with his fist, and leaves *V* unconscious on the ground. Later, *X* observes *V* on the road and exploits the situation by robbing *V*. *D* is the proximate cause of the battery. But, he would *not* be the proximate cause of the ensuing robbery (although it would not have occurred but for the battery), because *X*'s act of robbing *V* is a "free, deliberate, and informed" intervening human act.

III.   Review Questions

[Answers Provided in Appendix A, page 360]

1.   State the test for "actual cause."

2. Albert shoots Bob in the leg, intending to kill him. He leaves Bob helpless on a rural road, bleeding. An hour later, a fox from the nearby forest smells the blood, comes to Bob because of it, and kills Bob eating him. How would you characterize the fox (other than as a "hungry animal"!) in terms of causal analysis?

3. Is Albert the proximate cause of Bob's death?

4. What are the five elements of a crime that you have studied so far?

PART SIX

Defenses to Crime: Justifications

■ *ANALYSIS*

CONVERSATION WITH STUDENTS

Alright. You have learned the basic elements of a crime. Now we look at some of the most important defenses to crimes. (We have already discussed two potential defenses: "mistake-of-fact" and "mistake-of-law.")

As you will see, there are two major categories of defenses: justification defenses and excuse defenses. (There are other categories, but don't worry about them for now.) In regard to justification defenses, the current topic, most criminal law casebooks focus almost exclusively on defenses to the use of *deadly* force. This is because most appellate court opinions involve criminal homicide prosecutions. Therefore, this Outline, too, will center on deadly force.

I. Justification Defenses: Generally

A. Definition

A justification defense is one that indicates society's belief that the defendant's conduct was morally good, socially desirable, or (at least) not wrongful. Thus, the killing of another human being, ordinarily a morally wrong or socially harmful outcome, is considered proper (or, at least, a neutral outcome) if it occurs for a "justifiable" reason, such as self-defense.

B. Basic Structure of Justification Defenses

In general, a justification defense contains three components, each of which will be developed more fully in subsequent sections of this Part.

1. Necessity

Ordinarily, use of force against another is not justifiable unless it is necessary. That is, if a person can protect herself or her property without the use of force, then force is unjustified.

2. Proportionality

Ordinarily, a person may not use force that is disproportional to the threat that motivates the use of force. For example, deadly force should not be used to repel a non-deadly threat.

3. Reasonable Belief

Ordinarily, a defendant must possess a reasonable (even if incorrect) belief that the use of force is necessary and proportional to the supposed threat.

II. Self–Defense

A. Common Law

1. General Rule

Subject to clarification below, a person is justified in using *deadly force* against another if: (a) he is not the *aggressor*; and (b) he *reasonably believes* that such force is *necessary* to repel the *imminent* use of *unlawful deadly force* by the other person. The italicized words are discussed more fully below.

2. Definition of "Deadly Force"

The term "deadly force"—whether applied to the actions of the aggressor or the person resisting aggression—is typically defined as "force likely to cause, or intended to cause, death or serious bodily harm."

Example: A fires a loaded gun at B. This is "deadly force," whether or not B dies: the firing of a loaded gun at another person is force that is intended to cause, or likely to cause, death or serious bodily injury.

3. "Aggressor"

An aggressor may not use deadly force in self-defense. It is possible, however, for an aggressor to purge himself of his status as an aggressor and regain the right of self-defense.

a. Definition

An "aggressor" may be defined as a person who commits an "unlawful act reasonably calculated to produce an affray foreboding injurious or fatal consequences." *United States v. Peterson*, 483 F.2d 1222 (D.C. Cir. 1973).

Example: In *Peterson, supra*, P observed V removing the windshield wipers from P's parked car in an alley. After a verbal exchange, P entered his house, obtained a gun, and returned to the alley, only to find V leaving the area. P threatened to shoot V. In response, V secured a lug wrench and walked toward P, whereupon P shot and killed V in "self-defense." On these facts, P was the aggressor at the time of the shooting and, therefore, unjustified in using deadly force in self-defense. The court indicated that even if V was the original aggressor when he tampered with P's car (which is uncertain, since this conduct was not necessarily likely to cause an "injurious or fatal" conflict), *V* lost this status when he sought to leave the scene and do no more mischief. (See below.)

b. **Losing the "Aggressor" Status**

   i. **Nondeadly Aggressors**

   A, a nondeadly aggressor, may regain her right of self-defense against *B*, if *B* responds to *A*'s nondeadly aggression by threatening to use excessive—deadly—force in response. Courts differ, however, regarding how *A* regains the right to use deadly force in such circumstances.

   (1) **Majority Rule**

   If *B* responds to *A*'s nondeadly aggression by threatening to use deadly force against *A*, *A* *immediately* regains her right of self-defense.

   Example: *A* threatens to slap *B* in the face. In response, *B* pulls out a knife and threatens to use it on *A*. *A* may now use deadly force in self-defense: her "aggressor" status is purged due to *B*'s disproportionate response.

   (2) **Minority Rule**

   If *B* responds to *A*'s nondeadly aggression by threatening to use deadly force against *A*, *A* may not use deadly force in self-defense unless *A* first retreats, and *B* continues to threaten *A* with deadly force. If no safe retreat is possible, however, *A* may immediately use deadly force.

   ii. **Deadly Aggressor**

   A, a deadly aggressor, loses the right of self-defense in a conflict unless she abandons her deadly design and communicates this fact to *B*.

   Example: *A* wrongfully pulls a knife on *B* and threatens to kill her. *B* pulls out a gun in self-defense. As *A* is a deadly aggressor, she may not use deadly force against *B* unless she demonstrates to *B* that she no longer poses a threat, such as by dropping her knife and running away. If *B* chases after her with the continued intention of killing *A* in "self-defense," *A* now has a right to defend herself. At this point, *B* becomes the deadly aggressor!

4. Proportionality of Force: Deadly Against Deadly

Deadly force may never be used in response to a non-deadly threat, even if this is the only way to repel the non-deadly threat.

Example: Arnold and Bob are standing on a public sidewalk. Arnold unlawfully swings his fist at Bob. The only way Bob can avoid being struck is to push Arnold away, off the sidewalk onto a major highway where Arnold is likely to be struck by a fast-moving car. Bob may not respond to Arnold's unlawful force this way: to do so would constitute the use of deadly force to respond to a non-deadly attack.

5. "Unlawful Force"/"Unlawful Threat"

A person has no right to defend herself against lawful—justified—force. She may only respond to unlawful threats of force.

Example: Officer Betty is making a lawful arrest of Serial Murderer Carl. Carl breaks away and flees. Officer Betty pulls out her gun and calls out to Carl, "Stop or I'll shoot." Carl turns and fires his weapon at Officer Betty, killing her. At trial, Carl claims self-defense. Serial Murderer Carl will lose this claim. Although he *was* responding to a threat of deadly force by Officer Betty, Betty's threat was a lawful one. She would have been justified in shooting at Carl, to prevent his flight. (She is justified under a "law enforcement" defense discussed later.)

6. "Imminency"

Although modern courts are somewhat less strict than their predecessors, generally speaking a person may not use deadly force in self-defense unless the aggressor's threatened force will occur immediately, almost at that instant.

Example: Arthur tells Bernice, his wife, before going to sleep: "I will kill you when I get up in the morning." At common law, Bernice is not permitted to use deadly force in self-defense while Arthur sleeps, because his threatened use of unlawful force upon her is not imminent.

7. Necessity to Use Deadly Force

A person may not use deadly force unless it is necessary.

a. Use of Less Force

A person may not use deadly force to repeal an unlawful deadly attack if more moderate (non-deadly) force will do the job.

b. Retreat?

Must non-aggressors retreat—flee to a safe place—rather than stand their ground and use deadly force? Today, there is a conflict on this subject in non-Model Penal Code jurisdictions.

i. Majority Rule

A majority of non-MPC jurisdictions do *not* have a retreat requirement. These courts do not require a person to retreat because, they say, Right should never have to yield to Wrong; also, to flee (retreat) is cowardly or "unmanly."

ii. Minority Position

(1) Rule

Subject to the "castle exception" discussed below, a non-aggressor may *not* use deadly force to repel an attack if she knows of a completely safe place to which she can retreat. *Notice*: retreat is only required if there is an *entirely* safe place available, and only if it is known to the innocent person. It is not enough that she *should have been aware* of the avenue of retreat. The retreat requirement values human life and is consistent with the general necessity requirement: even aggressors should not be killed if there is a way to avoid the taking of life.

(2) "Castle" Exception

Even in retreat jurisdictions, a non-aggressor is never required to retreat from her own home. This rule is based on the ancient common law view of the house as "a man's castle"—a natural sanctuary from external aggression: "the King should not expected to flee his own castle."

8. **"Reasonable Belief"**

a. General Rule

The self-defense rules discussed above are modified by the "reasonable belief" principle, which provides that a person may use deadly force in self-defense is she has reasonable grounds to believe, and actually believes, that she is in imminent danger of death or serious bodily harm, and that use of deadly force is necessary to protect herself, *even if her reasonable beliefs in these regards are incorrect*. Put differently, D may justifiably use deadly force in "self-defense" against A although: A was *not* going to use force against D; A was only going to use nondeadly force (so that D's response is disproportionate); a deadly threat was *not* imminent; or deadly force was unnecessary to repel a deadly attack—as long as D reasonably believes that the facts support the defense.

i.   Imperfect Defense

In most common law jurisdictions, a defendant who acts on the basis of an unreasonable belief entirely loses her self-defense claim and, therefore, will be convicted of murder. Some jurisdictions, however, recognize an "imperfect" defense in homicide prosecutions: if D kills another in *unreasonable* self-defense, D will be convicted of the lesser offense of manslaughter.

b.   What Is a "Reasonable Belief"?

A reasonable belief is a belief that a reasonable person would hold. But, that only shifts the question to: who is a "reasonable person"? Courts have struggled with this issue. Ordinarily, the defendant's physical characteristics may be incorporated into the "reasonable person." Thus, for example, if the defendant is blind, she will be held to the standard of what a reasonable blind person would believe in similar circumstances. Many courts today also subscribe to the view that prior experiences of the defendant that help the defendant evaluate the present situation are relevant. *People v. Goetz*, 68 N.Y.2d 96, 506 N.Y.S.2d 18, 497 N.E.2d 41 (1986); *State v. Wanrow*, 88 Wash.2d 221, 559 P.2d 548 (1977).

Examples: If D was a prior mugging victim, this experience may be considered in evaluating the reasonableness of D's actions when he believes he is confronting another mugging situation. *Goetz, supra.* Even more significantly, if D has been a victim of unlawful attacks by X in the past—e.g., D is a battered wife of X—these prior experiences are relevant in determining whether a reasonable person would interpret X's actions in the current situation as threatening.

c.   Battered Women and Self–Defense

This last *Example* raises a new issue, which some courts have considered, and which your casebook may discuss: How should the law deal with the situation of a woman, physically abused for years by her husband or live-in partner, who kills her abuser at a moment when she is not, in fact, under imminent attack, for example, when the batterer is sleeping? Can we say that the battered woman *reasonably* believed that the batterer represented an imminent threat in such nonconfrontational circumstances?

i. Battered Woman Syndrome (BWS) Testimony

In homicide prosecutions of the sort described here, a defense lawyer may seek to introduce evidence that the woman suffered from BWS, a condition that is said to cause a woman "to sink into a state of psychological paralysis and to become unable to take any action at all to improve or alter her situation." *State v. Kelly*, 97 N.J. 178, 478 A.2d 364 (1984). The purpose of this evidence is to try to show that the woman *subjectively* believed that he represented an immediate threat, and to show that a reasonable woman suffering from BWS would also so believe.

ii. Legal Trends

Most courts prohibit an instruction on self-defense if the homicide occurred in nonconfrontational circumstances, on the ground that no reasonable juror could believe that the defendant, *as a reasonable person*, would believe that a sleeping man represents an *imminent* threat. But, some courts now do permit such cases to go to the jury, if BWS evidence is introduced to show that the defendant, as a battered woman, suffered from this condition.

iii. Observation

The battered woman controversy raises a significant additional issue: is the law correct in requiring that a threat be imminent (or, at least, that a reasonable person so believe) before deadly force may be used? The Model Penal Code, discussed below, moves away from this strict requirement.

B. Model Penal Code

1. General Rule

Subject to the limitations discussed below, a person is not justified in using deadly force against another unless she believe that such force is immediately necessary to protect herself against the exercise of unlawful deadly force, force likely to cause serious bodily harm, kidnapping, or sexual intercourse compelled by force or threat, by the other person on the present occasion. MPC §§ 3.04(1), 3.04(2)(b).

a. Comparison to Common Law

i. Belief Requirement

Notice that the rule above is not stated in terms of the defendant's *reasonable* belief, only in terms of subjective belief. However, *as with nearly all Code justification defenses*, the self-protection defense is subject to the provisions of Section 3.09(2), which provides that if the actor's subjective belief is reckless or negligent, then the defendant may be convicted of a homicide offense based on recklessness or negligence (such as manslaughter or negligent homicide). Thus, the Code is consistent with the minority of common law jurisdictions that recognize an "imperfect defense."

ii. Imminency

The most significant difference is that the MPC provides that a person may use deadly force in self-protection even if the aggressor will not use deadly force immediately. The issue under the Code is *not* when the aggressor's unlawful force will be used, *but when the non-aggressor will need to use force on the present occasion.*

Example: D, a battered wife, is in the kitchen making dinner. *A*, her abusive husband, enters and says, "Today is the last day for you to live. I am going to the bedroom in a few moments to get my gun, come back, and kill you." *A* turns his back on *D*, perhaps to go get his gun. *D*, reasonably fearing for her life, stabs *A* to death in the back with a steak knife. At common law, *D* would likely not have a valid self-defense claim, since *A* is still unarmed; the harm to *D* is not "imminent" as the common law defined this term. Under the Code, however, *D* has a plausible self-protection claim, as the use of force was *"immediately necessary"*—realistically, it was now or never.

2. Limitations on General Rule

Even if deadly force is otherwise permitted, it is impermissible in two key circumstances.

a. Defendant as Aggressor

As with the common law, the defense is not permitted if the actor is the aggressor, which the Code defines as one who "provokes" the use of force against herself "in the same encounter" for the "purpose of causing death or serious bodily injury." MPC § 3.04(2)(b)(i).

b. Retreat

The Code follows the minority common law position that a non-aggressor must retreat if she knows that she can thereby avoid the need to use deadly force with complete safety to herself. MPC § 3.04(2)(b)(ii). This retreat requirement, however, is itself subject to various exceptions, most notably that a person need not retreat from her own dwelling. See MPC § 3.04(2)(b)(ii)(1).

c. Other "Non–Necessity" Circumstances

The Code explicitly provides that deadly force may not be used if, subject to various exceptions, the defendant can avoid doing so "by surrendering possession of a thing to a person asserting a claim of right thereto or by complying with a demand that he abstain from any action that he has no duty to take." MPC § 3.04(2)(b)(ii).

Examples: A loans his car to D for a specified period of time. Later, A seeks its return. D believes that she is entitled to retain it under their agreement. A threatens to use deadly force to retrieve it. *Whether or not* A's claim to the car is justified, D must give up possession of it if this will prevent the need for deadly force.

A, who has no right to do so, tells D that he will kill D if D dates A's girl-friend. D refuses to abstain from this conduct and, therefore, arms himself with a weapon in case A goes through with the threat. Under these circumstances, however, D cannot use deadly force against A, since he had no duty *not* to comply with A's demand.

A threatens to kill D, a police office, if D lawfully seeks to arrest A for a crime. Here, D has a legal duty *not* to abstain from arresting A; therefore, he may use deadly force, if otherwise necessary.

III. Defense–of–Third–Parties

A. Common Law

1. General Rule

Also called "defense of others," a person is justified is using deadly force to protect a third party (someone other than herself) from unlawful use of force by an aggressor. The intervenor's right to use force parallels the third party's *apparent* right of *self*-defense. That is, the third party may use force when, and to the extent that, she reasonably believes that the third party would be justified in using force to protect herself.

Example: X is being lawfully arrested at gunpoint by O, an undercover police officer. D reasonably believes, however, that X is being unlawfully threatened with deadly force by "mugger" O. Based on D's reasonable (albeit incorrect) understanding of the situation, X would have a right to use deadly force in self-protection. Therefore, D may use deadly force to protect X from O.

2. Minority Rule

Sometimes characterized as the "alter ego" principle, some jurisdictions provide that a person may only use force to defend a third party if the person being defended would *in fact* have been justified in using the same degree of force in self-defense. That is, the intervenor is placed in the shoes of the party whom she is seeking to defend. If the other person has no right of self-defense, *even though the intervenor reasonably believes that she does,* the intervenor loses her claim.

Example: In the example above, D would be guilty of murder. The defense-of-third-party claim would be lost.

B. Model Penal Code

A person is justified in using deadly force to protect another if: (1) the intervenor would be justified in using such force to protect herself, if the facts were as she believed them to be; (2) according to the facts as the intervenor believes them to be, the third person would be justified in using such force to protect herself; (3) the intervenor believes force is necessary for the third party's protection; and (4) if the third party would be required to retreat under the Code self-protection rules, the intervenor must attempt to cause the third party to retreat before using deadly force. MPC § 3.05. As with self-protection, this defense is subject to the rule that if the intervenor's beliefs are reckless or negligent, she may be convicted of an offense based on recklessness or negligence, as the case may be. MPC § 3.09(2).

IV. Defenses of Property and Habitation

CONVERSATION WITH STUDENTS

We now turn to two related defenses. Indeed, some jurisdictions merge the two into a single "defense of property" claim. But, there is an important distinction between the use of force to protect one's property, personal or real, from being taken from you—from being dispossessed of property—and the separate interest in the secure and private habitation of one's home. Thus, we have two defenses here to discuss.

A. Defense of Property

1. Common Law

A person is never justified in using deadly force to defend her real or personal property. A person *is* justified in using *non*deadly force if she reasonably believes that such force is necessary to prevent the imminent, unlawful dispossession of the property. Some jurisdictions also provide that, prior to using force, the property defender must ask the dispossessor to desist from his conduct, unless such a request would be futile or dangerous.

a. Important Clarification

With one exception, the defender must be in lawful possession of the property at the time force is used. If she has already been dispossessed of the property, force may *not* be used to *recapture* the property. Instead, the victim of dispossession must seek judicial redress. The exception is that nondeadly force *is* permitted in fresh pursuit of a dispossessor of property. In such circumstances, the use of force to recapture the property is treated as an extension of the original effort to prevent dispossession.

Example: V steals D's car. The next day D observes V driving her car. D may not justifiably use force to regain possession of it. But, if D catches V in the act, D could pursue V (for example, in another car), and use moderate force, if needed, to recapture the stolen vehicle.

b. Another Important Clarification

The defender's right to use force is based on her rightful *possession* of the property; she does not need to have title to it. In fact, if the other elements of the defense are satisfied, a lawful possessor of property may justifiably used nondeadly force against the owner of the property, if the latter is seeking to unlawfully dispossess her of it.

c. Study Point

Although deadly force is never justified at common law in defense of property, a defense-of-property claim can sometimes merge into a self-defense claim where deadly force is justified.

Example: D uses proper nondeadly force in an effort to prevent X from stealing D's car. X pulls a knife and threatens D with it. D may now have a right to use deadly force against X *in self-defense*.

2. Model Penal Code

The MPC differs from the common law in various key respects.

a. Belief Requirement

As with other justifications defenses, the right to use force to protect property is based on the actor's subjective belief, subject to the provisions of § 3.09, previously discussed.

b. Recapture of Property

With one exception, the MPC goes further than the common law in that it generally authorizes use of nondeadly force to retake possession of land or recapture personal property, *even after fresh pursuit has ended*, if the actor believes that the dispossessor has no claim of right to the property. MPC § 3.06(1)(b)(ii). The exception is that in the case of land, a recapturer may *not* use force unless she believes that it would constitute an "exceptional hardship" to delay re-entry until she can obtain a court order.

Example: V, not acting on a claim of right to the property, wrongfully dispossesses D of her farm land. D may not re-enter and throw V off the land, but must seek a judicial remedy *unless* the delay will cause extreme hardship to D, for example, if the crops on the land require immediate harvesting.

c. Deadly Force

The Code authorizes the use of deadly force if D believes that V: (1) intends to dispossess D of his dwelling other than under a claim-of-right to possession; or (2) intends to commit arson, burglary, robbery or felonious theft inside the dwelling and (2a) V "has employed or threatened deadly force against or in the presence" of D or (2b) the use of *non*deadly force to prevent commission of the crime would expose D or another to substantial risk of serious bodily harm. MPC § 3.06(3)(d).

B. Defense of Habitation

1. Common Law

a. Deadly Force

As discussed below, a person *may* use deadly force to protect her right to inhabit her home in safe repose.

i. Study Point

As we saw, a person may *not* use deadly force to avoid dispossession from her land—the defense of property. But, the same person *may* sometimes use deadly force to protect her right to live in her home in privacy and security. Obviously, then, the defense of property often merges into the defense of habitation. If a lawyer makes the proper claim (or a student makes a proper argument on an examination!), it may be possible to bring a case within defense-of-habitation.

b. Older, Broader Rule

D is justified in using deadly force against *V* if the actor reasonably believes that: (1) *V* intends unlawfully and imminently to enter *D*'s dwelling; (2) *V* intends to commit a felony inside, or to cause bodily injury, no matter how slight, to any occupant; and (3) deadly force is necessary to prevent the entry.

i. Study Point

Notice that the right to use deadly force here is triggered by the threat of imminent entry of the dwelling. The intended harm inside—a felony or even minor bodily injury—need *not* be imminent! Thus, this defense applies sooner than a claim of self-defense or defense-of-third-party, and it can justify deadly force even when a nondeadly injury is threatened!

c. Narrower Rule

Many jurisdictions no longer apply the broad rule set out above and instead hold that deadly force is limited to circumstances in which *D* believes that *V* will commit an atrocious (violent) felony inside the dwelling if *V* enters.

Example: *V* attempts to enter *D*'s home in order to steal property. *D* knows that *V* is unarmed. Based on this information alone, *D* may still use deadly force under the *broader* rule, assuming that such force is the only way to prevent *V*'s entry. But, under the narrower rule, *D* would not be justified in using deadly force unless *D* has reason to believe that *V* intends to commit a violent felony inside the dwelling.

2. **Model Penal Code**

The Code does not recognize a separate interest in habitation, as distinguished from defense of property. See the comments above in regard to the MPC defense-of-property claim.

C. Special Issue: Spring Guns

An issue that sometimes arises is whether a home dweller may set up a mechanical device, such as a spring gun (a gun that will fire if an intruder opens a door that "springs" the device), to protect herself, her habitation, and/or her property. Spring guns, by definition, constitute deadly force.

1. Common Law

A person may use a spring gun to inflict deadly force on another "where an intrusion is, *in fact*, such that a person, were he present, would be justified in taking the life or inflicting the bodily harm with his own hands." *People v. Ceballos*, 12 Cal.3d 470, 116 Cal. Rptr. 233, 526 P.2d 241 (1974) (but rejecting this common law rule).

Example: D installs a spring gun in her home so that it shoots to kill any person who attempts to enter her home while she is away on vacation or is in the house sleeping upstairs. *V*, a would-be-rapist, attempts to enter D's home. The spring gun kills *V*. At common law, D has acted justifiably.

a. Critical Feature of the Rule

As the italicized words in the quoted statement of the rule above suggest, the user of the spring gun acts at her peril: the deadly force must be necessary. Reasonable appearances will not suffice.

Example: *V*, a small child, accidentally opens D's unlocked front door, believing that this is her own home. The spring gun kills *V*. Even if D, as a reasonable person, would not have realized that the intruder was a harmless child and, therefore would have been justified in *personally* using deadly force in defense of habitation, D will not be entitled to invoke the defense here, as D has used the indirect method of a spring gun.

2. Model Penal Code

The justifiable use of force does *not* extend to any mechanical device that is intended to use, or is known to create, a significant risk of causing death or serious bodily injury. MPC § 3.06(5).

V. Law Enforcement Defenses

CONVERSATION WITH STUDENTS

We now turn to two law enforcement defenses. The labels used to describe them differ by jurisdiction, but they will be described here as the defenses of crime prevention and arrest. As you consider these defenses, keep in mind that they may overlap other justification defenses. For example, an arrestee may threaten physical injury to a police officer conducting an arrest; if so, the officer is also entitled to act in self-defense. Or, in preventing a murder of another, the officer could invoke the privilege of defense-of-third-parties as well as the defense of crime prevention. When an occupant of a home uses force to prevent unlawful entry of an intruder, the home-dweller may simultaneously be involved in crime prevention (burglary), defense of property, and defense of habitation (and, maybe, self-defense). So, don't treat any fact pattern in a vacuum: consider alternative defenses. A careful comparison of the defenses demonstrates that there is not a perfect overlap between them. One of the defenses may apply in a situation when another does not.

A. Crime Prevention

1. Common Law

Deadly force is never justifiable in the prevention of a petty offense, *i.e.*, misdemeanor. Only moderate nondeadly force may be used in such circumstances. Deadly force is permitted in *felony* crime prevention under certain circumstances. The alternative approaches are discussed below.

a. Original (Now Minority) Approach

The original common law rule, followed today in only a few jurisdictions, is that a police officer or private citizen is justified in using deadly force upon another if she reasonably believes that: (1) the other person is committing a felony; and (2) deadly force is necessary to prevent commission of the crime. This rule applies to *all* felonies. As such, this version of the defense is controversial because it can authorize use of force grossly disproportional to the threat caused by the felon.

Example: F is about to steal D's automobile. Because of the value of the car, this theft constitutes a felony, rather than a misdemeanor. In a jurisdiction applying the original common law rule, D (or a police officer) is justified in killing F if this is the only way to prevent F from taking the car. This is true, even if F does not represent a threat to anyone's safety.

b. Modern (Majority) Approach

The majority rule differs from the original rule in one critical way: deadly force is only permitted if the officer or private party reasonably believes that the other person is about to commit an "atrocious" felony. Such a felony is one that involves a significant risk of serious bodily harm to an innocent person. Among the felonies that are considered atrocious are: murder, manslaughter, robbery, arson, rape, and burglary.

2. Model Penal Code

A police officer or private party may not use deadly force to prevent a felony unless she believes that: (1) there is a substantial risk that the suspect will cause death or serious bodily harm to another unless commission or consummation of the offense is prevented; (2) the force is immediately necessary to prevent commission of the offense; and (3) use of deadly force presents no substantial risk of injury to bystanders. MPC § 3.07(5)(a). As with other Code justification defenses, the defense is based on the actor's subjective belief, subject always to the provisions of § 3.09, which permit prosecution for reckless or negligent homicide if the actor's beliefs were reckless or negligent, as the case may be.

Example: D, a police officer, observes a robbery in commission in a very busy shopping mall. The only way D can prevent the crime is to shoot the robber from a considerable distance At common law, the officer would be justified in using deadly force. Under the MPC, he would not be justified unless he believes that such force creates no substantial risk to innocent bystanders.

B. Arrest

As with crime prevention, deadly force is never permissible to effectuate an arrest of a misdemeanant, even if the misdemeanant will successfully avoid arrest otherwise. But, deadly force *is* permitted in some felony cases to prevent the arrestee from escaping.

1. Common Law

a. Majority Rule

A police officer is justified in using deadly force against another if she reasonably believes that: (1) the suspect committed any felony; and (2) such force is necessary to immediately effectuate the arrest. As discussed in subsection C. below, this rule is now unconstitutionally broad as it relates to the actions of police officers.

i. Comparison to Crime Prevention Defense

Notice that under this majority rule, a police officer may justifiably kill a person whom she might not have the right to kill in crime prevention under *that* majority rule. The arrest rule applies to *all* felonies, whereas the modern crime-prevention defense is limited to atrocious felonies.

ii. Rationale of Rule

This harsh rule—permitting the use of deadly force to effectuate an arrest, when necessary, of any felony—was justified at early common law on the ground that the felon, by committing the crime, forfeited his right to life. Forfeiture, it was argued, occurred because *all* common law felonies were capital offenses. Therefore, the killing of a felon, if necessary to prevent his flight, was viewed as little more than the pre-trial execution of the penalty.

b. Special Problem of "Citizen Arrests"

Common law jurists were hesitant to permit private citizens, less trained in the use of firearms, to use deadly force in "citizen arrests." Therefore, although the rules vary considerably by jurisdiction, limitations on the use of deadly force by private parties are common. These may include: (i) limitation of the use of deadly force to atrocious felonies; (ii) a requirement that the private person give notice of her intention to make the arrest; and (iii) denial of the defense if the suspect *in fact* did not commit the felony, even if the private party reasonably believed that she did.

2. Model Penal Code

Deadly force may *never* be used by private citizens, acting on their own, to make an arrest or to prevent a suspect's escape. However, a police officer (or private citizen assisting the officer) may use deadly force to effectuate an arrest if she believes that: (1) the force can be applied at no risk to innocent bystanders; (2) such force is immediately necessary to make the arrest; and either (3a) the felony for which the person is being arrested included the use or threatened use of deadly force; or (3b) a substantial risk exists that the suspect will cause serious bodily harm to another if she is not apprehended immediately. MPC §§ 3.07(1), 3.07(2)(b).

C. *Tennessee v. Garner*

1. Constitutional Rule

The Supreme Court ruled in *Tennessee v. Garner*, 471 U.S. 1, 105 S.Ct. 1694, 85 L.Ed.2d 1 (1985), that it is unconstitutional for a police officer to use deadly force to prevent the escape of a fleeing felony suspect unless: (1) the force is necessary to prevent the suspect's successful flight; (2) if it is practical to do so, the officer warns the suspect of her intention to use deadly force (*e.g.*, "Stop, or I'll shoot!"); and (3), the officer has probable cause to believe that the suspect, if not immediately apprehended, poses a significant threat of death or serious injury to the officer or others. The term "probable cause" is a constitutional term of art: it is enough for current purposes to state that it involves less than a fifty percent degree of likelihood.

2. Rationale

The Fourth Amendment to the United States Constitution prohibits "unreasonable searches and seizures." A "seizure" of a person occurs when an officer, by means of physical force or show of authority restrains the liberty of a citizen. An arrest, therefore, is a seizure of that person. The seizure of person by *killing* the suspect is the ultimate form of seizure. According to the Court, "it is not always better that all felony suspects die than that they escape." The Court reasoned that the common law rule permitting the use of deadly force to effectuate the arrest of *any* felon was unreasonable for two reasons.

a. Disproportionality of Response

Many modern felonies, such as in the white collar area (*e.g.*, embezzlement), do not implicate a serious risk of physical harm to others if the felon escapes. Killing such a person is a disproportionate response to the danger.

b. Forfeiture

The original common law rule, based as it was on the principle of forfeiture, no longer applies. All common law felonies carried the death penalty; today, the death penalty only applies to the felony of murder, and even here most murders do not merit capital punishment.

3. Court Examples of Permissible Deadly Force

The constitutional rule is set out above, but the Court provided two examples of circumstances in which deadly force, if otherwise necessary (and assuming a prior warning is given, if possible), would be reasonable: (1) if the suspect threatens the officer with a weapon; or (2) the officer has probable cause to believe that the suspect has committed a crime involving the actual or threatened infliction of serious physical harm to another.

4. Scope of the Rule

The Fourth Amendment to the United States Constitution only limits the actions of government agents. Therefore, *Garner* does *not* apply to private citizens acting alone. As to them, the common law rules discussed earlier continue to apply.

VI. Necessity

CONVERSATION WITH STUDENTS

We have reached the last justification defense. Indeed, this defense—called "necessity" at common law and "choice of evils" in the Mode Penal Code—is properly characterized as the "residual justification." That is, this defense should only be considered if none of the traditional defenses speaks to the case. By "speaks to the case" I mean that none of the other defenses permits *or rejects* the justification claim being raised. We are talking here about rare cases that simply do not fit the usual justification defenses. Typically, "necessity" is raised when the actor violates the letter of the law because some emergency threatens the actor or another, and none of the usual defenses applies. For example, the defense might arise if a defendant trespasses on another's land to avoid a tornado. None of the other defenses, all of which focus on the use of force upon another, are relevant to this case, which does not involve the use of force upon another. We need a backup defense. Or, perhaps the defendant purposely uses force against an innocent party, and not against an aggressor, for some arguably justifiable reason. This type of case, which falls outside the usual defenses—none of the defenses either permits or prohibits such claims—might fall under the "necessity" or "choice of evils" umbrella.

A. Common Law

1. Elements of the Defense

There is no universally accepted definition of the common law doctrine of necessity. In general, a person whose conduct would otherwise constitute a crime acts justifiably if certain conditions, set out below, are met. As discussed in subsection 2., there is some support for the proposition that the defense of necessity never applies in homicide prosecutions.

a. Lesser–Evils Analysis

The actor must be faced with a choice of evils or harms, and he must choose to commit the lesser of the evils. Put differently, the harm that *D* seeks to *prevent* by his conduct must be greater than the harm he reasonably expects to *cause* by his conduct. The balancing of the harms is conducted by the judge or jury; the defendant's belief that he is acting properly is not in itself sufficient.

Examples: *D1* violates the speeding laws in order to get her seriously ill child to the emergency room of a hospital. Firefighter *D2* burns down *V*'s barn and trees in order to create a firebreak, to prevent a surging firestorm from burning down many houses in the area. In these cases, *D1* and *D2* have chosen the lesser of two evils.

i.   Reasonable Belief

In measuring the competing harms, the court or jury must put itself in the actor's shoes at the time the choice had to be made: the harms to be weighed and compared are those that a reasonable person, at that moment, would expect to occur.

Example: *D* is driving down a steep hill on a public road when, no fault of her own, her brakes fail. *D* realizes that her car, which is gaining speed, will soon run through a red light at a busy intersection, very possibly striking other cars at a very high rate of speed. *D* observes a parked car, apparently unoccupied, to her right. She decides to purposely run into the car, to stop her vehicle. Unknown to *D*, the vehicle contained two small children. (Left their by their parents, the children were too small to be seen through the car window.) In determining whether *D* chose the lesser of two evils, the issue is what a reasonable person in *D*'s shoes, at the moment of decision, would have believed was the better choice. The after-the-fact unforeseeable reality that two children were in the car is not relevant.

b.   Imminency of Harm

The actor must be seeking to avoid imminent harm, *i.e.,* harm that appears likely to occur immediately. This rule is strictly enforced: if there is sufficient time to seek a lawful avenue, the actor *must* take that route.

c.   Causal Element

The actor must reasonably believe that his actions will abate the threatened harm.

d. **Blamelessness of the Actor**

Although some judicial opinions and statutes are silent in this regard, many courts and/or statutes provide that the actor must not be at fault in creating the necessity. Thus, in the *Example* above, the necessity claim would not apply if *D* was at fault for the failure of her brakes.

2. **Homicide Prosecutions**

It is unclear whether the defense of necessity applies to the crime of murder. Fortunately, the issue has only rarely arisen. The leading case—and the one most likely to be in your casebook—is the English opinion, *Regina v. Dudley and Stephens*, 14 Q.B.D. 273 (1884).

a. **The Case**

Three adults and a 17–year-old youth were stranded on a lifeboat. After almost three weeks, near starvation and dehydration, two of the men killed the youth (who was already sick), so that the three men could eat his remains to survive. As it turned out, they were picked up by a vessel shortly thereafter. The two men who participated in the killing were prosecuted for murder. The court rejected their necessity claim. Some commentators interpret this case as rejecting the view that a person may ever justifiably kill an innocent person, even if this is necessary to save a greater number of lives.

b. **Legal Observations**

Dudley and Stephens may stand for the proposition just stated, but perhaps not. There are ways to limit the case: some feel that the emergency had not yet reached the point where such an extreme measure was required. Others feel that the method for determining who should die—the two men chose the youth because he was already the sickest and most likely to die first—was faulty: perhaps the use of lots to choose the victim might have changed the analysis.

c. **Theoretical Observations**

Assuming that the case *does* stand for the proposition that it is never justifiable to kill an innocent person, even to save a greater number of lives, this outcome is proper under retributive theory: it is always wrong to treat any person merely as a means to an end. (But, this does *not* mean that the retributivist would necessarily punish Dudley and Stephens. Remember, the issue here is whether the killing is *justified*—proper. It remains to be seen in Part Seven whether one might *excuse* the defendants, a separate issue!) A utilitarian, however, might justify some homicides: if the choice *really* is to take one innocent life in order to save a greater number of lives. Moreover, a strong argument can be made that persons in Dudley's and Stephen's predicament are undeterrable; therefore, their punishment would be inefficacious.

B. Model Penal Code

The MPC recognizes a "choice of evils" justification defense, MPC § 3.02. This provision has had considerable influence on state penal codes.

1. Elements

A person is justified in committing an act that otherwise would constitute an offense if: (a) the actor believes that the conduct is necessary to avoid harm to himself or another; (b) the harm that the actor seeks to avoid is greater than that sought to be avoided by the law prohibiting his conduct; and (c) there does not plainly exist any legislative intent to exclude the justification claimed by the actor. If the actor was reckless or negligent in bringing about the emergency, the defense is unavailable in a prosecution for any offense for which recklessness or negligence, as the may be, is sufficient to prove guilt.

2. Comparison to Common Law

Under the Code, the threatened harm need not be imminent. Moreover, the Commentary to the Code expressly states that this defense *is* available in homicide prosecutions.

VII. Review Questions

[Answers Provided in Appendix A, page 361]

1. In self-defense, at common law, what constitute a threat of "imminent" force?

2. The Model Penal Code defense of self-protection does not require that a person wait until threatened force is imminent. Instead, at what time may a person use deadly force against an aggressor?

3. T or F.   At common law, a person who unlawfully threatens to use deadly force against another may never regain the right of self-defense against that person.

4. T or F.   Under the Model Penal Code, a person who honestly, but negligently or recklessly, believes that deadly force is necessary to protect

herself will not be convicted of any homicide offense.

5. Donald observes a man pointing a gun at Carla, a stranger. Donald, believing that the man is about to unlawfully kill Carla, and seeing no evidence that Carla can protect herself, kills the man with a weapon lawfully in his possession. It turns out, however, that the man's gun was a toy, he was playing a practical joke on Carla, and Carla was aware of the joke but was pretending she was fearful. Donald is prosecuted for the murder of the man. On these facts, what is the majority common law position?

    a. Donald's defense-of-third-party claim should fail, whether his mistaken belief that Carla's life was in jeopardy was reasonable or unreasonable;

    b. Donald's defense-of-third-party claim should succeed if his mistake was reasonable, but not if his mistake was unreasonable; or

    c. Donald's defense-of-third-party claim should succeed as long as he honestly believed that Carla's life was in jeopardy.

6. T or F.   Deadly force is never justified to protect personal property outside the home.

7. T or F.   At common law, a person who has been unlawfully dispossessed of his personal or real property may never use force to regain possession.

8. Under the Model Penal Code, may a person use a spring gun to defend her property or right to inhabit her home in safe repose?

9. In most common law jurisdictions, when may a police officer or private party use deadly force in crime prevention?

10. How does the Model Penal Code "crime prevention" defense differ from the majority common law rule?

11. T or F.   The Fourth Amendment of the United States Constitution bars the use of deadly force to prevent the escape of a person suspected of felony computer fraud.

12. Betty kills Dr. Alice Abortionist to prevent the doctor from performing future abortions. Betty seeks to defend the killing on necessity grounds. What legal hurdles must she overcome to win a common law claim?

*

PART SEVEN

Defenses to Crime: Excuses

■ *ANALYSIS*

CONVERSATION WITH STUDENTS

We have just finished discussing the justification defenses. Now we look at excuse defenses. It is often important to distinguish a "justification" from an "excuse." Some professors spend *a lot* of time focusing on the distinction, while others do not. If your professor is in the former category (I am), pay great attention to what he or she says about it, and to any materials in your casebook that help explain the distinction. (Ahem, there is at least one treatise out there that also covers the distinction in some detail, but modesty requires me to leave it at that.)

I. Excuse Defenses: Generally

A. Excuse: Defined

An excuse defense is one that indicates that, although the actor committed the elements of the offense, and although his actions were unjustified—wrongful—the law does not blame him for his wrongful conduct. For example, insanity is an excuse defense. An insane person will be acquitted of a crime. The acquittal does *not* mean that what the person did was good, permissible, or tolerable—quite the opposite: the insane actor *has* caused a wrongful, harmful result, but the insane person is not punished because the law does not hold him morally and legally accountable for his actions.

1. Rationale

a. Utilitarian Argument

Excuses defenses are sometimes explained on utilitarian grounds: some people suffer from conditions (*e.g.*, severe mental illness) that make them incapable of being deterred by the threat of punishment. As punishment is only justified in a utilitarian system if it will result in a net reduction of pain in the form of crime, the imposition of punishment on an undeterrable person represents an unnecessary evil. Therefore, excuse defenses should be recognized in those circumstances in which the threat of punishment will not serve its legitimate purpose. This argument is weak, however. Even if a person cannot be deterred by the threat of punishment, the *actual* infliction of punishment may have the positive effect of taking a dangerous person off the street; and punishment of an undeterrable person may serve as a useful object lesson for other, *deterrable* individuals.

b. Retributive Argument

Excuses defenses are more easily defended on retributive grounds: "to blame a person is to express a moral criticism, and if the person's action does not deserve criticism, blaming him is a kind of falsehood and is, to the extent the person is injured by being blamed, unjust to him." Sanford H. Kadish. *Excusing Crime*, 75 Calif. L. Rev. 257, 264 (1987). That is, there are circumstances in which our moral intuitions suggest that a person should not be blamed for his wrongful actions—that the wrongdoer does not deserve blame and condemnation. Blame in a retributive system assumes that the actor freely chose to commit the wrong, so excuses are recognized when we are prepared to say that the person's free choice was significantly undermined, either by internal factors (such as mental illness) or external ones (coercive conditions).

B. Justification versus Excuse

A justification defense tends to focus on the wrongfulness of an *act* or a result; an excuse defense focuses on the *actor*. The distinction between the two categories of defenses—justifications and excuses—is an important one. It makes a considerable difference to say that an outcome, such as the death of another person, is good (or, at least, not bad), as with a claim of self-defense, as distinguished from the claim that the result of the defendant's conduct was wrong, but that we believe that the defendant should not be blamed for her wrongful conduct. Sometimes, as well, this distinction will have practical significance in the courtroom.

II. Duress

A. Rationale of the Defense: Justification or Excuse?

1. Duress as a Justification Defense

A few courts and treatises treat duress as if it were sub-species of the necessity defense and, thus, as a justification defense. That is, when a person is forced to commit a crime, the duress exculpates her on the ground that she did the right thing—the lesser of two evils—in light of the coercive threat. According to this view, the only meaningful difference between necessity and duress is that the former defense involves natural, *i.e.*, non-human, pressures (*e.g.*, starvation requiring a person to steal; weather-based emergencies, such as a tornado requiring a person to trespass on land; and health-based emergencies, such as appendicitis requiring a violation of traffic laws to get to the hospital), whereas duress involves human-based threats (*e.g.*, a terrorist demanding an innocent person to commit a crime against other innocent persons; a criminal forcing an innocent person to rob a bank).

2. Duress as an Excuse Defense

Most courts and treatises treat duress as an excuse defense, and not as a justification defense. Intuitively, most people believe that a coerced person (based on the definition of duress discussed below) is morally blameless, but not that she has done nothing wrong. The essence of the duress defense is that a person is not to blame for her conduct if, because of an unlawful threat, she lacked a fair opportunity to conform her conduct to the law.

Example: Coercer (C) threatens to cut off *D*'s finger and gouge out his left eye unless *D* rapes *V*. *D* succumbs to the threat. If *D* is acquitted of rape on the ground of duress, it is not because the jury has balanced the relative harms and concluded that *D*'s finger and eye are more deserving of societal protection than *V*'s bodily integrity. Instead, *D*'s acquittal would be based on the proposition that, in light of *C*'s unlawful threat, the person to blame for the social harm caused is *C*, and not *D*.

B. Common Law

1. Elements of Defense

Generally speaking, a defendant will be acquitted of an offense *other than murder* on the basis of duress if she proves that she committed the offense because: (a) another person unlawfully threatened imminently to kill or grievously injure her or another person unless she committed the crime; and (b) she is not at fault in exposing herself to the threat.

2. Breaking Down the Components

a. Nature of the Threat

i. Deadly Force
Notice that the common law duress defense is very narrow. The excuse only applies if the coercer threatens to use deadly force (force likely to cause death or serious bodily injury). A lesser threat, such as to cause minor physical injury or to cause economic or reputational harm, will not excuse.

ii. Imminency
The deadly force threatened must be "present, imminent, and impending" (as some courts have put it). These words suggest

that the threat must be operational on the actor's will at the time of the criminal act. And, the requirement of imminency effectively means that the coerced actor had no reasonable, lawful alternative to acceding to the threat.

iii. Reasonable Belief
Although few cases speak to the issue (in large part because the issue rarely arises), the defendant's actions must be based on a reasonable belief that the coercer is serious about the threat and has the capacity to inflict the harm immediately.

b. Non–Fault of Defendant
This element is also rarely raised, although courts often mention it as an element.

Example: D joins a terrorist organization, with knowledge of its activities and tenets. Later, she is ordered by leaders of the organization to rob a bank to obtain funds for their terrorist activities. She refuses, but accedes to the threat when the leaders threaten to kill her child. Because she knowingly joined the organization, D will not be excused if she claims duress.

3. Coerced Homicides
The common law duress defense does not apply to the offense of murder. *E.g., People v. Anderson*, 28 Cal.4th 767, 122 Cal. Rptr.2d 587, 50 P.2d 368 (2002); *Regina v. Howe*, [1987] 1 App. Cas. 417 (House of Lords).

a. Rationale
The no-defense rule is sometimes defended on the utilitarian ground that the drive for self-preservation, although strong, is not irresistible; therefore, people should be persuaded (by the threat of punishment) to resist such coercion. The rule is also defended on the moral ground that it is better to die than to kill an innocent person. However, this latter argument only serves to show that a person is not *justified* in killing an innocent person. It does not explain why a coerced actor should not be *excused* on the ground that virtually anyone, short of a saintly hero, might succumb to the coercion.

4. Intolerable Prison Conditions

a. The Issue
Some casebooks raise this special issue: Suppose a prisoner is threatened by another inmate with sexual or physical assault, is

denied critical medical care by prison officials, or is placed in some other intolerable condition. Therefore, the inmate escapes confinement. Later, she is caught and, of course, returned to prison. But, she is now prosecuted for the felony offense of prison escape. The inmate wishes to avoid conviction by arguing that she fled as a result of the intolerable prison condition. The frequently litigated issue is whether the inmate may make such a claim in court; and, if she may, is her claim one of necessity (justification) or excuse (duress)?

b. The Law

Originally, courts did not permit inmates to raise prison conditions as a defense to their escape. Today most courts recognize a limited defense. Some courts, however, require the escapee to turn herself in after the escape, once the prison condition "has lost its coercive force," or else the defense is lost. *United States v. Bailey*, 444 U.S. 394, 100 S.Ct. 624, 62 L.Ed.2d 575 (1980). Other courts are more lenient and treat's an escapee's failure to turn herself in as one factor to be considered by the jury in determining whether the escapee should be acquitted. *People v. Unger*, 66 Ill.2d 333, 5 Ill. Dec. 848, 362 N.E.2d 319 (1977). Some states will not recognize the defense if the prisoner uses any violence against other persons during the escape.

c. Nature of the Defense

Courts are fairly evenly divided on the question of whether the defense claim is basically one of duress or necessity.

  i. Conceptual Problems

  The escape cases do not neatly fit either defense. Escape cases are unlike typical *duress* claims, in that nobody ordered the prisoner to commit the crime of escape. Also, the decision to escape usually is a deliberate one, involving planning and more free choice than is typical in duress cases. But, neither do these cases usually fit the paradigm of *necessity*: many cases involve human threats, rather than natural ones; moreover, the inmate may not be claiming that escaping was the right thing to do from a societal perspective, but rather that she should not be blamed for escaping under the circumstances.

  ii. Practical Significance

  The duress-versus-necessity, excuse-versus-justification issue is a matter of practical significance.

Examples: Inmate Bill fears an imminent sexual assault by another inmate. Bill receives help in his escape from Inmate Charley. Assume Bill will be acquitted. Is Charley guilty of any crime for assisting in the escape? As you will see later, Charley is an accomplice, but if he was an accomplice in a *justified* act (because Bill gets a defense of necessity), Charley should be acquitted. If Charley was an accomplice in an *excused* act (Bill gets a duress defense), the law should punish him, on the ground that the excuse that exculpates Bill does not apply to Charley, who was not threatened with sexual assault.

What if Inmate Bill in the last hypothetical is confronted by a guard during the escape. Does the guard have the right to prevent Bill from escaping? Common sense suggests that the answer is "Of course!" But, if Bill is *justified* in escaping, does it make sense to say that the guard is justified in stopping Bill? If the inmate is only *excused* for the escape, the guard's right to stop the escape (and even use force in the process) is clear.

C. Model Penal Code

1. Defense

The Model Penal Code duress defense (§ 2.09) unambiguously treats duress as an excuse, and not a justification, defense. Thus, the defense may be raised although the defendant did not commit the lesser of two evils. Instead, the defendant must show that: (a) he committed an offense because he was coerced to do so by another person's use, or threat to use, unlawful force against him or a third party; and (b) a person of reasonable firmness would have committed the offense. The Code further provides that the defense is lost if the coerced actor put himself in a situation "in which it was probable that he would be subjected to duress." Furthermore, if he was negligent in placing himself in the situation, the defense is unavailable if he is prosecuted for an offense for which negligence is sufficient to prove guilt.

2. Breaking Down the Components

The Code version of duress is broader than the common law.

a. Nature of the Coercion

Neither the "deadly threat" nor imminency requirements of the common law apply here. It is enough that the coerced used, or threatened to use, any form of unlawful *physical* coercion. (As with the common law, economic and reputational threats do not qualify.)

i. Threat or Use

Notice that the Code permits a duress claim to be based on prior use of force, and not simply a threat of future harm.

Example: Battered woman Alice robs a bank when batterer-husband Harold orders her to do so. Even if Harold issues no threat in this case, Alice may be able to claim duress based on her fear of Harold as a result of his *prior* use of force.

ii. Unlawfulness of Threat or Force

Notice that the force used or threatened, as at common law, must be unlawful. This means that the duress defense, as at common law, is limited to human-caused coercion, because natural threats (*e.g.* a tornado) are not capable of being characterized as unlawful.

iii. Reasonable Firmness Standard

Although any type of threat or use of force can trigger a duress claim, the defendant will not be excused unless a person of reasonable firmness would also have acceded to the threat. This shifts the issue to the jury to put themselves in the shoes of the defendant.

3. Coerced Homicides

Unlike the common law, there is no bar to use of the duress defense in murder prosecutions. It is up to the jury to decide whether, in view of the facts of the particular case including the nature of the threat or force used by the coercer, a person of reasonable firmness would have killed an innocent person.

III. Intoxication

A. Common Law: Voluntary Intoxication

When may a person avoid conviction of an offense because he voluntarily became intoxicated? The answer (not surprisingly) is, "not often."

1. Definition of "Intoxication"

The criminal law of "intoxication" is not limited to ingestion of alcohol. Intoxication may be defined as a disturbance of an actor's mental or physical capacities resulting from the ingestion of *any* foreign substance, most notably alcohol or drugs (including lawfully prescribed medication). See MPC § 2.08(5).

2. Not an Excuse Defense

A person is never *excused* for his criminal conduct on the ground that he became voluntarily intoxicated. Indeed, because intoxicants tend to reduce a person's ability to control his aggressive feelings or antisocial impulses, intoxication serves as an "anti-defense." The act of getting intoxicated enhances, rather than mitigates, culpability.

3. *Mens Rea* Defense

Although voluntary intoxication is *not* an excuse for criminal conduct, most jurisdictions following the common law provide that a person is not guilty of a *specific-intent* offense if, as the result of voluntary intoxication, he lacked the capacity or otherwise failed to form the specific intent required for the crime. However, voluntary intoxication does *not* exculpate for general-intent offenses.

Example: D, severely intoxicated, attempts to have intercourse with V, but is arrested before consummating the act. D is prosecuted for assault with intent to commit rape. If D can show at trial that, due to intoxication, he honestly but unreasonably believed that V was consenting, he is entitled to acquittal because he lacked the specific intent to rape (*i.e.*, he did not intend to have nonconsensual intercourse). On the other hand, if D had completed the sexual act, he would *not* be entitled to acquittal of the general-intent crime of rape!

a. Rationale

Notice that the reasoning for exculpation is the same as with claims of mistake-of-fact: it is not that the defendant is excused for his actions, but rather that the prosecutor has failed to prove an essential element of the offense charged, namely, *mens rea*.

b. Exceptions to Rule

A minority of states today have statutes that bar a defendant from introducing evidence of voluntary intoxication to avoid conviction for any offense, including specific-intent offenses. Although such laws are unfair because they deny the defendant the right to prove that, in fact, he lacked a required element of the offense, the Supreme Court, by a 5–4 vote, has upheld the constitutionality of such laws, at least in the one case it has considered so far. *Montana v. Egelhoff*, 518 U.S. 37, 116 S.Ct. 2013, 135 L.Ed.2d 361 (1996).

4. "Temporary" Insanity

Sometimes a defendant would like to claim he was "temporarily insane" at the time of the crime. "Insanity," however, presupposes a mental illness and not mere voluntary intoxication. Therefore, a defendant is *not* entitled to argue that, due to voluntary intoxication (rather than mental illness), he did not know right from wrong, or did not know what he was doing at the time of the offense, although such a mental state *would* result in acquittal on *insanity* grounds if he suffered from a mental illness.

5. "Fixed" Insanity

Long-term use of alcohol or drugs can cause brain damage or cause the individual to suffer from chronic mental illness. In such circumstances, the defendant who seeks acquittal is not claiming he should be exculpated because he was voluntarily intoxicated at the time of the crime, but rather that, because of long-term use of intoxicants, he is insane (whether he is currently sober or intoxicated). Such a claim *is* recognized by the common law, but the applicable defense is insanity, and not intoxication.

B. Model Penal Code: "Self–Induced" (Voluntary) Intoxication

The MPC does not distinguish between "general intent" and "specific intent" offenses. As discussed earlier, the Code generally requires the prosecutor to prove a specific state of mind as to each material element of a crime. Therefore, subject to one exception, voluntary intoxication is a defense to any crime, if it negates an element of the offense. MPC § 2.08

1. Exception to General Rule

If the defendant is charged with an offense for which recklessness suffices to convict, she cannot avoid conviction by proving that, because of intoxication, she was unaware of the riskiness of her conduct. MPC § 2.08(2). That is, even if the defendant's actual culpability is that of negligence—she *should have been aware* that her conduct created a substantial and unjustifiable risk of harm—she may be convicted of an offense requiring recklessness (which ordinarily requires *actual awareness* of the risk), if the reason for her failure to perceive the risk is her self-induced intoxication.

Example: D, severely intoxicated, drives her car dangerously at a high rate of speed, weaving between lanes, resulting in the unintended death of *V. D* was so intoxicated she did not realize she was speeding and weaving, although she should have been aware. Thus, *D* negligently killed *V* (the offense of negligent homicide under the MPC). However, under § 2.08(2), she may be convicted of a *reckless* form of homicide (manslaughter, in the MPC). In essence, her recklessness in getting intoxicated is transferred to the homicide.

C. Involuntary Intoxication

The law is more lenient in regard to persons who commit crimes as a result of *involuntary* intoxication (or what the MPC calls "non-self-induced" intoxication).

1. What Makes Intoxication Involuntary?

True cases of involuntary intoxication are extremely rare. Intoxication is involuntary if: (a) *coercion*: the actor is forced to ingest the intoxicant, such as when he is made to take a narcotic by gunpoint; (b) *mistake*: the actor innocently ingests an intoxicant, such as when the person takes food that, without his knowledge, was spiked with a narcotic; (c) *prescribed medication*: the actor becomes unexpectedly intoxicated from ingestion of a medically prescribed drug, perhaps due to an allergic reaction; or (d) *pathological intoxication*: the actor's intoxication is "grossly excessive in degree, given the amount of intoxicant, to which the actor does not know he is susceptible." MPC § 2.08(5)(c).

2. When Does Involuntary Intoxication Exculpate?

a. Lack of *Mens Rea*

The defendant will be acquitted if, as a result of involuntary intoxication, the actor lacks the requisite mental state of the offense for which she was charged, whether the offense could be denominated as specific-intent or general-intent. This is the common law and MPC rule. MPC § 2.08(1).

b. "Temporary Insanity"

Unlike the rule with voluntary intoxication, a defendant *will* be exculpated on the ground of "temporary insanity" if, due to involuntary intoxication rather than mental illness, she otherwise satisfies the jurisdiction's insanity test (*e.g.*, she did not know right from wrong, or did not understand what she was doing, because of involuntary intoxication). This is the common law and Model Penal Code rule. MPC § 2.08(4).

IV. Insanity

CONVERSATION WITH STUDENTS

The insanity defense is the most controversial defense in the criminal law, yet it is one of the most ancient. Especially when a person is acquitted on insanity grounds in a high-profile case—such as when John Hinckley was acquitted on grounds of insanity in the attempted assassination of President Ronald Reagan in the 1980s—there are public calls for abolition of the defense. Today, four states *have* abolished the defense (although those states *do* permit a defendant to introduce evidence of mental illness to prove that she did not possess the required *mens rea* for the crime).

What makes the controversy around the defense so interesting is that there are critics of the defense—abolitionists—among both political liberals (we might call them dove abolitionists) and conservatives (hawk abolitionists). The liberals feel that a defense based on mental illness should not be recognized because other persons, with supposedly equal moral claims for acquittal (for example, people who commit crimes because they were brought up in a terrible social environment), are not provided a defense. Conservatives believe that the insanity defense is too easy to raise and too difficult to refute, so it is abused by undeserving persons.

Another interesting feature overlaying the defense is the disparate approaches of lawyers and mental health professionals to matters of mental illness. Psychiatrists, as scientists, tend to look for causal explanations for criminal conduct, which leads them to the actor's environment (such as parental upbringing or abusive treatment) or genetic predispositions to crime, away from the "free will" premise of the criminal law. They believe that persons with mental illness should be treated, not punished, and they consider it odd to talk about "justice" when dealing with "sickness." Therefore, there is a never-ending tension between the law and psychiatry, and the proper role of juries versus experts, in deciding guilt or innocence.

One last point: Do *not* confuse "mental illness" with "insanity." The first is a medical term, the second is a legal concept. A person is not insane unless he is mentally ill; but a person can be mentally ill without being insane.

A. Rationale of Defense

1. Utilitarian Argument

A person who suffers from a severe cognitive or volitional disorder, *i.e.*, a disorder that undermines the actor's ability to perceive reality (cognition) or to control her conduct (volition), is undeterrable by the threat of punishment. Therefore, punishment is inefficacious.

a. Counter–Arguments

i. Specific Deterrence

The *threat* of punishment will not deter the undeterrable, but a person's undeterrability demonstrates her dangerousness. Therefore, the *infliction* of punishment by incapacitation is justified. Consequently, the defense should be abolished.

ii. General Deterrence

Although the threat of punishment may not deter the insane person, her actual punishment can serve as a warning to *sane* people who might otherwise believe (correctly or not) that they could escape punishment by feigning mental illness.

2. Retributive Argument

The insanity defense distinguishes the mad from the bad; it separates those whom we consider evil from those whom we consider sick. A person is not a moral agent, and thus is not fairly subject to moral condemnation, if she lacked the capacity to make a rational choice to violate the law or if she lacks the capacity to control her conduct.

B. The *M'Naghten* Test of Insanity

There are various common law definitions of insanity. The first significant test of insanity was announced by the British House of Lords in *M'Naghten's Case*, 8 Eng. Rep. 718 (1843). It has been heavily criticized. Nonetheless, it quickly became the overwhelming rule in the United States. Criticism of it began to cut into support for the rule in the 1960s and 1970s. Many jurisdictions during this period abandoned *M'Naghten*, the narrowest insanity test, for the broader Model Penal Code approach discussed below. Indeed, for a brief period in the 1980s, the *M'Naghten* test became a minority rule. However, John Hinckley's insanity acquittal in the Reagan attempted assassination case, turned the tide, and many courts returned to *M'Naghten*. *M'Naghten* is again the majority rule.

1. Rule

A person is legally insane if, at the time of the act, he was laboring under such a defect of reason, from disease of the mind, as: (1) not to know the nature and quality of the act he was doing; or, (2), if he did know it, that he did not know what he was doing was wrong.

Examples: D1, mentally ill, believes that he is killing a wild animal when he actually is killing a human being. *D1* is insane because he does not know the nature and quality of his act. Notice, however, that this example would also qualify under the second prong of *M'Naghten*: because *D1* does not realize he is killing a human being, he presumably does not realize he is doing something wrong. Also notice that in this example, independent of the insanity claim, *D1* should be able to avoid conviction for intent-to-kill murder, since *D1* did not intend to kill a human being.

D2, mentally ill, kills *V*, whom *D2* believes (due to paranoid delusions) is about to kill him. Here, *D2* arguably knows the nature and quality of his act—that he is killing another human being—but does not realize that this killing is wrong (because he thinks he is acting in self-defense). Therefore, he may be insane under the second prong of *M'Naghten*.

2. Clarification of the Rule

a. "Know" versus "Appreciate"

Although the *M'Naghten* test originally was phrased in terms of whether the defendant "knew" the nature and quality of his action or "knew" right from wrong, many jurisdictions now use the word "appreciate." "Appreciate" is a word intended to convey a deeper, or broader, sense of understanding than simple "knowledge." A small child may "know" he is pointing a gun at another person, and "know" that shooting a person will cause the other person to "die," and know that killing a person is "wrong." But, that child is not likely to "appreciate" the significance of his actions in a deeper sense. He may see the action in cartoon fashion—he may not realize that "death" is permanent, and will not appreciate in any meaningful way the devastation he is causing. Just as a youth (due to age) may, therefore, lack appreciation of his actions, a mentally ill adult may also lack this deeper sense of what he is doing. Some jurisdictions, therefore, will not find a person sane—accountable for his actions—unless he has this deeper appreciation of what he is doing, and right from wrong.

b. "Right/Wrong" Prong

Courts have split fairly evenly on whether this prong refers to legal or moral wrongfulness. However, in jurisdictions that use the "moral wrong" test, the relevant issue is *not* whether the defendant believed that his act was morally right, but rather when he knew (or appreciated) that *society* considered his actions morally wrong. In most cases, the distinction between "moral wrong" and "legal wrong" will not matter, but sometimes it does.

Example: D stabbed his wife while she was asleep. According to psychiatric testimony a trial, D delusionally believed that he had a "privileged relationship" with God, that he was in direct communication with God, and that it was his divine mission to kill his wife. D knew that his actions were contrary to law, but he believed that his actions were morally justified in view of God's wishes. In a "legal wrong" jurisdiction, D is not insane. In a "moral wrong"state, the fact that D thought he was acting properly would not be the key. Instead, the jury would need to know this: did D believe that *society* would view his actions as proper? If D thought, for example, "people will applaud my actions because they realize I am God's messenger," he is legally insane.

i.   Deific–Decree Rule
     A few jurisdictions provide that a person who commits a crime because he believes that God has literally *commanded* him to do so is legally insane, even if he knows that the law and society condemn the act. *E.g., State v. Crenshaw*, 98 Wash.2d 789, 659 P.2d 488 (1983). Other courts, however, simply view a "deific decree" delusion as a factor in assessing a person's cognitive capacity to distinguish right from wrong.

3.   Criticisms of *M'Naghten*

a.   Outmoded
     The test, developed at a very primitive time in our understanding of the human mind, focuses exclusively on cognition. Under *M'Naghten*, a person is sane if he knows what he is doing and knows that what he is doing is wrong, even if he cannot control his conduct, *i.e.*, even if he suffers from a volitional disorder and, therefore, is undeterrable.

b.   "Know"/"Appreciate"
     Jurisdictions that use the word "know" apply a test that essentially recognizes no degrees of cognitive disability. It results in a finding of sanity—and moral condemnation—of persons whose cognitive capacities are substantially but not totally undermined.

c. **Expert Testimony Hampered**

Because the test is so narrow and so outdated (see above), psychiatrists may be prevented from giving the jury—the ultimate factfinders—the type of information needed to determine whether the defendant deserves blame and punishment.

C. The "Irresistible Impulse" ("Control") Test of Insanity

In an effort to go beyond the narrow cognitive-based *M'Naghten* rule, some states apply *M'Naghten*, but supplement it with a volition-based "irresistible impulse" test.

1. Rule

The precise wording of the test varies by jurisdiction. In general, this supplement to *M'Naghten* provides that a person is insane if, as the result of mental illness or defect, she "acted with an irresistible and uncontrollable impulse," *Commonwealth v. Rogers*, 48 Mass. 500 (1844), or if she "lost the power to choose between . . . right and wrong, and to avoid doing the act in question, as that [her] free agency was at the time destroyed." *Parson v. State*, 81 Ala. 577, 2 So. 854 (1887).

2. Criticisms of the Test

a. **All-or-Nothing Feature**

As the versions of the test set out above suggest, if taken literally, a defendant's ability to control herself must be totally lacking, a standard virtually impossible to satisfy.

b. **The "Impulse" Element**

The test seems to require proof that the defendant's conduct was impulsive. As such, it would exclude from its coverage a person who (due to mental disease) plans a crime, but who is otherwise unable to control her actions. Many courts, however, do not seem to apply this concept as literally as it seems.

c. **Reliability of Proof**

Some critics, including the influential American Psychiatric Association, assert that the mental health profession is not at the point that it can reliably distinguish between a person who *cannot* control her conduct and one who simply *does not* control it. Thus, the APA has recommended that states not include a volitional prong in the definition of insanity.

D. The "Product" (*Durham*) Test of Insanity

The "product" test originated in the nineteenth century but received little attention until the influential District of Columbia federal circuit court announced its landmark decision, *Durham v. United States*, 214 F.2d 862 (D.C. Cir. 1954). Twenty years later, the same court overruled *Durham*. *United States v. Brawner*, 471 F.2d 969 (D.C. Cir. 1972). Only one state currently applies a version of this test.

1. Rule

A person is excused if his unlawful act was the product of a mental disease or defect. As subsequently defined by the D.C. Circuit, "mental disease or defect" is "any abnormal condition of the mind which substantially affects mental or emotional processes and substantially impairs behavior controls." *McDonald v. United States*, 312 F.2d 847 (D.C. Cir. 1962). Thus, to be acquitted according to this rule, two matters must be proved: the defendant suffered from a mental disease or defect at the time of the crime; and, but for the mental disease or defect, he would not have committed the crime.

Example: D suffers from a mental illness. As a result of this illness, D believes that V is his arch enemy. Therefore, weighing his choices, D kills V. At the time of the crime, D knew what he was doing, knew that the law and society would consider his actions wrongful, and he experienced no irresistible impulse to kill V. Therefore, under *M'Naghten* or that test supplemented by the "control" standard, D is sane. Under *Durham*, however, D is not guilty by reason of insanity: there is a but-for causal connection between D's mental illness and the crime.

2. Support for the Test

Mental health professionals preferred this test. It focused attention on the actor's mental illness; they expected the test would channel sick persons into the mental health arena, rather than into prisons. Likewise, mental health professionals expected the test to permit them to testify more freely, without the need to fit their testimony within *M'Naghten*'s artificial cognitive prongs, or to testify regarding elusive irresistible impulses.

3. Criticisms of the Test

a. Penological Arguments

The test is unwise. It will result in acquittal of persons who could be deterred by the threat of punishment. It will also result in exculpation of some persons with sufficient capacity for free choice that they deserve condemnation. Indeed, if one looks at the *Example* above, there is no reason to believe that *D*'s mental illness made him (or others like him) undeterrable; and the fact that *D* considered his options—to kill or not to kill, knowing full well that his contemplated actions were legally and morally wrong—suggests he had sufficient free will to merit condemnation and be held responsible for his actions.

> #### b. Psychiatric Influence
> The product test gave experts too much influence, according to critics. A defense psychiatrist would testify that the defendant had a mental illness and that it caused the outcome. The prosecution would put on competing psychiatric testimony (the defendant did not have a mental illness, or he had one but it did not cause the crime). There was nothing left for the jury, the representatives of the moral views of the community, to decide except as to which expert's testimony to believe.

E. Model Penal Code Test of Insanity

1. Rule
The MPC test represents a broadened version of the *M'Naghten* and irresistible impulse tests. With modifications, it retains the second prong of *M'Naghten* and adds to it a volitional prong. MPC § 4.01 provides that is person is not responsible for her conduct if, at the time of the criminal act, as the result of a mental disease or defect (a term left undefined), she lacked the substantial capacity either: (1) to appreciate the criminality (or, in the alternative, wrongfulness) of her actions; or (2) to conform her conduct to the dictates of the law.

2. Closer Analysis

> #### a. Avoiding All-or-Nothing Judgments
> Both MPC prongs are modified by the phrase "lacks *substantial* capacity." This avoids the criticism of the original tests, namely, that they could be interpreted to require proof of total cognitive or volitional incapacity.

> #### b. Cognitive Prong
> Two points are noteworthy. First, the Code uses the word "appreciate" rather than *M'Naghten*'s "know," to permit the deeper, fuller

analysis discussed above. Second, the drafters chose not to decide between "legal wrong" and "moral wrong": they invited legislators, in adopting the Code provision, to choose between the words "criminality" (legal wrong) and "wrongfulness" (moral wrong). Much as with the common law of *M'Naghten*, states applying the MPC have divided fairly evenly between these options

c. Volitional Prong

This prong is phrased to avoid the undesirable or potentially misleading words "irresistible" and "impulse." A person who has a very strong, but not irresistible, desire to commit a crime, including one who acts non-impulsively after considerable thought, can fall within the language of the MPC.

V. Diminished Capacity

A. Putting "Diminished Capacity" in Context

Few terms in the criminal law cause more confusion than that of "diminished capacity." Some of the confusion lies in the fact that the term "diminished capacity" is used by courts to describe two different categories of cases in which a person suffering from a mental disability—but one less severe that would entitle the person to successfully assert a defense of insanity—may be partially (or, rarely, fully) exculpated for his criminal conduct.

1. *Mens Rea* Version

A defendant may raise a claim of "diminished capacity" in order to show that he lacked the requisite *mens rea* for an offense. In that manner, "diminished capacity" works like mistake-of-fact or voluntary intoxication—it does not excuse the wrongdoer, but serves to show that the prosecutor has failed to prove an essential element of an offense.

2. Partial Responsibility Version

"Diminished capacity" may also serve as a highly controversial excuse defense, used exclusively in criminal homicide prosecutions, as a basis for reducing the severity of the offense. For purposes of clarity, this version of diminished capacity will be characterized as a "partial responsibility" claim.

B. Diminished Capacity and *Mens Rea*

A sane person may suffer from a mental disability (*e.g.*, mental illness, mental retardation, Alzheimer's) that arguably prevents him from forming the mental state required for the commission of an offense.

Examples: D1 pushes V1 to the ground, with the purpose of having intercourse with V1. D1 is arrested before intercourse. D1 is charged with assault with intent to commit rape. He claims that due to a mental disability, he believed (albeit quite irrationally) that, after he pushed V1 to the ground, she wanted intercourse.

D2 has nonconsensual intercourse with V2. D2 is charged with rape of V2. D2 claims that due to mental retardation, he thought that V2 had consented to the intercourse. Therefore, he claims, he lacked the intent to have *nonconsensual* intercourse with V2.

1. Model Penal Code Approach

As a matter of logic, a defendant should be acquitted of any offense for which he lacked the requisite *mens rea*, including those cases in which he lacked the mental state because of a mental disability, whether that disability is permanent or temporary. This is the position taken by the Model Penal Code. MPC § 4.02(1).

Examples: In the examples above, if D1's claim is believed by the jury, D1 lacked the intent (or, in MPC language, purpose) to rape V1. Therefore, D1 cannot be convicted of the offense charged, but is guilty of assault, a lesser-included offense.

If D2's claim is accepted, he is not guilty of rape or any other offense that requires proof that he intended to have nonconsensual sexual relations.

2. Common Law

Logic notwithstanding, most states permit evidence of an abnormal mental condition, *if at all*, in order to negate the *specific* intent in a specific-intent offense. Psychiatric evidence is inadmissible in the prosecution of general-intent offenses. A minority of jurisdictions do not permit diminished capacity to be claimed in *any* case.

Examples: In the examples above, D1, charged with a specific-intent offense, will be permitted to put on evidence of his mental condition, whereas D2 will be barred because rape is a general-intent offense.

a. Reasons for Judicial Hostility

i. Doubts About the Sophistication of Psychiatric Testimony

Some courts believe that "the finely differentiated psychiatric concepts associated with diminished capacity demands a sophisticated (or as critics would maintain, a sophistic bent) that jurors . . . ordinarily have not developed." *State v. Wilcox*, 70 Ohio St.2d 182, 436 N.E.2d 523 (1982). In essence, psychiatrists may be able to assist jurors when the defendant's claim is that of insanity, but when the claim relates to the more fine-tuned issue of whether the defendant did or did not form a specific intent, these courts doubt that psychiatrists are capable of providing the needed insight.

ii. **Doubts About the Need for the Defense**

Some courts reason that mentally abnormal offenders will almost always possess the requisite criminal intent. Indeed, it is easier to prove insanity than it is to show inability to form a specific intent: a person may not appreciate the gravity of his actions or be unable to conform his actions to the law, *i.e.,* be insane, but he still will almost always have the requisite intent. Indeed, anyone whose mental condition truly renders him incapable of entertaining the requisite intent is likely to be suffering from a mental condition that will also establish his insanity. Therefore, the defense is essentially unnecessary; psychiatric testimony should be limited to matters relating to insanity.

iii. **Post-trial Implications**

A person found not guilty by reason of insanity is typically committed to a mental institution on the basis of the acquittal; a finding of diminished capacity does not provide that assurance. Therefore, neither the defendant nor society is benefitted.

iv. **Specific–Intent versus General–Intent**

Courts that limit diminished capacity claims to specific-intent offenses rarely explain why the defense does not apply to general-intent offenses. The reason appears to be that with specific-intent offenses, there usually is a lesser, general-intent offense for which the defendant may be convicted; with general-intent offenses, however, the defense would often result in outright acquittal, an outcome that "would open the door to consequences which could seriously affect our society." *Chestnut v. State*, 538 So.2d 820 (Fla. 1989). In order to avoid "arbitrary applications of the law" on the basis of the "nebulous distinction" between general- and specific-intent, some courts prefer to disallow the defense in *both* circumstances.

C. Partial Responsibility

1. Common Law

In this country, the partial defense was originated by the California Supreme Court, and adopted by a small number of other courts. In general, a person who commits a criminal homicide and suffers from some mental illness or abnormality short of insanity may have her offense reduced because of her diminished mental capacity. States that recognize the partial-responsibility claim usually permit reduction of the offense from first-degree to second-degree murder, or from murder to manslaughter. The underlying rationale of the partial responsibility doctrine is that a person who does not meet a jurisdiction's definition of insanity, but who suffers from a mental abnormality, is less deserving of punishment than a killer who acts with a normal state of mind. Therefore, she should be convicted of a lesser offense. The originator of the defense—California—has since abolished it by statute. Cal. Pen. Code § 28(b).

2. Model Penal Code

The Code provides that a homicide that would otherwise be murder is reduced to manslaughter if the homicide was the result of "extreme mental or emotional disturbance for which there is a reasonable explanation or excuse." MPC § 210.3(1)(b). This language is intended to cover two types of cases: (a) it broadens the scope of the common law provocation doctrine (a topic discussed later in this Outline); and (b) it permits courts to recognize a partial responsibility defense.

VI. Entrapment

A. Overview

Entrapment issues arise when law enforcement agencies use undercover police officers to investigate crimes. Most commonly, undercover officers are used in the investigation and prosecution of so-called victimless crimes, such as prostitution or drug offenses, in which it is unlikely a victim will come forward and report that he or she has been harmed. Undercover officers are also used to infiltrate groups suspected of organized crime or, today, terrorism. Sometimes undercover officers get sufficiently involved in criminal activities—suggest crime to suspects or participate in them—that courts become concerned that the police have gone too far. The issue is how far may the police go in such undercover activity. And, over time, two different approaches have developed, one called the "subjective" approach, which is followed in federal courts and many state courts; the other is the "objective" approach followed by some states.

B. Subjective Test

1. Origins of the Test

In 1932, in *Sorrells v. United States*, 287 U.S. 435, 53 S.Ct. 210, 77 L.Ed. 413 (1932), the Supreme Court recognized a defense of entrapment, applicable in the federal courts. The defense articulated in that case, and reaffirmed in *Sherman v. United States*, 356 U.S. 369, 78 S.Ct. 819, 2 L.Ed.2d 848 (1958), and *United States v. Russell*, 411 U.S. 423, 93 S.Ct. 1637, 36 L.Ed.2d 366 (1973), is commonly called the "subjective" test of entrapment because it focuses on the mental state of the defendant.

2. Test

Entrapment is proved if the government agent implants in the mind of an innocent person the disposition to commit the alleged offense and induces its commission in order that the government may prosecute.

Example: In *Sorrells, supra*, a government agent posing as a tourist, befriended S by claiming to be a member of the same military division in which S had served. Thereafter, the agent attempted to convince S to sell him whiskey, in violation of the National Prohibition Act. S initially refused, but on the third request he sold the agent a one-half gallon jug of "bootleg" liquor. The Court held that S was entrapped as a matter of law: S "had no previous disposition to commit [the criminal act] but was an industrious, law-abiding citizen . . . lured . . . to its commission by repeated and persistent solicitation."

a. Innocent Persons versus Unwary Criminals

According to the Supreme Court in *Sherman, supra*, the police may employ "artifice and stratagem" to trap an unwary criminal, but it is improper when a criminal design, originating with the government, is used to induce an innocent person.

b. Predisposition of the Defendant

Following the subjective test, entrapment is not proved if the government agent induces a "predisposed" person to commit the offense. A person is criminally "predisposed," if, when he is first approached by the government, he is ready and willing to commit the type of crime charged, should a favorable opportunity to do so present itself.

Examples: In *Russell, supra,* an undercover agent pretending to be a representative of a criminal organization interested in controlling the drug trade in the Pacific Northwest, offered to supply *R*, an illegal manufacturer of amphetamines, with a difficult-to-obtain chemical needed for the production of the drug. *R* agreed to the arrangement. The Court rejected *R's* claim that he was entrapped as a matter of law because *R* was predisposed to commit the type of offense for which he was charged; the government merely provided him with an opportunity to ply his illegal trade.

In contrast, in *Jacobson v. United States,* 503 U.S. 540, 112 S.Ct. 1535, 118 L.Ed.2d 174 (1992), *J* purchased child pornography at a time when it was legal to do so. After Congress made possession of such materials illegal, *J* became the 26–month target of various government agencies posing as fictitious private organizations, which mailed him materials intended to convince him that he had a moral and constitutional right to receive child pornography through the mail. Finally, one of the fictitious groups convinced *J* in a mailing to purchase such materials in violation of federal law. The Supreme Court held that the government action constituted entrapment as a matter of law. According to the Court, the fact that *J* had purchased such materials when it was legal was of little probative value in establishing predisposition to commit a now-illegal act. Therefore, for purposes of entrapment, *J* was "innocent" when the government first approached him.

3. Rationale of the Subjective Test

The Supreme Court justifies the subjective version of entrapment on the ground that Congress did not intend its criminal sanctions to be applied to innocent persons induced by government officials to commit criminal offenses.

a. Criticisms of the Subjective Test

i. Legislative Intent Argument is Fictional

There is no evidence that Congress ever considered the issue of entrapment when they drafted specific criminal statutes. Therefore, the stated justification of the rule is fictional.

ii. Unfairness of the Test

The "predisposition" element of the test is unfair because it permits a prosecutor to introduce otherwise inadmissible character and prior-crime evidence pertaining to the defendant—evidence that the defendant has committed crimes of the same sort in the past or otherwise is "a bad guy"—which prejudices the defendant in the jury's eyes.

iii. Inconsistent with Criminal Law Doctrine

A person who is acquitted according to this test has voluntarily committed the offense, albeit as the result of government inducements. An entrapped person has not been coerced to commit the offense, *i.e.*, no gun has figuratively or literally been placed at his head. If the same inducements had been offered to the defendant by a private party, he would have no defense, so why here?

C. "Objective" Test

1. Test

In states that apply this standard, the test is defined variously, but it generally seeks to determine whether, in Justice Frankfurter's words in *Sherman, supra*, "the police conduct falls below standards, to which common feelings respond for the proper use of government power."

Example: In one reported case, a large city police force attempted to induce female prostitutes to solicit their services by having non-uniformed male officers go into high-prostitution areas, stand in alleys, unzip their trousers, and expose themselves. Such conduct might constitute entrapment under the test stated immediately above, even though the prostitutes were "predisposed."

a. Variation on the Theme

Some states provide that entrapment only exists if the police conduct is sufficiently egregious that it would induce an ordinary law-abiding individual to commit the offense.

Example: In the prostitution case above, for example, it is implausible to argue that an ordinary law-abiding woman would be induced to solicit sex for money with a man under the circumstances described there, so no entrapment would be found.

2. Rationale of the Objective Test

a. Deterrence

The defense should be used to deter police overreaching. By acquitting an entrapped defendant, the police learn what police conduct society will not countenance. As a result, the police will be induced to behave more appropriately.

b. Judicial Integrity

Some argue that a court should protect "the purity of its own temple" by making sure that guilt is not proved by ignoble means. *Sorrells, supra.*

3. Criticisms of the Objective Test

a. Deterrence

The objective test is too vague to send a clear message to the police, particularly if the message comes in the form of a general jury verdict of acquittal in a criminal prosecution. Moreover, such deterrence as occurs comes at too great a cost because it results in the acquittal of predisposed—and thus culpable and dangerous—wrongdoers.

b. Judicial integrity

Critics argues that the public does not want judges to protect the "purity" of their "temple" at the expense of the safety of the community.

D. Procedural Aspects of "Entrapment"

Although entrapment is a criminal law defense, some jurisdictions (primarily those that apply the objective test) permit the defendant to raise the defense in a pre-trial hearing before a judge. If the judge determines that the defendant was entrapped, the prosecution is barred. No trial is held. In most jurisdictions, especially those that apply the majority subjective test, entrapment is treated like all other defenses: the defendant has the burden to raise the entrapment defense and present evidence in support of the claim at trial. If the factfinder determines that the defendant was entrapped, it brings back a not-guilty verdict.

E. Entrapment and the Due Process Clause

Although entrapment is not a constitutional doctrine, the Supreme Court has stated in dictum that police conduct could become so outrageous as to violate the Due Process Clause. More than once, however, the Supreme Court has refused to find a due process violation in entrapment-like circumstances.

Examples: In *Russell, supra,* the Court ruled that the Due Process Clause was not violated merely because the government furnished a lawful, but hard-to-obtain, chemical to an illegal manufacturer of amphetamines. The Court stated that the government was not inappropriately "enmeshed in the criminal activity."

In *Hampton v. United States*, 425 U.S. 484, 96 S.Ct. 1646, 48 L.Ed.2d 113 (1976), the Court rejected a due process claim where the police used an undercover agent to supply heroin to *H*, so that the latter could sell it to another undercover agent. Notice here that the government was involved in both the beginning and end of the transaction, but the Court said it did not offend due process!

VII. Review Questions

[Answers Provided in Appendix A, page 363]

1. T or F.   Justification defenses focus on the actor, excuses focus on the act committed.

2. How does the Model Penal Code version of the duress defense differ from the common law? Specify the differences.

3. T or F.   "Voluntary intoxication" is an excuse in the prosecution of a specific-intent offense.

4. At common law, in which one or more of the following cases will a defendant be acquitted on the ground of intoxication?

   a.   *D1* voluntarily ingests LSD, an hallucinogenic; as a result, she hallucinates that Bob, standing in front of her, is a dangerous polar bear; she shoots at Bob but misses. *D1* is charged with assault with intent to murder;

   b.   *D2* voluntarily ingests LSD; as a result he comes to irrationally believe that his wife, Carla, is trying to kill him, so *D2* purposely kills her "in self-defense"; or

   c.   The same as b., except that *D2* ingested the LSD innocently after someone put the hallucinogenic in his food.

5. How does the Model Penal Code differ from the common law in regard to voluntary intoxication?

6. Which test of insanity do (or did) mental health professionals prefer, and why?

7. Alice suffers from a mental illness that sometimes causes her to hallucinate. Alice, a tenant in Bob's apartment building, becomes incensed when he raises the rent on her apartment. Therefore, she plots to kill Bob the next time she is alone with him. A week later, when the opportunity arises, Alice kills Bob. Under which of the following insanity tests, if any, is Alice legally insane?

   a. *M'Naghten*;

   b. Control test;

   c. Product test; or

   d. None of the above.

8. David, an elderly man suffering from Alzheimer's disease, wanders into Bobbi's home one night, believing Bobbi's home is his own. David is charged with felony burglary, defined as "entering the dwelling house of another at night with the intent to commit a felony therein." The jurisdiction in which these events occurred also prohibits misdemeanor trespass, defined as "entering another's property." Based on this information, which of the following statements about diminished capacity is most correct according to the common law? (Ignore other possible defenses.)

   a. David suffers from diminished capacity and, therefore, is guilty of neither burglary nor trespass;

   b. David suffers from diminished capacity and, therefore, will be acquitted of burglary but is guilty of trespass;

   c. David suffers from diminished capacity, but is guilty of burglary; or

   d. Because Alzheimer's disease does not constitute a mental illness, David cannot claim diminished capacity.

9. T or F. The Model Penal Code does not recognize a diminished capacity defense.

10. Which test of entrapment, the subjective or the objective one, focuses on the predisposition of the defendant?

11. Which test of entrapment, the subjective or objective one, is based on concerns about police deterrence and judicial integrity?

*

PART EIGHT

Inchoate Conduct

■ *ANALYSIS*

CONVERSATION WITH STUDENTS

This Part deal with "inchoate"—"incomplete" or "unsuccessful"—criminal conduct. As we know already, in Anglo–American law a person is not punished for her criminal thoughts alone. To be guilty, she must put her thoughts into action. The question to be considered in this Part is: At what point does an incomplete or unsuccessful effort to commit a crime itself become a crime?

As a matter of policy, this is a difficult question to answer. If the criminal law enters the picture too quickly, individuals without criminal design might be arrested and punished for innocent, but suspicious appearing, conduct. On the other hand, the police must not be left helpless: if a person cannot be arrested for inchoate conduct until the last moment, it may be impossible to prevent commission of an intended offense.

You will see below how Anglo–American law has balanced these competing concerns. Three crimes are covered in detail: criminal attempts; criminal solicitation; and criminal conspiracy. Brief discussion of other offenses will be included. Among the primary inchoate offenses, "attempt" involves conduct that comes the closest to completion of the offense; a conspiracy involves much more preliminary conduct; and criminal solicitation comes into play earlier still. In a comparative sense, the three crimes look like this, in which "CT" represents "criminal thoughts," "S" is "solicitation," "C" is "conspiracy," "A" is "attempt," and "CO" is the "completed offense":

<u>CT S C A   CO</u>

Don't take the placement of the crimes on this line too literally. In particular, attempt is not necessarily midway between the criminal thought and the completed offense. In some cases, it may be much closer to "CO," whereas in other cases it will be further away.

As you consider these offenses, attempt (no pun intended) to do the following. First, decide whether you agree with the developed law. Does the law intrude too soon? Too late? Second, inchoate crimes, like completed offenses, have an *actus reus* and *mens rea*. Learn what they are. Third, there are various special defenses applicable only to inchoate crimes. Learn them. (All of the justification and excuse defenses discussed in Parts Six and Seven apply to inchoate crimes, as well.)

I. Attempt

A. Common Law

"Attempt" was first recognized as a criminal offense in English common law in *Rex v. Scofield*, Caldecott 397 (1784).

1. General Principles

a. Basic Definition

In general, an attempt occurs when a person, with the intent to commit a criminal offense, engages in conduct that constitutes the beginning of the perpetration of, rather than mere preparation for, the target (*i.e.*, intended) offense. As explained below, however, this distinction—perpetration versus preparation—is not very helpful, and courts have reached different conclusions as to when a criminal attempt begins.

b. Grading of Offense

A criminal attempt was a common law misdemeanor in England, regardless of the seriousness of the target offense. Thus, although murder was a capital crime, attempted murder was a mere misdemeanor. Today, modern statutes provide that an attempt to commit a felony is a felony.

i. Attempt as a Lesser Crime

Most states that are based on the common law treat a criminal attempt as a lesser offense than the target crime. Often, for example, an attempt is punished about one-half as severely as the target offense. Thus, if the maximum penalty for rape is 20 years' imprisonment, attempted rape would carry a maximum penalty of 10 years.

(1) Criticism of the Traditional Grading Approach

Many scholars argue that a person who attempts to commit a crime is as dangerous and morally culpable as the successful criminal; only good luck (bad luck from the offender's perspective) or poor implementation of the criminal design prevented the successful completion of the crime, so attempts should be punished as severely as completed offenses.

(2) Defense of the Traditional Grading Approach

A criminal attempt causes less social harm than a successful crime. A person who murders, for example, has caused greater harm than one who only wounds the victim. The attempter, therefore, has a lesser debt to pay for her wrongdoing. Therefore, punishment of an attempt *should* be less. Also, from a utilitarian perspective, the legal system may wish to give a person an incentive to desist from completing an offense, by mitigating the punishment for an attempt.

c. Merger Doctrine

A criminal attempt merges into the target offense, if it is successfully completed.

Example: D attempts to kill V, but is arrested before completion. D is guilty of attempted murder. However, if her attempt succeeds, the attempt merges into the completed crime. She may be convicted of *either* attempted murder or murder, but not of both.

2. *Actus Reus*

Courts have long struggled to identify the point at which conduct moves from the preparatory stages to one of perpetration. Thus, there is no single common law test, but rather a number of tests that courts consider. Most, but not all, of the common law tests focus on how close the actor is to completing the target offense. In considering the various tests below, it is well to remember the special competing concerns that apply to inchoate conduct: the danger of arresting and convicting innocent persons; and the law enforcement need to prevent real criminal conduct from coming too close to fruition.

a. Last Act Test

The rule used to be that a criminal attempt only occurred when a person performed all of the acts that she believed were necessary to commit the target offense. The undesirability of this rule is obvious. In most cases it will not be possible for the police to prevent the target offense if they must wait until the last act is committed in order to make an arrest. Today, there is general agreement that an attempt occurs *at least* by the time of the last act, but no jurisdiction requires that it reach this stage on all occasions.

Example: According to this test, *D* is not guilty of attempted murder unless, for example, she pulls the trigger of the gun, stabs the victim, or puts the poison in *V*'s coffee.

b. Dangerous Proximity Test

Oliver Wendell Holmes announced the "dangerous proximity to success" test. This standard is not satisfied unless the conduct "is so near to the result that the danger of success is very great." *People v. Rizzo*, 246 N.Y. 334, 158 N.E. 888 (1927). In this regard, courts consider three factors: the nearness of the danger; the substantiality of the harm; and the degree of apprehension felt. The more serious the offense, the less close the actor must come to completing the offense to be convicted of attempt.

Example: In *Rizzo, supra*, *R* and three other armed men drove around in their car looking for their intended victim, who did not show up. Because they lacked the ability to complete the crime—the victim was missing—the court concluded that were not yet dangerously close to success.

c. Physical Proximity Test

To be guilty of attempt under this test, an act "must go so far that it would result, or apparently result in the actual commission of the crime it was designed to effect, if not extrinsically hindered or frustrated by extraneous circumstances." *Commonwealth v. Kelley*, 162 Pa.Super. 526, 58 A.2d 375 (1948). Or, as it is sometimes explained, the actor's conduct must approach sufficiently near to the completed offense "to stand either as the first or some subsequent step in a *direct movement* toward the commission of the offense after the preparations are made." *State v. Dowd*, 28 N.C.App. 32, 220 S.E.2d 393 (1975).

Examples: *D1*, weapon in hand, has her victim in sight and can immediately proceed to rob her, absent external factors (such as the intervention of the police). *D1* is guilty of attempted robbery.

In *Kelley, supra*, *D2*, intending to trick *V* out of her money, convinces her to go to the bank and withdraw some of her cash. *D2* is arrested before the money is withdrawn, and before *D2* can make overtures to obtain the money from *V*. *D2* is not guilty of attempted "larceny [theft] by trick."

d. "Unequivocality"/"Res Ipsa Loquitur" Test

This test provides that a person is not guilty of a criminal attempt until her conduct ceases to be equivocal, *i.e.*, her conduct, standing alone, demonstrates her criminal intent. This test reduces the risk of a false conviction of an innocent person, but it may also increase the risk the police will be unable to act quickly enough to prevent the target offense.

Example: In *People v. Miller*, 2 Cal.2d 527, 42 P.2d 308 (1935), *M* threatened to kill *V*, whom he accused of harassing his wife. Later that day, *M*, armed with a rifle, entered a field where *C*, the local constable, and *V*, standing 30 yards further away, were present. *M* walked in their direction, stopped, loaded his rifle but did not aim it, and continued to walk. *V* fled at a right angle from *M*'s line of approach. *C* took possession of *M*'s weapon without resistance. Remarkably, the court held that *M* was not guilty of attempted murder, because "up to the moment the gun was taken from the defendant, no one could say with certainty whether [*M*] had come into the field to carry out his threat to kill [*V*] or merely to demand his arrest by [*C*]" for harassing his wife.

e. Probable Desistance Test

A person is guilty of attempt if she has proceeded past "the point of no return," *i.e.*, the point past which an ordinary person is likely to abandon her criminal endeavor. This test has been criticized because it provides little guidance to the police, and because it is odd to apply an objective test here: is the standard what a reasonable criminal would do? How does a jury determine that? If the standard is what a reasonable law-abiding person would do, it is nonsensical since, by definition, such persons never commence criminal activity in the first place.

3. Mens Rea

a. Dual Intent

It is often said that the mental state required for a criminal attempt is "the intent to commit some other crime." This is an accurate statement, as far as it goes. It is more complete to say, however, that a criminal attempt involves two "intents."

i. First "Intent"

The actor must intentionally commit the acts that constitute the *actus reus* of an attempt, as discussed above, *e.g*, he must perform an act that brings him in dangerous proximity to commission of the target crime.

ii. Second "Intent"
The actor must commit the *actus reus* of an attempt with the specific intent to commit the target offense. This latter state of mind is almost always the critical *mens rea* issue in attempt prosecutions.

Example: D intentionally aims a loaded gun at V, who is standing nearby. D is arrested before he can pull the trigger. Although D intentionally aimed the gun at V—the first intent—he is not guilty of attempted murder unless he did so with the specific intent of killing V. If he merely intended to scare V, he is not guilty of attempted murder.

b. Comparing *Mens Rea* of Attempt to Target Offense

i. Higher *Mens Rea*
An attempt often requires a *higher* level of *mens rea* than is necessary to commit the target offense.

Example: As a practical joke, D intentionally fires a gun into an occupied building to scare the occupants. If D kills an occupant, he can be convicted of murder, as his conduct would almost certainly constitute extreme recklessness, or "depraved heart," a state of mind that satisfies the element of "malice afore-thought," *i.e.*, the *mens rea* of murder. However, if nobody dies as the result of D's conduct, he is not guilty of *attempted* murder, as he did not have the specific intent to kill an occupant.

ii. Specific-intent versus general-intent
As the second "intent" noted above shows, "attempt" is a specific-intent offense, even if the target crime is general-intent. Thus, rape is a general-intent crime, whereas attempted rape is specific-intent in nature.

c. Special Problem: Attendant Circumstances
At common law, it is unclear what *mens rea*, if any, an actor must possess regarding an attendant circumstance to be guilty of attempt.

Example: D engages in conduct that brings him close to his intended goal, which is to have sexual intercourse with V, a 15–year-old girl, whom *D* believes is 17 years old. Assume that if *D* were to have intercourse with *V*, he would be guilty of statutory rape (assume that age 16 is the cut-off point) because statutory rape is a strict-liability crime in most jurisdictions. If *D* does *not* complete the offense, however, is he guilty of *attempted* statutory rape?

i. Alternative Approaches

Some courts hold that a person may be convicted of a criminal attempt if he is reckless with regard to an attendant circumstance. Other courts believe that it is sufficient that the actor is as culpable regarding an attendant circumstance as is required for that element of the *target* crime.

Example: In the statutory rape hypothetical, some courts will not convict *D* unless he knew that *V* was underage or was, at least, reckless in his belief that she was old enough to consent. Other courts would hold that, since statutory rape is a strict liability offense in regard to the female's age, *D* may also be convicted of *attempted* statutory rape, even if he possessed no culpable state of mind as to *V*'s age.

4. Special Defense: Impossibility

a. General Rule

The common law distinguished between "factual" and "legal" impossibility. The latter was a defense to an attempt; the former was not. Unfortunately, the line between legal and factual impossibility is not clear—indeed, there can be an overlap, as discussed below.

b. Factual Impossibility

Factual impossibility, which is not a defense, may be defined as occurring when an actor's intended end constitutes a crime, but he fails to complete the offense because of a factual circumstance unknown to him or beyond his control. One way to phrase this is: if the facts had been as the defendant believed them to be, would his conduct have constituted a crime? If yes, then this is a case of factual impossibility.

Examples: *D1*, a pickpocket, puts his hand in an empty pocket. *D1* is guilty of attempted larceny.

D2 sexually assaults *V*, but he fails to consummate the sexual intercourse because he is impotent. *D2* is guilty of attempted rape.

c. Legal Impossibility

Although most courts do not acknowledge the point, there are two varieties of "legal impossibility." (For a court that has noted the distinction, see *People v. Thousand*, 465 Mich. 149, 631 N.W.2d 694 (2001).)

i. Pure Legal Impossibility

This form of impossibility applies when an actor engages in lawful conduct that she incorrectly believes constitutes a crime. Just as ignorance of the law generally is no excuse, it is also true that one who incorrectly thinks he is committing a crime is not guilty of an attempt to commit a non-existent offense.

Examples: D1 puts his hand on *V's* shoulder. *D1* believes that this act constitutes the crime of rape. Of course, it does not. Therefore, he is not only not guilty of rape, but he is not guilty of attempted rape, as this is a case of pure legal impossibility.

D2 files her federal income tax forms on April 15. She believes that the legal deadline for filing is April 14, so she incorrectly believes that she is in violation of federal law. Nonetheless, she is not guilty of *attempted* violation of the tax law.

ii. Hybrid Legal Impossibility

The more typical case of legal impossibility occurs when an actor's goal *is* illegal (this distinguishes it from pure legal impossibility), but commission of the offense is impossible due to a mistake by the actor regarding the *legal* status of some *factual* circumstance relevant to her conduct. Thus, as this last sentence suggests, such cases of legal impossibility are hybrids—it may just as easily be characterized as one of factual impossibility (no defense) as legal impossibility (defense).

Example: D1 receives property that he believes was stolen. In fact, the property had not been stolen. Uncontroversially, *D1* is not guilty of the crime of "receiving stolen property," since an element of the *actus reus* of this offense has not been proven—the attendant circumstance that the property received was *stolen* property. According to some courts, however, *D1* is also not guilty of *attempted* receipt of stolen property. *People v. Jaffe*, 185 N.Y. 497, 78 N.E. 169 (1906). Because the property had the *legal* status of being unstolen, it was legally impossible for *D1*, when he took possession of the property, to receive *stolen* property; this legal impossibility prevents him from being guilty of attempt, as well. But, this also can be characterized as factual impossibility: if the facts had been as *D1* believed them to be—if the property he received *had* been stolen, then *D1* *would* be guilty of the crime of receiving stolen property.

In *People v. Dlugash*, 41 N.Y.2d 725, 395 N.Y.S.2d 419, 363 N.E.2d 1155 (1977), *X* shot *V*. While *V* was lying on the ground, *D2* fired more bullets into him. The coroner concluded that *V* may have been dead at the time of *D2*'s actions. This case could fit either form of impossibility. Arguably, it is factual impossibility: *D2*'s intended end (killing a human being) constitutes a crime, but he failed to complete the offense because of a factual circumstance unknown to him (*V* was already dead). But, just as arguably, this is a case of legal impossibility: It is legally impossible to kill a dead person, because the law of homicide only prohibits the killing of a "human being," which *V* was not at the time.

d. Should the Factual/Legal Distinction Be Followed?

Many states have followed the Model Penal Code approach, discussed below, and have purportedly abolished the "legal impossibility" defense, more accurately, the hybrid version. The reasoning for abolition includes: (1) the people who are acquitted on the ground of legal impossibility are as dangerous and culpable as those who are convicted on the ground of factual impossibility; and (2) as noted above, the distinction between factual impossibility and hybrid legal impossibility is largely non-existent—virtually any case can logically be characterized as either factual or legal impossibility.

B. Model Penal Code

1. General Principles

a. Definition

The MPC definition of a criminal attempt is set out in a particularly inartfully drafted provision, § 5.01(1). Rather than set it out here, you should look at it in your casebook. The relevant provisions will be quoted and considered below.

b. Grading of Offense

Unlike the common law and non-MPC statutes, which treat criminal attempts as a lesser offense, with lesser punishment, than the target offense, the MPC generally treats the inchoate offenses of attempt, solicitation, and conspiracy as offenses of the same degree, and thus subject to the same punishment, as the target offense. MPC § 5.05(1). The one exception is that, for a felony characterized as a "felony of the first degree" under the Code—basically, an offense that carries a maximum punishment of life imprisonment, MPC § 6.06(1)—an attempt to commit such an offense is a felony of the *second* degree, *i.e.*, a lesser offense.

c. Merger

The common law merger doctrine applies as well under the Code. MPC § 1.07.

2. *Actus Reus*

It is sometimes necessary to distinguish between a "complete" attempt and an "incomplete" one. This distinction is especially critical in understanding and applying the MPC attempt provisions. A complete attempt is one in which the defendant has done every act necessary on his part to commit the target offense, but has failed to commit the crime; an incomplete attempt occurs when the defendant has *not* committed the last act necessary on his part. There are no *actus reus* issues in the case of a completed attempt—the defendant has done everything, including the last act, but simply has failed to commit the crime. The *actus reus* issues arise with incomplete attempts.

Examples: D1 aims and fires her gun at *V1*, intending to kill *V1*. The bullet misses *V1*, or wounds but does kill *V1*. This is a complete attempt.

D2 aims her gun at *V2*, but is arrested before she pulls the trigger, or she changes her mind before pulling the trigger. This is not a completed attempt case, as *D2* has not yet committed the final act. The issue is whether this case of incomplete conduct has gone far enough to constitute an attempt.

a. Test

The Model Penal Code abandons all of the common law tests described above and replaces them with a *substantial step* standard. Specifically, one has gone far enough to constitute an attempt if the "act or omission constitut[es] a substantial step in the course of conduct planned to culminate in his commission of the crime." MPC § 5.01(1)(c).

i. **Important Clarification**

The term "substantial step" is not defined, but the Code states that it must be "corroborative of the actor's criminal purpose." MPC § 5.01(2). Furthermore, the Code provides a list of factual circumstances in which the defendant's conduct, if strongly corroborative of her criminal purpose, "shall not be held insufficient as a matter of law." *Id.* That is, if any one of the listed factual circumstances exists (*e.g.*, the defendant was "lying in wait, searching for or following the contemplated victim of the crime"), the judge *must* let the factfinder (the jury) consider the prosecutor's case. In turn, the jury will be told, simply, to determine whether the defendant's act/omission constituted a substantial step in a course of conduct planned to culminate in commission of the target offense.

ii. **Distinction from Common Law**

One significant difference between the substantial step test and the various common law standards is that, in general, the common law looked to see how close the defendant was to completing the crime, whereas the MPC looks to see how far the defendant has gone from the point of initiation of the target offense.

Example: Look at the line I set out in the **Conversation with Students** at the start of Part Eight. The common law focuses on how close the defendant is to "**CO**"; the MPC focuses on how far the defendant has gone past "**CT**."

3. *Mens Rea*

In order to apply the MPC criminal attempt statute, a lawyer (or student) needs to draw two important distinctions at the outset. First, look at the facts of the case and decide whether it implicate a complete attempt or an incomplete attempt, as defined earlier. *All* incomplete attempts are considered in MPC § 5.01(1)(c). Complete attempts are considered pursuant to MPC § 5.01(1)(a)-(b). Second, if one is dealing with a complete attempt, decide whether the target offense relates to a criminal *result* or to criminal *conduct*. Conduct crimes are handled by (1)(a), whereas results are considered in (1)(b).

Examples: *D1* aims a gun at *V1,* intending to shoot *V1. D1* is arrested and charged with attempted murder. This is an incomplete attempt. Apply MPC § 5.01(1)(c).

D2 aims her gun and shoots at *V2,* but misses. *D2* is charged with attempted murder. This is a complete attempt, and the target offense (murder) is a "result crime," in that it prohibits the *result* of the death of another person. Apply MPC § 5.01(1)(b).

D3, a would-be pickpocket, puts his hand in *V3's* pocket in order to take *V3's* wallet, but she fails to grasp the wallet. *D3* is charged with attempted "unlawful taking." This is a complete attempt (she has done everything she intended to do), and the target offense is a conduct crime (it prohibits the conduct of "taking" another's property). Apply MPC § 5.01(1)(a).

a.   Rule

The Code uses slightly different language than the common law, but the analysis is essentially the same. A person is not guilty of attempt unless he: *"purposely* engages in conduct that would constitute the crime." (MPC § 5.01(1)(a)); acts "with the *purpose* of causing" or "with the *belief* that it will cause" the criminal result (MPC § 5.01(1)(b)); or *"purposely* does . . . an act . . . constituting a substantial step" in furtherance of the offense. MPC § 5.01(1)(c).

b.   Special Problem: Attendant Circumstances

The analysis above tells us what *mens rea* is required—purpose—as to conduct and results, but what about "attendant circumstance" elements of an offense?

i.   Rule

The "purpose" requirement for an attempt does *not* apply to attendant circumstances; as to attendant circumstances, a person is guilty of an attempt if she "act[s] with the kind of culpability otherwise required for commission of the [target] crime." MPC § 5.01(1). In short, the MPC approach is similar to the approach taken by *some* common law courts: the actor need only be as culpable regarding an attendant circumstance as is required for the target offense.

Example: Reconsider the common law "attendant circumstance" *Example* dealing with statutory rape on page 249. If statutory rape is a strict liability offense regarding the attendant circumstance of the female's age, then the same applies as to this attendant circumstance in an *attempted* statutory rape charge. On the other hand, if the required *mens rea* as to the attendant circumstance of the female's age is, for example, negligence, then "negligence" is required for the crime of *attempted* statutory rape. Quite simply, one looks at the target offense, determines the required culpability as to an attendant circumstance, and then applies this same *mens rea* as to the attempt charge.

4. Special Defense: Impossibility

The Code provides that a person is guilty of an attempt if his conduct "would constitute the crime *if the attendant circumstances were as he believes them to be*." MPC § 5.01(1)(a). The effect of this language is to abandon the hybrid legal impossibility defense discussed earlier. The rationale for abolition of the defense is set out above in subsection A.4.d. Notwithstanding the Code language quoted above, *pure* legal impossibility remains a defense.

Examples: A person would be guilty of an attempt in both the *Jaffe* and *Dlugash* cases set out in the *Examples* above in A.4.c.ii, *supra*, as well as in all of the factual impossibility cases.

In the hand-on-shoulder "rape" and tax filing *Examples* noted in A.4.c.i., *supra*, the defendant would still be *not guilty* of a criminal attempt.

5. Special Defense: Renunciation of Criminal Purpose

The Code recognizes a defense of "renunciation of criminal purpose." MPC § 5.01(4). A person is not guilty of a criminal attempt, *even if her actions constitute a substantial step in the commission of an offense*, if: (1) she abandons her effort to commit the crime or prevents it from being committed; and (2) her conduct manifests a complete and voluntary renunciation of her criminal purpose. This defense is sometimes described as the "abandonment" defense.

Examples: While attempting to rob a bank, *D1* flees when she observes a police officer. *D1* cannot successfully claim the renunciation or abandonment defense, because *D1*'s abandonment of the robbery was not voluntary.

D2, a prison inmate, attempts to escape confinement. Just as he is about to climb over the prison fence, he thinks of his children and decides that he does not want to shame them further by his conduct. Therefore, he abandons his escape and returns to his cell. *Commonwealth v. McCloskey*, 234 Pa.Super. 577, 341 A.2d 500 (1975). In a Model Penal Code jurisdiction, *D2*'s conduct, if believed by the jury, would result in acquittal.

a. Rationale

A person who voluntarily and completely abandons her criminal endeavor is no longer dangerous. Moreover, this defense provides an incentive to an actor to turn away from her criminal enterprise before she consummates the offense.

b. Common Law Counter–Rationale

The common law did not recognize this defense. The rationale for this position is that once the social harm of an attempt has occurred, a person cannot undo that harm, just as a person cannot avoid guilt for a theft by returning the property to the victim.

II. Conspiracy

CONVERSATION WITH STUDENTS

Conspiracy is a hard crime to study. The Supreme Court has stated that the concept is "so vague that it almost defies definition." *Krulewitch v. United States*, 336 U.S. 440, 69 S.Ct. 716, 93 L.Ed. 790 (1949). It is also a controversial crime because it is "predominantly mental in composition." *Id..* That is, the crime consists of little more than a guilty meeting of the minds of two or more persons. Consequently, "conspiracy" is, as Judge Learned Hand has put it, "the darling of the modern prosecutor's nursery." *Harrison v. United States*, 7 F.2d 259 (2d Cir. 1925). (In this regard, you would do well to take another look at my **Conversation** at the start of this Part, to see where conspiracy fits in among the inchoate offenses.)

One other important point: "conspiracy" is both a crime and a theory of complicity, that is, a means of holding a person accountable for the criminal conduct of another. Put still more clearly, if *A* and *B*, for example, commit the *crime* of conspiracy to commit murder, and if *A* then commits the murder, not only are both persons guilty of the *crime* of conspiracy, but *B*—who did not commit the murder personally—may be convicted of this crime as well because "conspiracy" also serves as a basis for holding persons responsible for the actions of others (co-conspirators). This latter feature of conspiracy—as a doctrine of complicity—is discussed in the next Part. Don't worry about it for now. For now, we look only at the crime of conspiracy.

A. Common Law

1. General Principles

a. Definition

A common law conspiracy is an agreement between two or more persons to commit an unlawful act or series of unlawful acts.

b. Grading

At original common law, conspiracy was a misdemeanor. Today, conspiracy to commit a felony is usually a felony, but typically is a lesser offense than the target crime.

c. Rationale of the Offense

i. Preventive Law Enforcement

Like other inchoate offenses, recognition of the offense of conspiracy provides a basis for the police to arrest people before they commit another offense. With conspiracy, the police may intervene even before the parties reach the "attempt" stage.

ii. Special Dangerousness

Group criminality is considered by some observers as more dangerous than individual wrongdoing. Thus, a "conspiracy" involves its own aggravated social harm. The thesis is that when people combine to commit an offense, they are more dangerous than an individual criminal, because of their combined resources, strength, and expertise. They are also thought to be less likely to abandon their criminal purpose if they know that other persons are involved.

d. Merger

Unlike criminal attempts (and, unlike criminal solicitations, discussed below in III), a common law conspiracy does *not* merge into the attempted or completed offense that is the object of the agreement.

Example: D1 and D2 conspire to kill *V1*. They kill *V1*. Under these circumstances, they may be convicted of both conspiracy and murder.

i. Rationale of No–Merger Rule

The no-merger rule is based on the special dangerousness rationale of conspiracy. That is, the extra danger inherent in conspiratorial relationships is thought to justify punishment of the conspiracy, even if its criminal object is completed.

2. *Actus Reus:* Basics

The gist of a conspiracy is the agreement by the parties to commit an unlawful act or series of unlawful acts together. (Notice in this regard that the agreement—the *actus reus* of the offense—is little more than the meeting of the minds—which is the *mens rea* of the offense!) Although there is more to be said on the subject of the agreement, here are the basics.

a. Overt Act

A common law conspiracy is committed as soon as the agreement is made. No act in furtherance of it is required. Today, influenced in part by the Model Penal Code, many statutes provide that a conspiracy does not occur unless at least one party to the agreement commits an overt act in furtherance of it. The overt act need not constitute a substantial step in furtherance of the target offense. *Any* act will do.

Example: D1 and D2 agree to rob a bank. At common law, D1 and D2 are now guilty of conspiracy, even if they do nothing further. In an "overt act" jurisdiction, neither person may be convicted of conspiracy until one of them commits a single act in furtherance of the robbery, such as to map out the get-away route, or to obtain a gun to use in the later robbery.

b. Method of Forming the Agreement

The conspiratorial agreement need not be in writing, nor even be verbally expressed. It may be implied from the actions of the parties. (Remember, the agreement is really nothing more than a nebulous "meeting of the minds.") A conspiracy often looks as if the events were choreographed, with each party performing a different act in furtherance of the crime.

Example: D1, D2, and D3 drive to the City Bank together. D1 and D2 exit the vehicle, while D3 remains in the car, with the ignition on. D1 and D2 enter the bank. D1 points a gun at a teller. D2 stands at the door, preventing customers from leaving. When *D1* receives money from the teller, *D1* and *D2* flee to the automobile outside, and *D3* drives them away. By the very nature of these facts—working in unison—a jury may infer a conspiratorial agreement, even without written evidence or any testimony regarding the forming of a verbal agreement.

c. Nature of Agreement

Notice the common law definition of conspiracy set out above: the object of the agreement must be unlawful. For purposes of conspiracy, an "unlawful" act is a morally wrongful act; *it need not be a criminal act.*

Example: *D1* and *D2* agree to defame *V*. Their agreement is punishable as a common law conspiracy, although defamation is not a crime. *State v. Henry*, 117 N.J.L. 442, 188 A. 918 (1937).

3. *Mens Rea:* The Basics

a. General Rule

Conspiracy is a dual-intent offense. First, the parties must intend to form an agreement (the *actus reus* of the conspiracy). Second, they must intend that the object(s) of their agreement be achieved. This second intent makes conspiracy a specific-intent offense.

b. Purpose versus Knowledge

i. The Issue

An issue that arises in some conspiracy prosecutions is whether a person may be convicted of conspiracy if, with *knowledge* that another person intends to commit an unlawful act, *but with indifference as to whether the crime is committed*, he furnishes an instrumentality for that offense or provides a service to the other person that aids in its commission.

Examples: *A* rents out a room to *B*, a prostitute, with knowledge that *B* will use it in her illegal activities. Does this show an *A-B* conspiracy to commit prostitution?

C, a drug wholesaler, sells large quantities of *legal* drugs to *D*, knowing that the latter will use them for *illegal* purposes. *Direct Sales Co. v. United States*, 319 U.S. 703, 63 S.Ct. 1265, 87 L.Ed. 1674 (1943). Does this demonstrate a *C-D* drug conspiracy?

ii. **Case Law**

The law is split on the issue set out above. Most courts will not convict a person unless he acts with the *purpose* of promoting or facilitating the offense. Knowledge, coupled with indifference as to whether the offense is committed, is insufficient. But, be careful: sometimes one can infer purpose from knowledge.

(1) **Proving Purpose From Knowledge**

Even in jurisdictions that require proof of purpose, this mental state may be inferred from knowledge, if there is evidence that the party had a stake in the venture. *United States v. Falcone*, 109 F.2d 579 (2d Cir. 1940). This may be proven in many ways.

Examples: In the *Examples* above, if *A* rents the room to *B*, the prostitute, at a grossly inflated price, *A*'s purpose to facilitate the acts of prostitution may be inferred. That is, *A* now has reason to want *B* to succeed in her prostitution activities: to continue to receive the inflated rental fees.

If *C* obtains a disproportionate amount of his business from *D*, the drug purchaser, the requisite intent may be inferred.

4. Plurality Requirement

No person is guilty of conspiracy unless *two or more persons* possess the requisite *mens rea*: the intent to agree and the intent that the object of their agreement be achieved.

Examples: *D1* suggests to *X*, an undercover police officer, that they rob a bank together. *X* pretends to go along and says, "Fine." Later, *X* arrests *D1* for conspiracy. *D1* had the requisite *mens rea*: she intended to agree, and she had the specific intent to rob the bank. However, *X* did not have the requisite *mens rea*: he intended to agree, but he did *not* intend for the robbery to occur. Therefore, because two (or more) persons did not possess the dual intents, no conspiracy has occurred. *D1*, therefore, is not guilty of conspiracy.

D2 and *D3* agree to commit a crime. Later, it turns out that *D3* lacked the requisite *mens rea*, because he was insane. The plurality rule precludes conviction of *D2*.

D4, *D5*, and *Y* (an undercover officer, feigning participation) agree to rob a bank. Here, *D4* and *D5 may* be convicted of conspiracy. Even after *Y* is dropped out of the picture, the plurality requirement is met.

a. Important Clarification

The plurality doctrine does not require that two persons be prosecuted and convicted of conspiracy. It is satisfactory that the prosecutor proves beyond a reasonable doubt that there were two or more persons who formed the agreement with the requisite *mens rea*.

Example: *D* and *X* agree to murder *V*. Prior to trial for conspiracy, *X* dies or flees the jurisdiction. *D* may still be convicted of conspiracy, as long as the prosecutor proves beyond a reasonable doubt that *D* conspired with *X*.

b. Observations about the Plurality Requirement

The plurality rule may make some sense if one focuses on the supposed special dangers of conspiracies. If what makes a conspiracy more dangerous is the extra person involved in the criminal enterprise, then the fact that one of the "conspirators" is an undercover police officer negates the special dangerousness. On the other hand, the fact that one party feigns agreement, is insane, or is otherwise incapable of committing the offense, does not render the other person less dangerous or culpable. And, the preventive law enforcement purpose of conspiracy law—giving the police the chance to respond early—is frustrated by the plurality requirement.

5. Parties to an Agreement

a. The Issue

Even if it is clear that a conspiracy exists as defined and explained above, it is sometimes difficult to determine *who* is a party to the conspiracy.

Examples: In *Kotteakos v. United States*, 328 U.S. 750, 66 S.Ct. 1239, 90 L.Ed. 1557 (1946), *D*, a broker, assisted at least eight groups of persons to obtain federal loans in a fraudulent manner. Is this one conspiracy involving all of the parties (as the government alleged), or is this eight smaller conspiracies, with *D* as the common party in each of them?

In *Blumenthal v. United States*, 332 U.S. 539, 68 S.Ct. 248, 92 L.Ed.154 (1947), *O*, a liquor wholesaler, illegally distributed whiskey to two men, *A* and *B*, who in turn worked with *X* and *Y* to sell the liquor to local taverns. Is this a single conspiracy, consisting of *O*, *A-B*, and *X-Y* (as the prosecutor alleged), or are there two conspiracies: one between *O* and the people with whom he dealt (*A* and *B*); and the other between *A* and *B*, on the one hand, and the people with whom *they* dealt, *X* and *Y*?

In *United States v. Bruno*, 105 F.2d 921 (2d Cir. 1939), various persons smuggled narcotics into the Port of New York. The smugglers sold the narcotics to a number of middlemen, who in turn sold the drugs to retailers in New York and to another group of retailers in the Texas–Louisiana region. Is this a single conspiracy, including everyone from the smugglers to the local retailers, or do these facts suggest smaller conspiracies, *e.g.*, a conspiracy between the smugglers and the middlemen, and another between the middlemen and the New York and Texas–Louisiana retailers?

b. **Structure of Conspiracies**

In conspiracy prosecutions involving many layers of actors, it is useful to conceptualize the alleged conspiracy in diagrammatic fashion. Usually a conspiracy looks something like a wheel, a chain, or a combination of the two.

i. **Wheel Conspiracy**

A conspiracy may look like a wheel. In the center (the hub) is one person or group, who/which conducts illegal dealings with various other persons or groups (the spokes).

Example: In *Kotteakos, supra*, the most logical way to characterize the conspiracy is in the form of a wheel, in which *D* is in the center, with each of his clients for whom he obtained the loans functioning as spokes emanating from the hub. (You may see this by diagraming the situation: put *D* in the middle, and draw lines [the spokes] from *D* to each of the eight groups he assisted.)

(1) **Connecting the Spokes**

But, wait! In the description above, something is missing—there is no rim around the wheel. That is, although you have drawn lines between *D* and each client, there is no line around the wheel, connecting each client (spoke) to each other. In order to connect the spokes—to put the rim around the wheel—there must exist some *community of interest* between the spokes. If there is none, the wheel remains rimless, *and there cannot be a single conspiracy.* Instead, you would have a lot of smaller conspiracies (the spokes).

Example: In *Kotteakos,* there was no community of interest. None of the spokes cared about the loans *D* brokered for the others. Each spoke obtained personal assistance in obtaining a fraudulent loan, and then moved on. Therefore, the wheel had no rim. As a consequence, the Court held that the prosecutor was wrong in charging a single conspiracy; instead, there were multiple two-party conspiracies.

ii. **Chain Conspiracy**

Some conspiracies involve multiple layers of personnel, in which each person or group in the conspiracy has specialized responsibilities that link together the various aspects of the unlawful conduct. Thus, the parties are linked to each other as in a chain. The very nature of the conspiracy, with its multiple layers with specialized responsibilities, creates a *community of interest* among the parties. In such circumstances, it is justifiable to treat the arrangement as a single conspiracy.

Example: In *Blumenthal, supra,* if you were to diagram the conspiracy, it would look like a chain, because you have a business-like linkage: the owner who works with the distributors who in turn deal with their local contacts, and so on.

iii. **Chain–Wheel Conspiracy**

Sometimes a conspiracy will include a chain and a wheel.

Example: In *Bruno, supra,* it is plausible to treat some of the conspiracy as a chain: smugglers-to-middlemen-to-retailers, but to have the third link—the retailer link—split off, as if there were separate spokes, one spoke involving the New York retailers, and a separate spoke for the Texas–Louisiana retailers. Thus, we might see this as *two* chain conspiracies, each involving the smugglers and middlemen, but with a different retailer for each. (This is *not* what the court ruled in *Bruno*: it treated this, merely, as one chain conspiracy.)

6. Objectives of a Conspiracy

a. Issue

Another analytical problem is this: Since the gist of a conspiracy is an agreement, what if the parties to the agreement intend to commit more than one offense. Is this one conspiracy or more?

Examples: D1 and *D2* rob Bank 1 on Day 1. They rob Bank 2 on Day 2. They rob Bank 3 on Day 3. Assuming that it is clear that these robberies were the result of prior arrangement, is this a single conspiracy to rob three banks or are there three conspiracies to rob one bank each, thus resulting in three conspiracy prosecutions?

D3 and *D4* kill *X*, kill *Y*, and rape and kill *Z*, in a one-day crime spree. Is this one conspiracy? Or, two conspiracies, one for each section of the penal code that was violated (conspiracy to murder; and conspiracy to rape)? Or, three conspiracies (one per victim)? Or, four conspiracies (one per criminal incident)?

b. Rule

In general, there are as many (or as few) conspiracies as there are agreements actually formed. *Braverman v. United States*, 317 U.S. 49, 63 S.Ct. 99, 87 L.Ed. 23 (1942). In each of the *Examples* above, the number of conspiracy charges will depend on whether the parties formed one agreement to commit multiple offenses, or formed a number of separate agreements.

i. Comment on Rule

Although this rule makes sense—after, all, a conspiracy is an agreement, so there should be as many conspiracy charges as there are separate agreements—the rule is impractical. In view of the secretive nature of most conspiracies, there is rarely going to be direct evidence regarding whether the parties had a single agreement with multiple objectives, or multiple agreements with fewer objectives. Not only is the rule impractical, but it is apt to result in unfairness. Parties who form multiple agreements to commit a single crime each are subject to much greater punishment under this rule than those who have the foresight—or luck—to draw up a single multiple-objective agreement at one time. Yet, they are no more dangerous or culpable than the other group.

7. Special Defense: Wharton's Rule

a. Rule

If a crime *by definition* requires two or more persons as willing participants, there can be no conspiracy to commit that offense if the only parties to the agreement are those who are necessary to the commission of the underlying offense. This is Wharton's Rule, a common law defense to conspiracy.

Examples: By definition, adultery requires two willing parties: *A*, who has consensual sexual intercourse with *B*, who is married to another person. There is no way to commit adultery in the absence of an agreement between *A* and *B*. Therefore, under Wharton's Rule, *A* and *B* may not be prosecuted for conspiracy to commit adultery.

C agrees to sell heroin to *D*. *C* and *D* may not be prosecuted for conspiracy to sell heroin: a sale, by definition, requires two persons (a willing seller and buyer). However, they may be prosecuted for conspiracy to *possess* contraband, because the crime of possession does not *by definition* require two persons. For example, a person can pick up contraband she finds on the ground, and thus possess it without the intervention of a second willing party.

i. Justification of the Rule

To the extent that a conspiracy is thought to involve special dangers inherent in group criminality—it is worse for two people to agree to commit a crime than for one person to plan a crime—there is no extra harm in the cases in which Wharton's Rule applies, as the crime inherently involves group criminality. On the other hand, Wharton's Rule frustrates the law enforcement purpose of conspiracy laws: the police must wait for the crime to be attempted.

b. Wharton's Rule Exceptions

i. Unnecessary Party

Wharton's Rule does not apply if the two conspirators are not the parties necessary to the commission of the offense.

Example: A conspires with C, B's spouse, to commit adultery with B. Wharton's Rule does not apply here. Although only two persons are involved, the two who agreed are not both the adulterers. A and C may be convicted of conspiracy.

ii. **Third–Party Exception**

Wharton's Rule does not apply if more persons than are necessary to commit the crime are involved in the agreement to commit the crime.

Example: A, B agree to sell heroin to C. Because three persons are involved in the conspiracy—one more than it takes to agree to a sale—the extra-danger rationale of group criminality comes back into play. Therefore, all three persons may be prosecuted for conspiracy to sell heroin.

c. **Breakdown of the Rule**

Wharton's Rule is increasingly disliked by courts. The Supreme Court has announced that, in federal courts, the doctrine is no more than a judicial rebuttable presumption. If there is evidence that the legislature, in defining an offense that would otherwise bring Wharton's Rule into play, intended to reject the rule, then the doctrine will not be enforced. *Iannelli v. United States*, 420 U.S. 770, 95 S.Ct. 1284, 43 L.Ed.2d 616 (1975).

8. **Special Defense: Legislative–Exemption Rule**

a. **Rule**

A person may not be prosecuted for conspiracy to commit a crime that is intended to protect that person.

Example: Statutory rape laws are intended to protect young females from immature decisions to consent to intercourse. It would defeat the purpose of the statutory rape law if a young female could be prosecuted for conspiracy to commit statutory rape on herself. Therefore, she is considered legally incapable of conspiring to commit statutory rape of herself.

b. **Significance of the Rule**

Notice the implications of this rule. If one party to a two-party conspiracy is exempt from prosecution, there is now only one remaining party to the conspiracy. Under the plurality doctrine discussed earlier in the chapter, that remaining person must also be acquitted of conspiracy!

9. Special Defense?: Impossibility

Is there is a "legal impossibility" defense to the crime of conspiracy, as there is to the common law crime of attempt? Case law here is particularly thin, but it has been stated that neither factual impossibility nor legal impossibility is a defense to a criminal conspiracy.

10. Special Defense?: Abandonment

a. No Defense to Crime of Conspiracy

At common law, the crime of conspiracy is complete as soon as the agreement is formed by two or more culpable persons. There is no turning back from that. Once the offense of conspiracy is complete, abandonment of the criminal plan by one of the parties is not a defense to the crime of conspiracy.

b. Relevance of Abandonment

Although abandonment, or withdrawal, from a conspiracy is not a defense to prosecution of the *crime* of conspiracy, a person who withdraws from a conspiracy may avoid conviction for subsequent offenses committed in furtherance of the conspiracy by other members of the conspiracy, if the abandoning party communicates his withdrawal to every other member of the conspiracy (a near impossibility in many-member conspiracies).

B. Model Penal Code

The MPC law of conspiracy has had mixed results. Some aspects of it have been influential and resulted in movement away from common law doctrines discussed above. Other features have had much less impact. The Code "criminal conspiracy" provision—Section 5.03—is long and very complicated. If your professor intends to focus on it, look at it carefully in your casebook.

1. General Principles

a. Definition

The MPC provides that "a person is guilty of conspiracy with another person or persons to commit a crime" if that person, "with the purpose of promoting or facilitating" commission of the crime, "agrees with such other person or persons that they or one or more of them will engage in conduct that constitutes such crime or an attempt or solicitation to commit such crime," or if that person agrees to aid the other person or persons in commission of the offense, or of an attempt or solicitation to commit such crime. MPC § 5.03(1).

b. Grading

Unlike the common law, which treats conspiracy as a lesser offense than the targeted crime, the Code provides that a conspiracy to commit any offense other than a felony of the first degree is graded the same as the crime that is the object of the conspiracy. MPC § 5.05(1).

c. Merger

Unlike the common law, a conspirator may *not* be convicted of both conspiracy and the target offense(s), unless the conspiracy involves a continuing course of conduct. MPC § 1.07(1)(b).

Examples: D1 and D2 agree to murder V1, and do so. D1 and D2 may be convicted of one, but not both, conspiracy and murder,

D3 and D4 conspire to murder V2 and V3. They kill V2. They are arrested before they can kill V3. Under these circumstances, they may be convicted of the one murder, as well as of conspiracy to kill V3.

2. ***Actus* Reus: How It Differs from Common Law**

a. Overt Act

In contrast to the common law, an overt act is required, except for felonies of the first and second degree. MPC § 5.03(5).

b. Nature of Agreement

In contrast to the common law, the object of the agreement must be a crime, and not merely an "unlawful" act. MPC § 5.03(1).

3. ***Mens Rea***

As the definition set out above suggests, the Code provides that a person is not guilty of conspiracy unless she acts with the *purpose* of promoting or facilitating the commission of the conduct that constitutes a crime.

MPC § 5.03(1). One who furnishes a service or instrumentality with mere *knowledge* of another's criminal activities is not guilty of conspiracy.

4. Plurality Rule

The most influential feature of the MPC is its rejection of the common law plurality requirement. Notice that the Code defines the offense in unilateral terms: "*A person* is guilty of conspiracy with another person . . . [if he] agrees with such other person . . . ." MPC § 5.03(1). Notice: it takes two people to agree, but it takes only one person to be *guilty* of conspiracy. Therefore, the special common law plurality problems discussed above drop out under the MPC.

5. Parties to Agreement

Two aspects of the Code need to be kept in mind in determining the parties to a conspiracy. First, conspiracy is a unilateral offense, as discussed above. Second, MPC § 5.03(2) provides that if a person guilty of conspiracy knows that the person with whom he has conspired has, in turn, conspired with still another person or persons to commit the *same* crime, the first person is also guilty of conspiring with the other persons or person, "whether or not he knows their identity." This aspect of the Code approach to conspiracy is *very* difficult to analyze.

Example: Let's reconsider *Bruno*, discussed above, but with much easier facts for analysis. Assume *A*, drug importer, meets with *B*, and they agree that *A* will smuggle narcotics into the country, in violation of Statute X. In their meeting, they further agree that *B* will find retailers to sell the imported narcotics in their respective states. These sales would violate Statute Y. Later, *B* meets with *C*, a New York retailer, and later still with *D*, a Texas retailer, and each agrees with *B* to sell drugs in their respective states. Assume further that neither retailer knows that *B* is dealing with the other retailer, nor do the retailers know the details of the A–B agreement.

Based on these facts, here is what you do. Step One: Apply § 5.03(1), in order to identify each agreement to commit a crime that occurred. Here, we have four agreements: (1) *A* and *B* to violate Statute X; (2) *A* and *B* to violate Statute Y; (3) *B* and *C* to violate Statute Y; and (4) *B* and *D* to violate Statute Y. So far, therefore, we have four two-person agreements.

Step 2: Bring § 5.03(2) into play, to potentially bring additional links into the conspiracy. But, because the MPC treats conspiracy as a crime of which one person may be guilty, we have to analyze each person separately. Thus, *A* knew that *B*, with whom *A* conspired to violate Statute Y, would also conspire with others to commit the same offense. Therefore, *A* is guilty of conspiracy not only with *B*, but with *C* and *D* (although he did not know their identities), to violate Statute Y. But, looking at the parties from the other direction, in our hypothetical facts, *C* and *D* did not know of the *A-B* agreement to violate Statute Y, so neither *C* nor *D* is guilty of conspiracy with *A* in regard to Crime Y, *even though A is guilty of conspiracy with them* as to Crime Y!

Now consider the B–C conspiracy to violate Statute Y. Is *D* also a party to this conspiracy? Probably not: because *D* may not have had the "purpose of promoting of facilitating the commission" of *that* offense. (Ditto analysis on *C*'s part, in regard to *B-D* conspiracy to sell drugs in Texas.)

6. Objectives of a Conspiracy

The Code provides that there is only one conspiracy between parties, even if they have multiple criminal objectives, as long as the multiple objectives are part of the same agreement (this is the same as the common law) or part of a "continuous conspiratorial relationship." MPC § 5.03(3).

Examples: *D1* and *D2* rob Bank 1 on Day 1. They rob Bank 2 on Day 2. They rob Bank 3 on Day 3. This would be a single conspiracy, even if *D1* and *D2* had formed three separate agreements, if the crimes were committed as part of a continuous conspiratorial relationship.

D3 and *D4* kill *X*, kill *Y*, and rape and kill *Z*, in a one-day crime spree. Again, there should be a single charge of conspiracy if it is shown that the crimes were all committed as part of a continuing conspiratorial relationship between *D3* and *D4*.

7. Special Defenses

The MPC does not recognize Wharton's Rule, nor any impossibility defense.

a. Legislative–Exemption Rule

The Code provides that it is a defense to a charge of conspiracy (or solicitation) "that if the criminal object were achieved, the actor would not be guilty of a crime under the law defining the offense or as an accomplice." MPC § 5.04(2). The effect of this language is to permit a defense if enforcement of the conspiracy law would frustrate a legislative intention to exempt that party from prosecution.

Example: Statutory rape laws are intended to protect underage females. It would frustrate that intent, if an underage female could be prosecuted for statutory rape of herself, either as accomplice of the male, or a conspirator. Therefore, she will not only *not* be convicted of statutory rape, but she is also not guilty of conspiracy to commit statutory rape of herself. However, as the MPC rejects the plurality doctrine, the male *may* be convicted of conspiracy with the underage female, although she is exempt!

b. Renunciation of Criminal Purpose

A person is not guilty of conspiracy under the Code if he renounces his criminal purpose, and then thwarts the success of the conspiracy "under circumstances manifesting a complete and voluntary renunciation of his criminal purpose." MPC § 5.03(6).

III. Solicitation

CONVERSATION WITH STUDENTS

Thankfully, solicitation is an easier concept to learn that conspiracy. Indeed, the common law and the MPC differ in only small respects. Therefore, unless I indicate otherwise, you can treat the common law and MPC as basically the same.

A. General Principles

1. Definition

At common law, a person is guilty of solicitation if he intentionally invites, requests, commands, or encourages another person to engage in conduct constituting a felony, or a misdemeanor involving a breach of the peace or obstruction of justice.

a. Model Penal Code

The Code definition of "solicitation" (§ 5.02) is broader than the common law in that it applies to solicitation to commit *any* misdemeanor (as well as all felonies).

2. Grading

At common law, a criminal solicitation was a misdemeanor, even when the offense solicited was a felony. Today, a solicitation to commit a felony is often treated as a felony, but of a lesser degree than the felony solicited.

a. Model Penal Code

As with other inchoate offenses, the MPC treats a solicitation to commit any offense other than a felony of the first degree as an offense of equal grade as the target offense. MPC § 5.05(1).

3. Merger

The concept of merger applies to the crime of solicitation, just as it does to the offense of attempt.

Example: D solicits X to rob V. X refuses. D is guilty of solicitation. However, if X agrees and commits the robbery or attempts it, D will be convicted of the robbery (or its attempt, as the case may be), as an accomplice in its commission. (See Part Nine, which deals with accomplice liability.) The crime of solicitation merges into the robbery; D may be convicted of solicitation or robbery, but not of both. (Notice, also, that if X agreed, there is now a D-X conspiracy to commit robbery, which raises issues as to whether the *conspiracy* merges into robbery, a matter discussed in the Conspiracy section above.)

B. *Actus Reus*

1. General Rule

The *actus reus* of a solicitation is consummated when the actor communicates the words or performs the physical act that constitutes the invitation, request, command, or encouragement of the other person to commit an offense.

Example: D asks X, or inquires of X by letter, "Will you please kill V?" This is a solicitation.

2. Unsuccessful Communications

At common law, a solicitation does not occur unless the words or conduct of the solicitor are successfully communicated to the solicited party.

Example: D is not guilty of solicitation, even if he requests X to commit an offense, if X does not hear the words, does not understand their meaning (*e.g.*, X does not speak the same language), or if the solicitation message to X never reaches him. In some jurisdictions, however, D is guilty of *attempted* solicitation in these circumstances.

a. Model Penal Code

The Code provides that one who unsuccessfully attempts to communicate a solicitation is guilty of solicitation. MPC § 5.02(2).

3. Relationship of Solicitor to Solicited Party

At common law, a person is not guilty of solicitation if she merely asks another person to *assist* in the crime, that is, to be an accomplice in the crime. To be guilty, a solicitor must ask the other person to actually perpetrate the offense herself. In contrast, the MPC provides that a person *is* guilty of solicitation if she asks the other person to commit the offense (as at common law), *or* if she requests the other person to do some act that would establish the latter person's complicity as an accomplice in the offense. MPC § 5.02(1).

Example: D asks X to furnish D with a gun so that he (D) can kill V. D is not guilty of common law solicitation, as he did not ask X to kill V—he only asked X to aid in the crime. In contrast, D is guilty of solicitation under the MPC.

C. *Mens Rea*

1. Common Law

Solicitation is a specific-intent offense at common law. The solicitor must intentionally commit the *actus reus* (request, encourage, etc., another to commit the crime), with the specific intent that the person solicited commit the target offense.

Example: D jokingly asks Y to kill D's wife. D is not guilty of solicitation. Although he intended to communicate the solicitation, he did not possess the specific intent to have Y commit the crime.

2. Model Penal Code

The Model Penal Code does not deal in concepts of "specific intent" and "general intent." However, the analysis is the same: a person is not guilty of solicitation unless she acts with the purpose of promoting or facilitating the commission of the solicited offense. MPC § 5.02(1).

D. Defense: Renunciation

The Model Penal Code—but not the common law—provides a defense to the crime of solicitation if the soliciting party: (1) completely and voluntarily renounces her criminal intent; and (2) persuades the solicited party not to commit the offense or otherwise prevents her from committing the crime. MPC § 5.02(3).

IV. Other Inchoate Offenses

A. Assault

1. Common Law Definition

A common law assault is an attempted battery. (A battery is unlawful application of force to the person of another.) However, the common law recognized "assault" as an offense before criminal attempt laws developed, so attempt doctrines do not apply to it. To be guilty of assault, a person must engage in conduct that is in closer proximity to completion than is generally required for other attempt offenses.

Example: As seen earlier, a person may be convicted of attempted murder although she has not committed the last act necessary, *e.g.*, she has not pulled the trigger of a gun or begun stabbing the victim. However, to be guilty of assault (attempted battery), the actor must usually commit the last act, such as swinging her fist at *V*.

2. Modern Statutes

Nearly all states have broadened the definition of assault to include the tort definition of assault: intentionally placing another person in reasonable apprehension of an imminent battery.

Example: D swings her fist at *V*, in order to scare *V*. D is not guilty of common law assault, but she may be guilty of statutory assault, if her conduct placed *V* in reasonable apprehension of an unlawful touching.

B. Inchoate Offenses in Disguise

Various common law offenses and modern statutes may be considered, in some sense, inchoate crimes in disguise. They are worth brief note here, in this context.

1. Burglary

Common law burglary involves "breaking and entering the dwelling house of another at night with the intent to commit a felony therein." Thus, burglary only occurs if a person not only breaks into another person's dwelling at night, but has the further specific intention to commit a serious crime inside the dwelling. *The latter felony is inchoate at* the time that the *actus reus* of burglary (breaking and entering) occurs. Yet, at early common law, when burglary law was in formulation, it was not evident that the burglar could be prosecuted, at the moment he entered the home, for an attempt to commit the felony inside. He had to come closer to perpetration of *that* felony. The burglary offense, however, provided law enforcement the opportunity to arrest a suspected felon before he came dangerously close to committing the crime inside.

2. Larceny

Common law larceny is the trespassory taking and carrying away of the personal property of another with the intent to steal the property, *i.e.* permanently deprive the other of the property. As with burglary, the specific intent points to the inchoate aspect of the offense. The ultimate harm of theft comes when the wrongdoer *permanently* deprives the person of the property. *That* harm has not occurred at the moment when the thief nonconsensually "takes and carries away" the personal property of another. If all that we were concerned with is the taking and carrying away of property, there would be no need to add the specific intent to the definition of the crime: it is that latter intent, not yet brought to fruition, that converts the taking into a felony.

V. Review Questions

[Answers Provided in Appendix A, page 366]

1. T or F.   At common law, criminal attempt is treated as a lesser offense than the successful completion of the target crime.

2. Name and explain at least three common law tests for determining whether a defendant has done sufficient acts to constitute an attempt.

3. T or F.   Attempted rape is a specific-intent crime at common law.

4. Donald Despicable has sexual intercourse with a female he believes is unconscious from extreme intoxication. In fact, the female is dead. Donald is charged with attempted rape. At common law:

   a.   This is a case of factual impossibility;

   b.   This is a case of pure legal impossibility; or

   c.   This is a case of hybrid legal impossibility.

5. What result in Question 4, at common law: Is Despicable guilty or not guilty of attempted rape?

6. What result in Question 4, under the Model Penal Code.

7. Denise intends to kill Victor. She comes to Victor's house with a loaded gun and waits behind a bush for Victor to come out of his house. When Victor comes out, Denise decides not to kill Victor now or in the future, and leaves. Is Denise guilty of attempted murder under the MPC? What about the common law?

8. T of F. At common law, a person may be convicted of conspiracy with another to commit an act that, if he committed it alone, would not constitute a crime.

9. Alex, a licensed gun dealer, sells a gun to Bob at a regular price, with knowledge Bob intends to use the gun to murder Carl. At common law, is Alex guilty of conspiracy with Bob to commit murder? What about under the MPC?

10. Betty and Karen agree to duel, a crime. If they are serious about this, are they guilty of common law conspiracy?

11. Chester and Donald agree to rob First State Bank. It turns out later that Donald was involuntarily intoxicated at the time Chester and he formed the agreement and, therefore, he did not really know what it was he agreed to. Chester and Donald are charged with conspiracy to rob the bank. What result under the common law? What about the Model Penal Code?

12. Jack and Jill meet on Day 1 and decide to rob Bank1. The next day, they decide they should also rob Bank 2. (Assume they have not robbed either bank yet.) How many charges of conspiracy are permitted here? Try the common law, and then MPC.

13. Roger and Carl agree to murder the President. The next day, before either person has acted on this plan, Carl tells Roger, "forget it. I am out. I don't want to do this." Are Roger and Carl guilty of conspiracy to commit murder? Apply the common law.

14. Alex asks Richard to kill Carl. Richard says no. At common law, is Alex guilty of solicitation? Can you think of any other crime of which he might be guilty?

15. Gina writes an e-mail message she intends to send to Bill, requesting that Bill steal certain property from Harold. Gina then decides it is a bad idea. She

tries to push the DELETE button on her computer but accidentally pushes the SEND button. Harold receives and reads Gina's message. Is Gina guilty of common law solicitation?

16. Is there anything odd about charging a person with the offense of attempted assault?

PART NINE

Complicity

■ *ANALYSIS*

CONVERSATION WITH STUDENTS

We now turn to an issue we have only tangentially discussed so far: the circumstances under which a person who does not personally commit a crime may be held accountable for the actions of another.

There are two theories of so-called complicity liability. First, a person is accountable for the actions of another if she is an *accomplice* in the commission of the crime. Second, she is accountable if she *conspires* (as that concept was explained in Part Eight) with another person.

Usually, an accomplice in a crime is also a co-conspirator, in which case both complicity theories apply. However, it is possible to conspire without assisting, or vice-versa. Therefore, each theory should be considered separately. It is especially important that you do so because, as you will see, conspiracy liability potentially is broader than accomplice liability.

I. Accomplice Liability: Common Law

A. General Principles

1. General Rule

Subject to clarification below, a person is an accomplice in the commission of an offense if she intentionally assists another person to engage in the conduct that constitutes the offense.

2. Accomplice Liability as Derivative Liability

An important point to remember—as it will help you understand accomplice law—is that accomplice liability is derivative in nature. That is, an accomplice's liability derives from the primary party to whom she provided assistance. Put another way, there is no crime of "aiding and abetting." The accomplice is ordinarily convicted of the offense committed by the primary party.

Example: If *A* intentionally assists *P* to rob a bank by driving the get-away vehicle, *A* is guilty of the crime of robbery. She derives her guilt for robbery from *P*. It follows that if *P* is arrested in the bank while *attempting* the robbery, *A* is guilty of *attempted* robbery instead: as that is the crime *P* committed, this is the crime that she derives. If *P* is stopped before his actions reach the "attempt" stage—in which case, presumably, *P* is guilty of no offense—*A* is also guilty of no offense relating to the bank robbery, as there is no liability to derive from *P*. (Of course, *A* and *P* may be convicted of the crime of *conspiracy* to commit robbery.)

3. Justification for Derivative Liability

Accomplice liability is loosely based on the civil concept of agency. That is, when a person intentionally assists another person in the commission of an offense, she manifests thereby her willingness to be held accountable for the conduct of the other person, *i.e.*, she allows the perpetrator of the crime to serve as her agent.

4. Common Law Terminology

There are four common law categories of parties to criminal offenses. Nearly every state has abolished these categories, but the terminology persists in many judicial opinions.

a. Principal in the First Degree

He is the person who, with the requisite *mens rea*, personally commits the offense (*e.g.*, in murder, fires the gun that kills the victim; in rape, personally has sexual intercourse with the nonconsenting female), or who uses an innocent human instrumentality to commit it.

i. Innocent Instrumentality Doctrine

A person is a principal in the first degree if she dupes or coerces an innocent human being to perform the acts that constitute an offense.

Examples: P puts a gun to *I*'s head, and threatens to kill *I* unless *I* robs *V*. If *I* accedes to the threat, *I* will be acquitted of robbery on the ground of duress; *P* may be convicted of robbery, as the principal in the first degree, on the ground that she used *I* as her innocent instrumentality.

P says to *I*, "Please go next door and pick up my automobile, which I loaned to *V*, and bring it back to me." *I* agrees, and brings the vehicle to *P*, unaware of the fact that the car really belongs to *V*. *I* is not guilty of larceny, as he lacked the specific intent of the offense (he did not take and carry away *V*'s property with the intent to steal it). Instead, *P* will be convicted of larceny, as the principal in the first degree, because she duped *I* into performing the larcenous acts.

b. **Principal in the Second Degree**

She is the person who intentionally assists the principal in the first degree to commit the offense, and who is actually or constructively present during its commission. A person is "constructively" present if she is close enough to assist the principal in the first degree during the crime.

Example: P robs a bank, while *A1* stands guard at the door, and *A2* remains in the car, ready to drive them away. P is the principal in the first degree; *A1* is a principal in the second degree, as she is actually present. *A2* is also a principal in the second degree, as she is constructively present.

c. **Accessory Before the Fact**

She is one who intentionally assists in the commission of the offense, but who is not actually or constructively present during its commission.

Example: *A* is an accessory before the fact if she solicits a murder, or if she intentionally furnishes *P* with a gun for use in the homicide, but she is not present at the time of the crime. *Notice:* one who is guilty of the *crime* of solicitation is thereby an accomplice in the commission of the solicited crime.

d. **Accessory After the Fact**

She is one who knowingly assists a felon to avoid arrest, trial, or conviction. Although the common law treated an accessory after the fact as an accomplice in the commission of the crime and, thus, held her responsible for that crime, all states today treat accessoryship after the fact as an offense separate from, and less serious than, the felony committed by the principal in the first degree. Consequently, accessories *after* the fact will not be discussed further.

e. **Why the Distinctions Mattered**

The distinction between principals (of either degree), on the one hand, and accessories, on the other hand, was of substantial practical procedural significance in the common law era. The procedural distinctions have almost universally been abrogated.

i. **Venue**

A principal had to be brought to trial in the jurisdiction in which the crime occurred. An accessory had to be prosecuted in the jurisdiction in which her accessorial acts occurred.

ii. Proper Pleading

An indictment had to state correctly whether the party charged was a principal or an accessory. A person indicted as a principal could not be convicted as an accessory, or vice-versa.

iii. Timing of Prosecution

Principals and accessories could be tried jointly, or a principal could be tried first, but under no circumstances could an accessory be brought to trial before the principal was prosecuted.

iv. Acquittal of Principal

An accessory could not be convicted if the principal was acquitted, regardless of the reason for the principal's acquittal.

(1) *Important Study Point*

Although the common law procedural rules set out above no longer apply, this latter rule remains relevant in some circumstances. See subsection I.D. below.

B. What Makes a Person an Accomplice: Assistance

A person "assists" in an offense, and thus may be an accomplice in its commission, if she solicits or encourages another person to commit the crime, or if she aids in its commission.

1. If No Assistance

A person is not an accomplice unless her conduct *in fact* assists in commission of the crime.

Example: A, intending to help *P* burglarize *V*'s home, opens a window at *V*'s house so that *P* can enter. *P*, unaware that the window has been opened, enters by another route. *A* is not an accomplice on the basis of the window opening. Conceptually, *A attempted* to assist, but she did not *in fact* aid in the commission of the crime.

2. Trivial Assistance

If a person intentionally aids in the commission of an offense, she is liable as an accomplice, although her assistance was trivial. *Indeed, an accomplice is liable even if the crime would have occurred without her assistance, i.e., she is guilty although her assistance did not cause commission of the offense.* It is enough that the accomplice made commission of the crime slightly easier.

Example: In the window-opening *Example* immediately above, if *P* had entered the window that *A* opened, this assistance would render *A* liable as an accomplice (assuming that *A* had the requisite *mens rea*), even if *P* would have committed the crime anyway.

a. Encouragement

Because any actual assistance, no matter how trivial, qualifies, a person may be an accomplice merely by providing psychological encouragement to the perpetrator.

Example: *P* says to *A*, his wife, "I am going now to rob the bank." *A* to *P*, "That's wonderful dear. I love you." Remarkably, these words of encouragement can serve as the basis for treating *A* as an accomplice.

3. Presence at the Scene

It follows from what has been set out above, a person who is present at the scene of a crime, *even if she is present in order to aid in commission of the offense*, is not an accomplice unless she *in fact* assists in the crime. Although "mere presence" does not constitute assistance, it does not take much to convert presence into trivial assistance. In some circumstances, a person's presence could provide psychological encouragement to the principal, which is enough to trigger accomplice liability.

Example: *A* agrees to sit in a car and serve as a lookout for *P*, while *P* breaks into a home. *P* goes into the house. *A* falls asleep in the car and never serves as a lookout. Nonetheless, *A*'s offer provided encouragement to *P*, which is assistance. (Also, notice that *A* is a co-conspirator in these circumstances and may be held responsible under conspiracy theory, as discussed later in this Part.)

4. Omissions

Although a person is not generally an accomplice if she simply permits a crime to occur, one may be an accomplice by failing to act to prevent a crime, when she has a duty to so act.

Example: *A*, a police officer, observes a crime being committed. She stands by and does nothing. As it is her duty to intervene, *A*'s omission constitutes assistance. If *A* omitted her duty with the requisite *mens rea*—she wanted the crime to occur—she is an accomplice in its commission.

C. What Makes a Person an Accomplice: *Mens Rea*

1. Rule

A person is an accomplice in the commission of an offense if she possesses two mental states. She must: (1) intentionally engage in the acts of assistance; and (2) act with the level of culpability required in the definition of the offense in which she assisted. (This rule is subject to one exception, described below in subsection C.3.) The easy cases to analyze involve offenses for which "intent" is the required *mens rea*.

Examples: *A* is a customer in a bank when *P* is robbing it. *A* notices what is going on. Out of surprise, she exclaims, "I wonder if the robber notices the bank camera." Alerted by these words, *P* shoots out the camera and completes the offense. On these facts, *A* has assisted in the crime, but she is not an accomplice. That is, her words assisted *P*, albeit perhaps minimally, in the commission of the robbery. Furthermore, *A* intentionally uttered the words of assistance (the first *mens rea* described above). However, *A* did *not* act with the intent that *P* commit the robbery (the second *mens rea*).

Same as this last Example, but add one new fact: *A* says to herself when she spots *P* robbing the bank, "Good! These bastards didn't give me a loan when I asked for it. I want this guy to get away with millions." Then, speaking out loud, *A* warns *P* about the camera. Now *A* not only has the first *mens rea* described above, but also the second. *A* is an accomplice.

2. Crimes of Recklessness or Negligence

Notice that, whereas the first *mens rea* set out above requires proof of intent—the intent to perform the acts that in fact constitute the assistance—the second *mens rea* requirement, relating to the commission of the crime itself, is that the individual possess the level of culpability required in the definition of the offense in which she assisted. The prosecutor does not have to prove that the accomplice *intended* a crime of recklessness to occur: it is enough that she was reckless in regard to the ensuing harm; as for a crime of negligence, it is enough to show that the would-be accomplice was negligent in regard to the ensuring harm.

Example: *A* is in a rush to get to the airport. She tells *P*, a taxi driver, "I am very late for a plane. You will have to speed. I will give you a huge tip if you get me there on time." As a result, *P* drives at a negligent rate of speed, and kills *V*, a pedestrian. Assume from these facts that *P* is guilty of negligent manslaughter. On these facts, *A* may also plausibly be convicted of manslaughter. Here is why: she assisted *P* in commission of the offense by soliciting or encouraging *P* to drive above the speed limit; her words of solicitation or encouragement were intentionally expressed (the first *mens rea* element); as to the second *mens rea* requirement, she may be convicted if her assistance (offering a large tip and telling *P* to rush) constituted criminal negligence, the *mens rea* required for the offense committed by *P*. Quite arguably, she should have realized that her words would cause *P* to drive in a dangerous manner and, thus, risk human life. Consequently, *A* was negligent, the *mens rea* for the crime charged.

3. Natural–And–Probable–Consequences Doctrine

An accomplice is guilty not only of the offense she intended to facilitate or encourage, but also of any reasonably foreseeable offense committed by the person she aided. Put more precisely, once the prosecutor proves that *A* was an accomplice of *P* in the commission of Crime 1 (using the analysis discussed so far), *A* is also responsible for any other offense committed by *P* that was a natural and probable consequence of Crime 1.

Examples: *A* intentionally assists *P* in an armed robbery of *V* (Crime 1). To *A*'s surprise and dismay, *P* intentionally kills *V* during the robbery because *V* resists (Crime 2). *A* is an accomplice in the robbery by *P* based on the principles we have studied. She is also guilty of the intent-to-kill murder of *V*, even though she did not intend for the death to occur because the death of an armed robbery victim is a natural and probable—foreseeable—consequence of this crime.

In the same armed robbery example, assume that *P* also intentionally kills *X*, who is across the street from *V*, because *X* was having an affair with *P*'s spouse, and this was *P*'s first opportunity to exact revenge. *This* homicide is not foreseeable, so *A* will *not* be guilty of *X*'s murder, although she remains accountable for the robbery and *V*'s death.

D. Accomplice Liability: If the Perpetrator Is Acquitted

Remember that accomplice liability is derivative in nature. Therefore, ordinarily, but not always, acquittal of the principal in the first degree should result in acquittal of the alleged accomplice as a matter of logic.

1. If No Crime Occurred

If a jury finds that the alleged crime never occurred and, therefore, acquits the principal in the first degree, it logically follows that any accomplice must be acquitted as well, as there is no guilt to derive—one cannot be an accomplice to a nonexistent crime.

Example: P is prosecuted for rape of *V. A* is prosecuted as *P*'s accomplice. *P*'s defense at trial is that no rape occurred because *V* consented. The jury acquits *P*. It must also acquit *A. A* cannot be an accomplice to something (rape) that the jury has concluded didn't happen!

2. If Perpetrator Is Acquitted on Grounds of a Defense

If a jury acquits the alleged perpetrator of a crime on the ground that he was justified in his actions, then the accomplice should also be acquitted, as this means she aided in a justified (proper) act. But, if the jury acquits the perpetrator on the ground of an excuse, then the jury has determined that a crime *has* occurred. The perpetrator's excuse claim is personal to him, and should not protect the accomplice.

Examples: A assists *P* escape prison. In a subsequent prosecution for escape, *P* claims that he fled because of intolerable prison conditions. If *P* is acquitted on the ground of necessity—a lesser-evils justification defense—*A* should also be acquitted, because she cannot derive criminal liability from a lawful (justified) act. See *United States v. Lopez*, 662 F. Supp. 1083 (N.D. Cal. 1987).

On the other hand, if the jury acquits *P* on the ground of duress—an excuse—*A* may properly be convicted. Under such circumstances, the jury has concluded that a crime occurred, but that *P* should not be held accountable for it because she was coerced. Unless *A* was also coerced, there is no reason why *A* should not be held accountable for the crime that occurred.

E. Perpetrator and Accomplice: Degrees of Guilt

The common law rule used to be that an accessory before the fact could not be convicted of a more serious offense, or a higher degree of an offense, than that for which the principal was convicted. (It has nearly always been the case that an accomplice may be convicted of a *lesser* degree of crime than the principal in the first degree.) This rule is breaking down. Even in an earlier era, however, most courts treated criminal homicides differently: on the right facts, courts were and are prepared to convict an accomplice of a higher degree of criminal homicide than the perpetrator.

Example: A wants *P* to kill *V. A* knows that *P*'s spouse is having an affair with *V*, so *A* induces *P* to go home one afternoon when *A* knows that *P* will discover his wife in bed with *V. P* arrives home, discovers the act of adultery, and in sudden passion kills *V.* Based on criminal homicide doctrine, *P* is guilty of voluntary manslaughter. *A*, who not only intended the killing to occur, but acted calmly and premeditatedly, may be convicted of murder. *See People v. McCoy*, 25 Cal. 4th 1111, 108 Cal. Rptr.2d 188, 24 P.3d 1210 (2001).

F. Special Defense: Legislative–Exemption Rule

A person may not be convicted as an accomplice in her own victimization.

Example: A, an underage female, assisted *P* break into *V*'s home one night, so that *P* and *A* could use *V*'s home to have sexual intercourse. *P* was charged with burglary, on the ground that he broke and entered another person's home at night with the intent to commit a felony—statutory rape of *A*—therein. Although *P* was guilty of this offense, and *A* did assist in the burglary, she is not guilty of the burglary. *In re Meagan R.*, 42 Cal.App. 4th 17, 49 Cal.Rptr.2d 325 (1996). This is because statutory rape laws are intended to protect underage females; *A*, therefore, may not properly be convicted as an accomplice in her own statutory rape. As she may claim a "legislative exemption" defense to the charge of being an accomplice in the statutory rape, which was the underlying felony in the burglary, she is also legislatively exempt in the burglary prosecution.

II. Conspiracy Liability

A. The *Pinkerton* Doctrine

At common law, a person may be held accountable for the actions of others either as an accomplice, discussed above, or as a conspirator. A controversial feature of conspiracy law in many, but not all, jurisdictions is the *Pinkerton* doctrine, named after the Supreme Court ruling in *Pinkerton v. United States*, 328 U.S. 640, 66 S.Ct. 1180, 90 L.Ed. 1489 (1946). This doctrine provides that a co-conspirator is responsible for any crime committed by any other member of the conspiracy, whether or not he assisted, if the offense was an object of the conspiracy or a reasonably foreseeable consequence thereof.

Example: In *Pinkerton*, *A* and *P* conspired to violate certain tax laws. However, *A* did not assist in their commission because he was in prison on an unrelated offense when the tax crimes occurred. Under *accomplice* liability, *A* was not guilty of the tax law violations. However, under the doctrine announced in the case, *A* was guilty of the tax-law violations because they were the object of the conspiracy.

1. Breadth of the Rule

The *Pinkerton* doctrine can result in exceptionally broad liability. Conspiratorial agreements are often open-ended, such as a conspiracy "to rob banks," "to commit prostitution," or "to distribute narcotics." Thus, the conspiracy can last a very long time, involve many parties (both major and minor in involvement), and include many crimes. Under *Pinkerton*, *every* member of the conspiracy will be guilty of *every* crime committed by *every* other member of the conspiracy, as long as the crime is among the objects of the conspiracy (*e.g.*, a bank robbery, an act of prostitution, or a sale of narcotics), or is a reasonably foreseeable outgrowth of the broad conspiracy (*e.g.*, theft of a car to use in the bank robbery, a homicide to protect the drug dealers, bribery of a police officer to overlook the prostitution, etc.).

III. Model Penal Code

A. Forms of Complicity Liability

MPC complicity liability is set out in Section 2.06.

1. Innocent–Instrumentality Doctrine

A person is guilty of an offense that she did not personally commit if, acting with the requisite *mens rea*, she "causes an innocent or irresponsible person" to commit the crime. MPC § 2.06(2)(a). This is equivalent to the common law innocent-instrumentality rule discussed earlier. The same analysis applies.

2. Accomplice Liability

A person is guilty of an offense that she did not personally commit if she is an accomplice of another person in the commission of the offense. MPC § 2.06(2)(c).

a. Study Point

Notice: Under the Code, accomplice liability is conceptually independent of the innocent-instrumentality doctrine. Thus, when the Code uses the word "accomplice" in Section 2.06, it is *not* speaking of a person who uses an innocent or irresponsible person to commit an offense. Treat them separately!

3. *Pinkerton* Rule

The broad *Pinkerton* conspiracy doctrine discussed above is not recognized in the Code.

B. What Makes a Person an Accomplice: Assistance

1. Rule

To be an accomplice in the commission of an offense, the person must: (a) solicit the offense; (b) aid, agree to aid, or attempt to aid in its commission; or (c) fail to make a proper effort to prevent commission of the offense (assuming that she has a legal duty to act). MPC § 2.06(3)(a)(i)-(iii).

2. Comparison to Common Law

a. "Agree to aid"
This provision differs from the common law. It permits potentially *greater* liability than common law accomplice liability.

Example: A agrees to drive the get-away car in a bank robbery to be committed by *P*. *A* does not live up to her promise—she fails to show up on the day of the crime. *P* goes ahead with the robbery anyway. At common law, *A* would not be guilty of robbery under *accomplice* liability (she did not in fact aid), but she would be guilty under the Code, as she agreed to aid.

b. "Attempt to Aid"
This provision goes beyond the common law, as it permits accomplice liability if an actor tries, but fails, to aid in commission of the offense.

Example: Reconsider the window-opening *Example* (I.B.1., *supra*), in which *A* opened a window in order to assist *P* in entering a house to commit a crime, but *P* entered by another route. *A* would be guilty of the ensuing crime under the MPC. Although *A* did not aid in the crime, she attempted to do so.

C. What Makes a Person an Accomplice: *Mens Rea*

1. Rule
To be an accomplice, the person must act "with the purpose of promoting or facilitating the commission of the offense." MPC § 2.06(3)(a).

2. Exception to the Requirement of Purpose
The MPC handles the common law issue discussed above—liability for a crime of recklessness or negligence—with the following provision: A person who is an accomplice in the commission of *conduct* that causes a criminal *result*, is also an accomplice in the *result* thereof, if she has the level of culpability regarding the *result* required in the definition of the offense. MPC § 2.06(4).

Example: Reconsider the taxi-cab hypothetical discussed in I.C.2., *supra.* *A* would be guilty of negligent homicide as an accomplice of *P.* The MPC analysis will go as follows: First, ask whether *A* was an accomplice in the commission of the conduct (the speeding) that caused the result (the death). The answer would seem to be that she was: she encouraged the speeding (the assistance) with the purpose of promoting this conduct (the *mens rea*). Second, did *A* have the requisite *mens rea* (negligence) regarding the result (death)? On these facts, yes.

D. Accomplice Liability: If the Perpetrator Is Acquitted

MPC § 2.06(7) provides that an accomplice in the commission of the offense may be convicted of that offense, even if the alleged perpetrator "has been convicted of a different offense or degree of offense or . . . has been acquitted." One must be very careful in reading this provision: *if there has been no offense,* then one is not an accomplice "in the commission of *the offense.*" Therefore, although an accomplice may properly be convicted if the perpetrator is acquitted on the ground of an excuse defense, an accomplice should *not* be convicted if there was no offense, *i.e.,* the principal party was acquitted on the ground of a justification defense.

E. Special Defenses

1. Legislative–Exemption Rule

Like the common law, the MPC applies the legislative-exemption rule (see I.F. above). MPC § 2.06(6)(a).

2. Inevitable Incidence

An accomplice is not guilty of an offense if her conduct is an inevitable incident to the commission of the offense. MPC § 2.06(6)(b).

Example: A customer in the act of prostitution is not an accomplice in its commission.

3. Abandonment

A person is not an accomplice in the commission of a crime if she terminates her participation before the crime is committed, and if she either neutralizes her assistance, gives timely warning to the police of the impending offense, or in some other manner prevents commission of the crime. MPC § 2.06(6)(c).

F. Special Provision to Consider: Relationship of Accomplice Liability to Criminal Attempts

Note the relation between the MPC complicity provisions and the law of attempts. The Code goes well beyond the common law by permitting an accomplice to be convicted of criminal attempt, if she attempts to aid in commission of an offense, *although the other person does not commit or even attempt the offense.* MPC § 5.01(3).

Example: A furnishes P with a gun to kill V. Thereafter, P changes his mind and abandons his plan. At common law, P is not guilty of anything (except conspiracy, which for present purposes we can ignore). Because A derives her liability from P, A is also free of common law liability. Under the Code, however, A is guilty of attempted murder, although P is guilty of nothing! This is *not* a violation of the concept of derivative liability, because the Code is *not* convicting A on the basis of accomplice liability. Instead, A is the *perpetrator* of the offense of attempted murder (more conceptually accurately, the perpetrator of the offense of attempting *to aid* a murder), which MPC § 5.01(3) makes an offense!

IV. Review Questions

[Answers Provided in Appendix A, page 368]

1. Bob takes Carl's child hostage. Bob threatens to kill Carl unless Carl rapes Vanessa in his presence. To save his child, Carl rapes Vanessa. Which of the following best describes Bob's common law liability for the rape?

   a. He is the principal in the first degree;

   b. He is the principal in the second degree;

   c. He is an accessory before the fact; or

   d. None of the above.

2. Assume the same facts as the last question, except that Bob commands Carl to *kill* Vanessa. Carl kills Vanessa. Which of the possible answers above best describes Bob's common law liability for the criminal homicide?

3. T or F. Joshua accompanies Carla to the liquor store. Joshua knows that Carla plans to rob the store. Carla does not know Joshua is aware of this. Joshua intends to help, if needed. That is why he is there. His assistance is never needed: Carla robs the store without his help. Joshua is *not* guilty of the robbery.

4. Janice loans Xavier her car, although he is severely drunk. Janice was not aware of his condition, but should have been. Xavier drives the car and, due

to intoxication, recklessly kills a pedestrian. Assume that Xavier's recklessness is so extreme that he is guilty of murder. Of what MPC crime, if any, is Janice guilty?

5. Kelli, a fifteen-year-old female, helps Roger, a thirty-year-old male, have intercourse with Camille, another fifteen-year-old female. Roger is guilty of statutory rape. Is Kelli guilty of statutory rape?

6. Nellie, a drug peddler in Chicago, is a member of a nationwide drug conspiracy consisting of Smuggler, Middleman (who furnishes Nellie with the drugs she sells on the street), and drug peddlers in 50 other cities who also receive their drugs from Smuggler and Middleman. Overall, the other drug peddlers conduct 42,976 drug sales, 47 batteries and 1 murder of buyers who failed to pay for their drugs. Nellie in no way assisted in the crimes in the other cities. Is Nellie guilty of these non-Chicago criminal activities? Answer under the common law, and Model Penal Code.

7. Carlos furnishes a gun to Zelda so she can murder Kelly. Thereafter, Carlos has a change of heart and tells Zelda, "I want my gun back. Don't kill Kelly." Zelda ignores Carlos and proceeds to kill Kelly. Is Carlos an accomplice in the murder? Apply the MPC.

8. Let's turn the facts around a bit from Question 7. This time Carlos furnishes the gun to Zelda to kill Kelly, but *doesn't* has a change of heart, *but Zelda* does. Zelda does not kill Kelly, or even attempt the crime. Under the MPC, is Carlos guilty of anything?

*

PART TEN

Criminal Homicide

■ *ANALYSIS*

B. Murder

C. Manslaughter

D. Negligent Homicide

V. Review Questions

CONVERSATION WITH STUDENTS

We now discuss the common law crimes of murder and manslaughter, as well as the statutory variations on the common law, including the Model Penal Code.

Be careful: most or all of the homicide cases you read in your casebook are based on a particular state's homicide statute (perhaps the MPC version), which will *not* precisely mirror the common law version of the crime. Learning the common law here is just a starting point—an important one, however—to understanding modern homicide law.

One more point: The discussion below necessarily uses *mens rea* terms we discussed earlier. If you need to refresh your memory, look back at Part Three.

I. Criminal Homicide: Overview

A. "Homicide"

1. Definition

The English common law defined "homicide" as "the killing of a human being by a human being." In American common law, it is "the killing of a human being by *another* human being." Thus, the first definition, but not the second, treats suicide as a form of homicide. We will focus on the American version. Notice, too: "homicide" is a legally neutral term. A homicide may be justifiable, excusable or criminal.

2. "Criminal Homicide"

A criminal homicide is a homicide committed without justification (*e.g.*, in self-defense) or excuse (*e.g.*, as the result of insanity).

B. "Human Being"

1. At the Start of Life

The common law provides that a fetus is not a human being until it is born alive. *Keeler v. Superior Court*, 2 Cal.3d 619, 87 Cal. Rptr. 481, 470 P.2d 617 (1970). Therefore, a person is not guilty of criminal homicide if he causes a fetus to be stillborn.

Example: In *Keeler, supra*, K intentionally struck his estranged wife in the abdomen when he learned that she was pregnant by another man. The viable fetus was born dead. *K* was prosecuted for murder, based on a statute that did not define the term "human being." The state supreme court held that in the absence of a statutory definition, the common law definition prevailed. Therefore, *K* was not guilty of murder, as he did not kill a human being.

2. At the End of Life

At common law, a person is legally dead (and, therefore, ceases to be a "human being") when there is a total stoppage of the circulation of the blood and a permanent cessation of the functions of respiration and heart pulsation.

a. Brain Death

The common law definition has proven impractical in modern times. Due to life-support machinery, it is possible artificially to maintain the heart and lung activities of patients who have lost the spontaneous capacity to perform these functions. Therefore, the trend among the states, in part by common law but mostly by statute, has been to redefine death. Today, virtually every state provides that a person may be deemed legally dead if he experiences an irreversible cessation of breathing and heartbeat (the common law definition), *or* suffers from "brain death syndrome," which occurs when the whole brain (not just one portion of it) permanently loses the capacity to function.

C. Year–and–A–Day Rule

At common law, a homicide prosecution may only be brought if the victim dies within one year and a day of the injury inflicted by the accused.

Example: *D* stabs *V* in the stomach on March 1, 2000. If *V* dies on or before March 1, 2001 as the result of the stab wounds, a homicide prosecution may be brought. If *V* dies thereafter, a homicide prosecution is barred. In such circumstances, *D* may be prosecuted for a non-homicide offense, such as assault with intent to kill.

1. Rationale of Rule

In the early, medically unsophisticated common law era, courts were concerned that if a death occurred too long after the initial attack, the factfinder would be unable to determine reliably whether the death was the result of natural or criminal causes. Therefore, an arbitrary line was drawn: it was considered unfair to hold the defendant responsible for the death if a year and a day passed.

2. Modern Approach

Today, the cause of death can be ascertained far more easily than centuries ago, so the risk of unfair prosecution is reduced. Moreover, life-support machinery can artificially sustain a person's life well beyond a year and a day, thereby frustrating criminal prosecutions. Consequently, many states have abolished or modified the rule.

D. A Brief Touch of History

In early English history, criminal homicide was a single offense, punishable by death. Gradually, English judges determined that some homicides, although criminal, should not be punished by death. As a result, the offense was divided into two offenses: murder and manslaughter. The latter was a statutory non-capital offense in England. However, manslaughter is a common law offense in this country.

II. Common Law: Murder

A. Definition of "Murder"

Common law murder is a killing of a human being by another human being *with malice aforethought*.

1. "Malice"

A person acts with "malice" if she unjustifiably, inexcusably, and in the absence of any mitigating circumstance, kills a person with any one of four mental states: (a) the intention to kill a human being; (b) the intention to inflict grievous bodily injury on another; (c) an extremely reckless disregard for the value of human life (often called "depraved heart" at common law); or (d) the intention to commit a felony during the commission or attempted commission of which a death accidentally occurs (the "felony-murder rule"). These four categories of malice are considered below.

2. "Aforethought"

Originally, the term "aforethought" meant that the actor thought about the killing beforehand, *i.e.*, that he premeditated the killing. Over time, the term lost significance, except as a reminder of the obvious: that the "malicious" mental state must occur at the time of the homicide, rather than after the killing. The law doesn't punish people for killing with "malice *after*thought."

B. Murder: Intent to Kill

1. General Rule

In view of the definition of "malice aforethought" set out above, an intentional killing that is unjustifiable (*e.g.*, not committed in self-defense), inexcusable (*e.g.*, not committed by an insane person), and unmitigated (*e.g.*, not the result of sudden heat of passion) constitutes common law murder.

2. Proving Intent

"Intent" is a subjective form of fault. The prosecutor must prove beyond a reasonable doubt that the killer *purposely* or *knowingly* took another's life. How does the prosecutor determine that it was the conscious objective of the killer to take life, or that this person subjectively knew that death was virtually certain to result from his conduct?

a. Natural and Probable Consequences Inference

Until 1979, juries were often instructed in murder prosecutions that "the law presumes that a person *intends* the natural and probable consequences of his voluntary acts."

Example: D aims a loaded gun at *V*'s head, and fires the weapon, killing *V*. Unless *V* confesses, or there is strong evidence of a motive to kill, a jury might find it difficult to determine *D*'s subjective intentions. However, under the instruction quoted above, the jury would presume the "natural and probable consequence" of *D*'s conduct of pointing a loaded gun at *V*'s head and pulling the trigger: namely, that she intended to kill *V*.

i. Constitutional Law Intervenes

This instruction violates the Due Process Clause of the United States Constitution, because it improperly shifts the burden of proof regarding an element of the offense (malice aforethought, via a finding of intent-to-kill) from the prosecutor to the defendant. *Sandstrom v. Montana*, 442 U.S. 510, 99 S.Ct. 2450, 61 L.Ed.2d 39 (1979). (See generally Part One.)

ii. Common sense to the Rescue

The jury instruction simply points out the obvious. In the absence of evidence that the actor is of subnormal intelligence, is mentally unstable, or deeply intoxicated, it is reasonable to infer that a person intends the natural and probable consequences of her actions. Therefore, even without an instruction, a jury may infer (*but not presume*) intent.

b. Deadly Weapon Rule

A corollary of the natural-and-probable-consequences inference is the "deadly weapon" rule, which provides that a jury may infer an intent to kill, if the defendant intentionally uses a deadly weapon directed at a vital part of the human anatomy. In appropriate cases, jurors may be instructed that they may, but need not, draw this inference.

3. **Statutory Reform: "Wilful, Deliberate, Premeditated" Formula**

a. Historical Note

As noted above, English judges determined that not all criminal homicides justified the death penalty. So, they divided criminal homicide into two offenses. Murder carried the death penalty; manslaughter did not. In this country, legislatures took the process one step further. Starting in Pennsylvania (thus, the so-called "Pennsylvania Model"), many states concluded that not all *murders* merited the death penalty and, as a consequence, they divided murder into degrees. Only first-degree murder carried the possibility of capital punishment.

i. Study Point

Although most states followed the Pennsylvania Model and divided murder into two degrees, you must remember that **the common law had no degrees of murder.** So, if you are tested on the common law, you would be wrong to discuss "first-degree" or "second-degree" (or, for that matter, "tenth-degree" murder). **There was no such thing at common law.** The "wilful, deliberate, premeditation" formula about to be discussed **was not part of the common law analysis.** To decide whether a particular murder is "first-degree," "second-degree," or any other degree—or whether it is just plain old "murder"—can only be answered by *reading and interpreting the particular statute in question.*

b. The "Wilful, Deliberate, Premeditated" Formula

In states that have followed the Pennsylvania Model, which divides murder into degrees, a "wilful, deliberate, premeditated" killing is first-degree murder. What do these terms mean?

i. **Wilful**

In the context of murder statutes, this term means, simply, "intentional." (This is where we find the "malice aforethought" needed for murder.)

ii. **Premeditated**

To "premeditate" is "to think about beforehand." *People v. Morrin*, 31 Mich. App. 301, 187 N.W.2d 434 (1971). But, this does not tell us how long one much think about a killing beforehand to constitute "premeditation."

(1) **How Much Premeditation?**

Some courts state that "no time is too short" for a person to premeditate, *e.g., Commonwealth v. Carrol*, 412 Pa. 525, 194 A.2d 911 (1963); "an intent to kill need exist only for an instant." *State v. Schrader*, 172 W.Va. 1, 302 S.E.2d 70 (1982). In contrast, others courts require proof that the actor thought about the killing "some appreciable time." *E.g., People v. Anderson*, 73 Cal.Rptr. 550, 447 P.2d 942 (1968).

(2) **Critique**

The problem with the first approach is that if an "instant" constitutes premeditation, then every intentional (wilful) killing is a premeditated homicide. If so, why would the legislature have divided the crime into degrees, and required proof of premeditation and deliberation for first-degree murder?

iii. **Deliberate**

Unfortunately, courts rarely distinguish "premeditation" from "deliberation"—they treat it as a single entity. But, if this is so, why include both words in the murder statute? When courts do draw a distinction, as they should, the latter term means "to measure and evaluate the major facets of a choice or problem." *People v. Morrin, supra.* Notice: to satisfy this standard of deliberation, a person would have to premeditate longer than an instant.

(1) **Study Point**

Think of it this way: premeditation considers the *quantity* of time taken; deliberation concerns the *quality* of the thinking processes during that time. In general, deliberation is characterized by "cool, calm" thinking. Understood this way, it is possible to premeditate without deliberating, but deliberation requires premeditation. (Deliberate on that!)

iv. **What If . . .**

What if a jury concludes that the defendant acted wilfully—intended to kill—but did *not* premeditate and deliberate? Assuming there is no claim of justification, excuse, or mitigation, the defendant is guilty of *second*-degree murder in states with murder statutes of the sort being considered here. It is murder because the killing was intentional (remember: intent-to-kill is one form of malice aforethought); since the killing was not premeditated and deliberate, it is not first-degree murder. So, by matter of elimination, it drops to second-degree.

C. Murder: Intent to Inflict Grievous Bodily Injury

A person acts with malice aforethought if she intends to inflict grievous bodily injury on another human being. Therefore, if a death results from her conduct, she is guilty of murder.

Example: D stabs V in the stomach with a large knife. V dies. D states that she did not intend to kill V. Even if a jury were to believe her claim, which it need not, she could be convicted of murder because she intended to inflict grievous bodily injury on V.

1. "Grievous bodily injury"

Statutes sometimes fail to define "grievous bodily injury" (or other terms they sometimes use synonymously, "serious bodily injury" or "great bodily harm"). When the term is defined, either by statute or judicial opinion, the definitions vary. It has been defined as injury "that imperils life" or that "is likely to be attended with dangerous or fatal consequences." See *Wellar v. People*, 30 Mich. 16 (1874); *People v. Crenshaw*, 298 Ill. 412, 131 N.E. 576 (1921). Or, it is an injury that "gives rise to the apprehension of danger to life, health, or limb." *Jackson v. State*, 168 Tex.Crim. 51, 323 S.W.2d 442, 443 (App.1959).

2. Statutory Approach

In states that distinguish between degrees of murder according to the Pennsylvania Model, one who kills another person with this state of mind is usually guilty of second-degree murder. It constitutes malice aforethought (murder), but it is not a wilful, deliberate, premeditated killing (first-degree murder).

a. Study Point

This form of malice very often merges with the "extreme recklessness"/"depraved heart" type of malice discussed next.

D. Murder: "Depraved Heart" (Extreme Recklessness)

1. General Rule

A person who acts with what the common law colorfully described as a "depraved heart" or an "abandoned and malignant" heart is one who acts with malice aforethought. If a person dies as a result of such conduct, the actor is guilty of murder, although the death was unintended.

2. What is "Depraved Heart"/"Extreme Recklessness"?

Common law judges did not provide a clear definition of "depraved heart" or "abandoned and malignant heart" behavior. In general terms, it is conduct that manifests an extreme indifference to the value of human life. Although no single definition of such extreme indifference can explain all of the common law decisions, today most courts would probably agree that an actor manifests an extreme indifference to the value of human life if he *consciously* takes a *substantial and unjustifiable foreseeable risk* of causing human death. The common law characterized such conduct as "implied malice," as distinguished from intentional killings, which involved "express malice."

Examples: Although each case must be decided on its own merits, the following facts have supported a charge of extreme recklessness: leaving a pit bull tethered, but in an accessible area, near where children are known to play, *Berry v. Superior Court*, 256 Cal.Rptr. 344 (Ct. App. 1989); knowingly placing a loaded gun at the victim's temple, after which the weapon goes off accidentally, *People v. Love*, 111 Cal.App.3d 98, 168 Cal.Rptr. 407 (1980); playing "Russian roulette," *Commonwealth v. Malone*, 354 Pa. 180, 47 A.2d 445 (1946); shooting into a moving train for no apparent reason other than to cause mischief, *Banks v. State*, 85 Tex.Crim 165, 211 S.W. 217 (1919); and speeding, driving in an intoxicated condition, and ignoring stop signs and red lights. *Pears v. State*, 672 P.2d 903 (Alaska 1983).

3. Statutory Approach

In states that divide murder into degrees pursuant to the traditional model, a depraved-heart homicide ordinarily is second-degree murder.

E. Felony–Murder Rule

1. General Rule

At common law, a person is guilty of murder if she kills another person, even accidentally, during the commission or attempted commission of any felony. *Regina v. Serné*, 16 Cox. Crim. Cas. 311 (1887) (Eng.). This is the so-called "felony-murder rule."

Examples: At gunpoint, *D1* robs *V*, a man with a history of heart disease. After *D1* flees, *V* dies of a heart attack caused by fright from the robbery. *D1* is guilty of murder under the felony-murder rule. *People v. Stamp*, 2 Cal.App.3d 203, 82 Cal.Rptr. 598 (1969).

The police spotted *D2* and *D3* stealing tires from a used car lot. A high-speed chase ensued. As a result of the chase, *D1* and *D2* ran through a red light, killing the driver of another car. *D2* and *D3* were guilty of felony-murder. *People v. Fuller*, 86 Cal.App.3d 618, 150 Cal.Rptr. 515 (1978).

a. Statutory Approach

Many states that divide murder into degrees have a dual approach to felony-murder. The murder statute will often provide that a killing that occurs during the commission of certain specifically listed felonies (most commonly: arson, robbery, rape, and burglary) is first-degree murder; a death during the commission of any non-enumerated felony constitutes murder of the second-degree.

2. Rationale of the Rule

Various justifications for the rule have been suggested. The most common explanations for the rule are based on deterrence. Some seek to defend the rule on the ground that the threat of a murder conviction, and the punishment that follows from it, may deter felonies. But, this argument has been correctly criticized: if we want to use the threat of punishment to deter a robber or rapist or burglar or thief from committing their felony, the solution is to increase the potential punishment of *the felony* and not to deal with it indirectly by threatening greater punishment for the unintended (and relatively rare) homicide that may occur during the felony. The somewhat more plausible deterrence argument—the one that is used more often to defend felony-murder—is that the harshness of the rule will cause felons to commit their crimes in a less dangerous manner, thereby decreasing the risk that deaths will ensue. *People v. Washington*, 62 Cal.2d 777, 44 Cal.Rptr. 442, 402 P.2d 130 (1965).

3. Controversies Regarding Felony–Murder

a. Deterrence

Opponents of the rule contend that there is no serious empirical evidence to support the deterrence reasoning set out above. Indeed, statistics suggest that the felony-murder rule is used most often in cases in which the felon intentionally killed the victim, or in which he acted in an extremely reckless manner, *i.e.*, in cases in which the rule is unnecessary. In the few cases where the felony-murder rule is really needed, the felon likely did not expect anyone to die and, therefore, is not significantly deterred by the rule.

b. Retributive Criticism: Culpability

Retributivists often contend that the rule, when applied to accidental homicides, results in disproportional punishment. In effect, the intent to commit the felony is transferred to the homicide, which is unfair.

Example: Imagine two pickpockets. Pickpocket *A* takes money out of *V1*'s pocket. Pickpocket *B* does the same thing in regard to *V2*, but in her case *V2* has a heart attack from the experience and dies. The actors are equally culpable: each committed a theft; and each took the same risk (very little) that a person would die from the act. *A* will be convicted of theft; *B* is guilty of theft and murder. Yet, the death—the difference in result in the two cases—was accidental and unforeseeable. Unlucky Pickpocket *B* will now be treated as a murderer.

4. Limitations On Felony–Murder Rule

Because the felony-murder rule is unpopular, many courts have limited its scope. Among the most common limitations are those discussed below. *But, do not lose sight of the fact that some jurisdictions apply the felony-murder as described above without any of these limitations, and other jurisdictions may apply one or another, but not all, of these limits.*

a. Inherently-Dangerous-Felony Limitation

Although the "pure" felony-murder rule applies to homicides that occur during the commission of *any* felony, many states limit the rule to killings that arise during the commission of "inherently dangerous" felonies. Courts do not agree, however, on how to determine whether a felony is inherently dangerous. Some courts consider the felony in the abstract: they look at the definition of the crime and ask whether the offense *could* be committed without creating "a high probability" of loss of life, *People v. Patterson*, 49 Cal.3d 615, 262 Cal.Rptr. 195, 778 P.2d 549 (1989), or *could* be committed without creating a "substantial risk" that someone will die. *People v. Burroughs*, 35 Cal.3d 824, 201 Cal.Rptr. 319, 678 P.2d 894 (1984). Other courts consider a felony inherently dangerous if it is dangerous in the abstract *or* in light of the circumstances surrounding the particular case. *State v. Harrison*, 90 N.M. 439, 564 P.2d 1321 (1977).

Examples: The difference in approach is significant. Consider *People v. Phillips*, 64 Cal.2d 574, 51 Cal.Rptr. 225, 414 P.2d 353 (1966): *P* obtained money from *X* under false pretenses by claiming to have a medical cure for *V*, *X*'s terminally ill child. *V* died as the result of *P*'s fraud. *P* was prosecuted for felony-murder, based on the felony of grand theft. Applying the in-the-abstract test, the court determined that grand theft is not inherently dangerous because a person can commit a theft without creating a high probability of loss of life. Under the facts-of-the-case test, however, it would seem that *P* committed the theft in a dangerous manner. (But, notice: in the latter analysis, the felony-murder rule probably is unnecessary to convict *P* of murder. The depraved heart approach will do.)

In *People v. Henderson*, 19 Cal.3d 86, 137 Cal.Rptr. 1, 560 P.2d 1180 (1977), *H* falsely imprisoned *V* at gunpoint. The gun went off accidentally causing death. The court held that the felony-murder rule did not apply because, looking at the felony (false imprisonment) in the abstract, it was not inherently dangerous. It reached that conclusion because the statute prohibited imprisonment "effected by violence, menace, fraud, or deceit." The court pointed to the disjunctive "or" in the statute: a person could be guilty of the crime if she imprisoned the victim by the nondangerous means of fraud or deceit.

b. Independent-Felony Limitation

Some courts require that the felony that serves as the predicate for the felony-murder rule be "independent" of the homicide. A felony that is *not* independent is said to *merge* with the homicide.

i. The Easy Case

The most obvious and least controversial example of a felony that merges is assault with a deadly weapon.

Example: I shot and killed *V*, his wife, during a dispute. The prosecutor sought to convict *I* on the basis of the felony-murder rule: that is, *I* killed *V* during the commission of the felony of assault with a deadly weapon. *People v. Ireland*, 70 Cal.2d 522, 75 Cal.Rptr. 188, 450 P.2d 580 (1969). The court held that the underlying felony was *not* independent of the homicide—it merges into the homicide and cannot be used to support a felony-murder prosecution.

(1) Rationale

In light of the most plausible rationale of the felony-murder rule (to deter dangerous conduct during the commission of felonies), the independent-felony limitation makes sense. There is no way for an actor to commit an assault with a deadly weapon in a non-dangerous manner. Therefore, there is no deterrent value to the felony-murder rule in such circumstances. Moreover, some courts have reasoned, if a felony assault could be used as the basis for felony-murder, it would mean that *every* felony assault resulting in death would constitute murder, and this would "usurp most of the law of homicide," as it would "frustrate the Legislature's intent to punish certain felonious assaults resulting in death [less] harshly [as manslaughter] than other felonious assaults." *People v. Hansen*, 9 Cal.4th 300, 36 Cal.Rptr.2d 609, 885 P.2d 1022 (1994).

ii. The Difficult Cases

Many violent offenses include assaultive conduct. For example, armed robbery basically consists of the offense of larceny + assault with a deadly weapon; rape involves assaultive conduct. In order that the "independent felony/merger" limitation not eat up the felony-murder rule, courts have followed either of two approaches: some limit the merger principle to crimes of assault; other courts define a felony as independent—thus, a felony that will support the felony-murder rule, even if it is assaultive—if it involves an "independent felonious purpose." *People v. Burton*, 6 Cal.3d 375, 99 Cal.Rptr. 1, 491 P.2d 793 (1971).

Example: Armed robbery has an independent felonious purpose: to take property from the victim. Rape has an independent felonious purpose: sexual intercourse with the victim. Therefore, these felonies are independent although they involve assaultive conduct. The felony-murder rule applies.

(1) Observation

Again, the rule makes sense. You cannot induce a person who wishes to assault another person to commit that offense safely; but the law may be able to deter a robber from taking other people's property in a dangerous manner (convince him to steal nonviolently), or motivate a rapist to secure sexual intercourse from the victim in a manner that does not involve a significant risk of death.

c. *Res Gestae* Limitation

Many courts provide that the mere fact that a death occurs, in a temporal sense, "during" the commission of a felony, is insufficient to trigger the felony-murder rule. There must also be a causal connection between the felony and the death.

Examples: D1 robs a cashier in a grocery store. While this is occurring, a customer, unaware of the robbery, dies of a coincidental heart attack. The felony-murder rule would not apply.

D2, in felonious possession of an unlicensed firearm in the glove compartment of her vehicle, accidentally strikes and kills a pedestrian. The felony-murder rule does not apply, as there is no link between the felony and the car accident.

Pilot *D3* is flying a small aircraft containing 500 pounds of marijuana. Because of heavy fog, he becomes lost and crashes into a mountain, causing the death of *X*, a passenger also involved in the drug offense. In a case close to these facts, the court held that there was no causal connection between the felony of drug distribution and the death by plane crash. That is, although $D3$ and X presumably would not have been in the airplane but for their felonious behavior, the crash was not the result of any act in direct furtherance of the felony, *e.g.*, they were not flying low to avoid radar detection.

i. Important Clarification

Just as the preceding discussion shows that you cannot treat the phrase "during the commission of a felony" literally—some deaths that occur during the crime do not fall within the felony-murder rule—it is also true that most courts say that the "*res gestae*" of the felony (and, therefore, the scope of the felony-murder rule) continues, even after the felony is technically over, if the death occurs during the escape from the scene of the crime or otherwise seems to be part of the same, continuous transaction.

d. Killing by a Non–Felon

Some jurisdictions provide that the felony-murder rule does not apply if the person who commits the homicide is a non-felon resisting the felony. But, as discussed below, even among courts that take this position, their reasoning differs. Notice, also: the *victim* of the homicide at the hands of the non-felon might be one of the felons or another innocent person.

Examples: In *State v. Bonner*, 330 N.C. 536, 411 S.E.2d 598 (1992), $D1$, $D2$, $D3$, and $D4$ robbed a restaurant. During the robbery, O, an off-duty police officer, thwarted the crime by killing $D1$ and $D2$. May $D3$ and $D4$ be charged with felony-murder of their cohorts, although the shooter was O?

Or, suppose that X, the victim of the robbery attempts to shoot one of the felons, but instead accidentally kills V, an innocent bystander. May the felons be charged with felony-murder?

i. Initial Observation

In such cases, the felony-murder rule literally applies: a killing has occurred during the attempted commission of a felony. Indeed, there is a causal connection between the felony and the homicide, since the shooter was resisting the felony. Thus, the *res gestae* limitation discussed above does not come into play.

ii. Judicial Approach to Issue

(1) Agency Approach

Many courts apply the "agency" theory of felony-murder. That is, a felon is only responsible for homicides committed *in furtherance* of the felony, by a person acting as the felon's "agent." Therefore, a homicide committed by a police officer, felony victim, or bystander falls outside the felony-murder rule: they are antagonists, not agents of the felon; a homicide committed by one of them is *not* in furtherance of the felony.

(2) Proximate Causation Approach

Some court apply a "proximate causation" rule, which holds that a felon may be held responsible for a homicide perpetrated by a non-felon if the felon proximately caused the shooting. Essentially, this makes a felon responsible for the death of another, although the shooter was a police officer, felony victim, or good samaritan bystander, because the shooting is a foreseeable response to the felon's conduct.

III. Common Law: Manslaughter

A. Manslaughter: General Principles

1. Definition of "Manslaughter"

Common law manslaughter is an unlawful killing of a human being by another human being *without* malice aforethought.

2. Categories of Manslaughter

The common law recognized two type of manslaughter, "voluntary" and "involuntary." Once punished alike, today voluntary manslaughter is the more serious offense.

a. Voluntary Manslaughter

As discussed below, voluntary manslaughter is an intentional killing, but one in which the actor takes a life in "sudden heat of passion," as the result of "adequate provocation."

i. Study Point

A few jurisdictions also recognize a diminished capacity "partial responsibility" defense that will reduce a murder to manslaughter. (See Part Seven, section V. to learn or remind yourself about this principle.) Also, some jurisdictions recognize "imperfect" justification defenses (see Part Six, II.A.8.a.i.), which will reduce murder to voluntary or involuntary manslaughter (depending on the jurisdiction).

b. **Involuntary manslaughter**

As discussed below, an unintentional killing constitutes involuntary manslaughter if the homicide occurs in either of two ways.

i. **Criminal Negligence**

A homicide is manslaughter if it is the result of a lawful act performed (in Blackstone's words) "in an unlawful manner, and without due caution and circumspection." This means simply that the killing occurred in a criminal negligent (or what some courts have, unfortunately, loosely called "reckless") manner.

ii. **Unlawful–Act Doctrine**

A homicide is manslaughter if it is the result of the commission of an unlawful act. Somewhat less accurately, this is sometimes called the "misdemeanor-manslaughter" rule.

3. **Murder Versus Manslaughter**

a. **Intentional Killings**

Notice that an intentional killing, if criminal (not justifiable or excusable) can constitute either murder or manslaughter. An intentional killing will constitute murder—malice aforethought—unless a mitigating factor is present: that the killing occurred as a result of provocation, as explained below.

b. **Unintentional Killings**

An unintentional killing can constitute either murder or manslaughter.

i. **Recklessness versus Negligence**

In general, a reckless killing is murder, whereas a criminally negligent one is manslaughter. Sometimes courts describe the line between the offenses differently: an "extremely reckless" killing is murder, and a "reckless" killing is manslaughter.

ii. Accidental killings

An accidental killing does not constitute criminal homicide unless it occurs during the commission of a wrongful act. In general, if a death occurs during the commission of a felony, the homicide is murder; if it results during the commission of a misdemeanor or some other unlawful act, it is manslaughter.

B. Voluntary Manslaughter: Provocation ("Heat–of–Passion")

1. General Rule

An intentional, unjustified, inexcusable killing, which ordinarily is murder, constitutes manslaughter (or "voluntary manslaughter") if it is committed in sudden heat of passion, as the result of adequate provocation. Thus, the provocation doctrine functions as a full defense to murder, and as a partial defense overall (as the defendant is guilty of manslaughter).

Example: Hal returns home and finds his wife in bed with Victor. Enraged, Hal shoots and kills Victor. As discussed below, Hal may be guilty of voluntary manslaughter: although he killed Victor intentionally, he did so in sudden heat of passion, as the result of the provocation of observing his wife in an act of adultery.

2. Rationale of the Provocation Doctrine

Courts and commentators disagree regarding why an intentional killing in heat of passion is reduced to manslaughter.

a. Partial Justification

Although it is currently the minority view, some courts in the past seemed to believe—and some scholars have expressly argued—that the provocation doctrine functions as a partial justification for a killing, *i.e.*, that the death of the provoker-victim constitutes less of a social harm than the killing of an entirely "innocent" person. Some would argue that the victim, by provoking the killer, partially forfeits his right to life by his unlawful conduct.

b. Partial excuse

Most commentators today now characterize the defense as a partial excuse, as a concession to normal human frailty. That is, the social harm is unmitigated (the provoker does not deserve, even partially, to die) but the culpability of the actor is reduced because of the provocation. Why is this so? If the provocation is serious enough (what the common law calls "adequate provocation"), "we are prepared to say that an ordinary person in the actor's circumstances, even an ordinarily law-abiding person . . . , might become sufficiently upset by the provocation to experience substantial impairment of his capacity for self-control and, as a consequence, to act violently." Joshua Dressler, *Why Keep the Provocation Defense?: Some Reflections on a Difficult Subject*, 86 Minn. L. Rev. 959, 974 (2002).

c. Critique

The provocation doctrine is under attack today. As always, some have criticized the partial defense on the ground that it undermines utilitarian goals by "rewarding" (through lesser punishment) people who respond violently to non-violent provocations. But, in recent years, the doctrine has also been attacked by feminists (some who would abolish the defense, and by others who would narrow its scope), who argue that the defense serves to partially excuse male aggression at the expense of women: "men are by far the most frequent victimizers, and women the most frequent victims." Victoria Nourse, *Passion's Progress: Modern Law Reform and the Provocation Defense*, 106 Yale L.J. 1331, 1335 (1997). Although much of the criticism of the provocation doctrine is directed at post-common law expansions of the defense (especially by the Model Penal Code), the thrust of the criticism applies to the common law as well.

3. Elements of the Defense

a. Adequate Provocation

A person may not claim the defense simply because he was provoked. The provocation must be such that it might "inflame the passion of a reasonable man and tend to cause him to act for the moment from passion rather than reason." See *Girouard v. State*, 321 Md. 532, 583 A.2d 718 (App. 1991). Or, the provocation must be such that it "might render ordinary men, of fair average disposition, liable to act rashly or without due deliberation or reflection, and from passion, rather than judgment." *Maher v. People*, 10 Mich. 212 (1862).

i. Fixed Categories

At original common law, the judge, rather than the jury, determined the adequacy of the provocation. Only a few types of provocation were deemed adequate. The most common were: a serious battery; mutual combat; and observation by the husband of his wife in an act of adultery. "Adequate provocation" was *not* proved if the husband was informed of the adultery but did not see it. And, a rigid rule existed: words alone, no matter how insulting, were insufficient grounds for reducing a homicide to manslaughter.

ii. Modern Trend

Today, most jurisdictions go beyond the limited categories of "adequate provocation" of the original common law. The issue is now left to juries to decide whether the alleged provocation would render an ordinary person liable to act rashly. However, most jurisdictions continue to hold that words alone are never adequate provocation for a homicide.

(1) The "reasonable [or ordinary] person"

To the extent that juries have relatively free rein to determine what provocation is adequate, they must test the provocation against the standard of the "reasonable person" or "ordinary person." A significant issue is whether this objective standard should be subjectivized to the extent of incorporating any of the defendant's characteristics into the "reasonable/ordinary" person.

Examples: X sexually assaulted C, a 15–year-old boy, who responded by beating X to death. *Director of Public Prosecutions v. Camplin,* [1978] 2 All. Eng.Rep. 168. The court had to determine whether the jury should consider the provocation from the perspective of a person of C's age.

In *Commonwealth v. Carr,* 398 Pa.Super. 306, 580 A.2d 1362 (1990), C became inflamed when he observed two women in lesbian lovemaking at a camp site. C killed one of the women and seriously wounded the other. He sought to show at trial that the victims' conduct was highly provocative to him, in part because he had been traumatized earlier in life when his mother may have had a lesbian relationship.

(2) Law

The trend in the law, more evident in the United Kingdom, but also taking place in the United States, is to consider a defendant's characteristics if it is considered relevant in measuring the *gravity* of the provocation, but not to include it in assessing the *level of self-control* to be expected of the reasonable person.

Examples: An example of the old and more rigid approach is *Bedder v. Director of Public Prosecutions,* [1954] 38 Crim. App. 133, in which *B*, an impotent male, sought to have intercourse with *V*, a prostitute. When he failed, she taunted him and struck him. The court held that the issue before it was whether *V*'s conduct would have provoked a reasonable *non-impotent* man to act violently. A modern approach would permit the jury to take into consideration the defendant's impotence in measuring the *gravity* of the victim's taunting words and battery. His impotence would not be relevant, however, in determining the *level of self-control* to be expected of a reasonable person.

In *Camplin, supra,* the facts of which are set out above, the House of Lords held that the jury should be instructed that the "reasonable man referred to . . . is a person having the power of self-control to be expected of any ordinary person of the sex and age of the accused, but in other respects sharing such of the accused's characteristics as they think would affect the gravity of the provocation to him." Notice that this instruction not only subjectivizes the "reasonable person" standard in terms of the *gravity* of the provocation, but in terms of capacity for self-control would incorporate the defendant's age and sex!

Query: how far should courts go in this regard? What about the *Carr* case, discussed above? Should the jury be asked, in essence, to determine whether the "provocation" of observing lesbian lovemaking would cause a "reasonable person whose mother may have had a lesbian relationship" to become sufficiently upset that he might act violently? Or, does such a standard go much too far? This is the issue many courts must currently confront. Don't be surprised if your professor wants you to discuss this general issue.

b. State of Passion

For the provocation doctrine to apply, the defendant must kill the victim while in a state of passion. Although the typical "passion" is anger, any over-wrought emotional state, including fear, jealousy, or even deep depression, may qualify.

c. Suddenness

The killing must occur in *sudden* heat of passion. That is, the defendant must not have had reasonable time to cool off. Early cases required proof that the defendant acted almost immediately after the provocation. Modern courts leave the issue to the jury. A few cases even allow the jury to consider the defense in cases of brooding.

Example: In *People v. Berry*, 18 Cal.3d 509, 134 Cal.Rptr. 415, 556 P.2d 777 (1976), *B* was provoked off and on for two weeks by *V*, his girl friend. After the last provocation, *B* remained in *V*'s apartment during her absence for 20 hours, brooding. When she returned, she screamed at him, and he killed her. Clearly, the screaming was not adequate provocation: *B*'s provocation claim was based on the accumulation of events. The court allowed the defense to go to the jury.

d. Causal Connection

A causal link between the provocation, the passion, and the fatal act must be proved.

Example: *D* intends to kill *V*, her business rival. Coincidentally, her first opportunity to kill *V* occurs when she discovers *V* in bed with her (*D*'s) husband. *D* kills *V*. Even if *D* killed suddenly, while angry, and although adultery ordinarily constitutes adequate provocation, the decision to kill *V* antedated the provocation. Therefore, the defense would not apply.

C. Involuntary Manslaughter: Criminal Negligence

1. General Rule

A person who kills another person in a criminally negligent manner is guilty of involuntary manslaughter.

2. Murder versus Manslaughter

This offense often blurs into the depraved-heart version of reckless murder.

Example: In *State v. Williams*, 4 Wash.App. 908, 484 P.2d 1167 (1971), *Ws*, low-educated parents of *V*, did not take their seriously ill child to a doctor until it was too late to save his life. They behaved as they did, in part, because they were unaware of the seriousness of the child's condition, although the jury determined that a reasonable person in their circumstances would have realized that the child was seriously ill. (They also feared taking their child to a doctor because, as Native Americans living on a reservation, they believed their child might be taken away from them by the Welfare Department.) As characterized, their conduct constituted negligence. If they had been consciously aware that their child had a life-threatening condition—and, thus, they knew they were taking a substantial and unjustifiable risk by not seeing a physician—their conduct would have constituted recklessness and could have justified a depraved-heart murder conviction.

D. Involuntary Manslaughter: Unlawful–Act Doctrine

1. General Rule

In an analogue to the felony-murder rule, a person is guilty of involuntary manslaughter if she kills another person during the commission or attempted commission of an unlawful act that does not otherwise trigger the felony-murder rule.

Examples: *D1* unjustifiably pushes *V1* in the chest (a simple battery). *V1*, who is drunk, falls to the ground, strikes the back of his head on the sidewalk, and dies. In a jurisdiction that applies the unlawful-act doctrine, *D1* is guilty of manslaughter. *State v. Pray*, 378 A.2d 1322 (Me. 1977).

D2, a car driver, fails to stop at a stop sign, in violation of a traffic law, and strikes and kills *V2*. (On the facts, assume *D2*'s conduct did not constitute criminal negligence.) *D2* is guilty of manslaughter because the accidental death occurred during the commission of an unlawful act, a violation of the traffic law. *State v. Hupf*, 48 Del. 254, 101 A.2d 355 (1953).

2. Scope of the Rule

There are broad and narrower versions of the unlawful-act doctrine, as well as a few jurisdictions that reject the doctrine.

a. Broad Version

Some states apply the doctrine to all misdemeanors, as well as to any felony that is excluded from the felony-murder rule due to a limitation on the felony-murder rule. A few jurisdictions go so far as apply the doctrine if the conduct that causes the death is wrongful (immoral), albeit not illegal.

Example: C attempts to commit suicide. *V* intervenes to prevent the suicide, but in the process mortally injures herself and dies. If attempted suicide, although not criminal, is considered morally wrongful, *C* may be convicted of manslaughter of her rescuer! *See People v. Chrisholtz*, 55 Misc.2d 309, 285 N.Y.S.2d 231 (1967).

b. Limitations

Some jurisdictions limit the rule to *mala in se* misdemeanors, such as petty theft, or to "dangerous" misdemeanors, *i.e.,* offenses entailing "a reasonably foreseeable risk of appreciable physical injury." *Comber v. United States*, 584 A.2d 26 (D.C.App. 1990).

IV. Model Penal Code

A. Criminal Homicide: Overview

The MPC provides that a person is guilty of criminal homicide if she takes the life of another human being purposely, knowingly, recklessly, or negligently. MPC § 210.1(1). Unlike the common law, the Code divides criminal homicide into *three*, rather than two, offenses: murder, manslaughter, and negligent homicide.

1. "Human being"

A human being is a person born alive. MPC § 210.0(1). The Code does not indicate when a person ceases to be a human being, *i.e.,* what the definition of death is.

B. Murder

1. Rule

In general, a homicide constitutes murder if the killing is committed: (a) purposely; (b) knowingly; or (c) "recklessly under circumstances manifesting an extreme indifference to the value of human life."

2. Degrees of Murder?

Unlike many modern statutes, the MPC does *not* divide murder into degrees. The drafters believed that there is no defensible way to distinguish between first- and second-degree murder on the basis of either dangerousness or culpability.

Example: Compare an adult son who premeditates the mercy killing of his terminally ill father, *State v. Forrest*, 321 N.C. 186, 362 S.E.2d 252 (1987), with a reckless drunk driver who kills a pedestrian, or a person who, on whim and without premeditation, throws a child over a bridge to her death. Under traditional homicide statutes, the mercy killing is first-degree murder, whereas the other two crimes are second-degree murder, yet these outcomes probably do not conform with our intuitions about the dangerousness or culpability of the actors.

3. Common Law versus MPC

a. Types of murder

The common law term "malice aforethought" is abandoned in the Code. What about the underlying concept of malice aforethought? Consider the four common law forms:

i. Intent to Kill

This form *is* recognized under the MPC: as noted above, a criminal homicide is murder under the Code if the killing is committed purposely or knowingly. In essence, this is equivalent to the common law "intent to kill" form of *mens rea*. Because there are no degrees of murder, the Code—like the common law, but unlike many modern non-Code statutes—does not require proof of premeditation and deliberation.

ii. Intent to Commit Grievous Bodily Injury

Virtually any case that would qualify as common law murder according to this form of malice, will fit under the MPC "extreme recklessness" umbrella discussed below.

iii. Depraved Heart

The MPC extreme recklessness provision is similar to the depraved heart form of common law murder, except that it is explicit in requiring proof of advertent risk-taking, and that the risk-taking be "substantial and unjustifiable."

iv. Felony–Murder

The Code abandons the felony-murder rule. However, drafters of the Code feared that a felony-murder-less criminal homicide code would be rejected by legislatures. Therefore, as a compromise, the Code provides that reckless indifference to human life may be presumed if the person causes the death during commission of one of the felonies enumerated in the Code (robbery, arson, burglary, kidnapping, felonious escape, or rape or deviate sexual intercourse by force or threat of force). However, this is not a true presumption: the burden of proof remains on the prosecution. The jury is simply permitted to *infer* extreme indifference to human life from the commission of one of these felonies. And, the defendant may present evidence that she committed the felony in a manner that does not manifest extreme indifference to human life. If the jury has a reasonable doubt about the matter, it must find her not guilty of murder, even if the defendant committed the felony.

C. Manslaughter

Criminal homicide constitutes manslaughter (§ 210.3) in two circumstances.

1. Recklessness

A homicide committed recklessly constitutes manslaughter. The difference between reckless manslaughter and reckless murder is that here the conduct, although reckless, does *not* manifest an extreme indifference to human life.

a. Comparison to Common Law

The MPC definition of "recklessness" (§ 2.02(2)(c)), provides that the actor must be aware that she is taking a substantial and unjustifiable risk to human life. Therefore, the Code differs from the common law in that the common law permits conviction for involuntary manslaughter based on *inadvertent* risk-taking, *i.e.*, the defendant may be convicted although she was unaware of the risk she was taking.

2. Extreme Mental or Emotional Disturbance

The Code recognizes a much broader version of the common law provocation doctrine, and also allows states to recognize a "partial responsibility" diminished capacity defense (see Part Seven), if they wish to do so. MPC § 210.3(1)(b) provides that a murder constitutes manslaughter if the actor kills under the influence of an "extreme mental or emotional disturbance" (EMED), for which there is a "reasonable explanation or excuse." (Notice that the Code clearly sees this defense as a partial excuse and not a partial justification.)

a. Study Point

A common error of students is to say—and to believe—that the issue is whether there is a reasonable explanation or excuse *for the homicide*. Hardly so—if there were a reasonable explanation or excuse for the homicide, the defendant should be acquitted of any crime! Instead, the issue is whether there is a reasonable explanation or excuse *for the EMED*.

b. Comparison to Common Law

i. Common Law Rigidity/Narrowness Rejected

The EMED provision is wide open: The MPC permits a jury, if it chooses to do so, to reduce the offense to manslaughter without considering the rigid common law categories of adequate provocation; also, "words alone" can qualify. Indeed, the defense applies *even if there is no provocation at all*, as long as the jury concludes that there is a reasonable explanation or excuse for the actor's EMED. There is also no "reasonable cooling off" requirement.

ii. Mixed Subjectivity and Objectivity

The Code provides that the reasonableness of the defendant's explanation or excuse for the EMED should be determined from the perspective of a person "in the actor's situation under the circumstances as he believes them to be." This allows for considerable subjectivization of the objective standard, although the Commentary to the Code concedes that the words "in the actor's situation" are "designedly ambiguous," so as to permit common law development of the subjective/objective issue.

3. **What is "Missing"**

Notice that there is no "unlawful-act" manslaughter provision under the MPC. As for criminally negligent homicides, they represent a reduced offense, discussed immediately below.

D. **Negligent Homicide**

A criminally negligent killing—involuntary manslaughter at common law—is the lesser offense of "negligent homicide" under the Code. MPC § 210.4.

V. Review Questions

[Answers Provided in Appendix A, page 370]

1. T or F.   Homicide is a crime.

2. Carla, intending to kill, stabs Lisa in the heart with a knife. Through heroic medical care and a bit of luck, Lisa survives the assault. Two years later, while playing basketball with her son in the backyard, she has a heart attack and dies. The coroner reports that Lisa's heart had been severely weakened as the result of the wounds inflicted by Carla, and that but for Carla actions, Lisa would not have died. May Carla be prosecuted for murder at common law?

3. What are the four states of mind that constitute common law malice aforethought?

4. At common law, is an intentional killing first-degree or second-degree murder?

5. In states that apply the Pennsylvania Model of murder, of what degree of murder is a person guilty if, without justification, excuse, or mitigation, she intentionally kills a person after an instant of thought?

6. Why would it be that many commentators say that the second form of "malice aforethought" ("intent to inflict grievous bodily harm") tends to merge into the third form ("depraved heart")?

7. Doctor Alice conducts cardiac transplant surgery on 22–year-old Patient Pat, who will die within days if the surgery is not conducted, but who may live a normal life if the surgery succeeds. Doctor Alice knows (and has told Pat) that there is a fifty percent chance that Pat will die during the surgery because of his weakened condition. Pat does die. Based on these facts, is Alice guilty of murder? Why, or why not?

8. T or F.   The common law felony-murder rule applies to all felonies, even non-violent ones.

9. T or F.   The most common argument in favor of the felony-murder rule is that it is meant to deter felons from committing their felonies.

10. "Practicing medicine without a license constitutes a felony." Is this felony inherently dangerous in the abstract?

11. *"Child abuse.* Any person who, under circumstances likely to produce great bodily harm or death, inflicts unjustifiable physical pain on any child, is guilty of a felony." Is this felony independent of a homicide, or would it merge into the offense?

12. *F* burglarizes an apartment home (a felony). *P*, a police officer arrives as *F* is leaving. A chase takes place over the roof the apartment building. During the chase, *P* slips and falls off the roof and dies. Would the *res gestae* limitation bar application of the felony-murder rule?

13. Frank enters a liquor store to rob it. The cashier responds to the robbery by pulling a gun and shooting at Frank, but the bullet strikes and kills Carla, a customer. Does the felony-murder rule apply to these facts?

14. Jack tells Jerry, "You are a stupid, lazy, piece of vermin. I am glad I had sex with your whore of a wife." Jerry, outraged, immediately kills Jack. At common law, is Jack guilty of murder or manslaughter?

15. *V* sexually assaults ten-year-old *C*. *V* is arrested for the crime. In court two months later, *V* testifies, admits the attack, and laughingly says, "I enjoyed it." *C*'s mother is in the court, hears his remarks, pulls out a gun she smuggled into the court, and shoots and kills *V*. Murder or manslaughter, at common law?

16. T or F. Any wrongful death that would justify a finding of tort liability on the basis of negligence would justify conviction for involuntary manslaughter.

17. Make a list of all of the ways the Model Penal Code criminal homicide provisions differ from the common law and/or modern criminal homicide statutes.

PART ELEVEN

Rape

■ *ANALYSIS*

CONVERSATION WITH STUDENTS

Few subjects in law school, if any, evoke more heated discussion and controversy than rape. It is also the common law offense than has undergone the most extensive statutory and even common law transformation in the past two decades. These changes cannot be understood except in their social context: as social attitudes about sex roles, sexual harassment, and feminism in general, have changed, the law of rape has also evolved.

I. Common Law: Forcible Rape

A. In General

Blackstone defined rape as "carnal knowledge of a woman forcibly and against her will." 4 Blackstone, Commentaries on the Law of England * 210 (1769). Today, it is more accurate to characterize this as *forcible* rape. Rape is a general-intent offense.

1. Statutory Law

The elements of the offense statutorily vary by jurisdiction. Moreover, it is valuable to distinguish between traditional forcible rape statutes—those enacted when states shifted from the common law to statutory law, which generally did little more than codify the common law—and modern reform statutes, adopted in some states to deal with criticisms of the common law. Reform provisions are noted below, but the traditional rape statute is apt to provide that forcible rape is *sexual intercourse by a male, with a female not his wife, by means of force or threat of force, against her will, and without her consent.*

B. *Actus Reus* in Detail

1. Sexual Intercourse By Male With Female

The common law offense was not complete in the absence of penetration by a male of the female's vagina. Nonconsensual oral and anal sexual penetration constituted the separate offense of sodomy.

a. Modern Reform Statutes

Many states that have reformed their law have re-named the offense "sexual assault" or "sexual battery." These offenses typically prohibit *all* forms of forcible sexual penetration, and not simply vaginal intercourse. They also tend to be gender-neutral: male-on-male and female-on-female sexual penetration is included, as is nonconsensual female-on-male sexual penetration. Also, some states prohibit "sexual contact"—undesired contact that does not result in penetration—as a lesser degree of the offense.

2. Marital Immunity

At original common law, a husband was immune from prosecution for rape of his wife. He could be convicted as an *accomplice* in the rape of his wife, but could not convicted for personally committing the crime. On the other hand, he could be convicted of simple assault or battery of his wife.

a. Rationale

i. Consent

According to common law scholar Hale, "by their mutual matrimonial consent and contract the wife hath given up herself in this kind unto her husband, which she cannot retract." 1 Hale, History of the Pleas of the Crown (1736). It is unclear whether even seventeenth century jurists accepted this argument. Even if they did, it is impossible today to defend the principle that, upon marriage, a woman (and only she) loses her personal liberty to say no to intercourse with her husband on a given occasion.

ii. Property law

A female was considered the property of her father or husband in very early English common law. Therefore, she had no right to refuse her husband's wishes in this regard. This property-rights view was never accepted in the United States. Nor is it consistent with the fact that the immunity rule does not apply to the charge of assault or battery: if a wife was the property of her husband, it would seem that he could use his property any way he chose, and thus would be immune from assault or battery prosecution, as well.

iii. Protect Marriage

The marital-immunity rule, it is argued, is needed to protect against intrusion by the government into marital privacy, and to promote reconciliation of the marital partners. This argument is hard to defend: if the act of forcible intercourse by the husband is an isolated act, it is unlikely the wife would want to see her husband prosecuted for an offense that will result in a long prison sentence. If the husband is guilty of ongoing physical abuse, there is little or no chance of reconciliation. In any case, a wife's safety should outweigh any legitimate privacy concern.

b. Modern Law

England abolished the marital-immunity rule in 1991. The law in this country is in transition. Some states have abolished the rule outright, and other states have repealed the exemption if the husband and wife are legally separated or, at least, living apart at the time of the rape.

3. Nonconsent

The essence of rape is the nonconsensual nature of the sexual intercourse. Notice, however, that "nonconsent" is an element of the crime, rather than consent being a defense. This means that the prosecutor must prove nonconsent beyond a reasonable doubt.

4. Force

a. General Rule

The crime of forcible rape is not complete simply upon proof of nonconsensual intercourse. It must also be shown that the male acted forcibly or by threat of physical force. *Nonconsent and force are separate elements.*

Example: In *State v. Alston*, 310 N.C. 399, 312 S.E.2d 470 (1984), *F* and *M* were involved in what the court described as a six month "consensual sexual relationship." During this time, *F* had sexual relations with *M* whenever he wished to have intercourse. At times, *F* would "stand still and remain entirely passive while [*M*] undressed her and had intercourse with her." On the particular occasion at issue, *F* had moved out of *M*'s apartment. *M* accosted *F* in public, blocked her path, and grabbed her by the arm. *M* let go when *F* said she would walk with him if he released her. They walked together. *F* told *M* that their relationship was over. *M* said that he had a right to have intercourse with her again. They went into a house where they had previously had sexual relations. *M* had intercourse with *F*. The appellate court held that the evidence demonstrated that *F* did not consent to the intercourse; but it reversed the conviction on the ground that the state did not present substantial evidence of force.

b. **How Much Force**

At original common law, the prosecutor had to prove that the male used or threatened substantial force upon the female in order for a forcible rape prosecution to succeed. In this regard, the common law developed a resistance requirement.

i. **Resistance Rule**

As one court put it, "[f]orce is an essential element of the crime and to justify a conviction, the evidence must warrant a conclusion either that the victim resisted and her resistance was overcome by force or that she was prevented from resisting by threats to her safety." *Hazel v. State*, 221 Md. 464, 157 A.2d 922 (1960). Essentially, this means: if the male uses or threatens to use force likely to cause death or serious bodily injury to the female, she is not required to resist. If the male uses lesser force, the female *is* required to resist the rapist "to the utmost," or "until exhausted or overpowered." Thus, rape is not "forcible" unless the male uses force sufficiently great to overcome her resistance. The resistance requirement has been sharply criticized: it forces the female to escalate the danger to herself; it assumes that *verbal* resistance—saying no—is not enough; and it ignores the fact that many females may freeze up out of fear of the male aggressor.

Example: In *Commonwealth v. Berkowitz*, 537 Pa. 143, 641 A.2d 1161 (1994), *F*, a female college student, came to a male friend's dormitory room. He was not present, but *M*, the friend's roommate, was there. *M* asked *F* to stay, which she did, and asked for a back rub, which she refused. *F* sat on the floor, where *M* joined her and became sexually aggressive. *M* lifted *F*'s blouse, and fondled her breasts. Thereafter, the two rose to their feet, *M* locked the door, and then he "put her" on the bed. *F* testified that *M* did not throw her on the bed, but that it was "kind of like a push." During subsequent oral sex and intercourse, in which *M* was on top of *F*, *F* said "no" multiple times. The state supreme court reversed *M*'s conviction, on the ground that the facts did not support a finding of sufficient force to constitute forcible rape. Another way of looking at it in a common law context is that, although *F* may have *verbally* resisted *M*'s advances, she did not physically resist him, which was legally required.

c. Moving Away From Force

i. Requiring Less Force

Some states have begun to reshape forcible rape law by requiring far less proof of force, at least in cases involving unusual facts.

Example: F was asleep in a hospital bed. M entered the room, pulled up F's gown, pulled down her panties, and inserted his finger in her vagina. F awoke just before the last act; however, because she was still half-asleep and believed that M was a nurse performing an abdominal palpation, she did not resist. In a prosecution for forcible rape, the court held that the "actions in pulling back the bed clothing, pulling up the victim's gown, and pulling her panties aside amount to actual physical 'force' as that term is to be applied in sexual offense cases." *State v. Brown*, 332 N.C. 262, 420 S.E.2d 147 (1992). This case may be limited to the fact that F was surprised by M, and could not realistically resist.

ii. Changing the Resistance Requirement

A few states have abolished the resistance requirement. Most states still retain the requirement, but the extent of resistance required has been reduced in most states: resistance "to the utmost" is rarely required now; only "reasonable resistance" is required, which leaves it to the jury to determine the sufficiency of the female's resistance. The effect of these changes is to permit rape prosecutions based on less force by the male than in the past.

iii. Abandoning the Force Requirement Altogether

The New Jersey Supreme Court has gone so far as to hold that the force inherently involved in the sexual act itself is sufficient evidence of "force" to permit a forcible rape conviction. The effect of this decision is to make *all* cases of sexual intercourse "forcible." The only remaining issue is whether the intercourse was nonconsensual. Furthermore, the New Jersey court has held that forcible rape is proved upon evidence of sexual intercourse, unless the female, by words or conduct, reasonably appears to give permission for the intercourse. *In re M.T.S.*, 129 N.J. 422, 609 A.2d 1266 (1992). That is, not only is a "no" (in words or conduct) by the female sufficient to prove forcible rape, but *the absence of "yes"* (in words or conduct) also constitutes forcible rape. This places the onus on the person desiring intercourse to obtain permission before proceeding.

Example: In *M.T.S.*, *D* and *V*, two teenagers, had sexual intercourse. *V* gave permission for kissing and "heavy petting," but she did not give permission for intercourse. The New Jersey Supreme Court held that a forcible rape conviction could be supported on these facts.

(1) Observation

Not surprisingly, *M.T.S.* is controversial. As a matter of judicial interpretation of a forcible rape statute, the case is very hard to defend, even by those who like the decision as a policy matter. As a matter of policy, those who like the decision believe that the essence of rape is the nonconsensual nature of the offense; force should not be a prerequisite. Critics argue that nonconsensual forcible intercourse is worse than nonconsensual *non*forcible intercourse; even if the latter should be a crime, it should not be equated with the former. Other critics believe that a person alleging rape should be required, at the least, to express nonconsent, rather than for the law to require that affirmative permission be obtained.

C. *Mens Rea*

1. General Rule

Rape is a general-intent offense. Therefore, most jurisdictions provide that a person is not guilty of rape if, at the time of intercourse, he entertained a genuine and *reasonable* belief that the female voluntarily consented. Some courts now provide that a defendant is not entitled to an instruction on mistake-of-fact in the absence of equivocal conduct on the victim's part. *People v. Williams*, 4 Cal.4th 354, 14 Cal.Rptr.2d 441, 841 P.2d 961 (1992). Therefore, especially in jurisdictions applying the resistance rule, equivocal conduct will rarely exist: the female's resistance is an unequivocal act of nonconsent.

2. Minority Rules

a. No Mistake-of-Fact "Defense"
A few states provide that even a defendant's *reasonable* mistake of fact is not a defense. *E.g., Commonwealth v. Ascolillo*, 405 Mass. 456,

541 N.E.2d 570 (1989). This rule effectively converts forcible rape, an offense with very severe penalties, into a strict-liability offense.

b. Unreasonable Mistake-of-Fact as a "Defense"

At the other end of the spectrum, the English House of Lords ruled that even an *unreasonable* mistake of fact is a defense to rape. *Regina v. Morgan*, [1976] A.C. 182. Essentially, the House of Lords concluded that rape requires proof of intent, and that this *mens rea* element modifies all of the *actus reus* elements of rape, including the element of nonconsent. Therefore, a defendant cannot be convicted unless he not only intends sexual intercourse, but intends that it be nonconsensual. Effectively, the House of Lords treated rape as a specific-intent crime. No American state has adopted this reasoning. Moreover, the English public was so upset with the *Morgan* decision that Parliament redrafted its rape statute to permit conviction for rape if the male was at least reckless in regard to the female's lack of consent.

II. Common Law: Rape by Nonforcible Means

CONVERSATION WITH STUDENTS

Forcible rape is the primary, if not exclusive, topic you will discuss in class, in so far as the crime of rape is concerned. In large part this is because nearly all rape prosecutions "in the real world" are based on claims of force. Another reason for the emphasis on forcible rape is, simply, that the common law did not criminalize many forms of nonforcible sexual intercourse; indeed, this is one of the criticisms of the common law. Why should the law focus almost exclusively on *physical* force and threats of *physical* harm, and not also consider other forms of coercion—economic, reputational, and the like—used to obtain sexual contact? Increasingly, sexual assault law *is* moving into these areas, resulting in considerable controversy, but still relatively little case law. What follows, therefore, is brief discussion of two relatively "old" forms of nonforcible sexual intercourse that may be covered in your casebook and class.

A. Statutory Rape

1. Statutory Background

All states provide that intercourse by a male with an underage female to whom he is not married constitutes rape. Neither force nor the underage female's lack of consent is an element of the offense. The definition of "underage" varies considerably by jurisdiction. At its inception as a crime in 1275, the "age of consent"—when voluntary consent would be recognized—was twelve; in 1576, it was lowered to ten. In the early years in the United States, the age of consent was also ten; it was raised over time, in some jurisdictions to as high as eighteen or even twenty-one years of age. Michelle Oberman, *Turning Girls Into Women: Re–Evaluating Modern Statutory Rape Law*, 85 J. Crim. L. & Criminology 15 (1994). Today, many states divide statutory rape into degrees of offense, based on the age of the female and, often, on the basis of the difference in age between the female and the male. The most severe penalties are imposed when the male is an adult and the female is pre-pubescent.

2. Rationale

An early rationale of statutory rape laws, especially in the Victorian era, was that such laws were needed to protect "chaste maidens" from becoming "fallen women." As explained in less colorful language, "[a]n unwise disposition of [the young female's] sexual favor is deemed to do harm both to herself and the social mores by which the community's conduct patterns are established. The law of statutory rape intervenes in an effort to avoid such a disposition." *People v. Hernandez*, 61 Cal.2d 529, 39 Cal.Rptr. 361, 393 P.2d 673 (1964). In recent years, statutory rape laws—which largely remain gender-specific in that they protect only underage females, and not young males—have been defended on a different ground: recent studies reveal that there is a high pregnancy rate among underage females as a result of sexual relations with adult males. At least in these cases, prosecution of statutory rape laws arguably might serve as a deterrent against adult exploitation and resulting pregnancies of young females.

3. Mistake of Fact Regarding Age

Nearly all jurisdictions treat statutory rape as a strict-liability offense. Therefore, the defendant is guilty of the offense, even if he reasonably believed that the victim was old enough to consent.

B. Rape by Fraud

1. Fraud in the Inducement

At common law, a seducer is not a rapist. More specifically, a male is not guilty of rape even if he fraudulent induces the female to consent to intercourse with him.

Examples: D1, a look-alike of a famous actor, induces *V1* to have intercourse with him by impersonating the actor. *D1* is not guilty of rape.

D2 induces *V2*, a prostitute, to have intercourse with him by offering her counterfeit money in exchange for sex. *D2* is not guilty of rape.

D3 induces *V3* to have intercourse with him, by falsely claiming that intercourse will cure her of a serious illness. *D3* is not guilty of rape. *Don Moran v. People*, 25 Mich. 356 (1872); see *Boro v. Superior Court*, 163 Cal.App.3d 1224, 210 Cal. Rptr. 122 (1985).

2. Fraud in the Factum

In contrast to fraud-in-the-inducement, consent to engage in sexual intercourse is invalid if, as the result of fraud, the victim is unaware that she has consented to an act of sexual intercourse. Therefore, in these so-called fraud-in-the-factum cases, consent is vitiated and a rape prosecution will lie.

Example: *V*, a patient, signs a consent form in which she agrees to permit *P*, a surgeon, "to insert an instrument" in her vagina while she is under anaesthesia. The instrument turns out to be *P*'s penis. *P* is guilty of rape. See *Pomeroy v. State*, 94 Ind. 96 (1883).

III. Model Penal Code

CONVERSATION WITH STUDENTS

The Model Penal Code was drafted in the 1950s and adopted by the American Law Institute in 1962. At that time, the MPC rape provisions, like the rest of the Code, were perceived to be relatively progressive in content. But, social attitudes have changed so much in the intervening forty years that the sexual offense provisions of the Code now seem remarkably antiquated to most people.

A. Forcible Rape

Section 213.1, subsection (1), prohibits four forms of rape, of which one form is forcible rape.

1. Definition

"A male who has sexual intercourse with a female not his wife is guilty if . . . he compels her to submit by force or by threat of imminent death, serious bodily injury, extreme pain or kidnapping, to be inflicted on anyone." MPC § 213.1(1)(a).

2. Clarification

As the preceding definition shows, the Code is gender-specific and recognizes the marital immunity rule. The term "sexual intercourse," however, is defined elsewhere (§ 213.0(2)) to include oral and anal sexual relations, which is broader than the common law.

3. Looking a Little Deeper

Notice that the Code does not use the term "nonconsent." Instead, it uses the word "compels." Although, of course, compulsion by the male implies nonconsent by the female, the intent of the drafters was to shift the trial focus from the female to the male—a perspective appreciated by later rape reformers. That is, the drafters believed that, as with other violent crimes, attention should be focused on the alleged perpetrator's actions—here, his acts of compulsion—and not on how the alleged victim responded. Thus, the MPC does *not* include a resistance requirement.

4. Grading Rape

The Code grades rape as a felony of the second degree except in two circumstances, in which it is aggravated to a felony of the first degree. It is first degree if: (1) the male actually inflicts serious bodily injury upon anyone during the course of the rape; or, very controversially today, (2) the female was *not* a "voluntary social companion of the actor upon the occasion of the crime and had not previously permitted him sexual liberties." In short, if a female is voluntarily sexually intimate with a male and remains his "voluntary social companion," then her subsequent rape is considered less serious than if such intimacies had never occurred before.

B. Other Forms of Rape

The Code also prohibits nonforcible sexual intercourse by a male with a female not his wife in other circumstances: (1) if he "substantially impaired her power to appraise or control her conduct by administering or employing without her knowledge drugs, intoxicants, or other means for the purpose of preventing resistance"; (2) if she was unconscious at the time of the intercourse; or (3) if she is under ten years of age. MPC § 213.1(1)(b)-(d). In the latter case, it is no defense that the male reasonably believed "the child to be older than 10." § 213.6(1).

C. Gross Sexual Imposition

The MPC drafters defined a new sexual offense, less serious than rape (it is a felony of the third degree) to deal with three circumstances in which a male secures sexual intercourse with a female not his wife: (1) if "he compels her to submit by any threat that would prevent resistance by a woman of ordinary resolution"; (2) if he knows that she suffers from mental disease "which renders her incapable of appraising the nature of her conduct"; or (3) "he knows that she is unaware that a sexual act is being committed upon her or that she submits because she mistakenly supposed that he is her husband." MPC 213.1(2).

1. Clarification

Notice that the first version of gross sexual imposition set out above applies to compulsion by "any threat that would prevent resistance by a woman of ordinary resolution." This is intended to criminalize less serious *bodily* threats than are encompassed under the rape statute *as well as non-bodily threats—economic, reputational, and the like*. The limitation— that the threat would prevent resistance by a "woman of ordinary resolution"—is intended to reduce the risk that criminal prosecutions will be brought in cases of relatively trivial threats.

The third form above covers cases of fraud-in-the-factum and one specific issue that bedeviled common law courts: cases in which a female has intercourse with a man whom she incorrectly believes is her husband. (For example, there are cases in which a stranger has broken into a home at night, in the dark, and entered the bed of a woman whom, he knows, mistakenly believes that he is her husband.) The common law sometimes treated these cases as fraud-in-the-inducement (and, there- fore, no crime, as discussed above); other courts felt that the husband- wife relationship was so basic—no "good" wife would knowingly have intercourse with anyone other than her husband—that these cases should be treated as equivalent to fraud-in-the-factum. The MPC takes the latter approach.

IV. Review Questions

[Answers Provided in Appendix A, page 373]

1. T or F.   Forcible oral sex by a male of a female not his wife is prohibited by common law rape.

2. T or F.   At common law, if a male threatened to cause serious bodily injury to a female unless she acceded to intercourse, she had to resist him to the utmost, or else the subsequent intercourse did not constitute forcible rape.

3. Al has sexual intercourse with Betty, a female not his wife. Betty did not consent. Al believed that she did. Assuming all of the other elements of a rape

prosecution are proved, in which the following circumstances, if any, is Al *not* guilty of common law rape?

a. He reasonably believed that she consented;

b. He unreasonably but honestly believed that she consented;

c. In both a. and b.; or

d. In neither case.

4. What are some of the ways modern rape laws varies from the common law?

5. Police Officer Predator lawfully stops Sally for a traffic violation. He tells her that if she has intercourse with him, he will not give her a ticket. If she refuses, he will give her the ticket and also take her into custody, saying "you will be in jail overnight before anyone realizes you don't belong there." Sally has intercourse with Predator. Of what sexual offense, if any, is Predator guilty under the Model Penal Code?

*

PART TWELVE

Theft

■ *ANALYSIS*

CONVERSATION WITH STUDENTS

"Theft" is a shorthand term used to describe various property crimes, the most important of which are common law larceny and the statutory offenses of embezzlement and false pretenses.

In very early English history, the criminal law prohibited only the forcible taking of property, *i.e.*, robbery. Later, the law was extended to punish non-violent takings, *i.e.*, larceny. The law of larceny, however, has not developed smoothly. Courts devised various complicated legal fictions regarding the crime. On the one hand, they used the fictions to narrow the scope of the crime in order to reduce the use of the death penalty, which was the punishment for most larceny convictions. On the other hand, the judges cooperated with the economic power interests of the time to expand larceny law in certain contexts to meet changing economic conditions.

As the result of these conflicting trends, larceny law is replete with illogical rules and, at the same time, gaps in its coverage. To fill the gaps, the English Parliament enacted the offenses of embezzlement and false pretenses. These offenses, along with larceny, were carried over to this country.

Today, many states have consolidated the three crimes into a single offense of "theft." The purpose of the consolidation was to repeal the paper-thin, largely useless, distinctions between the crimes. Unfortunately, courts frequently interpret theft laws as if the reforms barely occurred: many of the common law doctrines persist to this day. Therefore, like it or not (and you probably will not like it) you need to learn the technical rules that developed centuries ago.

One other point: the Model Penal Code, while consolidating many property offenses under the category of "theft," recognizes various theft offenses, such as "Theft by Unlawful Taking or Disposition" (§ 223.2); "Theft by Deception" (§ 223.3); "Theft of Property Lost, Mislaid, or Delivered by Mistake" (§ 223.5); "Theft of Services" (§ 223.7); and others. Most professors focus on the common law, with a more cursory look at the MPC provisions. Therefore, we will emphasize the historic common law.

I. Larceny

A. General Principles

1. Common Law Definition

Larceny is the trespassory taking and carrying away of the personal property of another with the intent to permanently deprive the other person of the property (for shorthand, with the "intent to steal" the property).

a. *Actus Reus*

As so defined, the *actus reus* of larceny is the trespassory taking and carrying away of the personal property of another. That is, the law prohibits the conduct of taking and carrying away another's property; the offense is complete at that instant. Larceny is proved even if the property is not damaged, destroyed, or converted to the personal use of the taker.

i. Possession

Larceny is a crime of possession. That is, the *actus reus* of larceny occurs when a wrongdoer trespassorily takes *possession* of the personal property of another and carries it away. *Title* to the property is not the key. If a wrongdoer wrongfully obtains title to another person's property, the offense of false pretenses, discussed later, may be implicated.

b. *Mens Rea*

Larceny is a specific-intent offense. The defendant is not guilty of the crime unless he commits the *actus reus* with the specific intent to steal the property. As discussed below, the intent to steal must concur in time with the trespassory taking.

2. Grade of the Offense

Common law larceny was a felony. However, the crime was divided up between "grand" and "petty" larceny. The death penalty applied to grand larceny. In modern statutes, petty larceny is a misdemeanor; grand theft is a felony.

a. Value of Property Taken

At original common law, grand theft involved the taking of property valued in excess of twelve pence, which was roughly the value of a single sheep. Today, the line between petty and grand larceny differs by state, but often the value set for grand larceny is in excess of $500–$2000.

i. Thief's belief about value

Case law is scant, but apparently a thief's belief regarding the value of property is irrelevant at common law. That is, a thief is guilty of grand or petty larceny, depending exclusively on the objective value of the property. In contrast, the Model Penal Code provides that a person is guilty of grand theft, even if the property is worth less than $500 (the Code cut-off line), if he believed it was worth more. MPC § 223.2(2).

Example: D1 steals an original Picasso painting, believing it is a nearly worthless fake. This constitutes grand larceny at common law, even though he would have been guilty of only petty larceny if the painting had been as D1 had believed.

D2 steals a nearly worthless fake Picasso, believing it is an original. This would constitute petty larceny at common law, although D2 thought its value was such as would make the offense grand larceny. This would constitute grand larceny, however, under the MPC.

B. *Actus Reus* in Detail

1. Trespass

The taking of another person's personal property is not larceny unless the taking is trespassory in nature.

a. Definition of "Trespass"

For purposes of larceny law, a trespass occurs if the defendant takes possession of the personal property of another, *i.e.*, she dispossesses another person, without the latter's consent or in the absence of a justification for the nonconsensual taking.

Example: D, a police officer, takes possession of X's automobile pursuant to a court order. This is a non-trespassory taking, as she was justified in taking the property over X's objections.

i. Clarification

Notice that the term "trespass" in this context has nothing to do with the tort or crime of trespass to land. The term comes from the ancient writ of *trespass be bonis asportatis* (trespass for goods carried away).

b. Taking Possession by Fraud

A person who secures property deceitfully acts trespassorily, *i.e.,* the fraud vitiates the consent of the original possessor of the property. Larceny by fraud is sometimes called *larceny by trick.*

Example: In the historically important case of *King v. Pear,* 168 Eng. Rep. 208 (1779), *P* rented a horse upon the promise that he would return it in one day. In fact, when *P* hired the horse, he did not intend to return it. Later, he sold the animal. A majority of judges in *Pear* held that, although the taking of the horse outwardly appeared to be consensual, *P*'s hidden intent not to return the horse rendered the taking nonconsensual, *i.e.,* trespassory in nature.

i. Larceny versus the Crime of False Pretenses

It is important to distinguish larceny by trick from false pretenses, which is discussed later in subsection III. The key distinction is that larceny by trick involves the use of fraud to obtain *possession* of personal property, whereas false pretenses involves the use of deceit to obtain *title* to it.

2. Taking Possession ("Caption")

Larceny implicates the trespassory taking (or "caption") of personal property. More specifically, a "taking" involves the wrongful taking of *possession,* rather than mere *custody,* of property. This distinction—possession versus custody—is critical to understanding larceny law.

a. Possession versus Custody: Drawing the Distinction

i. Possession

A person is in "possession" of property if she has sufficient control over it to use it in a generally unrestricted manner. Possession may be actual or constructive. It is "actual" if a person has physical control over the property. It is "constructive" if she does not have physical control over it, but nobody else is in actual possession of it.

Example: X is in actual possession of her car when she drives it. When she parks it on the street and departs, she is in constructive possession of it, since nobody else has actual possession.

ii. Custody

A person is in "custody" of property if she has physical control of the property, but her right to use it is substantially restricted.

In the ordinary situation, a person has custody rather than possession of property if she has temporary and limited right to use the property in the possessor's presence.

Examples: A, a clothing merchant, permits *B*, a customer, to try on a piece of clothing. *B* has *custody* of the clothing, while *A* retains constructive *possession* of it.

C, a car dealer, permits *D* to test-drive the vehicle by himself. Because *C* is not in the car, *D* has *possession* of it.

E, a car dealer, remains in the car during a test drive by *F. F* has mere *custody* of the car, and *E* remains in *possession* of it.

iii. **Importance of the Custody/Possession Distinction**

The question of *whether and when* a person obtained possession of property is critical to determining whether a larceny has occurred.

Examples: In the *C-D* test-drive *Example* above, if *D* decides *during* the drive to abscond with the car, he would *not* be guilty of larceny, because he took possession of the vehicle the moment *C* let him drive it alone. As *that* taking of possession was consensual (he did not have a felonious intent at that time), it was not a *trespassory* taking.

In the other test-drive *Example*, if *F* decided to abscond with the car during the drive, and drove away as soon as *E*, the auto dealer, got out of the car, *F* would be guilty of larceny. This is because *F* originally had mere custody of the vehicle (because *E* was in the car with him); *F* took possession when *E* left the car and *F* drove away; this act of taking possession was nonconsensual, *i.e.*, trespassory.

b. **Special Possession/Custody Rules In Employment Relationship**

i. **Employer to Employee**

When an employer (the "master") furnishes his personal property to his employee (the "servant") for use in the employment relationship, the common law rule is that the employer retains constructive possession of the property. The employee has mere custody.

Example: R, the owner of a pizza-delivery business, allows E, his employee, to drive R's car to deliver pizzas. At common law, E has mere *custody* of R's automobile; R retains *possession.* Therefore, if E takes the vehicle beyond the scope of the job, she takes wrongful possession of it from R.

ii. Third Person to Employee for Employer
When a person furnishes personal property to *another* person's employee, in order that it will be delivered to the employer, he transfers *possession* of the property to the *employee.*

Example: X hands her money to E, a bank teller, so that E will deposit it in X's account in R Bank. Because there is no employment relationship between X and E, E obtains possession of the money from X. R Bank does not have possession of the money until E places the money in a bank drawer.

(1) Significance of This Rule

Because an employee obtains possession, not mere custody, of property when he receives it from a third person, the timing of the employee's felonious intent is critical.

Examples: E, bank teller, receives money from X, bank customer, for deposit. Assume that at that moment, E intends to pocket the money, which he does. E is guilty of larceny by trick: his felonious intent at the time of taking renders the taking of possession trespassory, as discussed in *Pear, supra.*

Assume the facts in the last example change slightly: E takes the money from X with the honest intention of depositing it in the bank drawer, but seconds later decides to pocket it. E is *not* guilty of common law larceny, as the original taking was lawful. See *King v. Bazeley,* 168 Eng. Rep. 517 (1799); *Commonwealth v. Ryan,* 155 Mass. 523, 30 N.E. 364 (1892).

Change the facts a little more. E properly puts the money in the bank drawer, but at the end of the day decides to take the money. This is now larceny. This is because: When the money was put in the drawer, possession of it shifted from *E* (who obtained possession from *X*) to Bank *R*; when *E* returns to the drawer at the end of the day and takes the money, *E* is now taking trespassory possession of the property, although this time from *R*, rather than *X*. If *E* carries the money away with the requisite *mens rea*, he is guilty of larceny.

(2) The Problem

Notice the unfair position the law places the prosecutor. The line between larceny and non-larceny often depends on whether an employee intended to steal property before or only after he received it from the third person. Yet, there is virtually no way to know when the intent was formed; nor is there any difference in culpability or dangerousness of the offender.

(3) The Solution

Because of the difficulty of obtaining larceny convictions in cases of the sort described here (in particular, as a result of the decision in *Bazeley, supra*, involving a dishonest bank employee), the Parliament enacted the offense of embezzlement, discussed below, and the United States followed suit.

c. Bailments: The Breaking Bulk Doctrine

When a bailee is entrusted by the bailor with a container for delivery to another person, the bailee receives possession of the container, but mere custody of its contents. Therefore, if the bailee wrongfully opens the container and removes its contents, *i.e.*, breaks bulk, he takes possession of the contents at that moment. *Carrier's Case*, Year Book 13 Edw. IV pl. 5 (1473). As with other areas of theft law, the precise facts of the case can turn a larceny into a non-larceny, or vice-versa.

Examples: *BE*, the bailee, obtains a container from *BR*, the bailor, to transport to *X*. Later, *BE* decides to sell the *unopened* container to *Y*, rather than deliver it as promised to *X*. *BE* is not guilty of larceny of the contents because he obtained lawful (non-trespassory) possession of the *container*, and at no time did *BE* obtain possession of the *contents*.

However, if *BE* opens the box and then sells the *contents* to *Y*, *BE* is guilty of larceny: when he broke bulk, *BE* wrongfully took possession of the contents from *BR*.

If *BE* properly delivers the unopened container to *X*, but then returns and takes the container from *X* without *X*'s knowledge, *BE* is guilty of larceny, but the "victim" would be *X*, as *X* obtained possession of the container when *BE* delivered it to him.

3. Carrying Away ("Asportation")

A person is not guilty of larceny unless he carries away the property. This is sometimes described as the "asportation" requirement. Virtually any movement of property away from the place where possession was taken constitutes asportation.

Example: *D* trespassorily takes possession of *V*'s parked automobile. She is arrested at that moment. She is guilty of *attempted* larceny, as no asportation occurred. If *D* drives the car away, even an inch, she is guilty of larceny (assuming the requisite *mens rea*).

a. Clarification

The asportation must consist of "carrying away" movement.

Example: *D* moves a box containing a video cassette recorder from the floor onto a table, so that she can more easily open the box and pull out the contents, which she intends to steal. This act is not a "carrying away" act. Therefore, if *D* is arrested at this moment, she is guilty only of attempted larceny.

4. Personal Property of Another

a. "Personal Property"

i. Personal versus Real Property

Larceny is not committed if a person takes property attached to the land, such as trees and crops, because such property is *real* rather than *personal* in nature. When real property is severed from the land, however, it becomes personal property, and the first person to take possession of it in that form is in lawful possession of it.

Examples: *D* wrongfully cuts down *V*'s tree and immediately removes the timber. *D* is not guilty of common law larceny.

When *D* cut the tree down, he acted wrongfully as to *real* property, which is a tort, but not a common law theft crime. When the tree parts were severed from the land, they became *personal* property in *D*'s possession. As he did not take possession of the *personal* property from anyone, it was a lawful taking.

Suppose, however, that *D* leaves the timber he has severed on *V*'s land and returns the next day to carry it away. *D* is now guilty of larceny. *D* left the personal property on *V*'s land; therefore, *V* obtained constructive possession of it. When *D* returned and carried away the property, this taking was trespassory.

ii. Animals

At common law, domestic animals were protected by larceny law; animals in the state of nature (*ferae naturae*), such as wild deer and birds, were not considered to be personal property belonging to another.

iii. Intangible property

Intangible personal property—property that, by definition, cannot be taken and carried away—is not protected by the common law of larceny. Nearly all states now prohibit the exercise of control over intangible property. *E.g.*, MPC § 223.2.

Example: *D* steals an "IOU" slip belonging to *V*. *D* has stolen a piece of paper, which is tangible property. Therefore, he is guilty of petty larceny of the paper. But, he is not guilty of common law larceny of the intangible right to secure the money owed.

b. "Of Another"

Larceny involves the taking of *another person's* personal property. For purposes of larceny law, the "another" is the person who has lawful possession of the property. Ownership is not the key.

Example: *D* takes her watch to *X* for repair. When she receives the bill, she decides not to pay for it. Instead, she takes the watch without permission. *D* is guilty of larceny: when she gave *X* the watch to be repaired, *X* took lawful possession of it; when *D* took it back without paying for it, she trespassorily took possession, even though she owned the watch.

C. *Mens Rea*: "Intent to Steal"

1. General Rule

A person is not guilty of larceny when he wrongfully takes and carries away another person's personal property, unless he possesses the specific intent to permanently deprive the other person of the property.

Example: D takes V's parked car without permission, with the intention of keeping it for a day. D returns it later that day. D is not guilty of larceny, as he lacked the specific intent to steal the car. (Today, D would be guilty of a lesser statutory offense such as "joyriding.")

a. Recklessness

Often, a court will find that the requisite intent is proven if the actor takes property, and then abandons it under circumstances in which he knows that the property will probably not be returned to its owner. In such circumstances, it is more accurate to describe the actor's *mens rea* here as "reckless deprivation of another person's property."

Example: D wrongfully takes V's automobile in Los Angeles, and abandons it in a high-crime area in San Francisco. In view of the likelihood that the vehicle will be re-stolen or that it will "stripped" of its parts before it can be recovered, a jury might convict D of larceny.

2. Concurrence Requirement

In general, the intent to steal must *concur* with the taking of the property.

Example: D lawfully borrows X's car for one day, intending to return it. During the day, she decides to keep the car, and she drives out of town with it. D is not guilty of larceny: the intent to steal did not concur with the taking, which was lawful. That is, D's felonious intent developed after she took possession of the property.

a. "Continuing Trespass" Doctrine

The concurrence requirement is subject to the "continuing trespass" doctrine. This legal fiction provides that when a person *trespassorily* takes possession of property, she commits a new trespass every moment that she retains wrongful possession of it. Therefore, even if the wrongdoer does not have the intent to steal the property when she originally takes it, the concurrence requirement is met if she later decides to steal the property.

Example: D takes V's car without permission, with the intention of returning at the end of the day. Later that day, D changes her mind and decides to keep the car. D is guilty of larceny. Notice: When D originally took the car, she took *trespassory* possession of it—she had no right to it—but she took possession without the intention to steal. However, as the result of the continuing-trespass doctrine, she "continued" to take the vehicle as long as she retained it. Therefore, when she later decided to keep the car—when her intention to steal was formed—there was a concurrence of the felonious intent with the trespass that occurred at that moment.

D. Special Problem: Lost or Mislaid Property

1. Lost Property

The rights of a finder of lost property depend on two factors: the possessory interest of the person who lost the property at the time the property is discovered by the finder; and the finder's state of mind when he retrieves the lost property.

a. Possessory Interest of the Owner

A person retains constructive possession of his lost property if there is a reasonable clue to ownership of it when it is discovered. A reasonable clue to ownership exists if the finder: (1) knows to whom the lost property belongs; or (2) has reasonable ground to believe, from the nature of the property or the circumstances under which it is found, that the party to whom it belongs can reasonably be ascertained.

Examples: F1 discovers a dollar bill lying on the street. If F1 observed O drop it, a reasonable clue to ownership exists; therefore, O retains constructive possession of it.

F2 discovers a dollar bill under a bush. It is unlikely that there is a reasonable clue to ownership: it would be very hard to discover the true owner. Therefore, the true owner does not maintain constructive possession of the property. When F picks it up, she is not *taking* possession from anyone so no larceny has occurred.

b. State of Mind of the Finder

As with other larceny cases, it is important to determine the finder's state of mind when he takes possession of the lost property.

Examples: O accidentally drops her extremely valuable watch on the sidewalk. It has her name and address etched on the back. *F* observes the watch on the ground, and decides to steal it. *F* picks up the watch. In view of the etching (and, perhaps even without it, in view of its value and the strong possibility that *O* would advertise for its recovery), there is a reasonable clue to ownership. Therefore, *O* retains constructive possession of the watch until *F* finds it, at which time possession transfers to *F*. As *F* picked up the watch with the intent to keep it, this taking was trespassory and felonious. She is guilty of larceny.

The same example, except that when *F* picks up the watch, she intends to find the owner. Later, however, she decides to keep it. Now there is no larceny, as the original taking on the street was nontrespassory. The felonious intent did not concur with the taking.

The same example, except that when *F* picks up the watch, she figures, "I am going to a fancy party tonight. I'll wear it, and then find the owner." Now the taking of possession is trespassory (wrongful), but the intent to steal is absent. However, in light of the continuing-trespass doctrine, *F*'s subsequent felonious intent concurs with the "later" trespass.

2. Mislaid Property

An object is "mislaid" if it is intentionally put in a certain place for a temporary purpose, and then accidentally left there when the owner leaves. The two factors just discussed regarding lost property also apply to mislaid property. However, in regard to the "reasonable clue to ownership" factor, the common law is more protective of the owner of mislaid property than of lost property.

a. Reasonable Clue to Ownership

The common law provides that there is *always* a clue to ownership of mislaid property: because it was misplaced, rather than lost, the owner knows where it is, and is considered likely to return to pick it up once he notices that he has forgotten it. The implication of this is that the lawfulness of the finder's conduct depends entirely on his state of mind when he takes possession of the property from the owner: if he takes the property with the intent to steal it, he is guilty of larceny; if he picks it up with honest intentions, he is not guilty of larceny.

II. Embezzlement

A. Elements of the Offense

In 1799, shortly after the acquittal of a dishonest bank employee in the *Bazeley* case, *supra*, the English Parliament enacted the first general embezzlement statute. Under the statute, embezzlement was a misdemeanor. Today, it is a felony or a misdemeanor, depending on the value of the property embezzled. Because the offense is statutory in nature, and differs from jurisdiction to jurisdiction, the precise contours of the offense cannot be stated. However, in general the offense requires proof of two or three elements:

1. Manner of Obtaining Possession

Embezzlement occurs when the actor takes possession of the personal property of another in a lawful—nontrespassory—manner.

2. Conversion

After securing lawful possession of the property, the actor converts the property to his own use, *i.e.,* he uses the property in a manner that manifests his intention to deprive another person of the property permanently.

3. Entrustment

Many embezzlement statutes provide that the actor must have obtained possession as a result of entrustment by another person.

Examples: X hands D, a bank teller, cash that X expects D to give to B, the bank, for deposit in X's account. X has entrusted the property to D for that purpose.

BR gives property to BE, a bailee, to be shipped to X. This is an entrustment.

O loses property. F finds it. There is no entrustment.

B. Larceny Versus Embezzlement

The line between these two offenses is very thin, and depends in large part on the state of mind of the actor at the time he takes possession of property.

Examples: E obtains a car from R, her employer, in order to deliver pizzas. E absconds with the vehicle. E is guilty of larceny. This follows from the fact that E originally had only custody of the vehicle, because she obtained it from her employer. When she violated the employment contract by driving the car away, she trespassorily took possession of it with the requisite *mens rea*.

BR, a bailor, entrusts a car to *BE*, the bailee, to deliver to *X* in another city. *BE* takes the vehicle with the intention of stealing it. *BE* is guilty of larceny by trick: the taking of possession was trespassory (see *Pear, supra*, discussed in section I.B.1.b. above).

The same as the last example, except that *BE* takes possession with the intent to deliver it as requested. Later, *BE* changes his mind and drives away with the car. *BE* is guilty of embezzlement: he was lawfully entrusted with the property, and he converted it to his own use.

D finds lost property, for which there is a reasonable clue to ownership. *D* intends to find the true owner, but later changes his mind. Notice: *D* has taken lawful possession of the property. Therefore, the continuing trespass doctrine does not apply, so that the subsequent intent to steal does not concur with the taking. Therefore, *D* is not guilty of larceny. But, neither is it embezzlement, if the embezzlement statute requires entrustment.

III. False Pretenses

A. Elements of the Offense

The crime of "obtaining property by false pretenses" is a statutory offense, enacted in England in 1757. Originally, it was a misdemeanor. Today, it is a felony or misdemeanor, depending on the value of the property taken. As with embezzlement, the statutory nature of the crime allows for only general description of the offense.

1. Title

With false pretenses, the victim transfers title, rather than mere possession, to the wrongdoer. This is the key difference between false pretenses, on the one hand, and larceny and embezzlement, on the other.

Examples: *D* drives to *V*'s "full-service" gas station for a fill-up. *D* has no intention of paying for the gasoline. After *V* fills *D*'s tank, *D* speeds away. This is larceny by trick. When *V* put the gasoline into *D*'s car, *V* intended to transfer only possession of the gasoline until he was paid. Therefore, false pretenses is not involved. See *Hufstetler v. State*, 37 Ala.App. 71, 63 So.2d 730 (1953).

The same as the last example, except that D pays for the gasoline with counterfeit money. Now the crime is false pretenses. When D handed V the counterfeit money, title to the gasoline transferred to D. This change in title occurred as the result of fraud.

2. Nature of Fraud

False pretenses involves a false representation of an existing fact.

a. How the Misrepresentation Occurs

The misrepresentation may be in written or oral form, or can be the result of misleading conduct. Silence—nondisclosure of a fact—does not usually constitute false pretenses, even if D knowingly takes advantage of V's false impressions.

b. Fact versus Opinion

The misrepresentation must be of a fact and not of opinion.

Examples: D sells V a car after telling him that the car is "the best automobile ever built." D does not believe this statement is true. The statement is pure puffery: it is a statement that cannot realistically be proved or disproved. Therefore, it is more in the nature of an opinion.

D sells V a car after turning back the odometer, so that it reads "100" instead of "1,000" miles. The act of turning back the odometer constitutes misrepresentation of a fact. Therefore, assuming the other elements of the offense are proved, D is guilty of false pretenses.

c. Existing Fact versus a Promise of Future Conduct

The majority rule is that, to constitute false pretenses, a factual misrepresentation must pertain to an existing fact, and not involve a promise of future conduct.

Example: D buys a car on an installment contract. At the time of purchase, D does not intend to pay the monthly installments. On these facts, D obtained constructive title of the vehicle when she signed the contract; she secured this title as the result of fraud. However, the misrepresentation is in the form of a promise of future conduct (future payment). The majority rule is that D is not guilty of false pretenses.

i. Rationale
A promise of future conduct is really a representation of an existing fact: the fact of a present intention to live up to a promise. Nonetheless, common law courts feared that is would be too easy for a simple breach of contract to be converted into a crime. Therefore, this special rule was devised.

ii. Model Penal Code
The minority rule, led by the Model Penal Code, is that a prosecution is permitted, even if the misrepresentation is in the form of a promise of future conduct. However, the intention to deceive cannot be proved solely on the basis of the promisor's failure to live up to his promise. MPC § 223.3(1).

3. *Mens Rea*
The deceiver must make the false representation "knowingly" and with "the intent to defraud." That is, the actor must know that the representation is false; and he must make the false statement with the specific intent of defrauding the other person. This approximates the "intent to steal" concept in larceny.

IV. Review Questions

[Answers Provided in Appendix A, page 375]

1. T or F.   Common law larceny is intended to protect owners from the wrongful taking of their personal property by a person who intends to keep the property.

2. Jane finds a valuable ring on the street. She picks it up intending to find the true owner. Gina comes to Jane and fraudulently convinces Jane that the ring belongs to her. Therefore, Jane hands the ring to Gina, who leaves with it. Larceny, embezzlement, false pretenses, or none of the above by Gina?

3. Unfortunately this is a real case: Lawyer tells Client, "You give me $1000 and I will bribe Police Officer to change his arrest report on you." Client to Lawyer, "Geez, that is a lot of money. Okay, I'll do it, but you be sure that you don't give the cop the money until he makes the change in the report." Lawyer agrees, but later decides to convert the money to his own use. Larceny, embezzlement, false pretenses, or none of the above?

4. Charles trespasses onto Larry's land and digs up Larry's beautiful begonias from the garden, and leaves with them, intending to give them to his girl

friend. Larceny, embezzlement, false pretenses, or none of the above?

5. Pizza deliverer (and very hungry) Jason receives a hot pizza to deliver to Sam from Jason's employer. In the car, on the way to Sam's, Jason eats a slice of the pizza. Larceny, embezzlement, false pretenses, or none of the above?

APPENDIX A

Answers to Review Questions

■ PART ONE: INTRODUCTORY PRINCIPLES

[ANSWERS TO QUESTIONS ON PAGES 129–130]

1. There is no agreed-upon definition. The best definition is that a "crime" is conduct that "if duly shown to have taken place, will incur a formal and solemn pronouncement of the moral condemnation of the community."

2. **False.** Thanks to the Double Jeopardy Clause (and, thus, the rule that acquittals are unappealable), jurors have the raw *power* to nullify the law, but they do not have the legal *right* to do so.

3. **b.** The speaker is using Albert's punishment as an object lesson for others, which is what general deterrence is all about.

4. **False.** Recidivist laws are generally defended on specific deterrence grounds (incapacitation) and perhaps general deterrence grounds (create fear in others of what happens if they continue to disobey the law). Retributivism ignores the risk of future punishment, and punishes only for the past action. Earlier crimes do not go into the calculation since the defendant has already paid for that crime.

5.   This is the principle that provides that a person may not be convicted or punished unless there is a pre-existing law. Today, it also means that such laws should be enacted by legislatures and not judges. Corollaries of the principle are that statutes should be sufficiently clear to put reasonable people on notice that their proposed conduct might violate the law; and statutes should not be so broad or standardless that the police have undue discretion in enforcing the law.

6.   c.   This is wrong. The Constitution is silent in regard to the question of who should carry the burden of persuasion regarding affirmative defenses. It is up to the legislature to decide on whom to place the burden.

   d.   There are two errors here. The constitutional rule is that the prosecutor must prove *beyond a reasonable doubt* (the first correction) any fact *other than the fact that the defendant was previously convicted* (the second correction) that increases the penalty for a crime beyond the prescribed statutory maximum.

■ PART TWO: *ACTUS REUS*

[ANSWERS TO QUESTIONS ON PAGE 141]

1.   Voluntary act (or, sometimes, an omission); and social harm.

2.   The common law definition is a willed muscular contraction. The Model Penal Code only gives examples of involuntary acts.

3.   **True.** Despite the general rule, Alex would have a duty to act: as a lifeguard he contractually would take on this duty. But, remember: to be convicted of a homicide offense, the prosecutor will also have to prove that Alex had the requisite *mens rea*. This is a subject for later lessons.

4.   a.   The words here that constitute the *actus reus* of the offense are every word except "intentionally," which is the *mens rea* term.

   b.   The words that constitute the social harm of the offense are the same words! How can this be? Because the other aspect of the *actus reus* is that the social harm must occur as the result of conduct that includes a voluntary act (or, rarely, an omission), but statutes rarely express this requirement in their definition of the crime. We can simply say that the taking of the life, which constitutes the social harm, must be the result of conduct that includes a voluntary act (such as firing a gun at the victim).

c. This statute has all three categories! We have a result: the death; we have conduct: "by means of poison"; and we have attendant circumstances: that the killer be a "person" (a human being and not, for example, an animal), and that the victim be "another" person (not oneself). I know it may seem silly right now to go through this process of categorization, but it will become important as we proceed.

■ PART THREE: *MENS REA*

[ANSWERS TO QUESTIONS ON PAGES 163–164]

1. The "culpability" meaning of *mens rea*, simply, is that the defendant committed the *actus reus* of the offense in a morally culpable manner. No particular state of mind is required.

2. Albert either wanted to kill Bob—it was his conscious object—or he knew that his actions were practically certain to cause Bob's death.

3. True. This offense requires that the person not only rape the victim but have a further intention (to kill) that goes beyond the *actus reus* of the offense. That is, the crime requires an intent to commit some act that is not part of the *actus reus* of the offense.

4. Recklessness is a higher level of *mens rea* than negligence. This is true under the Model Penal Code because recklessness involves consciously taking a risk (substantial and unjustifiable) that the actor knows that he should not take, whereas the negligent actor is unaware that is he is taking a substantial and unjustifiable risk. He is blamed for not being aware of the risk, but he is not consciously disregarding the risk, which is worse. As for the common law, the answer is either the same or, depending on the definition of recklessness, involves taking an even greater, more unjustifiable, risk than the negligent actor.

5. This is a tricky question. The answer is **no.** The Model Penal Code *does* permit strict liability as to "violations," which are "offenses," but not "crimes." As for crimes, Model Penal Code § 2.02(1) requires proof of *some mens rea* as to each element of the offense.

6. a. Model Penal Code § 2.02(4) answers this question—*mens rea* as to one term applies to all material elements unless a contrary legislation intention plainly appears. This is a straight-forward case.

7. False. Especially in the case of statutes with common law roots, courts presume that legislatures intended to require a *mens rea*. But, this is just a matter of a judicial presumption of legislative intent. Strict liability offenses are not presumptively unconstitutional.

■ PART FOUR: *MENS REA* AND MISTAKES OF FACT OR LAW

[ANSWERS TO QUESTIONS ON PAGES 175–176]

1. b. Burglary, as defined, is a specific-intent offense. Dennis's mistake negates the "purpose" to commit a felony inside the house—after all, he thought it was his own home. Therefore, even the most unreasonable mistake in the world (and this sounds like one!) negates that purpose.

2. b. Same answer and same reasoning. The common law applies an elemental analysis to specific-intent offenses; the MPC applies an elemental analysis to all offenses.

3. False. Although the general rule is that a reasonable mistake of fact is a defense to a general-intent offense, don't forget the moral-wrong and legal-wrong doctrines that permit conviction for reasonable mistake of fact if a court chooses to apply the doctrine.

4. An unreasonable mistake of law is potentially exculpatory when the offense itself requires knowledge and understanding of some law and the mistake of law negates that knowledge or understanding. This is true at common law and the MPC.

■ PART FIVE: CAUSATION

[ANSWERS TO QUESTIONS ON PAGES 185–186]

1. "But for the defendant's voluntary act [or omission, if relevant], would the social harm have occurred when it did?"

2.   Dependent intervening cause. It seems fair to assume that the fox is a but-for cause of Bob's death—Bob either was not going to die from the gunshot wound or he would have died later. The fox, at the least, accelerated the death. As the fox's causal involvement occurred after Albert's actions, the fox is an intervening cause. What kind? A dependent one, because the fox did not just happen to show up on that rural road: the facts say the fox smelled the blood and came.

3.   Who knows? Since the issue is one of justice, one of public policy, there is no sure answer. But: if we consider the fox to be a dependent intervening cause, under that analysis Albert remains the proximate cause of the death unless we consider the fox not only an unforeseeable intervening cause, but a downright freakish one. This was a rural road with a "nearby forest," so this seems not to be freakish. Albert: you are out of luck. But, what about the other factors? Under the intended-consequences doctrine, Albert wanted Bob dead, but did he want him dead *this way*? My sense of justice suggests that Albert should not get off under these circumstances, but I assume Albert's lawyer will make some argument to the contrary. As for the "free, deliberate informed human intervention" test—the fox obviously does not qualify, so we can get Albert under that theory!

4.   (1) Voluntary Act

(2) Social Harm

(3) *Mens Rea* (usually)

(4) Actual Cause

(5) Proximate Cause

■ PART SIX: DEFENSES TO CRIMES: JUSTIFICATIONS

[ANSWERS TO QUESTIONS ON PAGES 210–211]

1.   "Imminent" force is force that will occur immediately, at virtually that moment or instant.

2.   The MPC only requires that the defendant's self-defensive force be "immediately necessary . . . on the present occasion." Thus, the issue is not when the aggressor will use *his* force, but when the innocent party's self-defensive force is immediately necessary.

3.   False. It is not easy for a deadly aggressor to regain the right of self-defense, but it *is* possible: if the aggressor wholly abandons his deadly design and communicates this fact to the innocent party.

4.   False. Too many students think the answer is True, because MPC § 3.04(1) is written in terms of "belief" rather than "reasonable belief." But, this section expressly provides that § 3.09 of the Code applies as a limiting feature, and the latter provision holds that a person who has a reckless belief may be convicted of a crime of recklessness (*e.g.*, manslaughter), and a person with a negligent belief may be convicted of a crime of negligence (*e.g.*, negligent homicide).

5.   b.   Based on Donald's understanding of the situation, Carla was just about to be the victim of an unlawful deadly assault. Therefore, Carla would have had a right of self-defense. Although this was not, in fact, the case, Donald is entitled to act on the basis of his reasonable, but not unreasonable, belief that she was under real attack. A minority of jurisdictions would deny Donald any defense, even if his mistake was reasonable (answer **a.**).

6.   True. Please notice that I did not specify whether I was talking about the common law or Model Penal Code. But, here, the answer is the same. True, the MPC *does* permit the use of deadly force in some circumstances, but all of them pertain to entry of the dwelling, and not to property taken outside the premises.

7.   False. This question is *almost* true. The one exception, which makes the statement false, is that a person *may* use nondeadly force after dispossession, if in hot pursuit of the dispossessor.

8.   No. Assuming that the spring gun is intended to cause serious bodily harm or death, or is simply know to create such a risk, then spring guns are forbidden under the MPC. This is a sharp divergence from the common law.

9.   The modern and majority rule limits the use of deadly force to the prevention of felonies, and then only if the person using the force reasonably believes that (1) the other person is committing an atrocious felony; and (2) deadly force is necessary to prevent commission of the offense.

10.   If you compare the (majority) common law and MPC crime-prevention defenses (something I urge you to do generally), the biggest difference is the MPC limitation that deadly force may not be exercised if, to do so, would present a substantial risk of injury to bystanders. If you compare the felonies that fall within the rules, they are pretty much the same: the Code limits the use of deadly force to felonies that involve a substantial risk that the suspect will cause death or serious bodily harm if the felony is not prevented. That comes pretty close to the atrocious felony limitation of the majority common law rule.

11. False. The statement is very close to being true, but not quite. First: remember that *Tennessee v. Garner* only applies to the actions of law enforcement officers (and others helping them), and not to private citizens acting alone. Second: it is true that computer fraud would ordinarily fall outside the scope of permissible use of deadly force—such a suspect rarely poses a significant threat to the physical safety of others—but *Garner* makes clear that we must look at each case on its own facts. Suppose our computer geek pulls a knife or gun on the officer in an effort to escape? In that case, the situation would fall within one of the two Court examples where deadly force *would* be permissible.

12. Whatever one's views about abortion, this claim will likely fail for various reasons. First, based on the sparse description of the facts in this question, Betty cannot prove that the harm she seeks to prevent is imminent. Her stated purpose is to prevent "future abortions," not even an abortion taking place at that instant. Second, closely tied to the imminency problem, can Betty show that her actions will causally prevent the threatened harm? If Dr. Abortionist doesn't perform the abortions, are there other physicians who will fill this need? Third, there is a harm-balancing obstacle. The issue is not whether Betty thinks that fetuses are human beings, but whether the society or, at least, the jury, would so conclude. Presumably, if a fetus is not treated as equivalent to a live human being, the killing of the doctor in order to prevent the death of fetuses will create some significant calculation problems (how many fetuses equal one human life?). A final obstacle: as discussed in the Outline, the defense may not even apply to homicide prosecutions. By the way, remember that the defense does not apply if the law has already considered the issue (re-read my Conversation at the start of the Necessity section). And, here, we have such an answer: according to the Supreme Court, a woman has a constitutional right to abort her fetus. Therefore, Betty and, for that matter, the judge or jury, may not substitute their judgment for the law's specific answer to this question.

■ PART SEVEN: DEFENSES TO CRIMES: EXCUSES
[ANSWERS TO QUESTIONS ON PAGES 240–241]

1. False. The correct answer is exactly the opposite: justifications focus on the act; excuses focus on the actor. This is an easy and useful sentence to remember.

2. You might mention a number of points. First, the MPC defense is unambiguously an excuse defense; the common law is more muddled (although most courts treat the defense, as it should, as an excuse.) Second, the common law only applies to threats of force, whereas the MPC defense may be based on prior use of force without any further threat. Third, the common law only applies to threats of imminent harm; the MPC has no imminency requirement. Fourth, the common law only applies to *deadly* threats; the MPC has no such limitation. Fifth, the MPC applies a "person of reasonable firmness standard"; the common law has no equivalent test. Sixth, the MPC, but not the common law, permits the defense to be used in murder cases. Seventh, there are some minor differences in the language relating to person who are at fault for getting themselves in the coercive predicament (but I wouldn't lose a lot of sleep over those differences).

3. **False**. Voluntary intoxication is *never* an *excuse* for criminal conduct. Be sure to distinguish an excuse claim from the very different claim that the defendant should be acquitted because she lacked the *mens rea* of the offense charged.

4. **a.** and **c.**

In **a.**, *D1* should be acquitted because she believed she was killing a polar bear; therefore she did not have the specific intent to murder, since murder involves the killing of a human being, not a polar bear.

In **b.**, *D2* is basically arguing temporary insanity—he knows he is killing a human being, but does not realize it is wrong under the circumstances (he thinks it is right, due to self-defense). Temporary insanity, however, is no defense to voluntary intoxication.

In **c.**, however, the temporary insanity claim will work because this is a case of *involuntary* intoxication. (By the way, you have not yet studied insanity, so some of this may be a bit confusing now, but should be clearer soon.)

5. First, a minor point: the Code calls it "self-induced" intoxication, rather than "voluntary" intoxication. Second, and more critically, the MPC, unlike the common law, does not distinguish between general-intent and specific-intent offenses. Voluntary intoxication (or whatever it is called) can potentially exculpate for *any* offense under the MPC, and not just specific-intent offenses. (But, in this regard, don't forget the special MPC rule—negligence may be treated like recklessness.)

6. *Durham* or "product" test. The mental health professionals believed that this test properly focused on the defendant's mental illness, would permit more persons to be found insane and, therefore, directed to mental health care; it also seemed to give psychiatrists the opportunity to testify fully, without being compelled to fit their testimony into the volitional and cognitive pigeonholes of prior insanity tests.

7. d. Pretty clearly Alice is not insane under *M'Naghten*: there is no indication she did not know what she was doing or that what she was doing was wrong. (The fact that she planned to do it when she was alone with him might even suggest her awareness of the illegality of her actions.) Nor is there any evidence presented that she could not control herself. Indeed, she waited a week to act out her plans. But, this also does not seem to meet *Durham*, or the product test. Why not? Yes, she suffers from a mental illness, but there is nothing about her hallucinatory condition that seems to be causally linked to the crime. Indeed, there is no evidence she was hallucinating either when she formed the plan or when she committed it!

8. b. Diminished capacity applies to any abnormal mental condition, so it is unnecessary to worry whether Alzheimer's is considered a "mental illness." That eliminates **d.** David believed he had entered his own home, so he did not enter with the specific intent to commit a felony inside. Therefore, he is not guilty of the specific-intent offense of burglary. But, he is guilty of trespass. On its face, the misdemeanor is strict liability, so there is no *mens rea* to negate. But, this may not be the case—remember the common law bias against strict liability. But, at most this is a general-intent offense, and diminished capacity does not apply to general-intent crimes at common law. (By the way, notice that *if* Alzheimer's constitutes a mental disease, David might have a very plausible insanity claim, as he did not know that what he was doing was wrong due to his cognitive impairment. If so, he is not guilty of any offense on *that* basis. That is why some courts and scholars see no reason to recognize a separate defense of diminished capacity!)

9. Very False. The MPC is far more open to diminished capacity claims than the common law. It not only permits the introduction of psychiatric testimony to prove the absence of *mens rea* for any crime, but it also recognizes the partial responsibility version of diminished capacity in the homicide area: murder may be reduced to manslaughter if the defendant suffers from an extreme mental or emotional disturbance for which there is reasonable explanation or excuse.

10. Subjective test. Enough said.

11. Objective test. Also, enough said.

■ PART EIGHT: INCHOATE CONDUCT

[ANSWERS TO QUESTIONS ON PAGES 276–278]

1. **True.** At original common law, an attempt was punished as a mere misdemeanor, even if the target offense was a capital felony! Today, common law jurisdictions and states following the common law treat an attempted felony as a felony, but as a lesser one, with a lesser punishment.

2. The purpose of this question is to re-enforce the point that you should learn the various common law *actus reus* tests of attempt (last act; dangerous proximity; physical proximity; unequivocality; probable desistance)—the titles of these tests are less important, of course, than an understanding of the substance of the tests.

3. **True**. All crimes of attempts are specific intent, even if the target offense is general intent.

4. **c.** These awful facts are from a *real* case. This is a case of hybrid legal impossibility. If the facts had been as Despicable believed them to be—that she was alive—then this would have constituted a rape. So, that sounds like factual impossibility. But, it is also true that what Despicable did—have sexual intercourse with a corpse—is not a crime (or, more accurately, it is not the crime of rape), so this is also a case of legal impossibility. Put differently, this is a hybrid case.

5. **Unclear**. If a court treats this as legal impossibility, then Despicable will be acquitted. But, some courts will decide to treat this as a case of a factual impossibility (see above), and convict Despicable.

6. **Guilty**. The MPC has abolished the legal impossibility defense. More accurately, it has abolished the *hybrid* legal impossibility defense. Therefore, Despicable is guilty.

7. **Not guilty under the MPC; probably guilty under the common law.** There seems to be little doubt that a jury would find that Denise's conduct constitutes a substantial step in the culmination of a murder under the MPC, and lying in wait certainly is corroborative of her criminal intent. But, Denise can avoid conviction here because her conduct appears to satisfy the "renunciation of criminal purpose" defense: her abandonment of her criminal enterprise was voluntary and complete. The common law, however, does *not* recognize this defense, so Denise's last-moment renunciation will do her no good. Assuming, therefore, that a jury finds that Denise's conduct constitutes an attempt according to one of the common law tests of attempt, she will be convicted.

8. True. Using the example provided in the Outline, a person cannot be convicted of the crime of defamation, as there is no such crime. But, an agreement between two persons later to defame another *is* a crime (of conspiracy)! So, apparently it is worse for two people to agree to defame than it is for one to actually do it. Is that crazy, or what?

9. Definitely no under the MPC, probably no under the common law. Alex has knowledge of Bob's plans, but there is no evidence presented he wants the killing to occur. He did not sell the gun at an inflated price or in any other way indicate that it was his conscious objective that the crime occur. Under the MPC, therefore, there is no conspiracy, as he did not have the purpose of promoting or facilitating the killing. The common law is less clear, as there are some courts that will permit a conspiracy charge to be based on mere knowledge, but most courts reject this.

10. No. Wharton's Rule would bar prosecution. By definition, dueling requires at least two willing combatants. It takes two to tango, and two to tangle (by dueling). (Sorry. I couldn't resist.)

11. Common law: Both are acquitted. MPC: Chester is convicted, Donald is acquitted. Here is how to look at this. Donald, due to involuntary intoxication, did not know what he agreed to. Therefore, he lacked the specific intent to rob First State Bank. Therefore, he is not guilty of common law conspiracy, which requires that one not only intend to agree, but intend that the target offense be committed. Since Donald gets off, so does Chester because of the plurality rule. But, the MPC rejects the plurality rule. So, Chester will be convicted of conspiracy, although nobody else is guilty.

12. Common law: two counts of conspiracy; MPC: one count. At common law the issue is simple to state: how many agreements were formed. In most cases it will be nearly impossible to answer, but here the facts seem reasonably clear. They made one agreement on Day 1, and then formed another agreement on Day 2. That is bad luck for them. If they had agreed on Day 1 to rob both banks, there would be guilty of only one count of conspiracy, not two. The MPC would presumably say that there existed a "continuing conspiratorial relationship" between Jack and Jill, so there is just one conspiracy. (It would be different if they had robbed Bank 1 on Day 1, divided the proceeds, and "broke up," only to get back together at a later date.)

13. Both are guilty. Notice, first, that there was no overt act in furtherance of the conspiracy. At common law, however, none is needed. But, on an exam, if you are working with a statute, see if there is such a requirement. If so, neither would be guilty here unless you can point to some act in furtherance of the plan by one of them. The facts show that Carl withdrew his support from the conspiracy. At common law, however, this is no defense to the crime of conspiracy. (Carl's withdrawal, however, *would* free him from guilt for the President's murder, if Roger went on without him.)

14.   Yes, he is guilty of solicitation. That is the easy question. (However, please remember that his guilt assumes that he genuinely wanted the killing to occur and was not joking.) The tricky answer here is this: **Isn't a solicitation an "attempted conspiracy"?!** After all, if Richard had said yes, they would be guilty of conspiracy. Alex wanted Richard to say yes, so this is an attempt to conspire! But, the law just treats this as solicitation.

15.   No. She did not intend to communicate with Bill. True enough, she originally had the intent to communicate with Bill to encourage him to commit a crime, but when she performed the voluntary act of pushing the SEND button, she no longer had the requisite *mens rea*.

16.   Okay, okay. I put this question in as a sort of brain teaser to end our discussion of inchoate crimes. Here is what I am getting at. At common law, an assault is an attempted battery. So, an attempted assault is an attempt to attempt a battery! That *does* seem odd, and some courts have said there is no such offense. Two counter-points. First, there is nothing odd about "attempted assault" if "assault" is defined as it is in tort law. Basically, that would mean that the wrongdoer tried, but failed, to put the victim in apprehension of a battery. Second, even with the common law definition of assault, there *might* be some logic to an attempted assault charge: as I noted earlier, an assault ordinary requires that the defendant perform the last act necessary to commit the battery. So, perhaps an attempted assault would be a way to punish a person who has *not* committed the last act. Maybe, just as the person is about to swing his fist, this would constitute an attempted assault!

■ PART NINE: COMPLICITY

[ANSWERS TO QUESTIONS ON PAGES 292–293]

1.   a.   Carl is not guilty of rape (duress). Bob used Carl as his innocent instrumentality. Bob is the principal in the first degree.

2. b. This is a tough one: it requires you to remember what you (hopefully) learned about the duress defense: the common law does not recognize the duress defense in homicide cases. So, Carl is guilty of the murder despite the coercion. That means he is *not* an *innocent* person. Therefore, Bob is a principal in the second degree (since the facts say he was present when the killing occurred).

3. True. Mere presence at the scene of a crime is not enough to make one an accomplice. Presence plus the intent to aid is also not enough! Joshua had the *mens rea* to be an accomplice, but to be an accomplice you must aid in some way, and he didn't. We can't even prove encouragement here, as Carla has no idea that Joshua was aware of her intentions. Joshua may not be a good guy, but he is not guilty of robbery.

4. Negligent homicide. Janice clearly assisted in the crime by handing over the keys to her car to Xavier. The issue is her *mens rea*. She intentionally committed the act of assistance; but what was her *mens rea* in regard to the outcome (the death)? The facts suggest she was negligent, not reckless. (The facts tell us she was unaware of Xavier's condition, so she is not reckless.) So, she is not guilty of murder or even manslaughter. The MPC (§ 2.06(7)) provides that an accomplice can be convicted of a different crime or degree of crime than the principal, so she is guilty of negligent homicide.

5. You bet she is! The legislative-exemption rule gets Camille off the hook—she cannot be an accomplice in her own statutory rape—*she is considered the victim*. But that doctrine does not apply to Kelli. She is not the victim here. So, Kelli, an underage female can be convicted (via accomplice liability) of statutory rape of another underage female.

6. You bet she is under the *Pinkerton* doctrine, but not under the MPC. You can't convict Nellie as an accomplice in any of those non-Chicago crimes. The facts say she did not assist in any way. But, she can be convicted as a member of the broad conspiracy, assuming a jurisdiction chooses to apply *Pinkerton*: those other crimes are very much a part of the conspiracy—a conspiracy to sell drugs results in the sale of drugs! And violence with one's drug customers is hardly unforeseeable. But, as for the MPC, the MPC rejects the *Pinkerton* doctrine, so the only way to convict Nellie of these crimes is if she aided, agreed to aid, or attempted to aid in the specific offenses that occurred in the other cities, and none of this happened.

7. Yes. Abandonment is a defense under the MPC, but only if the accomplice neutralizes his assistance (here, by retrieving the gun), calling the police or otherwise preventing the crime from occurring. Here, Carlos didn't do any of this.

8.   Yes, attempted murder. This is where MPC § 5.01(3) comes into play. Carlos did commit an act—furnishing the gun—that would have made him an accomplice if Zelda had committed the offense (or attempted it). Therefore, Carlos attempted to aid in a murder. Therefore, he is guilty of attempted murder.

■ PART TEN: CRIMINAL HOMICIDE

[ANSWERS TO QUESTIONS ON PAGES 323–324]

1.   False, as stated. The only point I want to register by this question is this: "homicide" is a neutral term. Many homicides are not criminal (for example, a killing in self-defense; an execution by the State; the taking of life at war).

2.   No. The year-and-a-day rule would bar prosecution. Realistically, today, a coroner could make the type of causal determination involved here, but not at common law, so the rule was strict—366 days after the homicide, a prosecution is barred.

3.   First, intent to kill (a human being). Second, **intent to commit grievous bodily injury.** Third, **depraved heart murder,** which is an extremely reckless killing. Fourth, **the felony-murder rule,** that is, a killing (even an unintentional one) that occurs during the commission or attempted commission of a felony.

4.   Trick Question Alert: *NEITHER.* Remember. Remember. Remember. *There are no degrees of murder at common law.* Also, remember that an intentional killing need not constitute murder at all: if the intentional killing justified, excused, or the result of a mitigating factor (the provocation doctrine).

5.   Either first-degree or second-degree, but it ought to be the latter. As the Outline points out, some courts have effectively negated the element of premeditation by saying that even an instant of thought constitutes premeditation. But, if the term is treated seriously, as many courts do, an instant would not be long enough to deliberate (to reflect meaningfully and calmly on the pros and cons of committing the crime), so this person would be guilty of a wilful killing that is neither premeditated nor deliberate. So, the murder would be second-degree.

**6.   The reason is that any person who intends to inflict grievous bodily injury upon another—not to kill the victim, but to inflict injury that "imperils life" or "is likely to be attended with dangerous or fatal consequences"—almost surely is acting in a manner that manifests an extreme indifference to the value of human life. Anyone who tries to come close to killing without killing (assuming, as will usually be the case, that he has no good reason for such conduct) is taking a hugely unjustified, foreseeable risk of causing death. And, such an actor almost certainly is aware that he is taking such a risk. So, all of the elements of "depraved heart" are proven.

7. **No.** Rather clearly Doctor Alice did not intend to kill or inflict grievous bodily injury: we can say this because it was not her conscious object to kill or grievously harm Pat, nor did she know that such an outcome was virtually certain to occur. Knowledge that something is 50–50, is a case of taking a risk, not a case of virtual certainty. So, the only plausible basis for a murder claim would be "depraved heart." (There is no felony, for felony-murder, so we can skip right by that.) But, nothing here manifests an extreme indifference to the value of human life—quite the opposite. Dr. Alice is trying to save a life. We can see this by looking at the basic elements of depraved heart: Did Dr. Alice consciously take a substantial, foreseeable, unjustifiable risk in doing the surgery? Notice the components: (a) conscious awareness; (b) a risk that is foreseeable; (c) a risk that is substantial; and (d) a risk that is unjustifiable. It is the latter element that is missing here—this was a *justifiable* risk. Weighing the options: someone who would die *for sure* in just a few days versus a 50% chance of providing a heart that would allow Pat a relatively normal long life—the risk here seems justifiable.

8. **True.** It is worth remembering, however, that at original common law, when the felony-murder rule developed, there were only a small number of felonies (unlike today when most penal codes have tens or hundreds of felonies on the books), and all of them were considered serious enough to carry the death penalty.

9. **False.** The primary argument for the felony-murder rule is not that it will deter felonies but that it will cause felons to commit their crimes in a less dangerous manner.

10. **No.** In the abstract we look, simply, at the statute as defined. It does not matter whether the defendant practiced medicine by "prescribing" aspirin for a headache or sought to diagnose a child for cancer. (The facts *would* matter if the jurisdiction applies the "the circumstances of the case" test.) Looking, then, at the statute, we ask: *can* this offense be committed without creating a high probability or substantial risk of death? Quite clearly, this offense *can* be committed without carrying that high a risk. First, the defendant might be trained as a physician but simply lack the license. And, even a charlatan can act reasonably safely, as long as she practices medicine on people who are not seriously ill.

11. This offense merges. This is basically the statute interpreted by the court in *People v. Smith*, 678 P.2d 886 (Cal. 1984). This is basically a crime of assault, even though the label is "child abuse." And, there is no independent felonious purpose here—there is no way for the abuser to commit the felony in a less dangerous manner. (By the way, notice that this offense *is* inherently dangerous, so it would qualify for felony-murder under *that* limitation, but it would not be available if the jurisdiction also apples the independent felony/merger limitation.)

12. No. True, the felony burglary was over (in fact, it was over as soon as *F* broke into the apartment in question), but the felony-murder rule extends to the flight after the felony, as long as there is a causal connection between the felony and the death. Here there is the requisite causal link.

13. Yes, if the jurisdiction applies the proximate causation theory; no if it applies the agency theory. Here, the shooter is not one of the felons. If a court applies the agency theory of felony-murder, as the cashier is not the felon's agent, Frank is not responsible for the homicide. But, he did proximately cause the death, so in a minority of jurisdictions, the felony-murder rule *would* apply.

14. Murder. This is obviously an intentional killing, so this is murder unless the provocation doctrine comes into play. At common law, however, this does not constitute adequate provocation. This is a case of "words alone"—which the original common law, and even most non-MPC courts today, do not recognize as adequate. As for the adultery—Jerry must observe it for the provocation to be considered adequate. (In a jurisdiction that divides murder into degrees, this ought to be second-degree murder: the killing seems unpremeditated and, in any case, it lacks the characteristics of a "cold-blooded" first-degree killing).

15. Probably, murder. As sympathetic as the mother's case seems, I would hope you would see the potential obstacles. First, is the provocation adequate? No, if the words-alone rule applies here. But, what if a court looks at this as a case of "sexual assault + words"? Now, it is not a case of words alone. The problem with *that* analysis, however, is that the sexual assault happened months earlier, so the mother had a reasonable time to cool off (another element of the defense). But, notice the comment in the Outline that some courts permit juries to consider the possibility of brooding. Is it not plausible that a parent would brood about the sexual attack, that the anger would be just below the surface for a very long time, and then when the testimony occurred, the explosion would take place? Perhaps, but such an approach greatly expands on what is otherwise a narrow defense. Finally, and perhaps most critically from the mother's perspective, is the premeditated act of smuggling the gun into the court (no easy matter these days), which suggests she planned to kill *V* when she entered the courtroom. That means that his testimony really did not trigger the homicide: the causal element of the defense is absent.

16. False. Tort liability is based on civil negligence. Common law involuntary manslaughter is based on *criminal* negligence, which is a higher level of negligence than is necessary in a tort action. (By the way, there may be another difference between a tort negligence suit and a criminal negligence prosecution: although "proximate causation" is an element of both criminal and tort law, the doctrines do not precisely overlap.)

17. Hmmm. Let's see. (Of course, your list and mine may differ, depending on whether you subdivide some of the differences.) Here is my list: (1) The MPC divides criminal homicide into three crimes, rather than two. (2) The critical distinction between common law murder and manslaughter—the presence or absence of "malice aforethought"—does not apply under the Code. (3) There are no degrees of murder in the MPC, unlike many non-Code statutes. (4) The MPC explicitly excludes inadvertent risk-taking from the category of murder; this is the approach of most, but not all, common law jurisdictions. (5) The MPC would abolish the felony-murder rule. (But look carefully at what it *does* do.) (6) The MPC does not recognize unlawful-act manslaughter. (7) The MPC treats inadvertent risk-taking homicides as "negligent homicide," whereas the common law treats such homicides as involuntary manslaughter. (7) The EMED provision of the MPC differs considerably from the common law provocation doctrine in that: (a) the common law forms of adequate provocation are rejected; (b) the "words alone" rule is abolished; (c) the "reasonable cooling off" rule is abolished.; (d) the issue is simply whether there is a reasonable explanation or excuse for the actor's EMED; and (e) the MPC invites somewhat more subjectivization of the "reasonable person" test.

■ PART ELEVEN: RAPE

[ANSWERS TO QUESTIONS ON PAGES 336–337]

1. False. At common law, the crime of rape only prohibited vaginal intercourse.

2. False. This statement is true if the male did not use force, or used only "moderate" force. But, a female did not have to resist a male's use (or threatened use) of force likely to cause death or serious bodily injury.

3. a. Rape is a general-intent crime at common law. Therefore, the general rule is that a reasonable mistake of fact is a defense, but an unreasonable one is not a defense.

4. Among the differences: (1) the crime is now characterized as "sexual assault" or "sexual battery"; (2) it includes other forms of sexual relations beyond vaginal intercourse; (3) the offense is gender neutral; (4) the marital immunity rule is abolished; (5) the resistance requirement is abolished or substantially reduced; (6) the law has been broadened to punish other forms of nonconsensual intercourse beyond the forcible variety. There are other differences, but these are among the most significant.

5. Probably, gross sexual imposition or nothing. Rape is a longshot. Looking first at the rape statute, Predator did not compel the intercourse by use of any force. The rape provision also covers *threats* of "imminent death, serious bodily injury, extreme pain or kidnapping." He did not threaten imminent death, imminent serious bodily injury, or imminent extreme pain. A closer issue is whether he threatened her with kidnapping. You have not looked at that statute, but here is what one learns if one looks at it. (Study lesson: don't assume you know what "kidnapping" is—look at the specific statute! Sometimes you cannot determine if Crime 1 [here, rape] has been committed without deciding whether Crime 2 [here, kidnapping] has occurred.] Kidnapping (§ 212.1) is limited to confining another "for a substantial period in a place of isolation"—does overnight in a jail with other prisoners qualify?—for any of the following reasons: in order to hold her for ransom (nope), facilitate commission of some other felony (nope), interfere with the performance of a governmental function (nope), or inflict bodily injury or to terrorize the victim (hmmm, maybe). My own sense is that Predator is guilty of false imprisonment (§ 212.3), which is defined as "knowingly restrain[ing] another unlawfully so as to interfere substantially with his liberty." If I am right in this regard, a rape charge is inappropriate. What, then, about gross sexual imposition? The issue—one for the jury—is whether this threat "would prevent resistance by a woman of ordinary resolution." By the way, I would argue that his offer not to give her a ticket if she had intercourse with him is just that—an offer, not a threat—and should drop out of the picture. The issue is not what he will do for her if she accedes, but *what he will do to her if she refuses.*

■ PART TWELVE: THEFT

[ANSWERS TO QUESTIONS ON PAGES 355–356]

1. False. Most obviously, this statement is false because it suggests that larceny law protects ownership rights, but it actually protects a person's possessory interest in property, even at the expense of the owner. A second, far more subtle point: the intention of a larcenous wrongdoer is to permanently deprive the original possessor of the property; *it is not necessary that the wrongdoer intend to keep the property himself.* If a thief takes your property intending to destroy it or bury it underground never to be seen again, he intends to permanently deprive you of your property; he does not intend to keep the property. But, he is still guilty of larceny.

2. Larceny (by trick). The first matter to ask yourself is whether Jane intended to transfer title to the ring or mere possession. This is a good place to start because the answer to this question will either put you on the false pretenses side of the line (in which case you can analyze that offense to see if Gina is guilty), or the larceny/embezzlement side (in which case you can drop false pretenses). The answer, at first blush, seems to be title: after all, Jane believed that Gina was the owner of the ring. But, that is exactly the point: Jane did not intend to transfer title, as she knew that she did not have the title to transfer. So, out goes false pretenses. So, we must now decide if it is larceny or embezzlement. What we know from the facts is that Jane took possession of the ring when she picked it up. Gina then took possession from Jane when Jane gave it to her. That possessory taking was trespassory because of fraud, so it is larceny by trick, and not embezzlement.

3. Embezzlement. This is not false pretenses: Client did not transfer title to the money when he handed it over. Notice from the facts that he did not intend to part with the money until a condition was satisfied, so when the money changed hands from Client to Lawyer, all that Lawyer received was possession. Since Lawyer intended at the time of taking possession to live up to the deal, that taking was lawful, so that eliminates larceny. This seems to be embezzlement: lawful possession; entrustment by Client to Lawyer; later conversion of the money.

4. None of the above. Of course, title did not transfer, so false pretenses is out. The key here, however, is that Charles took real property—the begonias are part of the land. Larceny and embezzlement involve the taking (and in the case of embezzlement, conversion) of *personal* property. So, none of these crimes are implicated.

5. Petty pizza larceny! Jason, as an employee, received mere custody, not possession, of the pizza from the employer. Once he ate the slice, he took trespassory possession of that piece. (It is pretty obvious he intended to deprive Sam of that slice on a permanent basis!) I guess the eating is a "carrying away" act, although I must admit I have not quite seen a case like this, and if I were Jason's lawyer, I would argue that point. (And I would wonder why the prosecutor brought criminal charges, and even more wonder why Jason paid big bucks for me to represent him on this *really* petty larceny misdemeanor case!)

APPENDIX B

Sample Essay Questions

ESSAY ONE (One hour)

On January 15, Leroy borrowed $100 from a friend in order to purchase a small quantity of cocaine for personal use. He ingested some of the cocaine and placed the remainder of the cocaine in his dresser drawer. (His continued possession of this small quantity of cocaine constituted a felony.)

On January 30, an exceedingly cold day, Leroy lit a torch made up of rolled newspapers in order to thaw frozen water pipes beneath his kitchen floor. In doing so, he created an unseen fire that smoldered under the kitchen floor. Shortly thereafter, Leroy's friend called and demanded repayment of the $100. Leroy left the house to go to repay the debt. Fifteen minutes later, during Leroy's absence, the house suddenly and quickly became engulfed in flames and smoke. His two-year-old son, left alone, became trapped in the house and died of smoke inhalation.

It never occurred to Leroy, emotionally devastated by the loss of his beloved son, that a fire might start in the manner in which it did.

Question

These events occurred in a state with the following criminal homicide statute:

§ 750.316   First degree murder; definition

A person who commits any of the following is guilty of first degree murder and shall be punished by imprisonment for life:

(a) Murder perpetrated by means of poison, lying in wait, or any other willful, deliberate, and premeditated killing.

(b) Murder committed in the perpetration, or attempt to perpetrate, arson, criminal sexual conduct, robbery, breaking and entering of a dwelling, home invasion in the first or second degree, larceny of any kind, extortion, or kidnapping.

§ 750.317   Second degree murder

All other kinds of murder shall be murder of the second degree, and shall be punished by imprisonment in the state prison for life, or any terms of years, in the discretion of the court trying the same.

§ 750.321   Manslaughter

Any person who shall commit the crime of manslaughter shall be guilty of a felony punishable by imprisonment in the state prison, not more than 15 years or by fine of not more than 7,500 dollars, or both, at the discretion of the court.

Discuss Leroy's criminal responsibility, if any, for the death of his son pursuant to this homicide statute. You may assume that the state otherwise applies common law doctrine. You may also assume that no affirmative defenses apply to these facts.

ESSAY TWO (One hour)

Albert was a 24–year-old male, 6'2" tall, muscular, and weighed 220 pounds. Albert earned money on the street by selling drugs. Albert often had fist fights in bars and on the streets. A *false* rumor on the street was that he had once cut a woman with a knife when she refused to have sex with him in exchange for drugs.

Albert was attracted to Francesca, a 19–year-old, 5'0", 105–pound clerk in a liquor store in the area in which Albert sold drugs. In the past, Francesca had rebuffed Albert's efforts to spend time together. However, Francesca was addicted to cocaine, which she purchased from Albert on occasion. One day, when Francesca sought to buy more cocaine from Albert, he said, "I will give it to you free, if you will sleep with me." Francesca refused and offered him cash for the drugs. Albert angrily said, "You either have sex with me or you are out of luck. No sex, no drugs now or ever." The addicted Francesca, desperate, and fearful of Albert because of the false rumor that he had used violence with another female drug addict, agreed to have intercourse with him. They had intercourse at Albert's apartment later that night.

The next day, Louis, Francesca's father, learned what happened. Outraged, Louis obtained a knife and went looking for Albert. When he discovered Albert on the street, he pulled the knife on him, said, "You are going to pay for what you did to my daughter." Albert laughed, pulled a gun and intentionally shot Louis to death.

Question

Discuss Albert's criminal responsibility, if any, for the intercourse with Francesca and the death of Louis. Apply the Model Penal Code. For your information, these are the pertinent sexual offense and criminal homicide statutes to use:

Section 213.1. Rape and Related Offenses

(1) *Rape.* A male who has sexual intercourse with a female not his wife is guilty of rape if:

> (a) he compels her to submit by force or by threat of imminent death, serious bodily injury, extreme pain or kidnapping, to be inflicted on anyone; or

> (b) he has substantially impaired her power to appraise or control her conduct by administering or employing without her knowledge drugs, intoxicants or other means for the purpose of preventing resistance; or

(c) the female is unconscious; or

(d) the female is less than 10 years old.

(2) *Gross Sexual Imposition.* A male who has sexual intercourse with a female not his wife commits a felony of the third degree if:

(a) he compels her to submit by any threat that would prevent resistance by a woman of ordinary resolution; or

(b) he knows that she suffers from a mental disease or defect which renders her incapable of appraising the nature of her conduct; or

(c) he knows that she is unaware that a sexual act is being committed upon her or that she submits because she mistakenly supposes that he is her husband.

Section 210.2. Murder

(1) Except as provided in Section 210.3(1)(b), criminal homicide constitutes murder when:

(a) it is committed purposely or knowingly; or

(b) it is committed recklessly under circumstances manifesting extreme indifference to the value of human life. Such recklessness and indifference are presumed if the actor is engaged or is an accomplice in the commission of, or an attempt to commit, or flight after committing or attempting to commit robbery, rape or deviate sexual intercourse by force or threat of force, arson, burglary, kidnapping or felonious escape.

Section 210.3. Manslaughter

(1) Criminal homicide constitutes manslaughter when:

(a) it is committed recklessly; or

(b) a homicide which would otherwise be murder is committed under the influence of extreme mental or emotional disturbance for which there is reasonable explanation or excuse. The reasonableness of such explanation or excuse shall be determined from the viewpoint of a person in the actor's situation under the circumstances as he believes them to be.

Section 210.4. Negligent Homicide

(1) Criminal homicide constitutes negligent homicide when it is committed negligently.

*

APPENDIX C

Answers to Essay Questions

ESSAY ONE INITIAL COMMENTS

1.   Notice that you are given a statute here, perhaps one you have never seen before. Professors often do this on an examination. Why? Because the professor wants you to demonstrate that you can use and adequately interpret a statute, a very important legal skill. And, even if the statute is new to you, it is likely to look like some statute you have seen in class (maybe a variation on the Model Penal Code), or the statute will use a lot of common law terms, so you will end up bringing common law analysis into the statutory discussion.

The statute here comes verbatim (with a few deletions to save time) from the Michigan Penal Code. Notice that "murder" is not defined in the statute: you are simply told what constitute first-degree and second-degree murder. Second-degree murder, it says, is "all other kinds of murder" (meaning that everything that is *not* first-degree murder is second-degree). But, that does not tell us what "murder" is. So how do you resolve this? The rule you will have learned by this time of the semester is: *when a statute uses common law terminology without defining the terms, you ordinarily use common law definitions.* ***That is precisely why you learned the common law in class.*** So, on this examination (as a lawyer in Michigan would do), you apply the common law definition of murder, and then apply the statute to determine whether the murder is first-degree or second-degree. Likewise, notice that the manslaughter provision of the Michigan Penal Code provides the punishment for manslaughter, but doesn't define the crime. So, again, you apply the common law!

2. Notice that you are told to "assume that no affirmative defenses apply to these facts." So, of course, you should not spend even one minute discussing affirmative defenses. This points up my advice (see the Perspective section of this Outline) about reading the call of the examination question with great care.

3. Some professors (including me) want students to discuss each element of a crime—voluntary act/omission; social harm; *mens rea*; actual cause; and proximate cause—even if some of these issues can be handled in a sentence or two. Other professors will tell you, "just talk about the *real* issues." These professors will argue that an issue that only requires a sentence or two is not a "real" issue. To the extent that you can, ask your professor in advance which approach he or she prefers.

4. What follows is not intended as a model answer. I am simply going to lead you through the basics of the question, giving you advice as I go along.

STATE VERSUS LEROY (CRIMINAL HOMICIDE)

[*Remember the advice I gave in Perspectives about examination taking. When a question calls for you to discuss criminal homicide, I urge you to "start at the top"—murder—and then work your way down to manslaughter, if relevant. Also, I suggested that this is the one place where it makes sense to discuss both crimes—murder and manslaughter—together under the title "Criminal Homicide." The only difference between the two crimes comes when you discuss mens rea. That is where 90% of your answer here will come.*]

Because this statute does not define murder, the common law definition applies. Murder is the killing of a human being by another human being with malice aforethought. Manslaughter is the unlawful killing of a human being without malice aforethought. Further clarification will be set out below, as needed.

1. VOLUNTARY ACT/OMISSION

As first glance, there is nothing difficult here. After all, a voluntary act is a willed muscular contraction, and Leroy did this when he lit the newspapers to thaw the frozen pipes. However, there is more to this matter than initially meets the eye, and you will see this from later discussion (and if you think out your answer before starting to write, as I recommended in the Perspective, you will be aware of this already). After all, what is the "conduct" that bothers the prosecutor (or us) about Leroy's behavior? Is it the act of lighting the torch under the house (a voluntary act), or is it that he left his child in the house alone? One problem here is that if you focus only on the act of lighting the newspapers, there may not have been anything reckless (or perhaps even negligent) on his part in regard to starting the fire. The real criticism we have with Leroy is that he left his two-year-old child unattended, which is dangerous in any case!

I think the latter is the *real* basis for the prosecution. If so, I would see this as a case involving an omission, and not a voluntary act: Leroy *failed* to take proper care of his son by leaving his two-year-old in the house. As a father, he has a duty to act in the best welfare of his children, which duty he breached by leaving him home alone. So *this* is the relevant place to start!

2. SOCIAL HARM

This is straight-forward: the social harm of criminal homicide is the death of another human being. Here we have a death of the child. Of course, the child was killed by the fire, but if we can link Leroy to the fire, then we prove the social harm.

3. *MENS REA*

A. Murder

This state does not define murder, so the common law definition will be used. Murder requires proof of malice aforethought. A person acts with malice aforethought if he possesses any one of four states of mind: (1) intent to kill; (2) intent to commit grievous bodily harm; (3) depraved heart; or (4) intent to commit a felony, in which a death occurs. [*Notice, I have defined the key term (malice) here—I have defined it fully, to show the professor I know the definition. Defining legal terms on an exam is critical.*] Turning to these four categories, can the prosecutor prove any one of them beyond a reasonable doubt?

Intent to kill. There are no absolutely facts to support a claim that Leroy intended to kill his son. The facts suggest a terrible accident; the facts also tell us that Leroy was devastated by the loss of his child, whom he loved deeply. So, you would note these facts and quickly demonstrate that intent to kill is missing.

Intent to commit grievous bodily harm. Again, this can be ruled out on the same basis as intent-to-kill.

Depraved heart. Aha, *this* is a highly viable issue. Essentially, "depraved heart" is the common law's way of talking about extreme recklessness, that is, manifesting an extreme indifference to the value of human life. At common law, as with the MPC, basically we ask whether the actor **consciously** took a **substantial** and **unjustifiable risk** to the lives of others. [*This is not the only way to define "depraved* *heart" at common law—unfortunately there is no single accepted definition. But, this is probably the best one.*] There is a lot one can do here. We really have two sets of events. First, was his decision to try to thaw his frozen pipes in the manner in which he did. How reckless was this? How depraved was this? More specifically, was he taking an unjustifiable risk here? After all, he had to do *something* about the water pipes before they burst. How substantial a risk did he create by these actions? And, was Leroy *consciously* aware that this conduct risked causing a fire or otherwise endangering himself and others? The facts state explicitly that it never occurred to him that his actions would start a fire "in the manner it occurred." So, since recklessness requires a *conscious awareness* of a risk, *this* risk-taking cannot constitute depraved heart. (And, frankly, once we put aside the 20:20 vision of hindsight, I doubt many people would have foreseen the fire.)

But, wait! We have a second set of facts: that he left his two-year old alone for 15+ minutes (we don't know how long he was away). *This* surely was risky. As a father, don't you think he must have been aware that doing this created *some* risks, even if a fire "caused in the manner it did" was not in his mind: he must have been aware of risks from leaving his young son, such as a dire medical emergency, a burglary in which his son might he harmed or kidnapped, a fire caused in some manner, etc.? Also, we have to consider his reason for leaving his child alone: he wasn't leaving, for example, to go next door to help a neighbor who was having a heart attack. He was going to pay back a friend for his drugs. This is where the depraved heart analysis, if it will work, almost certainly must center. This is where your discussion must go. Of course, your professor will not care much, if at all, how you resolve the issue, as long as you provide full analysis. Ideally, you would break down your analysis into: (a) magnitude of the foreseeable risk (remember not to use 20:20 hindsight); (b) likelihood of the foreseeable risk occurring; (c) reason for taking the risk; and (d) Leroy's awareness of the risk. Ultimately, I think a jury might—not necessarily would—find depraved heart murder. **If we go with this, this constitutes second-degree murder.** How do we know this? Because we know that depraved heart killing is murder; and, according to the statute you must apply, first-degree murder is limited to a killing committed by poison (not here), lying in wait (not here), or "any other willful, deliberate, and premeditated killing" (not here). It is also first-degree murder if the killing occurs during the commission of one of the enumerated felonies. That means that a depraved-heart killing is *not* first-degree murder, but it is murder, so it second-degree murder ("all other kinds of murder shall be murder of the second degree").

Felony-murder. A person is guilty of murder if, during the commission or attempted commission of any felony, a person is killed even accidentally. One might ask oneself whether Leroy committed any of the felonies listed in the first-degree murder statute. Is this arson? No. Arson is the malicious destruction of *another person's* dwelling. This is a non-starter.

We are told, however, Leroy committed the felony of cocaine possession. As this is a felony, and at common law the felony-murder rule applies to *any* felony, this would seem to make Leroy guilty of second-degree murder under the felony-murder rule, even if the depraved-heart theory fails. But, a few matters ought to be noted here. Can we say that the killing here occurred *"in the perpetration or attempt to perpetrate"* the felony? At first blush, the answer would seem to be no. But: the crime is not the purchase of the cocaine, which occurred 15 days earlier, but *possession*. Possession is a continuing act: it goes on from the moment that Leroy obtained the cocaine until the moment when all of the cocaine had been disposed of. Therefore, in a purely technical sense, *any death that occurs during that period of time (lasting 15+ days already) is a death that occurred during the commission of the offense.*

But, that seems crazy, doesn't it? Here is a place where a student can, and I believe should, focus on the potential unfairness of the felony-murder rule, and to see whether a defense attorney can avoid its use. One very possible legal argument is to suggest that there is no *causal* connection between the wrongdoing of the felony—possession of cocaine—and the death. As noted in the Outline, this involves the so-called *"res gestae"* potential limitation of the felony-murder rule. After all, we are not dealing here with, for example, someone who died using cocaine. We are not even dealing with the death of the child because, say, Leroy was under the influence of cocaine and, therefore, failed to notice the fire. The prosecutor would say that, but for the purchase of the drugs, Leroy would not have been out of the house paying the debt and, therefore, unable to save his son. But, that argument should fail because the crime is not the purchase of the drugs, but *possession*. In this case, "possession" is nothing more than the passive "act" of having cocaine in the house. How is there any causal link between *that* and the deaths? I think the defense has a strong argument here.

Also, a student might raise the issue of whether the jurisdiction in question limits the felony-murder rule to inherently dangerous felonies. If so, analysis of that limitation on the felony-murder rule merits discussion. This might also take this case outside the felony-murder rule.

So, to conclude: This clearly is *not* first-degree murder. It arguably constitutes second-degree murder if a jury finds depraved heart extreme recklessness. There are arguments to support this, but it is not a sure thing. A second way to find second-degree is through the felony-murder rule, but there are pretty good arguments for not using that doctrine here. But, it is a possibility.

B. Manslaughter

Why discuss manslaughter when you have found two potential bases for finding murder? The reason is that it is not a sure-thing that a jury will convict of murder. Particularly if Leroy comes across to the jury, either in testimony or just in body language, as a grieving father, the jury might choose not to find depraved heart, etc. On the other hand, they may be so angry that a father would leave his two-year-old son unattended, especially to pay off a drug debt, that they will convict of murder. But, a good lawyer (and good law student) will cover all of the reasonable possibilities, and one possibility is that murder won't work.

The statute provides no definition of manslaughter, so we must use the common law. The common law, as we learned, consists of voluntary manslaughter (heat of passion) and involuntary manslaughter (criminal negligence, and unlawful-act doctrine). This clearly cannot be voluntary manslaughter, but it might be (involuntary) manslaughter. Indeed, if Leroy did not act recklessly (murder), he can very likely be convicted of manslaughter. The case for criminal negligence seems very strong, and you would show why, bringing to bear much of the discussion you already provided in your depraved heart discussion.

4. ACTUAL CAUSATION

Your brief analysis here should coincide with your discussion of "voluntary act/omission" above. Don't switch in midstream. Notice: it is true that, but for Leroy's voluntary act of starting the fire to thaw the water pipes the lethal blaze would not have occurred. But that is arguably not the proper road for analysis: it is unlikely that this is part of the basis for claiming he acted with a depraved heart. (Moreover, if all we consider is that he started the fire, and look at nothing else, then we cannot say for sure he caused the death. All you can say is that he caused the fire. If he had stayed at home, he might not have been able to save his son anyway given how fast the fire and smoke engulfed the home.) That is why the prosecutor in this case would likely focus on the omission—abandonment of his son. But for *this omission*, would the child have died? Of course, it still is not certain, but this seems to be the question we should ask.

5. PROXIMATE CAUSATION

There does not seem to be anything in the facts meriting discussion here.

As stated in the Perspective, I do not recommend taking time to write a conclusion. Use your time to discuss the heart of the exam. Your discussion above should stand on its own.

ESSAY TWO INITIAL COMMENTS

Most casebooks today provide the MPC in an Appendix. A professor who asks you to answer an examination question based on the Model Penal Code will either allow you to bring your casebook to class so you can use the Appendix or will otherwise provide you with the pertinent provisions (unlike here, where I only gave you the definitions of the relevant crimes). You will never be expected to memorize the Code, although a professor who has emphasized the MPC during the semester *will* expect you to come to the exam sufficiently familiar with the Code to use it with reasonable facility.

STATE VERSUS ALBERT (RAPE)

1. VOLUNTARY ACT

This is not a major issue. Your professor might say skip it. If it counts at all, it is worth only a few moments. If you had the MPC in front of you, you would note that § 2.01 provides that a person is not guilty of any offense in the absence of a voluntary act (or an omission, where that is relevant). Here, there is nothing to suggest that the intercourse was other than voluntary.

2. SOCIAL HARM

Here is where you take the rape statute and apply the *actus reus* elements. Section 213.1(1) defines rape. Obviously, we have a male (Albert) who had sexual intercourse with a female not his wife (Francesca). The heart of the issue is subsection (1)(a): did he compel her to submit by force or by threat of imminent death, serious bodily injury, extreme pain, or kidnapping?

Compel. As discussed in the Outline, "compel" is the other side of the coin of "nonconsent," and is intended to focus our attention on what the male did, not what the female did or did not (resist) do. One can certainly argue that Francesca did not want to have intercourse with hm: she had previously rebuffed him; she sought to pay for her drugs; she feared Albert based on the prior rumor. Of course, she was also deeply addicted. Although all of this may show that her consent here was less than free, the law requires that the "compulsion" be the result of something that the male did (not just her addicted condition). That leads us to the remainder of the *actus reus*.

Compel . . . by force or by threat of imminent death, serious bodily injury, extreme pain, or kidnapping. There is no evidence whatsoever of the use of "force" to obtain intercourse. The only way to find force would be to apply the New Jersey common law approach of saying that the intercourse itself constitutes the requisite force. But, that can't be what the MPC had in mind, because the statute already includes the element of "sexual intercourse"—if intercourse also constitutes force, why include the word "force" in the statute? For that matter, if sexual intercourse = force, then we don't need the "threat" language. All we need is for the statute to read, "A male who compels sexual intercourse with a female not his wife is guilty of rape." That is not what the statute reads. So, the Code clearly intended for the prosecutor to prove that the force be enough to compel intercourse. No additional force is alleged here.

So, we turn to the threat issue. Here, too, we have a serious problem: he did not threaten imminent death. He did not threaten imminent serious bodily injury. He did not threaten imminent kidnapping. The only threat here was: no sex, no drugs ever. Can we make a case for arguing that he was threatening "extreme pain"? I would hope you would raise this (a prosecutor might try), but I think it loses. First, the imminency aspect is missing. Second, he is not threatening to impose extreme pain on her, *i.e.*, to torture her; he is threatening *not* to provide her with drugs that might reduce the extreme pain she will be feeling from her own addicted condition! So, as I see it, the *actus reus* of rape, as defined here, is missing.

The other approach is to say the following: she was compelled by an *implicit*— unstated—threat, perhaps on the ground that he would cut her with a knife if she refused him, as Francesca believed had happened before to another woman who refused him sex (the false rumor). Or, is there an implied threat of violence on his part simply from his fist fights on streets and in bars? One problem: Does the Code apply to an implicit threat? Perhaps, but notice how unfair that is—we are holding the defendant on the basis of something he *didn't* do (he *didn't* use a knife on another woman). It would be one thing if she had said to him, "If I say no, will you hurt me like you did that other woman?" That would put him on notice of her belief in the false rumor. If he just smiled and said nothing in response to her question, we would have an implied threat. But, we have nothing here. Nor does it seem proper to find an implied threat from the fact that he gets into unrelated fights on the street and bars.

Now, of course, you could try to bring this under one of the other subsections of (1). But look at them. None of them apply here. (He did not, for example, administer drugs to her to prevent her resistance; it was the opposite—he failed to administer drugs, etc.)

3. *MENS REA*

Frankly, I think the case for rape has been pretty solidly ruled out above. You might properly stop there and move on to the next crime. But, when I gave this as an exam question, about 25% of my students thought that the *actus reus* was proven or provable. Therefore, if you found the social harm above, or if you think there is *some* plausible argument there, you should *assume arguendo* the *actus reus*, and move on to the *mens rea*.

On *mens rea*, the statute does not identify any *mens rea*. But, you should know by the end of the semester from learning the MPC, that the Code generally requires proof of a *mens rea* as to each material element of an offense. Also, when no *mens rea* is listed, we are supposed to incorporate "purposely, knowingly, or recklessly" into the statute. (Go back to MPC § 2.02 in this regard.) Therefore, he is not guilty unless he purposely, knowingly, or at least recklessly compelled Francesca by force or threat (etc.). If you found a threat of "imminent extreme pain" (I think unlikely), it seems clear he did compel her purposely in that matter. If you found an *implied* threat above (less unlikely), the issue would be whether he purposely, knowingly, or recklessly compelled her by such an implied threat, which would mean the prosecutor would have to prove beyond a reasonable that Albert was consciously aware of the risk that she feared him, either due to the rumor (was he aware of the rumor?) or his violent character.

4. CAUSATION

No serious issue.

So, did you find rape? I would say no, but some might say yes. There is a backup:

STATE VERSUS ALBERT (GROSS SEXUAL IMPOSITION)

In a case like this, where you are discussing a second crime based on precisely the same facts, there is really no reason to repeat what you just said about issues such as "voluntary act" or "causation." Get right to the heart of the question. Here, we are changing crimes so we are changing the discussion of the social harm/*actus reus*.

1. SOCIAL HARM

This offense can be proved if Albert compelled Francesca "by any threat that would prevent resistance by a woman of ordinary resolution." Aha! There was a real threat here—perhaps not one that fits rape, but a threat: no drugs ever if you do not have sexual intercourse. That creates a jury issue of whether a woman of *ordinary resolution* would be compelled by this treat. Your answer should do more than spot this issue or reach some bald conclusion—you should discuss this, and the arguments that might be made, which could include policy issues about what we have (or don't have) a right to expect of a "woman of ordinary resolution." Notice, by the way, the extra problem: is the standard what a drug addicted woman would do? Is *that* a woman of *ordinary resolution*?

2. *MENS REA*

There seems to be no problem here. Albert purposely used the threat in order to compel her to have intercourse.

STATE VERSUS ALBERT (CRIMINAL HOMICIDE)

Your discussion here should proceed through the requisite elements. But, it should be very easy to prove the *prima facie* case. Indeed, if you are running out of time, you probably can skip some aspects. There *is* a voluntary act here—firing the gun. There *is* the social harm: Louis's death. As for *mens rea*, this is also clear: Albert killed Louis purposely, and that is murder. Nor is there any basis to reduce it to manslaughter—Albert was not experiencing an extreme mental or emotional disturbance at the time of the crime. Louis was, but he is not the defendant. So *mens rea* for murder is proven; and there are no serious causal issues here.

So, you can move rather quickly to the defenses, and the obvious defense issue here is self-protection (§ 3.04). On a real exam you would have that section in front of you. You would want to handle this just like you do everything else—go through each relevant element of the defense, as set out in the MPC, and discuss them.

The Code permits deadly force when the actor believes that force is immediately necessary on the present occasion to protect himself against death or serious bodily harm (among other grounds). § 3.04(1) and (2)(b). Albert should be able to make this argument given Louis's knife threat. Other issues: Can we make Albert the aggressor, by the fact that he compelled Francesca into intercourse? No, as the Code only treats one as an aggressor if "the actor, *with the purpose of causing death or serious bodily harm*, provoked the use of force against himself in the same encounter." § 3.04(2)(b)(i). That won't work: Albert may have provoked Louis in some sense, but it was not with the purpose of causing death or serious bodily harm to Louis, not was it "in the same encounter."

The Code also requires retreat if the actor "can avoid the necessity of such force with complete safety by retreating . . . " § 3.04(2)(b)(ii). This might work for the prosecution: this altercation happened on the street (so the castle exception does not apply). Louis had a knife, not a gun, so retreat is more realistic. Why couldn't Albert have retreated—run away from Louis? Louis is Francesco's father, presumably a lot older than 24–year-old Albert, so it seems plausible to think that Louis could not have outrun Albert. If retreat works, then the self-protection defense is lost, and a murder conviction would stand. But, note that this provision only applies if Albert knows—actually knows, not simply should have known—that he can retreat in *complete* safety. We would need to know more facts to decide this issue. It is enough for you to make these points, and leave it there.

*

APPENDIX D

Glossary

A

Accessory before the fact. At common law, she is a person who intentionally assists in the commission of an offense, but who is not actually or constructively present during its commission.

Actus reus. The physical, or external, component of a crime.

Adequate provocation. In voluntary manslaughter cases, it is provocation that might render an ordinary person, of average disposition, liable to act rashly, or without due deliberation or reflection, and from passion, rather than judgment.

Aggressor. In self-defense context, it is a person who commits an unlawful act reasonably calculated to produce an affray foreboding injurious or fatal consequences.

Atrocious felony. A forcible felony, *i.e.*, a felony that involves the use or threat-ened use of force or carries a substantial risk of physical harm to another.

Attendant circumstance. A fact in existence at the time of the conduct and/or result that constitutes the *actus reus* of an offense, and which is required to be proven in the definition of the offense.

B

Bench trial. A trial in which a judge, rather than a jury, is the factfinder and renders a verdict.

Burden of persuasion. The obligation of the prosecutor or the defendant, as the case may be, to persuade the factfinder regarding a particular issue.

Burden of production. The obligation of the prosecutor or the defendant, as the case may be, to introduce evidence on a given issue, so that the issue may be properly be considered by the factfinder.

C

Common law. Judge-made law.

Conspiracy. In general, an agreement between two or more persons to commit a crime or unlawful act. A conspiracy is an inchoate crime, and also a theory of complicity (a basis for holding a person accountable for the actions of another).

Crime. Conduct that, if shown to have occurred, deserves to incur a formal and solemn pronouncement of the moral condemnation of the community.

Criminal homicide. A homicide committed without justification or excuse.

D

Deadly force. Force likely to cause, or intended to cause, death or serious bodily harm.

Direct cause. An actual cause of resulting harm in which no other actual cause occurs to intervene between it and the social harm.

E

Excuse defense. An excuse defense is one that indicates that, although the actor committed the elements of the offense, and although his actions were unjustified—wrongful—the law does not blame him for his wrongful conduct.

F

Felony-murder rule. The rule that provides that a person is guilty of murder if she kills another person, even accidentally, during the commission or attempted commission of any felony.

G

General-intent offense. Any offense that requires proof of a culpable mental state, but which does not contain a specific intent, is a "general intent" offense.

Grievous bodily injury. Injury that imperils life, is likely to be attended with dangerous or fatal consequences, or that gives rise to the apprehension of danger to life, health, or limb.

H

Homicide. The killing of a human being by another human being. A homicide may be criminal or lawful.

Human being. A "human being" is a living person; at common law, this status begins when a fetus is born alive; it ends either when the individual experiences an irreversible cessation of breathing and heartbeat (the common law definition), or suffers from "brain death syndrome," which occurs when the whole brain permanently loses the capacity to function.

I

Imminent. In self-defense context, threatened force is imminent when it will occur immediately, at the present moment, almost instantly.

Inchoate. Incomplete or unsuccessful. The crimes of attempt, solicitation and conspiracy are example of inchoate conduct that is criminal.

Intentional. As to a result, a person acts intentionally if it is the individual's conscious object to cause the result or if the person knows that the harm is virtually certain to occur.

Intervening cause. An actual cause of social harm that arises after another person's causal contribution to the result.

Intoxication. A disturbance of an actor's mental or physical capacities resulting from the ingestion of a foreign substance, most notably alcohol or drugs (including lawfully prescribed medication).

J

Jury nullification. When a jury decides that the prosecution has proven its case beyond a reasonable doubt, but for reasons of conscience disregards the facts and/or the law and acquits.

Justification defense. A defense that indicates society believes that the defendant's conduct was morally good, socially desirable, or (at least) not wrongful.

K

Knowingly. As to an attendant circumstance, one knows a fact if the person is aware of the fact, correctly believes it exists, or suspects that it exists and purposely avoids confirming the suspicion.

L

Legality. A basic principle of American law that no crime or punishment should be imposed in the absence of pre-existent law defining and setting the punishment for such conduct.

M

Malice. Generally, one acts with malice if she intentionally or recklessly causes the social harm of an offense.

Malice aforethought. At common law, in murder prosecutions, a person acts with "malice" if she unjustifiably, inexcusably, and in the absence of any mitigating circumstance, kills a person with any one of four mental states: (a) the intention to kill a human being; (b) the intention to inflict grievous bodily injury on another; (c) an extremely reckless disregard for the value of human life (often called "depraved heart" at common law); or (d) the intention to commit a felony during the commission or attempted commission of which a death accidentally occurs (the "felony-murder rule").

Malum in se conduct. Conduct that is (morally) wrongful in itself, *i.e.*, inherently immoral.

Malum prohibitum conduct. Conduct that is wrongful only because it is prohibited by law.

Manslaughter. Common law manslaughter is an unlawful killing of a human being by another human being without malice aforethought.

Mens rea. The mental, or internal, component of a crime.

Model Penal Code. A code drafted by the American Law Institute in 1962, and intended to serve as a model for state legislative penal code reform.

Murder. At common law, a killing of a human being by another human being with malice aforethought.

N

Negligence. When a person should know that he is taking a substantial and unjustifiable risk of causing harm.

O

Omission. A failure to act where there is a legal duty to act.

P

Principal in the first degree. At common law, he is the person who, with the requisite *mens rea*, personally commits the offense or who uses an innocent human instrumentality to commit it.

Principal in the second degree. At common law, she is the person who intentionally assists the principal in the first degree to commit an offense, and who is actually or constructively present during its commission.

R

Rape. In Blackstone's time, it was "carnal knowledge of a woman forcibly and against her will." Statutes define forcible rape as sexual intercourse by a male, with a female not his wife, by means of force or threat of force, against the will, and without her consent.

Recklessness. Modern view: when a person consciously takes a substantial and unjustifiable risk of causing harm.

Retribution (retributivism). A theory of punishment that holds that punishment is justified as a deserved response to wrongdoing and should be imposed even if it will not reduce future crime.

S

Social harm. The destruction of, injury to, or endangerment of, some socially valuable interest.

Specific intent. Any one of three states of mind set out in the definition of an offense: (a) the intention to commit some act not part of the *actus reus* of the offense; (b) a special motive for committing the *actus reus*; or (c) awareness of an attendant circumstance.

Strict liability offense. An offense that can be committed without proof of any *mens rea*.

U

Unlawful. Morally wrongful or illegal.

Utilitarianism. A theory of punishment that holds that the general object of all laws is to augment the total happiness of the community by excluding, as much as possible, everything that subtracts from that happiness. Punishment, a form of pain, is only permitted to the extent that it will reduce a greater amount of pain, in the form of crime.

V

Voluntary act. A willed, muscular contraction or bodily movement of an actor.

APPENDIX E

Table of Cases

*

Index

†